THE NEW WINES
OF MOUNT ETNA

An Insider's Guide
to the History and Rebirth *of a* Wine Region

BENJAMIN NORTH SPENCER

Foreword by Susan Hulme MW

GEMELLI PRESS

Text copyright © 2020 by Benjamin North Spencer

Cover photo by: Piermanuele Sberni

All photos not credited are © Jason Johnson

Cover design and typesetting by Enterline Design Services

Requests for permission to make copies of any part of the work should be submitted online at www.gemellipress.com/contact or mailed to the following address:

Gemelli Press

9600 Stone Avenue North

Seattle, WA 98103.

ISBN 978-0-9864390-6-3

An application for Library of Congress Cataloguing-in-Publication Data has been filed

For my father

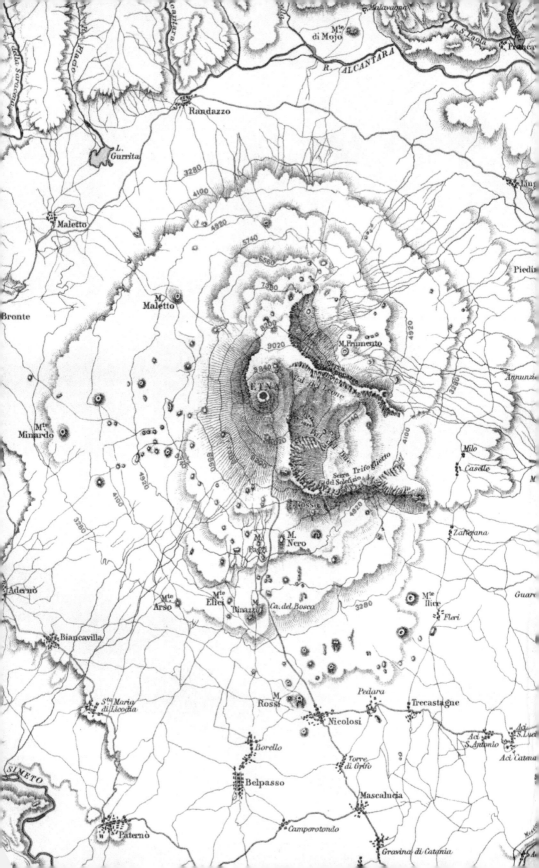

FOREWORD

To me, Sicily has always been a magical place, full of unexpected encounters and serendipity. My first meeting with Ben seems to have followed a similar pattern. In 2013, I was judging wine in the Finger Lakes, in Upstate New York, and I heard one of the other judges say that he lived on Mount Etna. Having lived in Sicily for some time, I introduced myself and we immediately began swapping experiences and ideas.

Since then, I have come to know Ben much better. As he kindly drove me around Mount Etna, to visits with leading Etna producers, I came to appreciate his quietly unassuming and non-judgemental manner that belies a wealth of knowledge and rich experience, including time as a winemaker in California and Sicily. He writes with an obvious love and passion for Etna and its wines, but also with a calm, thoughtful approach that I have come to respect greatly.

I write this having just returned from Francavilla di Sicilia, in the green Alcantara Valley on Etna's northern slope. The view of the volcano, with its various different smoke colors, patterns, and changes of light, held my attention for many an hour while I reflected on the changes of fortune of the Etna wine region, which Ben has captured so well in this book.

From ancient times, Sicily as a whole has had a tumultuous history. Its strategic position in the heart of the Mediterranean attracted one invader after another. The island was in a constant state of flux and rarely settled for long. Etna's wine culture has experienced its own highs and lows, including long periods of neglect.

Now, Etna is thriving. Many have rushed to invest in this boiling-on-the-inside, cool-on-the-outside mountain region, with its mineral-rich volcanic soil and views of the Ionian Sea. Thirty years ago, there were less than ten wineries that bottled their wines with regularity. That number has grown to more than one hundred today, and with it, the cost of grapes and land. The wines are also fetching ever-higher prices.

In the nineties, home-grown wine producers like Benanti and enologist Salvo Foti were instrumental in creating a buzz about Carricante and Nerello Mascalese. Their efforts inspired scores of others to try making wine on *mungibeddu* or *à muntagna*—"the mountain." Among the early pioneers, the Calabretta family, Andrea Franchetti, Frank Cornelissen, Marc de Grazia, the Biondi family, and Alberto Graci gave energy to a wine renaissance that continues to grow and evolve like the mountain itself.

Against this ever-changing backdrop, Ben's book is timely and much needed. It is a personal book, with Ben's love of Etna, its wines, and its people apparent on every page. But it is also an essential guide to the area, giving you all you need to make your own personal discoveries and create your own Etna story.

Susan Hulme MW

ACKNOWLEDGEMENTS

I never intended to live on a volcano. Where I grew up, in Upstate New York, it was generally accepted that volcanoes are dangerous places. Nor was wine a big part of my childhood. Sure, my mother liked the bag-in-box White Zinfandel that she tapped at the end of the day, and my relatives enjoyed Cold Duck or martinis on the holidays, but the rest of the time everyone drank beer. As far as I was concerned, wine was just another bad beverage choice.

As fate would have it, years later I accepted an apprenticeship at a winery in California. The ten-week job evolved into an obsession for wine. Over the course of a decade, I perfected the techniques used in the winery; enrolled in viticulture and enology courses at the University of California, Davis; trained in and then managed the winery laboratory; completed my studies with the Wine & Spirit Education Trust; moonlighted as a sommelier; launched my own boutique wine label; and began writing regularly about wine for online and print magazines.

It was a busy time.

I also met and married my wife during this period. Throughout our courtship, Nadine spoke affectionately about Sicily and the small seaside village at the base of the volcano Etna, where she grew up. I finally got a chance to see it when Nadine and I flew to the Mediterranean island, in 2007.

It was hot the day we arrived in Catania. The temperature at the airport was a seething 44°C (111°F). That afternoon we went for a walk at the seaside to cool off. It was a good opportunity to get my bearings. Looking north from the Port of Riposto, the Peloritani mountain range climbs from the surf, across the strait of Messina from the southern cape of Italy. To the east and south, the graphite-blue Ionian Sea stretches to the horizon. Turning west, Mount Etna rises above the rooftops like a steaming, malformed pyramid. I stole a glance at the volcano every chance I had.

After our walk, we stopped at a restaurant along the waterfront and sat outside. The proprietor brought a carafe of house wine to the table. The color was a dubious, cloudy yellow-orange. I was hesitant, but I brought the glass to my nose and then took a sip. The wine was marked with understated aromas of wild flowers, savory herbs, tropical fruit, and citrus, but the sensation of mineral salts outmaneuvered these other qualities. When the owner came back to take our orders, I asked about the wine. Nadine translated.

Unfortunately, he didn't know what vineyard it came from or who made it. He bought the wine in bulk from a reseller who bought it in bulk from a wholesaler. All he could manage was a gesture toward the volcano. "It came from the mountain."

Nadine explained my interest. "Il mio marito fa vino in California." My husband makes wine in California.

"Ah, America," he said. "What can I tell you? This city was built to sell the mountain wine. Like the one you're drinking. But that was a long time ago. Today, all we sell in Riposto is fish."

I looked at the liquid in my glass. The wines we were making in California were intended to impress—long hang times, new oak barriques, designer yeasts, heavy bottles. As far as I could tell, the only thing the stuff in my glass ever did was roll down the mountain. It seemed impractical for a wine that inviting, delicious, and complex to be so irreverently marketed, but there we were. It was a freeing and frightening sensation, because if this nameless wine was so good, what was all the fuss in California about? It was a question that stayed with me for the next five years, including a second trip to Etna in

2010. After all the wine I'd tasted, and all the wine regions I'd studied, I could not get Etna out of my mind.

In 2012, Nadine and I made the move to Mount Etna. The following day I began an apprenticeship with Ciro and Stephanie Biondi, and their nephew Manfredi, in Trecastagni. Working in the little mountainside neighborhood, pocked with micro-volcanoes and steep vineyards, was like a waking dream, but I didn't know how to approach Carricante or Nerello at first. My limited experience with these grapes was on the consumer end, when the wines were already developing in the bottle. I approached the fermentation and aging of the wines as a study. Every day in the cellar was another masterclass on Etna.

Whenever I had a free day or week, I threw myself up and down the mountain. I took notes on the weather, variations in the soil, the locations of small towns, color changes in the hillsides, vegetation, forests and hidden valleys, extinct craters, walkways, cloud formations, and eruptions. I took photographs, asked questions, and eventually I began making a few assessments of my own. Not only were the vineyards and wines infinitely intriguing, the producers were reinventing the region in real time. Whenever I learned something new, I shared it. Eventually, I started packaging the information into wine courses.

One year later, I was invited to give a presentation about the soils of Mount Etna, in Spain. The presentation—given under the auspices of the Etna Wine School—was paired with a broad tasting of Etna Bianco, Etna Rosso, and Etna Spumante from different parts of the mountain. In a hall full of options from every corner of the Mediterranean, the Etna Wine School table was rarely quiet or slow. The enthusiasm for the wines was unmistakable. Unfortunately, there is no way to convey the totality of Mount Etna in a lecture or a walk-around tasting in a ballroom. I knew the courses that I was developing had to move out of the "classroom" and into the landscape. The volcanic terrain, vineyards, and cantinas are the real campus.

My intention in writing this book is to do something similar. I've chosen to move out from behind the data, to step away from our scorecards, so that we can discover these volcanic wines on Etna's terms. Certainty, for example, arrives in small measures here. Frequent changes in topography, elevation, sunlight, wind, and soils influence the color, aromas, and flavors of a wine, but every neighbor also has an idea of how best to interpret the grapes, terrain, and vintage. This is part of what makes these volcanic wines so exciting. They often escape the crosshairs of precise definition.

That said, everyone who makes an effort is contributing answers to the question, "What is Etna?" Only one generation ago, the answers were dubious. Today, those charged with revitalizing Etna's wine economy are simultaneously the pioneers of a wild landscape and the torchbearers of an ancient tradition. As a result of the sacrifices they are making, wines from the mountain that dominates Sicily's eastern coastline have reclaimed some of the international spotlight. I say reclaimed because Etna has always produced wine. It was merely the spotlight that moved.

Of course, I wouldn't know any of this if we hadn't made the move to Etna. On my first trip to the mountain, there were no books like this. I wish there had been. Only a handful of texts have been written about the mountain and her wines. While historians transcribed reams about the politics and culture of nearby cities, few bothered to write about the farms where their food was grown. Despite my fascination with Etna, it was obvious to me very early on that I needed to follow things where they led me and accept the kindness of others whenever it was offered. As a result of this slow going, I've been given unfettered access to the insights and lives of unexpected friends and a growing family of talented, forward-thinking colleagues. Their sacrifices and continued successes are behind the *Why* of this book.

In particular, I would like to acknowledge and thank the Badalà, Baglioni, Biondi, Benanti, Bevilacqua, Bosco, Caciorgna, Cala, Calcagno, Cambria,

Carlisi, Cipolla-Licciardello, Coffa, Cornelissen, Costantino, Costanzo, Destro, DiBella, Franco, Gallo, Giammanco, Graci, Grasso, Guarrera, Hargrave, Leotta, Maestrelli, Mannino, Messina, Mulone, Munforte, Nicolosi-Asmundo, Platania, Raciti, Raiti, Romeo-Vigo, Russo, Scammacca, Scilio, Scirto, Tasca, Tokash, and Vassallo families for their unflinching support, guidance, and generosity during the preparation and writing of this book.

I am infinitely blessed to have worked with photographer Jason Johnson on this book, which could not have come to fruition without the support of my editor, Sally Carr; my publisher Kari Hock and Gemelli Press; my bride, Nadine; my family; and those of you who have taught me anything along the way.

Benjamin Spencer
Mount Etna, Sicily—December 2019

The Camarda family's alberello vineyard in Feudo di Mezzo is hemmed in by the 1566 and 1879 lava flows. It's one of the lucky places on the mountain, not only because the site has survived two of Etna's devastating eruptions, but because the vines have been worked organically, by hand, for more than 150 years.

HOW TO USE THIS BOOK

PART ONE

You really don't get to know an area until you start looking around and asking questions. Sicily is not an easy place to get fast answers. Even as we approach ten years here, people still ask me how my vacation's going. I'm not a tourist. I live here. I've become a part of this place and Etna has become part of me. The mountainous terrain and indigenous varieties are infinitely inviting, but the thing that still gets me is that the producers are reinventing these volcanic wines in real time. We are all witness to the rebirth of one of the oldest wine regions in the world. It's not the first time Etna has changed. Perhaps that's what I find most intriguing. Mount Etna is transfixed by evolution. In a way, we are taking cues from the volcano. Sometimes we change. Sometimes we remain the same.

INNOCENT BEGINNINGS 1
WINE GRAPES OF MOUNT ETNA 11
    Mount Etna's Primary Wine Grapes 14
    Supporting Grape Varieties 20
THE WINES 37
    Etna's White Wines 40
       • *Non-DOC white wines to try* 42
    Etna Bianco DOC 43
       • *Etna Bianco DOC wines to try* 43
    Etna Bianco Superiore DOC 45
       • *Etna Bianco Superiore DOC wines to try* 47

Rosé Wines 48

• *Rosé wines to try* 49

Etna Rosato DOC 49

• *Etna Rosato to try* 50

Red Wines 51

• *Non-Nerello red wines to try* 54

• *Non-Etna DOC Nerello wines to try* 54

Etna Rosso DOC and Etna Rosso Riserva DOC 55

• *Etna Rosso /Etna Rosso Riserva DOC wines to try* 57

Spumante and Etna Spumante DOC 59

• *Spumante wines to try* 65

Sweet Wines 65

• *Sweet wines to try* 68

A Summary 69

THE VINEYARDS 71

TERRA VULCANICA 89

THE WEATHER 99

PART TWO

There is a sense of calm that settles over you, living on the largest active volcano in Europe. You come to terms with your own mortality, the importance of living in the moment, and making that moment the best it can possibly be. It's a choice. You stay because you want to. Every person and civilization who made that decision to call Etna home has contributed to the wines in some way. As much as this section is dedicated to a history of Mount Etna's wines, it is a genealogy of the liquid in your glass.

THE HISTORY IN YOUR GLASS 111

The Greeks. 112

The Romans 115

The Vandals & Goths 117

Local Beers to Try 118

The Eastern Roman Empire. 118

Islamic Sicily. 119

The Normans 124

The First Best Vineyards. 125

Laws & Disorder 128

The Monasteries 130

Wineries Among the Southeast Craters 133

The Late Middle Ages. 134

The New World 135

The Birth of Mascali. 136

Etna Erupts 139

Late-Modern Etna 141

The Nineteenth Century. 145

The Risorgimento 150

Phylloxera—The Stowaway 154

The Twentieth Century 157

Passopisciaro wineries worth the effort 160

Places to Visit in Randazzo .161

The Specialists 161

End of An Era 164

Sicily's First DOC 166

Leveling the Terraces 170

A New Way Forward 173

The New Wines of Mount Etna 183

PART THREE

Over the last three decades, everything about wine on the mountain has changed. Where there were scores of functioning farms leading into the nineties, there were only a few bottlers, and very few were offering guests the sort of hospitality we see on the volcano today. The new wineries of Mount Etna have changed the rules. Not only is every cantina making wine from the local grapes, on their own terms, they are offering luxurious services and educational tastings for anyone interested in learning about the mountain and her wines. This section is dedicated to giving you access to and stories about the people and businesses producing some of the most inimitable wines in the world. Along with contact information and personal details, I offer information about the services offered at each location (if any), and wines to try while you're there.

Quick Tips for Tasting 219
    Places to Stay 219
    Planning Your Visit 220
    Tastings and Etiquette. 221
    Getting Social 222

The large black rocks protruding from the water off the coast of Aci Trezza are considered the above-water birthplace of the composite volcano we call Etna. Before 220,000 years ago, Etna was a shield volcano, building on itself under the water. The author Homer explained the occurrence of these rocks in *The Odyssey*, alleging that they were thrown there by a mammoth Cyclops by the name of Polyphemus.

PART ONE

In March, as the weather warms, grape vines begin to push out new buds. Every bud point carries the DNA to create shoots, leaves, tendrils, flowers, and grape clusters.

INNOCENT BEGINNINGS

n all likelihood, wine was an accidental discovery on Mount Etna. Perhaps someone ate a few grapes that they found on the ground. Or maybe grapes were collected for food and the skins ruptured, exposing the juice and pulp to oxygen-initiated fermentation, converting the sugars in the juice to alcohol. Any number of things could have happened. This is one of wine's great mysteries. No one knows when wine was really born. Archeological evidence suggests humans have been making wine in Sicily for 6000 years.[1] But that wasn't the birth of wine. The origin of wine happened long before that. And once it was discovered that eating grapes late in autumn or drinking the fermented juice presupposed sensations of euphoria, every effort was made to replicate that primordial "wow" moment.

It's not difficult to "make" wine. You can do it at home with grapes you bought at the market. All you have to do is squish the clusters into a large bowl and wait. A few days later you'll have a glass of wine. This is precisely what ancient Etneans did, only they used hollows found in nature. The first wines on Etna were made from grapes that were macerated in recesses of wood and rock. Simple basins and nooks of large rocks offered the most secure niches where grapes and juice could ferment without leaching into the container. As particular stones proved worthy, bigger and broader holes were gouged out of larger boulders. Typically, a broad and shallow treading area (*pista*) was carved at the top of a massive boulder. Immediately beside the pista, a collection vat (*tino*) was cut deep into the same stone. By cutting a slight decline into the pista it encouraged the juice to flow from the pista into the tino by gravity.

At the moment of harvest, the grapes were collected by hand and carried to these stone fermentation areas (*palmenti rupestri*). Removing the sweet juice from clusters of grapes was easy enough. The weight of a person treading grapes by foot is the perfect amount of pressure to pop the berries without crushing the bitter seeds and stems. More advanced production areas used tree limbs to squeeze piles of grapes to yield more wine. Pressed grapes would render wines with additional color and structure derived from the grape skins, seeds, and stems.

Overnight and into the next day, the newly pressed juice rested in the tino while yeasts in the environment began quietly feasting on the sugars. A few hours later, there were thousands of bubbles breaking open as they surfaced, carrying wonderful aromas into the air. The juice appeared to be boiling.

This naturally occurring commotion is where we get the word *ferment*. It comes from the Latin *fervere*, which means "to boil." No one would explain the dynamics of fermentations for several thousand years, but our ancestors didn't need science. They were fascinated by the process and its results. That it happened at all must have seemed like pure magic.

Wine evoked such curiosity that early Etneans spent months and years chipping away at ever larger boulders where wine could be produced on an annual schedule. They planted farms and built homes around these sites. They worshipped gods and buried their dead there too. Apart from the volcano herself, these open-sky fermenters were among Etna's mystical places. They represented a precise location in the real world where man could communicate with nature in a way that transcended day-to-day living.

The Giant's Eyes—In Salvatore Puglisi's book *La Valle Dei Palmenti* he writes about an intriguing discovery he made in the Alcantara Valley, on Etna's north slope. While hiking through the foothills north of Francavilla di Sicilia, he stumbled on what appeared to be an ancient palmento carved into a very large boulder.

The palmento is composed of two vats—one shallow and another that is deep. The shallow treading pista feeds a fermentation tino by gravity through a hole bored through a common wall. In the far wall of the pista is a deep groove where one end of a lever would be braced, making it easier to press the grapes.

It's a winemaking site, Puglisi notes. But the structure is carved into the vertical face of a boulder that stands more than 10 meters (30 ft.) tall.

What he came to realize was that the palmento was not carved where the boulder now stands. Rather, the enormous stone had been transported to its current position in December 1972, during a rainstorm and a landslide. As the large stone was carried by the mudslide, it came to a final resting position that stood the once-horizontal boulder on its end.

As he stood at the bottom of the boulder, looking up at the hand-carved pista and tina, Puglisi thought the two ancient vats resembled the eyes of a giant face. He called the palmento "The Giant's Eyes."

These rudimentary vinification sites were so popular throughout the Etna landscape that they defined how and where grapes were grown and processed for thousands of years. An estimate by Giuseppe Mannino, winemaker at Tenute Mannino di Plachi and the former president of Consorzio per la Tutela dei Vini Dell'Etna, there are 2,000 palmenti on and around the mountain. Many of these modern buildings were constructed between the eighteenth and twentieth centuries, with walls and roofs, massive lever presses, and aging rooms.

Some of the facilities were used to make wine as recently as the early 1990s. In fact, scores of wineries include a palmento tour as a part of a visit.

Mount Etna is not especially unique because of these sites. Stepped winemaking facilities, which used gravity to move grape pulp and wine through its phases, were used from the end of the Neolithic period (5,000 BCE) forward. Mechanized presses of wood and strap were in common use at the beginning of the first millennium BCE. As the Phoenicians and Greeks began exploring the western Mediterranean, trade routes were established on the Sicilian coast, and wine became something more than magic juice.

Phoenician and Greek merchants were the primary torchbearers of winemaking technology, which they shared with local Sicilians (the Sicels and Sicani) in order to benefit their own trade. I'm not talking about organized viticulture, certainly not the way we think about it today. Even something as simple as training the vine to grow toward the sky, instead of across the ground, exposed the grape clusters to more sunshine and breezes. It was a novel idea, really, and it worked. Wines that were made from trained vines tasted better and fetched higher prices too. From the Greek period (eighth century BCE) forward, vines were trained upward, with the support of a wood stake. Many vineyards are still organized this way on Mount Etna. We call these vines *alberelli* (little trees) for the way they look.

Palmenti also saw some modernization. In about 200 BCE, the Roman statesman and author Cato reengineered the lever press to include a pulley system that drew down on a pile of grapes wrapped in *fascia* (rope) and topped with an *orbis* (wood disk). It was a genius innovation. But the pulley-on-lever system was dependent on human and animal strength. What the merchants wanted was something that could really squeeze the heck out of a grape, for more wine.

Two centuries after Cato, Pliny the Elder modified the pulley system with two of his own designs. The first replaced Cato's pulley with a vertical screw that was attached to a large stone. Together, the screw and counterweight drew down the lever arm with significant force, releasing additional juice or wine in the process. It's this design that we find in most of Mount Etna's palmenti, which were used for consumer wines until 1991. Pliny's second design was a gentler system. By removing the long lever arm, a vertical screw pressed down on an orbis placed on top of the fascia-wrapped grapes. This design acted as the prototype for the modern-day basket press.

Both of the Plinian designs focused on gravity and sloped architecture to direct the must and wine, using channels that had been sculpted into the floors or walls of a building. *Amphorae*, *tini*, and *dolia* (large clay vessels) were used to store the wine until it could be moved or sold.

Storage containers were often made from *terracotta* (baked earth) and closed with tallow or wet clay. When poured onto the surface of wine, olive oil also prevents oxygen from aging the wine prematurely. Olive or mineral oil was the perfect seal, because it floats on wine, effectively separating it from the air above it. It sounded strange to me too, at first, but you can just scoop the oil away whenever you want. This was a trick I used frequently in California at the turn of the twenty-first century.

Wine barrels were not introduced on Mount Etna until the Middle Ages. The wood they chose was the local chestnut.

By 1,100 CE, the Hospitallers and Benedictine monasteries cultivated Etna's southern flank. With them arrived the collective experience of modern farming and winemaking in Europe. Vineyards were commonly planted to five or six grape varieties. At first glance this appears to be an agricultural choice, a way to add biodiversity into the vineyard and present variety from a single farm. In fact, this was a winemaking decision. I won't argue that some of these grapes were made separately; they most certainly were. But in the palmento, without temperature control, fermentations were fast. You can't extract a lot of character from a grape in two days, so what you do obtain from the grape is important.

Planting mixed varieties with different qualities simply made "better" wines. A farmer in the late medieval period would have planted one grape because it produced high sugar levels and another because it retained acidity. A third variety added color while a fourth had thicker skins, which offered more tannin when the grapes were pressed. A fifth supplied fruity aromas, while a sixth contributed quantitatively with high yields. Harvesting and processing the grapes in one moment transmitted all of these qualities to the wines.[2] Today, we call this a "field blend." Medieval Etna farmers believed it was the best way to make wine on Etna.

Pistamutta—Well into the early modern age, many of Etna's wines were made with very little skin contact, in a method called *pistamutta* (crush the grapes and separate the juice). Grapes were macerated, and juice was sent to containers to ferment. The pistamutta method also made it possible for local farmers to get must from their grapes and be on their way.

The color of pistamutta wines ranges from amber to pale ruby, depending on the percentage of black or white grapes used. In this way, we think of pistamutta as the precursor to and equivalent of Etna Rosato, or *rosso da pesce* (a lighter red wine that pairs great with fish). When compared to their bottled counterparts, pistamutta wines sold *sfuso* (in bulk) have an added cache for merchants and consumers, largely because a local farmer made it in the traditional way. To an unsuspecting buyer, pistamutta wines resemble a rosato, but they are, in fact, one of Etna's great traditions, a daily sipper with complexity.

See a selection of wines made in this way on pages 45–49.

By the late 1770s, the port of Riposto—on the Ionian coastline, at the base of Mount Etna—had evolved into a thriving community dedicated to wine and other goods. Decades later, Etna was a firebrand.

The onset of phylloxera in continental Europe (circa 1864) confirmed Etna's potential to supply good *vino da taglio* (blending wine). While plants in Europe withered and died, Etna producers increased production to satisfy the demand. Sophisticated equipment helped to increase the pace. It was no longer efficient to tread the clusters by foot when a destemming bin and roller crushers could remove the stems and macerate the grapes in a fraction of the time, without putting them in contact with the dirty floor. Tini were still used for fermentation and staging, but in many Etna palmenti the heavy Plinian lever press was replaced by a modified basket press. When a pneumatic or electric ratchet was added, a load of grapes could be managed in hours. By minimizing the amount of time that fresh grape juice and wine remained in contact with oxygen, the wines tasted fresher longer.

These modernizations may have helped the merchants sell more wine, but they removed the ceremony from the mountain's ancient tradition. Singing in the palmento was replaced by the cackle of gasoline-powered engines and clanking metal parts. It made the work faster, to be sure, but it also dulled the magic of this completely natural process.

Etna's vineyards, palmenti, and depots had supplied Europe with wine for generations, but phylloxera waned through grafting,[3] and struggling European wine regions rebounded. Politics and economics had also changed.

Sicily was now a part of Italy, and Mount Etna was but another one of her many impoverished farming communities.

During World War II, the local wine economy plummeted. Families and farms were decimated in 1943, during a military campaign in which the Axis powers lost control of Sicily to the Allies. After the war moved north, into the Italian Peninsula, winemaking on Etna was put on the back burner. The vineyards still produced grapes, but interest in any kind of quality winemaking was gone. What people needed was relief. Having any wine at all was enough.

Some families simply stopped working. Year in and year out, the vines grew without pruning. Forests encroached on the terraces, which became overgrown or suffocated under brambles. Walking through some of Etna's old palmenti, it feels as though the laborers simply finished their work, leaned their shovels along the walls, removed their boots, and walked away. They probably imagined they would come back to continue the tradition. But they didn't. They couldn't. With every delay, the machines rusted and rotted. The palmenti grew dusty. Termites ate the wood of the presses. The *botti* (barrels) and tini cracked. Eventually, the roofs collapsed. Once again, the palmenti were open to the sky. But there was no one there to work.

Following the war, at Barone di Villagrande, in Milo, the use of refrigerated containers for fermentation began in earnest. This research proved essential for understanding a new baseline of aromas and flavors that could be obtained from the local grapes. In 1968, the Etna DOC legislation was signed into Italian law, giving Sicily its first legal wine region. The regulations were intended to define and maintain Etna's recent traditions by delimiting an area where blends of local grapes—Carricante, Catarratto, Nerello Cappuccio, and Nerello Mascalese—could be turned into quality wines with a legal status. Unfortunately, a lot of the subsequent work was done in a vacuum. The tools and technology for improving the potential quality of wine were available, however, most of the wines were still being made in palmenti, in unsanitary conditions. The wine was "good enough," but there was very little passion in it. A lot of the production was consumed locally, sold by the liter at low prices, while larger quantities were shipped off the island.

The first concerted high-level experiments into modern Etna winemaking didn't occur until the end of the 1980s. Dr. Giuseppe Benanti was one of the first to apply a new kind of scientific acuity to the local grape varieties. Down the road at Murgo, Michele Scammacca was perfecting his own recipes for Etna Bianco and Etna Rosso. He was also experimenting with international varieties and a bottle-fermented sparkling wine from the local black grape, Nerello Mascalese. On the north slope, producers like Cantine Russo, Cottanera, Grasso Fratelli, and Antichi Vinai were testing Sicilian and local varieties. Over the next twenty-five years, other wineries followed suit.

As the twentieth century ended, a new wave of curious wine producers started interpreting Etna in their own ways. As you might expect, there is more than one approach to winemaking on Etna. In fact, there are scores of them. For now, Etna seems to be on a crawl toward making minimal-intervention wines, using modern technology at least part of the time. I know that covers a lot of ground, but critical consensus suggests that it's working. The mean quality of Etna wines is good to very good, and there are also truly exceptional wines being produced. Unfortunately, flawed products carrying the Etna flag still enter the market. Thankfully, the frequency of this is decreasing as winemakers tweak their methods and buyers come to terms with what Etna does best. More importantly, it comes down to which wines sell in a market of increasingly educated consumers who know that they have choices. As strange as this might sound—for a six-thousand-year-old wine region—Mount Etna is still in the process of determining what it wants to be when it grows up. Fortunately, there is one thing that every producer can agree on: everything starts in the vineyard.

One of Mount Etna's greatest resources is its archive of wine grapes. From the ancient world to the present, the best grapes for wine growing have been planted on the volcano's fertile slopes. Many of them are still here, hiding in plain sight. This centuries-old diversity is part of what makes Etna *Etna*.

Chiara Vigo called me on the phone. She was excited. "I made an amazing discovery. You have to see." The Romeo del Castello-Vigo family has lived and worked in Contrada Allegracore for centuries. Since 2007, Chiara has been restoring the estate. In that time, she's found artifacts from the family palmento in the yard, munitions and ration kits left behind by World War II soldiers, and countless tokens of a distant time. As much as Fattorie Romeo del Castello is a working farm, the family has transformed it into a living museum.

We talked as Chiara led me into the vineyard. "I couldn't believe it when I saw them," she said. She pointed at the wall of lava that buried more than sixty acres of their farm and vineyards in 1981. Young green tendrils and leaves were growing from the spongy basalt.

I was gobsmacked. "They found a way," I said.

"After thirty-five years? From under twenty feet of lava? How can this be?"

I examined the shoots and leaves. It wasn't the super-weedy American species, which are often used for grafting. Those have red stems and rounder, flatter leaves. These were verdant green and soft. "This is *vinifera*," I said.

"From the old vineyard," Chiara added.

"Survivors."

This is one of the most intriguing things about wine. It's a beverage made from the fruit of a plant that refused to give up. The grapevine has had one of the most incredible adventures of any living thing on the planet. We don't think about this when we uncork a bottle or put words to the emotions they give us. But it's true. Their saga began about 200 million years ago, on the geological supercontinent Pangaea, where a wild, deciduous, perennial flowering vine—Vitaceae—was slowly creeping across the prehistoric landscape. Over eons, Vitaceae mutated into different families and genera.[4] One genus of Vitaceae is called "Vitis." It's a flowering and fruiting vine with about eighty unique species of its own.[5] As perpetual tectonic shifts fractured Pangaea into smaller continents, Vitis spread out over the surface of the planet. With every new zip code, the vines evolved. Vitis is found in North America and Eastern Asia, but it's the Eurasian species, *Vitis vinifera*, that we use for quality wine production on Mount Etna, and around the globe.[6]

Vinifera vines that got trapped on the chunk of Earth we call Sicily evolved on their own, separated from the other bits and pieces of the evolving world as the island was dragged into its current position on the shoulder of Africa. Every time the African and European tectonic plates collided, there was a spark. One of those sparks gave birth to Mount Etna. For the next 300,000 years, she erupted under water, building on herself in a stratum of lava. As she surfaced from the water and merged with the rest of Sicily, the ancient grapevines already populating the island began to climb her flanks. Over millennia, edible grapes became wine grapes, and the best tasting, most resilient varieties were propagated. In the end, it was the elegant and pernicious *Vitis vinifera* that won out.

Looking at the vines reaching out from the wall of lava with Chiara, it was easy to see how sturdy our preferences have become.

One of Mount Etna's greatest resources is its archive of wine grapes. From the ancient world to the present, the best grapes for wine growing have been planted on the volcano's fertile slopes. Many of them are still here, hiding in plain sight. Nearly every vineyard on the mountain has a unique assortment of grapes. This centuries-old diversity is part of what makes Etna *Etna*.

Carricante and Nerello Mascalese are the standard bearers, but the law that defines Etna DOC wines also encourages the inclusion of small percentages of old Sicilian varieties in a blend. Older vineyards are notoriously spiced with heirloom cultivars that end up in the wine. New vineyards dedicated solely to Carricante, Catarratto, Nerello Mascalese, Nerello Cappuccio, and popular international varieties are changing this very old scheme. If you take the long view, decisions like this conform perfectly with the arc of Etna's traditions. Wine grapes have been popularized, replaced, revived, and forgotten on the flanks of the volcano since the Bronze Age. It's very likely that even contemporary blends may shift course over time. Someday, maybe there will be new grape crossings based on the wines we see today. Some type of Nerello Mascalese-Cappuccio, for example. What will that taste like?

Grape crossings are not new. Many of the wines we drink today are the result of ancient genetic marriages. Recent inquiries into the pedigrees of wine grapes, using DNA analysis, have yielded priceless information about the wines we love. The descriptions of those listed below are derived from my personal experience with these grapes and wines, years of study by the Department of Agriculture, Food, and Environment at the University of Catania, work being done by the Regional Institute of Wine and Oil of Sicily, and two books that have combined years of research conducted by hundreds of individuals. In place of contiguous footnotes, which would otherwise make these descriptions unbearable to read, I include the names of the two collections here: *Native Wine Grapes of Italy*, by Ian D'Agata (University of California Press, 2014); and *Wine Grapes: A Complete Guide to 1,368 Vine Varieties, Including Their Origins and Flavours,*" by Jancis Robinson, Julia Harding, and José Vouillamoz (Allen Lane, Penguin, 2012).

In alphabetical order, the following section includes Etna's principal wine grapes, secondary cultivars, international varieties that now call the mountain home, and relics of a distant past.

MOUNT ETNA'S PRIMARY GRAPES

Carricante

Carricante is the primary white wine grape on Mount Etna. It produces pale yellow wines with beautiful freshness and savory flavors. It is most often blended with Catarratto, Minella Bianca, and non-aromatic Sicilian varieties, for a sophisticated still table wine with potential for aging.

Carricante was named for its ability to produce massive quantities of wine. The verb *caricare* means "to load or carry." *Carricante* suggests something that is "overloaded." Near the seaside, a single vine was rumored to be capable of producing four gallons of wine. Where the vines grow today, at elevation and without irrigation, yields are typically a few kilos per vine. When Carricante grows above 400 meters above mean sea level (AMSL), the load decreases and quality improves.

The municipality of Milo, on Etna's east slope, is generally considered the best area to cultivate Carricante, though the grape also performs well in other locations on the mountain.

Also called Catanese Bianco and confused for Catarratto, Carricante appears to be the result of a natural crossing between Montonico Pinto and Scacco. Montonico Pinto contributes to Pollino DOC wines, in the province of Cosenza, in north Calabria. Scacco is no longer used for quality wines anywhere.

Carricante is Mount Etna's dominant white grape variety. Its name is suggestive of the grape's potential for high yields. On steep slopes and well-drained soils yields are lower and flavors are better. Carricante's home is on the east slope of the mountain, but it also performs well in other sites around the volcano. Cool, anaerobic strategies in the cellar yield wines that are delicate, savory, and age worthy.

Nerello Mascalese is Mount Etna's racy black grape. It has several phenotypes that share a profile of fruit and herbs, fresh acidity and firm tannins. Low yields in the vineyard and gentle treatment in the cellar attract the best flavors. Nerello Mascalese is often blended with Nerello Cappuccio, but it also shines on its own in rosé, red, and sparkling wines.

The Carricante Riesling Connection—When I arrived on Etna, I quickly noticed a resemblance between the aromas of aged Carricante and aged Riesling. In particular, there is a slight petrol or kerosene scent in some wines.

Contrary to these chemical descriptors, the compound that creates these aromas is not offensive in small doses. If anything, it can add depth and complexity to the bouquet of a wine. Some of us find it seductive. For others, it's a deal breaker.

The aroma at the heart of this fascinating phenomenon is TDN, an acronym for its laboratory name, Trimethyl Dihydronapthalene.

This aromatic connection between Riesling and Carricante isn't the result of genetic familiarities. While both Carricante and Riesling are hearty, low-sugar, high-acid white grapes, they have no connecting lineage. What they do share is a tendency to produce TDN when they have been exposed to intense sunlight during a specific period of their growing cycle.

In order to assist ripening, vineyard workers often remove leaves around the fruiting zone to expose grape clusters to additional hours of sunlight.

When the fruit zone of a Carricante vine is deleafed one month after flowering is complete, there tends to be a notable increase in TDN. Vines that are deleafed about sixty days from fruit set tend to show an increase in overall quality and a decrease in the occurrence of TDN. Of course, no two growing seasons are ever the same. Vineyard managers decide for themselves how to manage the canopy.

Catarratto Bianco

I like to present my guests with two white wines. One has Catarratto Bianco, the other doesn't. More times than not, the wine with Catarratto is the favorite. This white variety is Sicily's most planted grape. On its own, Catarratto makes a wine that has the potential to boast. Together with Carricante, Catarratto softens acidity while shifting the fruit profile of the wine toward the tropical. It's this lush fruit profile that we sense in basic Etna Bianco, where it can represent up to 40 percent of the blend.

Most Etna producers prefer the Catarratto Comune for the body and fruit it donates to a blend, but it's not the only Catarratto on the mountain. There are three distinct phenotypes identified—Comune, Lucido, and Extra Lucido. Their names are derived from the appearance of the bunches. Catarratto Comune berries have a plump, golden, and frosted look, while Lucido biotypes shy toward verdant green, increased acidity, and some vegetal characters.

In fertile soils, Catarratto can be vigorous and yields can be high. In sites above 400 meters AMSL, crops are smaller and flavors are more delicate. Regardless of the vineyard site, Catarratto's home is in an Etna Bianco blend.

Due to the prolific nature of its planting, Catarratto has many aliases. DNA analysis shows a relationship with Garganega, another prolific Italian white wine grape, from the Veneto.

Nerello Cappuccio

Nerello Mascalese's backup singer is the darker, richer, and mellower Nerello Cappuccio.

Cappuccio literally translated means "hood." The name supposedly derives from the thick powdery bloom (pruinose) that covers the plump, purple clusters, but they are also shaded by large leaves, and it was a variety popular within monastic vineyards managed by the Capuchins. One of the aliases is also Nerello Mantellato. *Mantello* translates as "coat or cover."

The bunches are tightly packed, making it a tough grape to work with in damp or wet vintages, or areas where this kind of weather is common. In general, it's not the farmer's favorite variety. Fungal attacks are normal, so additional attention must be given to create ventilation around the bunches.

DNA research into the origins of Nerello Cappuccio, which included old vineyards in eastern Sicily and Calabria, commercial vineyards in Sicily, and isolated sites on Mount Etna, have no clear lineage. As it often happens in Etna's vineyards, Nerello Cappuccio has a few unique phenotypes, with each communicating something special to a given blend.

There are currently only a handful of wineries who bottle pure expressions of Nerello Cappuccio—Al-Cantàra, Benanti, Calabretta, Feudo Vagliasindi, and Tenuta di Fessina—though I anticipate this number to grow.

Nerello Mascalese

Nerello Mascalese is Mount Etna's most important variety and the mountain's claim to fame. The black cultivar is named for the wine's gentle red color and the village of Mascali, which is largely regarded as its birthplace. Though we have this starting point to work from, Mascalese's pedigree is a curious one.

Nerello Mascalese appears to be a natural crossing between the black grape Sangiovese and the white Mantonico Bianco. These two grapes are not native to Sicily. Mantonico Bianco has been produced in Eastern Sicily for centuries, but its home is in southern Calabria, where it has been cultivated for its ability to retain acidity, especially when used for *passito* wines, since the eighth century BCE. Sangiovese produces a delicious tannic, medium-bodied red wine with a savory, earthy, cherry, and huckleberry fruit profile. Sangiovese is also grown on Mount Etna and elsewhere but the grape calls central Italy home.

Not surprisingly, Nerello Mascalese has nine synonyms, and several phenotypes exist. Its characteristic acidity, pale ruby color, red fruit profile, and peppery tannins are highly dependent on elevation, soil type and epoch, age of the vine, weather during the vintage, and the techniques of the producer.[7] Because of this, it reflects the changes within the mountain landscape better than any other grape that grows here.

Not only are the wines reflective of the environment, there can be stark changes in flavor between grafted and ungrafted Nerello Mascalese. Grafted vines have a profile of fresh cherry and forest berries. The wine has a soft ruby color, striking acidity, fine-grain tannins, and a dry brackish finish. Wines made with fruit from ungrafted vines have a brooding appeal. They show a deeper color, dark fruit aromas, mouth-watering flavors of black cherry, plum, and spice, with fatter tannins than their grafted counterparts.

SUPPORTING GRAPE VARIETIES

I love discovering new wine grapes. With each sip comes another discovery and a broader understanding of this thing we call Wine. But, it goes deeper than a tasting note for me. Wine grapes are part of history; they track shifts in culture, economic powers, and the rise and fall of empires.

Among Etna's supporting cast are ancient, lost, and popular grapes that were once sold widely in the international market, if only as part of a blend. While the inclination for most Etna winegrowers is to follow the Etna DOC legislation, which limits the majority blending components to the varieties listed above, the grapes actually grown in each vineyard varies from site to site. This nuanced spicing, in concert with the unique lava flows and climate, adds something special, and inarticulable, to these wonderful wines.

The **Aglianico** is a popular southern Italian black grape variety grown on Mount Etna at one winery, Wiegner. DNA profiling gives us very little evidence of an origin, though legends credit the Greeks or Spaniards with bringing the grape to Italy. Wiegner's bottling of 100 percent Aglianico is from vines planted in 2004. Though the vineyard is still finding its footing, the wine shows promise when yields are low, weather is good, and the wine ages in wood. Nevertheless, it is an unimportant grape for the rest of Etna.

One of Eastern Sicily's oldest white grape varieties is **Albanello.** It is still in production on Etna, albeit in very limited quantities. Albanello ripens late, and the heady wines made using the *appassimento* method (sun drying) have fallen out of fashion. Santa Maria La Nave has approximately 500 young vines planted outside of the DOC, near Maletto in Contrada Nave, at 1,100 meters. The young vines are the result of a mass selection made from local vineyards. They will make several experiments before releasing a wine to the public.

One of my non-traditional favorites is **Alicante**. It's also known as Grenache in France, Garnacha in Spain, and Cannonau in Sardegna. When blended with Nerello Mascalese or Cappuccio, which ripen one month later, Alicante adds depth, intensity, and body to the wine. It would be nice to see

Over years, the trunks of young vines strike elaborate poses. When Nerello Mascalese is trained in cordon, the bunches of grapes find a good balance between flavor and freshness. Here, the black grapes are going through veraison, an important moment in the growing season when grape clusters change color, signaling the onset of ripening.

more Etna *cantinas* (wineries) using this grape in small portions with the Nerello. SRC, I Custodi delle vigne dell'Etna, and Mirella Buscemi include Alicante as an important part of the blend. For now, only Guido Coffa regularly produces a pure, high-quality Alicante.

Alicante Bouschet is a Teinturier crossing with Alicante (see above). The red flesh of the black grape makes for intensely colored wines. There are sprinklings of this grape throughout Etna's northern flank, but very rarely does the variety get any serious recognition. Frank Cornelissen includes the grape in a red blend.

Ansonica adds a delicate stone-fruit profile to white wines on Mount Etna. The grape is also called **Inzolia**. The discrepancy in the name of the grape and its origins (Sicily or the mainland) has kept Ansonica/Inzolia in limbo until recently, when DNA tests showed a connection to other Sicilian varieties.

Cabernet Franc and **Cabernet Sauvignon** have no importance for Etna DOC wines. The few producers who work with Cabernets do so in a way that the table wines resemble Cru Bourgeois Bordeaux rather than a premiere Napa or a fine Chinon. One notable exception is Castello Solicchiata, located near Adrano, on Etna's southwest flank. Bottlings are based on quality and unique locations in the vineyards. Murgo also bottles a delicious Cabernet Sauvignon from vines grown on the lower southern slope, in the Piana di Catania.

Chardonnay is one of the world's most reputable white grapes and one of my favorite varieties, for how easily it reflects the intention of the winemaker. On Etna, only Passopisciaro and Tasca d'Almerita use it with success for a table wine. Terrazze dell'Etna grows Chardonnay for two fine classic method spumante wines. One is aged on lees for thirty-six months, the other for fifty. Chardonnay is a natural crossing of Pinot and Gouais Blanc, placing its origins firmly in Burgundy, France. Plant material was brought to Etna by producers who believe in the variety.

Rumors suggest that **Cesanese d'Affile** was delivered to the area around Rome by a Sicilian monk. On Etna, only Passopisciaro grows Cesanese, including it in a blend with Petit Verdot when the vintage requires it. Yields and quality can be variable, but in the best years the wine has great color, rich mulberry aromas, and flavors of black pepper, plum, and black cherry, with silky, ripe tannins. It fits well with the volcanic terroir. It would be interesting to see it blended, in small quantities, with Nerello Mascalese.

Another of Etna's heirloom varieties is **Coda di Volpe Bianca** (tail of the fox). The elongated clusters of white grapes can be found in older vineyards, but it is out of fashion for modern vineyard schemes. Those who claim it as an element in a white wine feel as though it contributes something special. I find it adds spice, body, and flavors of ripe peach or apricot.

Fiano is a popular southern Italian white grape with elongated berries, which has an affinity for stony and volcanic terrain. On Etna, Fiano is produced by a single winery, Wiegner, in a stylish modern way. The vineyard is planted at 750 meters above sea level in Contrada Marchesa.

Gewürztraminer and **Traminer** are mutations of the Savagnin grape, which is grown in the Jura region of France, near the French-Swiss-German border. There are no genetic or historical ties to Etna viticulture. Two wineries use the grapes to make a blend and a monovarietal bottling. Al-Cantàra produces a Gewürztraminer-Carricante blend from grapes grown at 600 meters. Enò-Trio makes a lovely pure Traminer Aromatico from vines planted at 1,100 meters in Contrada Nave.

The **Grecanico Dorato** is a white Sicilian variety that was recently proven through DNA analysis to be Garganega, a popular wine grape grown in Veneto. It is one of the ten most popular grapes on the island. Today, Grecanico Dorato is found in countless Etna vineyards, particularly on the north slope. It plays a reliable supporting role in Etna white wines. The Al-Cantàra, Buscemi Calcagno, Eduardo Torres Acosta, Filippo Grasso,

Francesco Modica, I Custodi delle vigne dell'Etna, Scirto, and Valenti wineries are using notable quantities of Grecanico Dorato for blended wines. Only Santa Maria La Nave is focusing on a pure, low-yield, quality Grecanico Dorato from high elevation vineyards on the northwest slope of Etna. They have also begun producing a delicious *metodo classico* (traditional method) sparkling wine from the grape, which spends more than two years on lees.

On the west coast of Sicily, **Grillo** is used to make beautiful white wines. On Etna, the grape makes random appearances. Recent DNA profiling has named Catarratto and Moscato d'Alessandria as Grillo's likely parents. Only one winery, Quantico, includes Grillo as an important part of their Etna Bianco blend. Even if the total approaches a mere 5 percent, the wine benefits from Grillo's presence.

Madama Bianca is believed to have arrived on Etna during the flourish to find disease-resistant cultivars after the phylloxera outbreak in the latter part of the nineteenth century. Its origin isn't confirmed, but it is thought to be France. The clusters are light and airy, with small berries and three separate small bunches on two wings. Ripening is achieved by the end of September. However, the natural acidity is low, which makes this and its black counterpart, **Madama Nera,** purely a blending grape in minor proportions. They are both popular on Etna's eastern flank, on Monte Ilice, and between Puntalazzo and Piedimonte Etneo, where the clusters can be compact and weighty.

Malvasia delle Lipari is considered an aromatic variety and is therefore not permitted for any Etna DOC wines. The grapes have delicate aromas and flavors that intensify through sun drying. A handful of Etna producers make this wine with regularity. The better wines carry the Malvasia delle Lipari DOC label. Barone di Villagrande makes a divine example of Malvasia delle Lipari from their vineyards on the island of Salina, blending 5 percent black Corinto Nero grapes to enhance the color.

Merlot is one of the most-planted black grapes in the world, but it barely forms a blip on Etna's radar. This early budding and early ripening variety—a natural cross between Cabernet Franc and Magdeleine Noir des Charentes—were smuggled to Etna from Bordeaux in a suitcase, so I'm told. Only three wineries, Barone di Villagrande, Enò-Trio, and Cottanera produce wines where the best qualities of Merlot shine.

Minella Bianca is a little-known and ever-present indigenous white variety that also has a black mutation, **Minella Nera**. They are quickly being replaced by other Etna varieties. While the grapes can be found in almost every vineyard on the volcano, quantities are sparse. On the vine, Minella quickly loses acidity, becomes flabby, and oxidizes, so the general rule of thumb is to harvest earlier rather than later. Only one winery, Calabretta, continues the production of Minella Bianca for a pure example of this wine. It has lovely aromas of citrus zest, a soft, spicy palate, and vibrant acidity. Minella comes from *minedda*, or "breast" in the local dialect, because of the elongated shape of the grapes. No DNA work has been completed on these cultivars.

The only plantings of **Mondeuse** on Etna are at Cottanera, where it is made into a single-variety, single-vineyard red wine that spends more than a year in large oak botti before bottling. Mondeuse comes from Savoie, in southeastern France. The inky wines have aromatic black fruit and bitter cherry flavors with a lingering acidity and a soft finish. It's a wonderful surprise when the wine arrives unannounced during a tasting, but it remains to be seen if Etna has any use for it.

The aromatic **Moscato Bianco** has several aliases, including Moscadella, Moscato Giallo, and, not surprisingly, Moscato dell'Etna. In truth, there are multiple members of the Moscato family found around the volcano. In the nineteenth and twentieth centuries, it was a favorite among merchants, but it has since fallen out of favor. Only La Gelsomina makes a luscious dessert wine derived from the appassimento process.

At the end of the 20th century, **Nero d'Avola** (the black grape from Avola) rose to international fame as Sicily's modern red wine variety. It is one of the most planted grapes on the island, in the Val di Noto, in particular, but it does not find a lot of love on Etna. That said, Nero d'Avola accounts for the second-most planted variety in the province of Catania—after Nerello Mascalese and before Carricante. DNA profiling proved a proliferation of clones, mutations, and distinct varieties being called Nero d'Avola, or its legal name, Calabrese, which also happens to be a pseudonym for Nerello Mascalese.

The black Bordeaux variety **Petit Verdot** makes a case for its inclusion in high-quality wines on Etna. On its own, the dark ruby-color wines have a haunting array of rich, ripe fruit, and spice. As a blender, Petit Verdot could easily stand in for Nerello Cappuccio, although in smaller quantities. Terrazze dell'Etna has raised this very question with a thought-provoking wine that blends Petit Verdot (20%) with Nerello Mascalese (80%). The effect of Petit Verdot is instantly recognizable. I can't help but wonder how it would perform at about 10 percent, or less, of the blend. One winery, Passopisciaro, makes a fetching and serious wine from Petit Verdot with varying quantities of Cesanese d'Affile, depending on the vintage.

Pinot Noir/Pinot Nero is an imported variety that gained fame on Etna when Italy's top enologist, Giacomo Tachis, said that the Pinot Nero being produced on the mountain "had the potential to rival Burgundy." Tachis tasted a lot of wines on his trip around Mount Etna. The Pinots made at Castello Solicchiata, near Adrano, on the south flank, and by Dr. Rocco Siciliano of Azienda Siciliano, in Contrada Marchesa, on the north slope, created a craze that continues quietly today. Pinot Nero is not an easy grape to grow or vinify. On Etna, it takes a delicate hand to make a good one. Clones vary and, in truth, very few producers know or want to know what clones are in the vineyard. They care that the wine has a dull ruby color and that it retains the noble aromas and flavors of the grape. If they can do that, it's enough. Etna usually puts such an imprint on the wine that it's hard to say with clarity that these are truly Pinot. Apart from those listed above, Murgo, Enò-Trio, Duca di Salaparuta, and Terrazze dell'Etna make still table wines that strive to hit the mark. Terrazze dell'Etna makes a metodo classico sparkling wine from Pinot Nero, using Nerello Mascalese to accent the blend.

Riesling is another international variety that's being tested around the mountain. Riesling likes cool, bright climates and stony environments. As a blender, the grapes add acidity with pleasant aromas and flavors of white and yellow flowers, green plum, and stone fruit. Planeta is the only winery making a pure Riesling from young vines, using a spacious guyot training system on a plateau at 800 meters AMSL, in Contrada Sciara Nuova. When used as a part of the estate's Carricante blend (at 10%), the Riesling dominates the organoleptics of the young wine. After a few years in bottle, the Carricante begins its enchanting evolution. It will be interesting to see how this Sicilia DOC blend evolves in the bottle. Both Carricante and Riesling have a predilection for improving with age.

Sangiovese's origin on Etna falls firmly into the hands of the monasteries around the end of the Middle Ages, with its first official reference appearing in a text by Giovan Soderni, at the end of the sixteenth century. The first cuttings of this vine that would become known as Sangiovese arrived on Mount Etna in the fourteenth century, when Franciscan monks fled northern Italy and were given sanctuary in Mount Etna's rural Benedictine monasteries. Sangiovese is credited as being a parent of Nerello Mascalese, Etna's most important cultivar (see Nerello Mascalese) and is found throughout Sicily and randomly on Etna, save one vineyard dedicated solely to the black grape. Tenuta Benedetta bought the vineyard, in Feudo di Mezzo, believing the grapes to be Nerello. They were certified as such by the previous owner, the Region of Sicily, and the nursery where they were raised. But the ripe bunches of grapes matured three weeks before Nerello. Subsequent DNA analysis showed it to be Sangiovese Grosso. The single-vineyard Sangiovese is a persuasive interpretation of this noble Italian grape.

Syrah has an affinity for rocky terrain and cool climates where there is intense sunlight and heat for short periods of time. Syrah did not appear in Etna's diaspora until recently. It is likely that the "Hermitage" vines, planted in the late nineteenth century at the Ducea di Nelson, included some Syrah. Unfortunately, almost all of those vines surrendered to phylloxera. Syrah vines on Etna are young and trained for moderate yields. Likely a spontaneous crossing of Mondeuse Blanche and Dureza that occurred in the Rhône-Alpes, it makes sense that Syrah might do well on Etna. Cottanera is the only winery on the mountain to make a pure Syrah.

Terribile was a popular black grape cultivar in vineyards around Pedara, Nicolosi, and Trecastagni, high on Etna's southeast slope. Terribile is still producing miniscule quantities, but it is included in field blends, particularly in the old alberelli on Monte Ilice. This name is strange considering its potential for consistent yields and a resistance to oidium, peronospora, and phylloxera, but the berries and clusters can be small, making it less popular than the larger clusters Nerello Mascalese can produce. That said, Terribile gives good color and fresh acidity with the potential to increase the alcohol and body of a red wine.

The white variety **Trebbiano** was popular on Etna, in particular for its high yields. Its subsequent use by Etna distilleries during the eighteenth and nineteenth centuries gave buoyancy to a brandy and fortified wine industry. It was included in the 1968 Etna DOC legislation as one of the favored cultivars used for blending. Vines can still be planted for inclusion in Etna DOC wine, though quantities are generally being decreased in favor of others with more character.

Viognier happens to be one of my favorite white wine cultivars, but on Etna it gets a little lost. When Viognier does find a way, aromas and flavors are delicate, elegant, and the wines improve with some aging. Only Cottanera produces a wine that blends small quantities of Viognier grown on Etna with Inzolia and/or Catarratto. Like Syrah, with which Viognier shares a mother (Mondeuse Blanche), the white wine grape likes rocky terrain with intense sunlight and moderate amounts of heat if it is to perform at its best. Etna seems like a logical place for it to excel. In small quantities, it seems an obvious blender for Carricante, though I have not found a good example of this.

The white grape **Zu' Matteo** appears regularly in old mixed vineyards around the spent southeastern craters, where it's been blended with Carricante since the end of the nineteenth century. Prior to this, it added delicate aromas of fruit and herbs to the field blend, which would have included Nerello. The berries are small and clusters are airy. When planted in fertile soils, yields and flavors are enhanced.

While no vineyard hosts Etna's entire archive of grape varieties in one location, wineries that feature a handful of cultivars inevitably add dimension and "spice" to the wines they are producing. A single vineyard with a solitary phenotype of one variety cannot do the same. This is not a bad thing. Mount Etna's potential is also found in hyper-territorial expressions of single varieties. In fact, it looks like that's the way things are headed. By exploring one grape in one plot we are able to study the terroir in ways that previous schemes, which only combined contemporary and relic varieties in field blends, have as yet been unable to achieve.

Etna's traditional palmento is an enclosed building that uses gravity to make wine. There is a top level *pista* for treading grapes; a second area for the *conzu*, which was used to press grapes and spent skins; a fermentation *tino*; and a *dispensa* where wine was stored. The palmento is no longer permitted for quality wine production. This restored palmento can be found at Terrazze dell'Etna, near Randazzo.

The subterranean aging room (*dispensa*) at Barone di Villagrande, in Milo, includes old, large chestnut botti, smaller chestnut tonneaux (left), and French oak barrels (right). The larger vats were built in place or were rolled downhill from the previous winery, which was destroyed in an earthquake at the end of the eighteenth century. The Nicolosi-Asmundo family has made wine at this site for three centuries.

In many Etna wineries, the old and new congregate. Centuries-old structures are considered historical sites. Any modernization has to be done carefully.

Giuseppe Scirto and I taste a young Nerello from their old-vine vineyard in Contrada Feudo di Mezzo. Stainless steel makes a regular appearance on Mount Etna. The inert container protects the subtle aromas and flavors of Etna grapes.

Frank Cornelissen uses Spanish amphorae in his Passopisciaro cellar for some wines, when the vintage requires it. Burying clay pots in the ground creates a natural, cool environment that slows evolution of a wine. Other producers on Mount Etna are making their own experiments with earthen containers.

Fabio Costantino (Terra Costantino) crouches in the window through which the grape clusters were deposited into the pista of the family palmento. Beside him, old chestnut vats serve as a reminder of Etna's history.

Terra Costantino's cement vats replicate the old palmento system of fermenting in volcanic rock, with a modern cooling system and no exposure to oxygen. The porous quality of the un-coated volcanic basalt contributes an authenticity to wines, which makes these tanks very popular for fermentation and some aging.

THE WINES

I t's been years since I last walked into a professional kitchen to work, but I still liken the winemaking process to cooking. How the dish comes out depends on the attention of the chef. Fresh ingredients prepared with care inevitably taste better than something you walk away from. You have to be there, to guide it, from the vineyard to the bottle. I discuss Etna's wines in the following sections, but there are a few things I'd like to address before moving on.

First, Mount Etna is a sunny, windy, and rainy wine region with vineyards growing at elevation on the side of an active volcano in close proximity to the sea. No vintage is ever the same.

All wineries harvest their grapes by hand. Etna's sloped terrain does not allow for mechanical harvesting. This means that every winery starts the vinification process with fresh grape clusters. What the winemaker chooses to do with those grapes has everything to do with the wine they intend to make.

White wines are generally the result of the fermented pulp that's been squeezed from grapes. Pink and Red wines are derived from hours to weeks of contact between macerated grapes.

Fermentation is initiated in a few different ways. Wineries that prefer to ferment without the assistance of modern additives frequently do so with the help of a *pied de cuve*. In a pied de cuve, a small harvest is done a few days before the main harvest is scheduled, and the grapes are macerated and left to begin fermenting. When the bulk of the grapes arrive in the winery, they are processed and a portion of the pied de cuve is added to the new must. In this way, the fermentation is pre-started with its own yeasts. Spontaneous ferments forego the pied de cuve, allowing the natural yeasts to populate the must when they get around to it. In both cases, the resulting wines have increased territorial aromas and flavors.

These local cultures speak of Etna in ways that laboratory yeasts cannot, but they are incredibly easy to buy. Winemakers select strains from a catalog, based on the characters they want most in a wine—enhanced fruit, low phenolics, increased tannins. Simply put, these designer options offer consistency and something akin to a branded style, but they are cultivated from yeasts found in other parts of the world.

Vintage after vintage, yeasts populate the walls, floors, barrels, and other winery equipment. In the traditional palmento of Etna, everything is constructed in stone and wood, allowing many opportunities for unique, wild, local cultures to settle into cracks and pores of every surface. A few wineries—Benanti, Palmento Costanzo, and Tenuta delle Terre Nere—have gone so far as to collect and research yeasts from old palmenti around Etna, isolating the best local strains for use in their wines. Everyone else depends on the other three schemes.

These aren't the only choices that Etna winemakers face. Just as certain yeasts affect a wine, the speed and temperature of a fermentation divine the characters that arrive in your glass. More and more cantinas prefer temperature-controlled vats or cold rooms to moderate the speed of fermentation, rendering a wine that is both expressive and territorial. Hot and fast fermentations kill yeasts or literally cook the aromas and flavors out of the must. The containers in which a wine is made and stored also matter.

Stainless steel, fiberglass, and cement are the most important inert containers currently being used on the mountain. Stainless steel and fiberglass create a virtually perfect anaerobic environment for slow aging. Oak *tonneaux* (500 L) and botti of varying sizes are popular, but first-passage, toasted barriques (225 L) are losing favor for the way they cover up the supple territorial qualities of Etna's wines. Historically, local wines have been made in large chestnut vats. Today, only one company, Barone di Villagrande, has maintained this practice exclusively for their Etna Rosso. Others are dabbling with the idea.

Affinamento (aging) is done in full containers so there is little or no air. Oxygen along with heat and light are the three cavaliers of aging. Fluctuations in the intensity of these three elements can improve or destroy a wine. Inert vessels like glass, fiberglass, and stainless steel help the wine to evolve in isolation, without losing volume. It's like bagging food for freshness. By limiting the influence of the natural elements, the wine evolves more slowly. Wood containers require regular topping up as water molecules in the wine move through the staves to the less-humid cellar, and the wine loses volume. This "angel's share" replaces the water loss with oxygen. And because oxygen ages the wine, most producers will top up the containers frequently.

You may be wondering why these porous vats are used at all. They serve a purpose. As small quantities of oxygen bind with the wine, they aid its stability and development. Inert containers, on the contrary, do not permit any contact with oxygen. Most winemakers introduce oxygen judiciously, as a tool to guide the must and wine through fermentation and aging.

Wines are racked once or twice during their aging and most often clarified by gravity or bentonite. Other fining agents (gelatins, egg whites, isinglass) are generally eschewed. Tartaric stabilization—a process that lures tartaric salts (wine diamonds) out of the liquid—happens naturally over the winter, after the harvest. Filtration has been normalized throughout the community. Producers do their best to make sure the wine is clear, but if a little sediment gets into the bottle, that's fine too.

Bottling is done using anaerobic and aerobic methods, depending on the intention and equipment at the winery. Bottling by hand is less frequent than systematic machines, which clean, sparge, and fill the bottles before sealing them. Closures include natural cork and technical stoppers that permit miniscule quantities of oxygen into the bottle. I have seen screw caps, but glass stoppers or crown caps (beer caps) have yet to make an appearance for any Etna wine in the market.

Chestnut Barrels—Mount Etna was introduced to wood wine barrels over centuries. As wood moved from fad to standard practice, it became necessary to have a ready and affordable source.

The slopes of Mount Etna were teeming with forests. Timber was plentiful, with chestnut trees everywhere. They were felled and aged and formed into small *barili*, medium *botticelli*, and large *botti*.

Recent trends have replaced chestnut with French, Austrian, and Slavonian oak in an almost unanimous way. However, Barone di Villagrande has opted to shirk the French fad for their portfolio of Etna Rosso. Both wines manage to hit all of the best intentions of Etna Rosso while remaining one of the last opportunities to taste a modern version of what Etna once was.

According to unpublished research done by the winery, the chestnut helps to stabilize the color of the red wines for longer than any other wood that they have trialed. Their wines are on the darker side of royal ruby and crimson. The sweet aroma of toasted chestnut infuses nicely with the fresh red fruit profiles of Nerello Mascalese and Nerello Cappuccio.

For merchants shipping wines throughout Europe over the centuries, the chestnut helped their wines appear fresher for longer. This was a huge selling point.

WHITE WINES

It seems fairly simplistic to say that white wines grown on Mount Etna are pale lemon-lime to gold in color with aromas and flavors of stone fruits, ripe citrus, savory herbs, a juicy acidity, and lingering finish that is both mineral and salty, but this is the target that producers are trying to hit. While many of Etna's white wines are based on Carricante, indigenous Sicilian varieties and internationally recognized grapes make this one of the mountain's most exciting and delicious categories. Those who sidestep the Etna DOC recipe do so with the purpose of producing white wines that carry an Etna signature.

The process of making the wines is similar across the board. Ripe, white grapes are collected and destemmed before pressing. Whole-bunch pressing is rare. Mechanical basket and pneumatic bladder presses are standard, though some wineries still implement screw and ratchet presses. The pulp is sent to a vat to clarify over one to two days by gravity before being removed (racked) from the sediment and transferred to fermentation vessels. Alcoholic fermentation can take days or weeks to complete. Malolactic fermentation (MLF) is exploited, to soften the acidity of a wine, but its use varies from cantina to cantina, grape to grape, and vintage to vintage.

White wines made using extended contact between the juice and grape skins show the potential complexity that arrives from aging Carricante but without the wait. For some producers, longer skin contact communicates everything of the terroir into the wine. Through this procedure additional potassium from the grape skins leaches into the must, increasing the pH slightly. In my own experiments over the years, allowing some skin contact is a wonderful technique for creating sophisticated, easy-drinking wines sooner. However, by increasing the pH, there is the danger of losing long-term freshness and introducing strong, musky vegetal odors into the wine. These odors can mask the delicate natural perfumes of Carricante. The best practices for skin-contact Carricante focus on ripe-to-mature grapes that are left to macerate in anaerobic conditions for a short period of time (twelve hours or less).

Aging white wines on fine lees with some *bâttonage,* or lees stirring, is the most accepted practice. Many producers lean toward using inert containers with some aerobic winemaking practices (*rimontaggio* and racking) to introduce oxygen where needed. Ideally, bottling occurs when the wines are young, within a year after the harvest.

While most cantinas follow their own version of the above practices, others prefer to experiment. Blends are one way of shifting the profile of a wine. Another is by prolonging grape skin contact before or during fermentation. Wines made with Albanello, Chardonnay, Coda di Volpe, Fiano, Grecanico Dorato, Grillo, Inzolia, Minella Bianca, Riesling, Traminer Aromatico, Viognier, and even Nerello Mascalese (vinified as a white wine) are yielding enchanting results. Some of these trials have led to internationally recognized branded products that are now made year in and year out.

Non-DOC white wines to try (Winery – Name / Variety)

Buscemi – *Il Bianco* / Blend

Calabretta – Vino Bianco / Minella

Camarda – Vino Bianco / Blend

Cantine Scudero – *Sedicidieci* / Blend

Destro – *Nausica* / Blend

Enò-Trio – Traminer Aromatico

Federico Graziani – *Mareneve* / Blend

Filippo Grasso – *Carrico 68.8* / Blend

Francesco Modica – *Terre dei Modica Bianco* / Blend

Frank Cornelissen – *MunJebel Bianco* / Blend

Guido Coffa – Catarratto

Passopisciaro – *Passobianco* / Chardonnay

Pietradolce – *Sant'Andrea* / Carricante

Planeta – *Eruzione 1614* / Riesling

Santa Maria La Nave – *Millesulmare* / Grecanico Dorato

Serafica – *Mirantur* / Catarratto

Tascante – Chardonnay

Tenuta Monte Ilice – *Asia* / Blend

Vigneti Vecchio – *Sciare Vive* / Blend

Vini Scirto – *Don Pippinu* / Blend

Vino Nibali – *Butterfly* / Blend

Wiegner – *Elisena* / Fiano

ETNA BIANCO DOC

Etna Bianco is a white wine with immense potential. It can be made from white grapes grown anywhere within the defined areas of the Etna DOC.

The basic recipe for Etna Bianco must include a minimum of 60 percent Carricante. Etna Bianco Superiore has to be made from a minimum of 80 percent Carricante grapes that are grown around Milo, a *comune* high on Etna's eastern flank. The remaining percentage of the blend can be any of an approved list, including Catarratto Comune and Catarratto Lucido, Trebbiano, Minella Bianca, Inzolia, Grillo, and other non-aromatic varieties. The minimum alcohol by volume (ABV) is 11 percent and 11.5 percent respectively.

These are not heady wines. In fact, young Carricante is quite shy. It has a pale color with subtle aromas and flavors of white flowers, pear, and citrus. It's usually blended with Catarratto. Most old vineyards also have some Minella Bianca, which can add a spicy, white peach profile to a blend. Together, these grapes form the traditional Etna Bianco being produced today.

Etna Bianco DOC wines to try

Alta Mora – Etna Bianco / Carricante

Benanti – Etna Bianco / Carricante

Biondi – *Pianta*, Contrada Ronzini / Blend

Cantina Malopasso – Etna Bianco / Blend

Cantine Russo – *Contrada Rampante* / Blend

Contrada Santo Spirito di Passopisciaro – *Animalucente* / Blend

Cottanera – *Contrada Calderara* / Blend

Destro – *Isolanuda*, Contrada Montelaguardia / Carricante

Donnafugata – *Sul Vulcano* / Blend

Eudes – *Bianco di Monte*, Contrada Monte Gorna / Blend

Famiglia Statella – Etna Bianco / Blend

Federico Curtaz – *Gamma* / Carricante

Feudo Cavaliere – *Millemetri*, Contrada Feudo Cavaliere / Carricante

Fifth Estate – Etna Bianco / Blend

Filippo Grasso – *Mari di Ripiddu*, Contrada Calderara / Carricante

Firriato – *Le Sabbie dell'Etna* / Blend

Generazione Alessandro – *Trainara* / Blend

Giovanni Rosso – *Contrada Monte Dolce* / Blend

Girolamo Russo – *Nerina* / Blend

Graci – *Arcurìa*, Contrada Arcurìa / Carricante

I Custodi delle vigne dell'Etna – *Ante* / Blend

Irene Badalà – Etna Bianco / Blend

Massimo Lentcsh – Etna Bianco / Carricante

Monteleone – Etna Bianco / Carricante

Murgo – Etna Bianco / Blend

Nicosia – Etna Bianco / Blend

Palmento Costanzo – *Bianco di Sei*, Contrada Santo Spirito / Carricante

Pietradolce – *Archineri* / Carricante

Planeta – Etna Bianco / Carricante

Quantico – Etna Bianco / Blend

Rupestre – Etna Bianco / Carricante

Santa Maria La Nave – *Re d'Ilice* / Blend

Sciara – *Lacrima di Luna* / Blend

Serafica – *Grotta Della Neve* / Blend

Tenuta Boccarossa – Etna Bianco / Carricante

Tenuta di Fessina – *A' Puddara*, Contrada Manzudda / Carricante

Tenuta Ferrata – *Cielo Cèneris* / Carricante

Tenuta Masseria Setteporte – *N'Ettaro* / Blend

Tenuta Tascante – *Buonora*, Contrada Piano Dario / Blend

Terra Costantino – *Contrada Blandano* / Blend

Terre di Nuna – Etna Bianco / Blend

Tornatore – *Contrada Pietrarizzo* / Carricante

Vini Gambino – *Tifeo* / Blend

Vivera – *Salisire, Contrada Martinella* / Carricante

ETNA BIANCO SUPERIORE DOC

Etna Bianco Superiore has to be made from a minimum of 80 percent Carricante grapes that are grown in contrade within the comune of Milo, high on Etna's eastern flank. The wine must consist of at least 80 percent Carricante, yet most producers increase the quantity to near purity. The result is a crisp Etna Bianco with increased acidity, temperate fruit, and saline flavors that benefit from extended aging in the bottle. Though many Etna Bianco Superiores are released one year after the harvest, the finest wines begin to show their best after about four years in the bottle.

A pure Carricante can take years to relax if it's made right. This is part of its charm. It requires patience. For the merchants of Riposto, this was also one of its greatest assets. Carricante could withstand long sea voyages without losing its freshness. We can chalk that up to the grape's naturally high acidity; it acts as a preservative. As Carricante ages, however, the light citrus profile of the wine evolves to sun-dried citrus zest, ginger, herbs, and

A new vintage of Etna Rosato rides a conveyor belt between the corking and capsuling machines. The pale color of many rosé wines is a tribute to the tradition of pistamutta, which was made from very short maceration of black and white varieties. These days, producers are increasingly using Nerello Mascalese to achieve pale wines with a supple profile.

toasted almond. Delicate aromas of petrol, similar to those found in aged Riesling, can also develop as Carricante ages.

The best flavors arrive through extended aging. In the cellar, Carricante has an affinity for aging on fine lees, and its high concentration of malic acid makes it a good candidate for some malolactic fermentation (MLF). During MLF, malic acid is converted to lactic acid. The process enhances the depth and character of Carricante. Many winemakers avoid complete MLF, because they prefer their Etna Bianco to be light and fresh, the perfect *aperitivo* or accompaniment for seafood.

There are always going to be quick solutions for winemakers. Every year offers new opportunities to make the trip to great wine shorter. With Carricante, however, the best path is often the longest. Slow and gentle pressing followed by cool anaerobic clarification and fermentation, with bâttonage and aging on fine lees, renders an elegantly structured and savory wine with incredible potential for aging.

Etna Bianco Superiore DOC wines to try

Barone di Villagrande – *Contrada Villagrande* / Blend

Benanti – *Pietra Marina* / Carricante

Calcagno – *Primazappa* / Carricante

Cantine Edomé – *Aitna* / Carricante

Eredi di Maio – *Affiu* / Carricante

Federico Curtaz & Eredi di Maio – *Kudos* / Carricante

Iuppa – *Lindo* / Blend

Maugeri – *Frontebosco* / Carricante

Sive Natura – *Biancomilo Caselle* / Carricante

Tenuta Delle Terre Nere – Blend

Tenuta di Fessina – *Musmeci* / Carricante

I have a soft spot for Etna's pale red wines. The mountain rosé is rosy in color and light- to medium-bodied with aromas and flavors of cranberry, cherry, strawberry, brambles, earth, and wet stone. They are inviting and food friendly, but more importantly, these reddish wines are one of Etna's oldest traditions.

Pink wines can be made from almost any combination of white wine and red wine, or black grapes and white grapes, or simply black grapes. In blends of red and white wines, the winemaker adds one to the other to create a pale red wine. Etna cantinas avoid this method, preferring instead to press or macerate black grapes to extract a small amount of color and structure from the skins before discarding them. The grapes are often harvested earlier than they would be for a robust red wine, to feature more acidity and less alcohol in the finished product.

Another method is called *salasso*. Black grapes are harvested and brought into the winery at full ripeness. They are destemmed and sent to the fermentation vat. Immediately, small amounts of pigment begin to redden the must. Within the first twenty-four hours, it's pink but not entirely red. A portion of the liquid is drawn off from the vat and fermented apart from the black grapes. While salasso is a good practice for cool years, or when there is rain at harvest, it also offers an opportunity to produce two wines from a single lot of grapes. But a salasso also has a higher potential alcohol level, because it is derived from fully ripe grapes that have been harvested for a full-bodied red wine. They will have a darker color and a fuller body.

These pink wines rarely spend any serious time aging in the winery. They are released into the market when the wines are light, fragrant, and thrilling. It's part of their charm. They bring us back to the beginning of Etna's winemaking story, when the liquid in our glass was a gateway to euphoria rather than the certified totality of its parts.

Rosé wines to try

Az. Agr. Siciliano – *Rosato del Dottore* / Nerello Mascalese

Enò-Trio – *Rosato* / Pinot Nero

Frank Cornelissen – *Susucaru* / Blend

Giuseppe Lazzaro – *Spariggiu* / Nerello Mascalese

Masseria del Pino – *SuperLuna* / Blend

SRC – *Rosato* / Blend

Terra Costantino – *Rasola* / Blend

ETNA ROSATO DOC

Etna Rosato is a wine done by the numbers. The Etna DOC mandates a minimum of 80 percent Nerello Mascalese. The remaining 20 percent can be composed of Nerello Cappuccio, or 10 percent Nerello Cappuccio and 10 percent non-aromatic Sicilian grapes.

Depending on the blend and processing of the grapes, Etna Rosato has a range of colors, from onionskin to strawberry and amber. Pale colors are generally linked to very short pressing cycles of black grapes. Deeper colors are an indication of longer skin contact and maximum percentages of Nerello Cappuccio. The Mascalese brings structured red fruit, tannins, and spice. Cappuccio contributes subtle violet colors and a fuller body. As a unit they resemble the diversity that exists within many vineyards. It's one of the reasons the two black grapes are legally joined in the DOC legislation for Rosato and Rosso wines. They almost need each other.

The simplest way of making Etna Rosato is to harvest and press ripe (not mature) black grapes and treat the must like it's a white wine. Some winemakers follow a different strategy. Instead of pressing black grapes immediately after harvesting, clusters are destemmed and sent to a vat where they spend up to forty-eight hours[8] in contact with the juice at cold temperatures, in an oxygen-free environment, before being sent to the press. The pigmented juice that exits the press is fermented at cool temperatures. While warm temperatures and MLF add complexity to the wine, most winemakers avoid these practices in favor of the primary fruit with some territorial flavors.

Etna Rosato DOC wines to try

Al-Cantàra – *Amuri di Fimmina e Amuri di Matri* / Nerello Mascalese

Barone di Villagrande – Etna Rosato / Blend

Benanti – Etna Rosato / Nerello Mascalese

Calcagno – *Romice delle Sciare* / Blend

Cantina Malopasso – Etna Rosato / Nerello Mascalese

Destro – *Zàhra* / Nerello Mascalese

Donnafugata – *Sul Vulcano* / Nerello Mascalese

Fattorie Romeo del Castello – *Vigorosa* / Blend

Feudo Vagliasindi – *Millemetri* / Nerello Mascalese

Fifth Estate – Etna Rosato / Nerello Mascalese

Filippo Grasso – *Ripiddu in Rosato* / Nerello Mascalese

Firriato – *Le Sabbie dell'Etna* / Nerello Mascalese

Graci – Etna Rosato / Nerello Mascalese

I Custodi delle vigne dell'Etna – *Alnus* / Blend

Massimo Lentsch – *Oma* / Nerello Mascalese

Nicosia – *Vulka* / Nerello Mascalese

Oro d'Etna – *Vena Ætna* / Nerello Mascalese

Pietradolce – Etna Rosato / Nerello Mascalese

Palmento Costanzo – *Mofete* / Nerello Mascalese

Roberto Abbate – Etna Rosato / Nerello Mascalese

Serafica – *Grotta Dei Lamponi* / Nerello Mascalese

Tenuta Antica Cavalleria – *Dame* / Blend

Tenuta di Fessina – *Erse* / Blend

Tenute Bosco – *Piano Dei Daini* / Nerello Mascalese

Terra Costantino – *deAetna* / Blend

Terrazze dell'Etna – *Rosato* / Nerello Mascalese

Theresa Eccher – *Ariel* / Nerello Mascalese

Tornatore – Etna Rosato / Nerello Mascalese

Travaglianti – Etna Rosato / Nerello Mascalese

Vini Gambino – *Tifeo* / Nerello Mascalese

Vini Scirto – *All'Antica* / Blend

Zumbo – *Ciùriciùri* / Nerello Mascalese

RED WINES

When people ask why I came to Etna, I often tell them I fell in love with a grape. Nerello Mascalese, to be precise. Though it is the dominant berry planted on Etna, scores of other black grapes have been grown on the volcano for millennia. I like those too, just not as much as Nerello. The landscape—stony and sandy soil, bright warm light, and constant cool breezes—lends itself to the production of elegant pigmented wines. Virtually every winery on the mountain makes one.

In the cellar, grape clusters are destemmed, and the berries are sent to a fermentation vat. Most recipes follow stepped protocols that protect the must from oxidation, enhance the absorption of aromas and flavors, and initiate a strong, slow fermentation that renders a dry red wine with good acidity, noble colors, pleasant aromas, and inviting flavors. Once the yeasts begin to work, the cellar team pushes the floating grape skins (cap) down, making a soup of grapes and fermenting juice, or they use a pump to draw off a portion of the young wine, spraying it over the top of the skins (*rimontaggio*). As the must passes among the grapes it picks up more color, aromatics, and character from the skins. The more time the skins and fermenting juice spend in contact, the more character the must absorbs. Once most of the sugars have been converted to alcohol, the tank is drained, the grapes are pressed, and the new wine is transferred to aging vessels, where it goes through MLF. Red wines can be clarified and filtered, but not everyone chooses to make that effort. Trial and error proves the best methods.

Non-Nerello reds fare well in the warm, sunny Mediterranean climate, but Etna's volcanic terrain often trumps the flavors we expect to find in popular varietal wines. Some of these are vinified and bottled separately, while others are grown in such small quantities that they get included in field blends as a tribute rather than adding anything meaningful to the wine. Wines that dedicate a notable percentage of the blend (5% or more) to other red grapes, or that create their own proprietary blends, do so with the intention of showcasing the potential of these varieties.

As experiments on Etna go, Nerello Cappuccio is one of the most exciting studies to follow. Nerello Cappuccio is a plum-colored wine with aromas and flavors of dark forest fruits, blueberry, and plum. On the palate, the wine has a moderate body with satin tannins. This is a byproduct of its upbringing. Nerello Cappuccio has soft, fleshy fruit and high levels of malvin and acylated anthocyanins, which intensify color and antioxidant properties in the must and wine. As red wines oxidize, they lose color (crimson moving to pale brown). Musts with higher levels of acylated anthocyanins typically hold their color longer, even under high temperatures. Looking at local fermentation practices and the merchant culture over the last few centuries, short, hot fermentations and oxidation could easily undermine Mascalese's sensory appeal. By adding Nerello Cappuccio, the red wine of Etna looked, smelled, and tasted healthier longer. When fermented together, as opposed to blending two finished wines, the tannins from the Mascalese and the anthocyanins from the Cappuccio combine to form a perpetual handshake that improves the stability of the wine. As a result, Nerello Cappuccio has been interplanted in nearly every Etna vineyard. It was only a matter of time before winemakers started to wonder what it could do on its own.

Producers bottling Nerello Cappuccio focus on recipes that include cool-temperature fermentations and aging in inert containers. Cappuccio performs best when a portion of the wine goes through MLF in used wood containers. Reduction[9] proves to be a problem when the wine is stored solely in inert vats or it isn't given enough air during fermentation and aging. It's a wine that needs to breathe.

One of the most underused black grapes on Etna is Alicante, known internationally as Grenache Noir (and many other names). Alicante is an anomaly on Etna. It matures quickly, ripening around the middle of September in a normal year. It takes Nerello one more month to complete ripening. In a blend, Alicante adds potential alcohol, rich fruit, and a depth of character to the finished wine. Those who include it on their labels do so with the intention of promoting the grape as an asset to the blend.

Four producers make Alicante a primary player in their red wines. Guido Coffa makes a pure Alicante from a small vineyard on the east slope, near Pisano, not far from his organic farm and luxury resort, Monaci delle Terre Nere. Mirella Buscemi adds 30 percent Alicante to her Nerello blend, grown in Contrada Tartaraci, on the volcano's northwest flank. From a vineyard near Randazzo, on the volcano's north slope, SRC augments Nerello Mascalese with Alicante at 20 percent. And I Custodi delle vigne dell'Etna names Alicante as a notable part of one Nerello blend.

Red wines made without Nerello regularly make a splash when they are included in a tasting, but too few wineries are producing these to suggest that they are currently important for the future of Mount Etna.

I tend to seek out the following wines when I want something inviting and different.

Non-Nerello red wines to try

Azienda Agricola Siciliano – *Rossoeuphoria* / Pinot Nero

Barone di Villagrande – *Sciara* / Merlot

Calabretta – Pinot Nero

Castello Solicchiata – *Dagala del Barone* / Pinot Nero

Cottanera – *L'Ardenza* /Mondeuse

Duca di Salaparuta – *Nawàri* / Pinot Nero

Guido Coffa – *U'Ranaci* / Alicante

Murgo – Cabernet Sauvignon; and *Tenuta San Michele* / Pinot Nero

Passopisciaro – *Franchetti* / Petit Verdot, Cesanese d'Affile

Planeta – *Eruzione 1614* / Pinot Nero

Tenuta Benedetta – *Vigna Benedetta* / Sangiovese

Terrazze dell'Etna – Pinot Nero

Wiegner – *Artemisio* / Cabernet Franc

The following list of wines are made on Etna, but because the blend does not fit the recipe for most Etna wines, or the vineyards fall outside the defined boundaries, sometimes by only a few meters, they cannot carry the Etna DOC classification. It's a sticking point for some producers. Some wineries within the Etna DOC simply choose not to apply for Etna DOC certification for a part or all of their portfolio, bottling their wines using DOC/DOP Sicilia or IGT/IGP Terre Siciliane instead. The wines may be every bit representative of Mount Etna, but because of the way they are labeled, consumers only know that they come from Sicily or Italy. On Etna it's important to know the producer, where their vineyards are, and how the wines are being made.

Non-Etna DOC Nerello wines to try
Sciara – *Centenario* / Blend

Benanti – Nerello Cappuccio

Buscemi – *Tartaraci* / Blend

Calabretta – *Piede Franco* / Nerello Mascalese

Camarda – Nerello Mascalese

Feudo Vagliasinidi – Nerello Cappuccio

Frank Cornelissen – *MunJebel Rosso* / Nerello Mascalese

Graci – *Quota 1000 Barbabecchi* / Nerello Mascalese

Guido Coffa – *Le Viti di Minico* / Blend

Masseria Setteporte – Nerello Mascalese

Passopisciaro – *Contrada Rampante (Contrada R)* / Nerello Mascalese

Serafica – *Mirantur* / Nerello Cappuccio

Sive Natura – *Nerello Dei Cento Cavalli* / Nerello Mascalese

SRC – *Rivaggi* / Blend

Tenuta Aglaea – *Aglaea* / Nerello Mascalese

Tenuta Rustica – *Sparviero* / Nerello Mascalese

Terrazze dell'Etna—*Cratere* / Nerello Mascalese, Petit Verdot

Terre dei Modica – *Vino Rosso* / Nerello Mascalese

ETNA ROSSO DOC AND ETNA ROSSO RISERVA DOC

The red wines on Mount Etna have a cache of red fruit aromas and flavors, with tenacious tannins, elegant but striking acidity, and a saline finish, which are fundamentally tied to the high-elevation, volcanic terrain and the objective of the winemaker. This is one of the most exciting parts of the Etna scene. No two wines are ever the same.

Based on a minimum of 80 percent Nerello Mascalese, Etna Rosso and Etna Rosso Riserva follow the same blending protocols as Etna Rosato, with a few exceptions. First, the Rosso and Rosso Riserva spend more time in contact with the grape skins—as long as thirty days. As a result, the wines are dark ruby in color. Second, the Rosso Riserva category mandates lower yields than is required for Rosso and Rosato wines. Third, Rosso Riserva spends a minimum of one year in wood and four years aging within the Etna zone before it can be released. The type of wood is not specified. Those who produce an Etna Rosso Riserva usually do so with extended aging beyond the minimums.

Etna Rosso can be made from grapes grown anywhere within the delimited Etna zone. The most striking contrasts in Etna Rosso occur between flanks and elevations. Vines planted at the extremes of growing have a tendency to produce fewer, lighter clusters than vines at lower elevations. Considering that Etna is one large cone, we find the most fertile soils at changes in slope (i.e., at the base of craters, in valleys, or on plateaus). As fertility improves, so too does the potential yield per plant.

Fermentations under temperature control that are minimally managed (less aggressive punch downs and fewer pump overs) tend to extract more savory fruit and less tannin. Musts that are fermented at higher temperatures or without temperature control show more territorial qualities derived from the pulp. Extended skin contact adds complexity and tannins, but the wines can be a little astringent if un-fined or consumed too young. These harsh components in the wine are managed by gentle fermentations, pressing the grapes off before primary fermentation is completed, or by managing the press wine separately from the first wines drafted off the vat.

MLF is universally practiced on Etna Rosso and Riserva wines. Depending on the producer, MLF occurs in inert containers, in wood, or sometimes during alcoholic fermentation. When the grapes are pressed and sent to wood to undergo MLF, Nerello takes on additional noble aromas and flavors, and the wood is better integrated in the wine. If the acids are converted before being put into wood, the synchronicity between the wine and the container can seem disjointed. New barriques, tonneaux, and botti are used for Nerello. Depending on the origin and age of the wood, and how it's been bent—flame, vapor, dry-heat—and toasted, all vats have an effect on the wine that rests inside.

Etna Rosso shows best when it's aged in second- and third-passage tonneaux or botti with thick staves and a fine grain. Most cantinas choose French oak from the central and eastern departments of France (Tronçais, Nevers, Allier, and Vosges). Slavonian and Austrian oak have made inroads in the form of botti of 1,000 liters or more. Wines that age in stainless steel or fiberglass have less contact with oxygen in the winery. Cement vats without a lining tend to enhance the fruitiness, textures, and long-term stability of the wine, while cement vats with an epoxy lining act as an inert container. Antichi Vinai, Graci, Pietradolce, SRC, Terra Costantino, and Tornatore are among a growing number of producers who use cement vats for vinification and aging with positive results.

Etna Rosso / Etna Rosso Riserva DOC wines to try

Al-Cantàra – *O'Scuro O'Scuro* / Blend

Alta Mora – *Guardiola* / Nerello Mascalese

Antichi Vinai – *Koinè* / Blend

Barone di Villagrande – Etna Rosso / Blend

Benanti – *Serra della Contessa* / Blend

Biondi – *Cisterna Fuori* / Blend

Bizantino – Etna Bianco / Blend

Calcagno – *Feudo di Mezzo* / Nerello Mascalese

Cantina Malopasso – Etna Rosso / Blend

Cottanera – *Riserva Zottorinoto* / Blend

Destro – *Sciarakè* / Blend

Edomé – *Vigna Nica*, Contrada Feudo di Mezzo / Blend

Eduardo Torres Acosta – *Versante Nord* / Blend

Enò-Trio – *Pussenti* / Nerello Mascalese

Eudes – *Milleottocentoquaranta* / Blend

Famiglia Statella – *Pettinociarelle* / Blend

Fattorie Romeo del Castello – *Allegracore* / Blend

Feudo Cavaliere – *Millemetri* / Blend

Fifth Estate – Etna Rosso / Nerello Mascalese

Filippo Grasso – *Ripiddu* / Blend

Firriato – *Signum Aetnae* / Blend

Francesco Modica – *Nonno Ciccio* / Nerello Mascalese

Generazione Alessandro – *Croceferro* / Nerello Mascalese

Giovanni Rosso – Etna Rosso / Blend

Girolamo Russo – *San Lorenzo* / Blend

Graci – Etna Rosso / Nerello Mascalese

I Custodi delle vigne dell'Etna – *Aetneus* / Blend

La Gelsomina – *Rosso della Contea* / Blend

Masseria del Pino – *i nove fratelli* / Blend

Masseria Setteporte – Etna Rosso / Blend

Massimo Lentsch – *San Teodoro* / Nerello Mascalese

Mecori – *Duo* / Blend

Monteleone – Etna Rosso / Blend

Monterosso – *Sisma* / Nerello Mascalese

Nicosia – *Riserva Monte Gorna* / Blend

Palmento Costanzo – *Nero di Sei* / Blend

Passopisciaro – *Passorosso* / Blend

Patria – Etna Rosso Riserva / Blend

Pietradolce – *Archineri* / Blend

Quantico – Etna Rosso / Blend

Roberto Abbate – Etna Rosso / Nerello Mascalese

Rupestre – Etna Rosso / Nerello Mascalese

Santa Maria La Nave – *Calmarossa* / Blend

Sciara – *760* / Nerello Mascalese

Serafica – *Grotta del Gelo* / Blend

Tenuta Antica Cavalleria – *DAM* / Blend

Tenuta Benedetta – *Vigna Laura* / Blend

Tenuta Boccarossa – Etna Rosso / Nerello Mascalese

Tenuta delle Terre Nere – *Guardiola* / Blend

Tenuta di Aglaea – Etna Rosso, Contrada Santo Spirito / Blend

Tenuta di Fessina – *Erse* / Blend

Tenuta Monte Gorna – Etna Rosso / Blend

Tenuta Pietro Caciorgna – *N'Anticchia* / Blend

Tenute Bosco – *Vigne Vico* / Blend

Terra Costantino – deÆtna / Blend

Terrazze dell'Etna – *Cirneco* / Nerello Mascalese

Theresa Eccher – *Altero* / Blend

Tornatore – *Trimarchisa* / Blend

Travaglianti – Etna Rosso / Nerello Mascalese

Vigneti Vecchio – *Sciare Vive* / Blend

Vini Ferrara Sardo – *'nzemmula* / Nerello Mascalese

Vini Gambino – *Petto Dragone* / Blend

Vini Scirto – *A'Culonna* / Blend

Vivera – *Martinella* / Blend

Wiegner – *Treterre* / Blend

Zumbo – *Manata*, Contrada Trimarchisa / Nerello Macalese

SPUMANTE AND ETNA SPUMANTE DOC

I made my first sparkling wine in the traditional method from Chardonnay, in California, in honor of my wedding year. Making traditional method, or

Etna Spumante is a true metodo classico. After a base wine is made—from a minimum 60% Nerello Mascalese—the wine receives a mixture of sugar and yeast to initiate a second fermentation that takes place in bottle. Here, the bottles are being inverted to move the yeast toward the neck for disgorgement.

metodo classico, sparkling wine is like walking a tightrope. One misstep is all it takes to lose your grace, equilibrium, or worse.

After five years aging on their lees, I started moving the sparkling wedding wine to the riddling rack. Two bottles inadvertently touched, breaking one of them, sending the jagged neck of the bottle flying past my throat. If I had moved one or two centimeters to the right, I would not be writing these words.

Those who have worked with sparkling wines know it can be dangerous. Fermenting anything in a closed container is basically a bad idea. Putting a still wine through a second, controlled fermentation in glass requires attention. Once the bottle fermentation is complete, the pressure inside can reach 45 psi. or more. Any imperfection in the glass or a subtle collision, the bottles can explode.

But I'm getting ahead of myself.

When the freshly harvested grapes arrive at the winery, they usually have low sugar and elevated acidity levels. The grapes are pressed softly to release the juice but not hard enough to extract the bitter qualities of the grape skins (less than 5 psi.). From there the must is treated as though a still wine is being produced. The first fermentation (alcoholic) renders a "base wine" with good acidity, low alcohol (approximately 10–11 percent ABV), and delicate aromas and flavors of the grapes.

A blend (*liqueur de tirage*) of yeasts, sugar, and often a little bentonite clay is mixed into the still wine. The wine is bottled immediately and topped with a crown cap, the same closure used on a bottle of beer. Over the next days to weeks, the wine inside the bottle goes through a second fermentation. The process increases the alcohol by 1 percent or more, but because the crown cap is fixed to the bottle, the gas cannot escape, and the wine absorbs all of the carbon dioxide created. For several months to years, the wine is left to age on the lees of dead yeasts.

While the wine ages inside the bottle, on its lees, it undergoes a process called "autolysis," which contributes rich, complex flavors. When the wine is ready for drinking, the bottles are jiggled (*remuage*, or riddling), by hand or machine, so that the lees move toward the neck of the bottle.

By the time the lees has fallen, all the bottles are standing on their heads. The heads and necks are frozen to suspend the lees and the crown cap is released (*sboccatura*). The pressure trapped inside the bottle pushes out the plug of sediment. The bottle is then topped off with a house blend of wine and sugar (*dosaggio*) and corked. The precise recipe of the *dosaggio* (dosage) varies from winery to winery, vintage to vintage, and wine to wine.

As important as it is for producers to maintain a house style year in and year out, it is imperative for Etna spumante producers to feature the vintage. All Etna Spumante DOC must be from a single growing year.

Metodo classico sparkling wines are among the most technical wines in the world. Etna producers have gotten very good at this complicated process. The Etna DOC added a special category for these bottle-fermented sparkling wines, beginning with the 2011 vintage.

Etna Spumante DOC is a metodo classico sparkling wine made from a single vintage and a minimum of 80 percent Nerello Mascalese that has been vinified as a white wine (no skin contact) or a rosato (skin contact). The rest of the blend may include any other Sicilian grapes, but most Etna producers choose to use only Nerello Mascalese. The wines must be aged for a minimum of eighteen months. They are only required to have 9.5 percent ABV. Most tend to fall between 12–13 percent. Etna Spumante must also be closed with the traditional sparkling wine cork and cage. Wineries are focusing on Nerello Mascalese, but Carricante, Catarratto, Chardonnay, Grecanico Dorato, and Pinot Nero are also used on Etna.

Earnest efforts to make quality sparkling wines on the slopes of the volcano began in the 1860s, at Castello Solicchiata, on Etna's southwestern flank. Within the castle walls, Barone Spitaleri di Muglia used Pinot Nero and the metodo classico to make Champagne Etna. By 1870, his wines were being marketed internationally but the project was discontinued.

One hundred years after the first successful forays into sparkling wine, Michele Scammacca, of Murgo, began his own experiments using Nerello Mascalese. The first wines were released from the 1989 vintage. For the next twenty years, the Murgo team worked to improve the recipe. Not every year was good, but with each vintage the practice of making high-quality sparkling wine became easier.

Thinking back about the process of becoming Etna's first sparkling wine producer, Scammacca said, "The best years for Etna Spumante are the worst years for table wines. It takes time to learn these things. And we continue learning."

Today, the Murgo Extra Brut Metodo Classico Spumante is a dry pure Nerello Mascalese vinified as a white wine, which goes through some MLF and is aged in the bottle on lees for five years. Since 2011, others have joined Murgo in the expedition for more bubbly. Each winery is pursuing a house blend while contributing something to the discussion of Etna's potential for making these classic wines.

The Nerello-based sparklers have an acute acidity and savory fruit with a briny, spicy palate. The longer the wine ages in the bottle on lees, the more complex and elegant the flavors and *mousse* become. While most producers age their wines from twenty-four to thirty-six months, there is a growing trend toward longer aging for small lots of special vintages.

Spumante from Etna's white wine grapes have a racy acidity and supple autolytic tones, with essences and flavors of white pear, peach, herbs, and wild grasses. But, Carricante, Catarratto, and Grecanico Dorato take longer to achieve true excellence through autolysis and bottle aging after sboccatura. The Benanti *Noblesse* and Santa Maria La Nave's *Tempesta* are perfect examples of classic method sparkling wines made from white grapes that have the potential for extended bottle aging.

Clusters of Moscato Bianco dry in the sun at La Gelsomina near Presa. The appassimento process is intended to dehydrate the grapes, resulting in a sweeter wine with higher acidity. Photo by Benjamin Spencer.

Qualitatively, Etna Spumante DOC is on pace to turn heads. The greatest obstacle is the quantity of sparkling wines available. In 2014, Etna Spumante DOC wines accounted for only 2 percent of total production. Each year, the numbers increase, but it's hard to get traction in the international market with numbers like these, so the impact must be sensory. In other words, the wines must be delicious.

Spumante wines to try

Benanti – *La Moremio* Brut Rose / Nerello Mascalese*; *Noblesse* / Carricante

Cantine Russo – *Mon Pit* / Nerello Mascalese

Destro – *Saxanigra* / Nerello Mascalese*

Firriato – *Gaudensius Blanc de Noir* / Nerello Mascalese*

Gambino – *Brut* / Nerello Mascalese*

La Gelsomina – *Brut* / Nerello Mascalese, Nerello Cappuccio*

Murgo – *Extra Brut* / Nerello Mascalese

Nicosia – *Sosta Tre Santi* / Nerello Mascalese*

Palmento Costanzo – *Brut* / Nerello Mascalese*

Patria – *Pàlici* / Nerello Mascalese

Planeta – *Brut* / Carricante

Santa Maria La Nave – *Tempesta* / Grecanico Dorato

Tenute Mannino di Plachi – *Caterina di Plachi Brut* / Nerello Mascalese*

Terrazze dell'Etna – *Cuveé Brut* / Chardonnay

* Etna DOC Spumante

SWEET WINES

Sweet wines were one of the first stylized fermented beverages ever made. All anyone had to do was let the grapes dry in the sun before macerating them.

Graci's Nerello vineyard, on the north slope of the volcano in Contrada Arurìa at 600 meters AMSL, has a north-south planting scheme that allows even ripening on the east and west sides of each vine. The soil here is sandy-rocky with medium-size ripiddu stones.

In ancient Greece, the process was called *elisaton*.[10] Eventually, it became common knowledge that sweeter wines tasted amazing and stayed fresher longer than their drier counterparts.

Some Etna wineries do produce sweet wines, usually by the *appassimento* method. This ancient practice of sun drying, or otherwise allowing clusters to desiccate, causes dehydration within each grape. The sugars and acids become less diluted as the water inside the grape evaporates. Potential alcohol and perceptible acidity rises as a result. If the process continued, you would eventually have raisins, but most cantinas ferment their wines before all of the moisture inside the grape is lost.

In Etna's modern cellars, clusters are brought to the winery after the drying period and pressed. The sweet must is left to ferment. Slowly, the yeasts begin to populate the must. This isn't the rapid boiling we see in most fermenters. Overly sweet must ferments slow and steady, until it stops spontaneously. Aging protocols vary, but the finished wine is fragrant, fresh, luscious, and most often labeled *passito* (a shortening of *appassimento*).

Depending on the grape variety or blend, passito wines that use white grapes are gold to amber, and the red wines that use black grapes are ruby to opaque. Only a handful of producers are currently making quality passito from grapes grown on the volcano, though it's not for lack of trying. There is no possible legal status for these wines within the Etna DOC. They are bottled as IGT/IGP Terre Siciliane or DOC/DOP Sicilia Passito.

It seems strange that Etna would omit passito from the local legislation when wines have been made this way, on Etna, in Sicily, and particularly in the Mediterranean islands for millennia, but that is the situation. When the DOC legislation was drafted and approved (1965–1968), very few of these wines were being made. The local communities were still reeling from the Second World War. Farmers were no longer desiccating their grapes to make a sweet product for the market. They needed wine. Passito was and still is a luxury.

Al-Cantàra, Destro, Sciara, and Scilio make serious passito wines from black grapes grown and vinified on Etna. Each of the three wines is sweet and refreshing, with aromas and flavors of rich, dark fruits, spice, licorice, vanilla, and cocoa. The residual sugar in each wine varies from year to year, as do the alcohol levels, but the wines rarely rise above 15 percent ABV.

La Gelsomina, in Presa, on Etna's northeast flank, produces Moscato Bianco and Moscato dell'Etna for a luxurious passito.

Five generations ago, Moscato dell'Etna was one of the most important products grown on the mountain. Today, it's been relegated to a few plants per vineyard or table grapes, or it's been torn out completely because it falls into the "aromatic" category, for which there is no tolerance under the Etna DOC legislation.

Sweet wines to try

Al-Cantàra – *Lu Disìu* / Nerello Mascalese

Destro – *Anuar* / Nerello Mascalese

La Gelsomina – *Passito* / Moscato

Sciara – *Passito* / Nerello Mascalese

Scilio – *Sikèlios* / Unknown

Vino Nibali – *Vinazzu* / Nerello Mascalese

> **The Sweet Side of Nerello Mascalese**—No one can say that Etna producers aren't innovative. The Nibali family has made wine for more than sixty years, in Feudo di Mezzo and Contrada Moganazzi, on Etna's north slope. They produce wines from traditional varieties under the Etna DOC and IGT/IGP labeling schemes, but one of Nibali's wines has intentionally taken another path.

Vinazzu is a heady wine made from 100 percent Nerello Mascalese that goes through the appassimento process on the vine. By the end of November, the grapes are harvested by hand and fermented at cool temperatures for at least one week before pressing and aging.

The finished wine is dark, lush, and sweet, with 16 percent alcohol and an opulent profile. It resembles a traditional Amarone, but the *Vinazzu* features higher acidity and brighter flavors of dried forest berries, plum, and dried black cherry, with restrained tannins. It's a mouthful of wine, but it is unsulfured, so it tastes best when the wine is young (five to seven years).

The Nibali family suggests that the *Vinazzu* is a *vino di meditazione* (literally translated as a "meditation wine," it calls for reflective drinking, whether you have it with or without food), but it pairs well with a range of meats and cheeses too, making it a bold choice for a table wine or after a meal.

A SUMMARY

It's difficult to write a summary of a wine region that is only beginning to bloom. Methods are unrefined, strategies are uncertain, and the definition of what Etna does best is not yet proven.

We could go back and forth about modalities and ideals, but what most wineries are aiming for is a "good" to "really good" glass of wine. Sometimes, "good enough" is all that comes through. In others, it fails to meet the mark. It's not difficult to make a wine that has some appeal to someone somewhere but arriving to a point where a wine region yields one continuous "wow" moment after another doesn't come easy. It requires patience, understanding, attention to detail, and a sustained commitment to doing what the region as a whole does *best*.

Carricante and Nerello Mascalese are obvious answers, but producers cannot rely on the grapes alone. They need to ask and answer important questions. What is it about these wines that make them successful? How should they be aged? When do they taste best? It's possible that these questions will fall on a circular line. It would be better, however, if they lead somewhere. One thing we know with certainty: wineries that sustain a consistent high quality will be the ones that define Etna's future.

THE VINEYARDS

Mount Etna's first modern vineyards were planted near the sea, in the lower Alcantara Valley, at Capo Schisò, around 730 BCE. I use the word *modern* because it was the moment that organized winegrowing became a consistent part of the local culture. Within a decade, vineyards spanned the coastline, from Giardini Naxos to the Valley of Catania, and the slow climb up the volcano began. By the late nineteenth century, more than half of Etna's arable land was under vine. There is a vertical limit, however. Grapes don't ripen much higher than 1,300 meters AMSL. A few producers test Etna's limits with plantings above the *quota mille* (1,000-meter mark). Wines made from vineyards at high elevations can be delicate or stunning. The authors of the Etna DOC knew this. They also realized that the profile of Etna's wines changed if they were grown at too low of an elevation, or too far west.

Because of this, the Etna DOC takes the form of a semicircle band between 400 and 1,000 meters AMSL, stretching from Biancavilla, on the volcano's southern flank, along the steep eastern slope and around to the undulating north side. As the DOC approaches Randazzo, the border drops to 800 meters AMSL. While there are high-quality vineyards planted outside the DOC border, the authors of the legislation felt that the wines they made were dissimilar enough to those produced in other vineyards that they weren't included. This is one reason the DOC doesn't connect on the western pitch of the mountain. The exposure and warmer weather contribute to powerful wines that don't fit the profile of those grown closer to the sea.

For me, wines made from vineyards that border the Etna DOC are some of the most interesting. They speak of Etna in every way, but they are not permitted to carry the Etna name on the label. Instead, they are identified as a Sicilian wine and classified under the IGP/IGT Terre Siciliane or DOC/DOP Sicilia scheme. There have been discussions about expanding the borders and applying for DOCG status, but it's uncertain as of this writing what will come of it.

THE CONTRADE—MOUNT ETNA'S NEIGHBORHOODS

Feudo di Mezzo, in Passopisciaro, is one of my favorite places to visit. The *contrada* (neighborhood) plays host to several cantinas producing wines grown across multiple lava flows from different epochs at variable elevations in a compact space. The contours of hardened lava and dramatic changes in soil are their own type of boundaries. Individual vineyards are often segregated following nature's logic—a change in slope, the depth of soil, an increase in the percentage of rock. It's one of many places where the complexities of Etna's facade coincide.

This kaleidoscopic terrain covers about 80 percent of the mountain and 90 percent of the Etna DOC, including thirty-six unique compositions of rock, ash, and soil. But most of what we see is no more than 15,000 years old. As far as vineyard soils go, Etna is a perpetual baby. While most wine regions around the world are the result of prehistoric changes in the landscape, Etna's soils are refreshed regularly in the form of ash and molten lava. They are not distributed uniformly, however.

The southern flank of the volcano—from Belpasso to Adrano—is composed of four ancient soils with soft to sharp slopes the farther west one travels. The southeastern flank—between Nicolosi and Pisano—counts thirty-five spent volcanic craters and a patchwork of fourteen soil compositions that include heavy metals, sand, and silica. The eastern flank—below the

Valle del Bove—is marked by precipitous gradients and twelve soils that flow in sandy, rocky ribbons toward the sea. On Etna's north side—from Piedimonte Etneo to Randazzo—hills, forests, and lush valleys give way to gentle inclines with swaths of eleven overlapping deposits that include rock, pumice, and sand.[11] When we wrap these variables over a circular, sloped landscape, and include the staggered phases of erosion, the commonalities and differences between each vineyard site matter even more. For this reason, the Etna DOC authorized the use of place names on wine labels beginning with the 2011 vintage.

Within the Etna DOC there are portions of several *comuni* (municipalities) and 133 *contrade* (neighborhoods). In most cases, wines with a named contrada are single-vineyard wines. In contrade where many cantinas have vineyards, the nuances between wines can be subtle or dramatic, but there are commonalities among them. Differences become increasingly noticeable when wines from different contrade are compared.

Legally, contrade are defined by altitude, aspect, and geology, as well as their administrative borders. While one contrada name is usually featured on a wine label, to denote that the grapes were grown in a particular neighborhood, secondary names can be included as well. In these instances, the vineyard is likely located where a portion of the contrada overlaps with smaller historic areas (Feudo di Mezzo, Feudo di Mezzo-Porcaria, Feudo di Mezzo-Sottana, Calderara Sottana). Unfortunately, it is possible that a proprietary name can give the illusion of a site-specific wine while being an appellation blend. To avoid any confusion, I include the legal names and general locations of Etna's contrade in the back of this book.

Contrade Dell'Etna—Every April, the tents go up, the wines come out, and the gates to the Contrade dell'Etna open. This is the annual tasting of new Etna wines from the recent vintage.

According to Andrea Franchetti, the founder of Passopisciaro winery and the event, when he launched the idea, in 2008, it was a way for the local wineries to taste all of the wines, colleague to colleague.

More than a decade later, the Contrade dell'Etna is a gauntlet of consumers, journalists, and buyers all angling for a sip of the newest wines of Mount Etna.

In most cases the producers are only presenting their en primeur wines, but many keep an extra bottle or two under the table to share. It's an amazing opportunity to taste the full spectrum of wines from the mountain in a single moment and meet the people who are making them.

WORKING THE VINES

We used to live on a Cabernet Sauvignon vineyard in California. This gave me a unique view into seasonal and annual cycles of winegrowing, and how the work was done.

The vines were organized on wires in tall rows, with an irrigation system that turned on every few days to give the roots a soaking. Once a month, the tractor entered the vineyard to cut the grass, blast fungicides on the green part of the plant, or spray herbicides on the ground beneath the vines. Little attention was given to the arrangement of the clusters or canopy management; the grapes ripened effortlessly. During the harvest, fieldworkers removed the overripe clusters by hand and tossed them into a half-ton bin (the average quantity-by-weight in grapes that each bin can hold). That's how the grapes arrived at the winery, rather unsanctimoniously piled on top of each other in a mound weighing as much as a grand piano. It was quite normal for the grapes at the bottom to burst, creating a shallow pool of juice in the bins as they awaited processing.

This is the way things are done in many places, but not on Mount Etna. The volcano's steep slopes and rugged terrain require almost-exclusive manual labor for every vine. Gradients of any kind are typically stepped with terraces that are too small for a tractor to maneuver. Vineyards on precipitous inclines of deep, loose volcanic sand make it difficult or impossible for machines to gain any traction at all. Mechanization only becomes feasible on gentle

The Contrade dell'Etna is the annual tasting of new Mount Etna wines. It's an amazing opportunity to taste a spectrum of wines from the volcano and connect with the people who are making them.

slopes and plateaus. The tight spacing of Etna's traditional *alberello* (short bushes planted at about 1 m x 1 m) makes it necessary to use smaller, simple tools. What I see in most vineyards are *zappe* (hoes), string trimmers, and skinny gasoline-powered *motozappe* (rotavators).

Not only does this slow down the processes of managing a vineyard, it increases the necessity to have more workers on hand to make time-sensitive adjustments at precise moments. For producers who work with the celestial calendar, timing is even more precious. Hiring skilled laborers costs money, and every detail must be addressed by hand. For me, this is an important point to pause on. Not only does the amount of handwork explain the elevated price of many Etna wines, it gives sommeliers and consumers a symbolic assurance that every Etna vine receives personalized attention. Imagine trained

workers addressing every detail of each plant—shoot and leaf thinning, green harvesting, cluster selection—as they talk, sing, and laugh. There may not be a way to measure this element of interaction in a qualitative way, but it sure beats an occasional drive-by chemical bath administered by a monstrous machine.

There are no half-ton bins on Etna. During the harvest, wine

Giuseppe di Vincenzo uses a motorized tiller in Tenute Bosco's Vico vineyard. Turning the soil injects oxygen and nitrogen into the soil, and minimizes competition for water as the growing season begins.

grapes are handpicked into shallow crates weighing about fifteen kilograms when full (the weight of a car tire). In this way, the berries on the bottom don't burst, workers can carry the crates through the vines without much trouble, and every grape cluster arrives at the winery intact.

Once the grapes have been harvested, vines go into a winter slumber and many of the fluids of the plant descend to the trunk and roots. Workers allow several weeks to pass before reentering the vineyard. The first job is cutting the grass sometime before January. Tilling the grass instead of cutting it has the added effect of increasing nutrients and oxygen in the topsoil and creating paths for rainwater. Plowing also cuts a vine's surface roots and encourages them to search for water deeper underground. This is particularly important for a vine's sustainability; irrigation is not permitted for Etna DOC wines. Each plant must find its own way to survive.

Vines are typically pruned (*potatura*) in January, during the waning-descending moon. The timing is specific for two reasons. First, the pruning wound needs to heal, and the vine requires time to adjust to its new form before the plant reawakens in March, when the weather is warmer. Second, liquids in the plant are attracted to the movements of the moon. As the moon moves toward the horizon, the fluids in the plant descend. With all the energy in the roots or trunk of the vine, it doesn't lose energy when the old growth is removed. Where and how the cuts are made depends on training protocols, the yields desired, and the location of the vineyard (a rocky or fertile site). The pruned canes are usually burned or saved for propagating vines. Some vineyards are prepared in anticipation of pruning, to receive the cuttings immediately after they've been removed from the plant.

With the canes pruned and collected, a cavity is dug around the base of each vine. This shallow depression allows access to the surface roots, which are cut back using strong *forbici* (scissors), forcing the vine to seek water deeper underground. The cavity also captures water and airborne organic material (leaves, grasses, etc.). The soil from each depression (*conca*) is collected in small dunes (*munzeddi*) between the vines. In the spring and early summer, any vegetation that has grown on the surface of the mound is raked into each hollow, to introduce nitrogen to the plant. On average, this is done until the vineyard floor is once again level and there is very little if any vegetation competing for water during the hottest part of the summer.

Etna's volcanic soils lack natural nitrogen, which is of primary importance for all of the vine's green growth. In a modern planting scheme, the alleys between rows of vines are often seeded with nitrogen-rich plants that are tilled into the soil on a schedule. Overstimulation of the soil can be a problem in this case, so the rows and the type of seeds are alternated. This makes it possible to work the vines while assuring that they have a healthy diet. Nature has a way of doing this on a regular schedule, on Etna. Each year, the spontaneous vegetation changes. One year, for instance, the mountain was awash in red poppies. In another it was white chervil. During the 2019 growing season, the vineyard floors were white with chamomile. It's not hard to imagine that a population of flowers adds more than just nutrients to the soil. Their seductive aromas become a part of the air that every leaf on every vine breathes.

Vines begin to draw on their stored energy in February. This is also when new vines are planted—after the cold, but during the rainy season. By March, a nutrient-rich sap is moving through the plant, and small fuzzy leaves begin to appear at each bud point. They are sweet, I'm told. It's why the deer in California like them so much. Living on the vineyard for so many years I regularly sprinted through the morning fog in my pajamas, yelling obscenities at very fast high-jumping silhouettes. It's a good thing we don't have deer on Etna. There aren't any fences to keep them out.

The vines go through a period of fast green growth before *fioritura* (flowering) in June. *Vitis vinifera* are self-pollinating plants. They depend on the gentle influence of breezes, bugs, and bees to assist in the pollination process. Would-be grapes that are disrupted during fertilization can cause "shatter"—gaps between grapes. Rain, hail, and wind are of particular concern during this time. They can reduce the total yield of a vineyard dramatically, by depleting the amount of available pollen.

Flowering is usually complete by the end of June. This is when the grape bunches begin to form, and everyone's attention shifts to balancing the canopy and the amount of fruit on the vine. Wet years or fertile vineyard sites require additional hand work because the plants can be more vigorous. If the vine spends too much energy on vegetation, the grape flavors can suffer. On the flip side, a healthy canopy of leaves can protect grape clusters from sunburn in dry, hot years. Even a small adjustment can have an effect on aromas and flavors.

Into July and August, workers focus on removing non-fruiting shoots, so a vine is able to concentrate its energy on those shoots with grape clusters. Reducing the number of leaves in the fruiting zone, the grapes are exposed to breezes and sunlight, which can assist in balanced ripening. If the plant produces too many grape clusters, secondary bunches will be removed during *vendemmia verde* (a green harvest), after the berries have gone through *invaiatura* (ripening), an important moment in development, when the grape skins change color—green to gold or black (veraison), depending on the variety.

Any decisions and the timing of work are determined by the site, the vineyard manager, and the intention of the winery. Sunny, ventilated areas on slopes generally require less management, but that doesn't mean you should let the vineyard decide what it will be. The winegrower's job is to encourage each vine to produce the best grapes possible. The finest wines are made from bunches that are selected while they are growing on the vine, not only at the harvest moment.

Etna wineries typically harvest between September and October, though shifts in the weather can push these dates forward or back. The most important thing is to get the grapes into the cantina before the rains come, at the end of October.

QUANTITY VS. QUALITY

I've heard several stories. In each, there's a discussion between the new landowner and the old farmer who has worked the vineyard for years. The landowner tells the farmer that in order to make better wine, they must reduce the amount of fruit on the vine by doing a *vendemmia verde*, intentional shoot thinning, or both. The farmer contests, the owner insists, and they go back and forth until the farmer walks off the job or weeps as extraneous bunches of fruit drop to the ground. Other stories are less dramatic but the end is the same. The yield of each vine is reduced.

By reducing the number of grape clusters that each plant must ripen, we are able to see improved aromas and flavors in the wines. Grape yields at harvest vary depending on a number of factors, including weather, aspect, elevation, rootstock, grape variety and cultivar, planting and training schemes, and whether or not there was a green harvest after veraison. Some producers don't do a green harvest. Others consider it mandatory. Ultimately, it depends how vigorous the vines are and what the target is—quantity or quality.

Valley floors retain more water and organic material in the soil. This is where vines are inherently more vigorous. A vigorous vine will produce additional shoots, leaves, and bunches of grapes. High elevation vineyards or stonier sites tend to be less vigorous. While Nerello and Carricante have the capability to produce bulk-wine quantities, by locating the Etna DOC at higher elevations the vines put their energy into smaller loads. This simple change of address can have a marked improvement in the flavors and territorial qualities in the glass. This may not sound nouveau to a wine connoisseur—low yields are a hallmark of fine wine—but for Etna, the concept is relatively new. Without question, quality has improved as a result.

TRAINING SYSTEMS

There are numerous ways and whys to train a grapevine. On Etna, the predominant systems are *alberello* (little tree) and *cordone* (cordon). Both schemes are intended to lift grape clusters off the ground to expose them to sunlight and breezes while maintaining the shortest distance possible between the roots and the fruit.

Newer vineyards are often organized in cordone in *filare* (lines). Each vine is shaped like a T with two arms (bilateral) and bound to a horizontal wire for support. The cordon system can also have one arm (unilateral). Along each arm are knuckles, called "spurs" (growth points), where annual shoots emerge every spring. Above the vines, a system of parallel wires aids their

Young alberelli vines are trained up chestnut stakes in Quantico's Contrada Lavina vineyard, in the hills above Linguaglossa. Photo by Benjamin Spencer.

climb and yields are easily managed. The vines are separated at one pace, or more, with an alley between each row. It's a ubiquitous scheme that makes it possible for some mechanization.

That said, an increasing number of wineries are planting vines in alberello. This three-dimensional system has been in use on Mount Etna since at least Roman times. When vines are young, they're trained upward from the ground and tied to a vertical chestnut stake for support. The stakes are two meters long, but the trunk of the vine is typically kept short so that it stands about half a meter (1.6 ft.) after winter pruning.

The alberello is also called "gobelet" or "bush" in other places, for the three-dimensional shape it assumes. The intention is to develop freestanding vines that do not require trellising after the chestnut stakes rot away. Each alberello typically has two or three short arms with one main spur on each. It's a beautiful training system, for how elaborate the vines become over time, but it is also one of the most laborious methods to manage.

Alberello vineyards are organized in *quinconce* (quincunx), quadrilateral, or rectangular patterns. The quadrilateral and rectangular systems are the most popular, but the quinconce arrangement is the more traditional option. It places four vines in the form of a square with a single vine in the center. (The number five on six-sided game dice, the stars on the American flag, the bases and pitcher's mound of a baseball diamond all take this form.) At its most simple, this arrangement optimizes planting area and creates enough space for manual laborers to work by hand without bumping into the vine next to them. But it's also a high-density planting scheme that creates self-regulation among the vines. Due to their stature, form, and proximity, alberelli in quinconce compete for water and nutrients. Yields are reduced, but flavors improve.

Hundreds of hectares of alberelli vineyards were transformed in the second half of the twentieth century. Every other vine row was grubbed up, and one arm was removed so that the remaining two could be trained along wires, like cordone, so farmers could work their vineyards in an easier way. Some cantinas note this in their marketing materials as "alberello in *spalliera*." In essence, these are old vines that have been reorganized in a modern way.

Wineries also utilize the guyot system and cane pruning. This method relies on skilled workers to select one or two canes from the recent vintage and remove the others. Each cane extends from the trunk carrying bud points for the coming seasonal growth. It can be trained horizontally along a wire or vertically up a stake. This system is ideal for reducing yields in fertile areas.

THE VINES

Until the phylloxera infestation of the late nineteenth century, Etna's vineyards were planted using mass selection or *propaggine* (layering). Phylloxera is a louse that attacks a vine's roots, debilitating its ability to take up water from the soil. It arrived in Europe from North America in the 1860s and devastated *Vitis vinifera* vines across the European continent until it was discovered that, by physically joining an American rootstock and a European vine, the plant could survive and even excel.

Today, all new *Vitis vinifera* arriving from a certified nursery have an American rootstock grafted to a noble variety like Carricante or Nerello. American vines (*Vitis rupestris*, *Vitis berlandieri*, and the lesser *Vitis riparia*) are tolerant of phylloxera, while the European *Vitis vinifera* is not. Grafting is the process of bonding two vines together by lopping off the top of a living, rooted American vine and attaching a fruiting variety (scion). As the root and scion fuse together, they create a single vine with the characteristics of the scion and the capabilities of the root system. By planting the tolerant rootstock in the soil, the phylloxera louse will not kill the vine. It sounds like

Young Carricante vines await planting in Benanti's Contrada Rinazzo vineyard, near Milo. Grafted vines like these are grown in nurseries. Wineries can select the root stock and fruiting scion based on the weather, soils, and yield preferences for that specific site.

a terribly arduous solution, but the efficiency of Frankenstein-ing two vines together literally prevented wine from ruin.

Farmers on Etna purchase these grafted vines from a nursery on the island, in Italy, or in France. Or they can do field grafting (top grafting) directly in the vineyard, vine by vine. Some Etna wineries choose to plant the American rootstocks first. This tempers them to the environment before a scion is grafted.

Grafted vines reduce the risk of perpetuating another phylloxera outbreak, but it's a dicey subject on Etna. There are those who believe pure vinifera vines produce better wines. Others have another opinion. In my experience, the differences are noticeable, especially once we begin considering the options of rootstock, and how they interpret the volcanic soil. The trouble with the argument for or against either practice is that no single Etna producer has published controlled research to test the hypothesis.

There are, however, proven economic benefits to grafting. By selecting the rootstock and vinifera scion based on the soil and environmental factors, wineries can depend on normalized results at harvest. Etna producers have a choice going forward. Vineyard sites with less than 3 percent clay[12] could potentially repopulate using *propaggine* or via selection. Phylloxera does not like the elevated level of silica in volcanic sand. When the louse burrows underground to incubate over winter the amount of rain saturating the soil drowns it. In the spring, the volcanic soil remains cool and wet. It does not crack open the way clay does, to let survivors propagate among the vines.[13] Winter weather upslope, where most of Etna's vineyards are located, is also harsher and colder than areas closer to the base of the mountain. Phylloxera prefers more temperate weather if it's going to ruin a vineyard. Planting ungrafted *Vitis vinifera* vines is a risk, since phylloxera has been known to adapt and mutate. But, for the sake of understanding Etna's wide-ranging potential, it may be imperative to try.

Buying New Grapevines—New vineyards can be purchased over the telephone. The vine nursery will help you make educated decisions based on soil and weather assessments and yield preferences. You can either supply your own plant material for the fruiting scion or you can buy the nursery's all-in-one disease-resistant package.

Paulsen 1103 (1103P) is the most popular phylloxera-resistant American rootstock on the mountain, followed by 775P, 779P, and Ruggeri 140 (140R).

Created in 1895, 1103P is best suited for dry-farmed vineyards. The roots burrow deep into the ground in search of water and nutrients. Given that 1103P is a cross between *Vitis berlandieri* and *Vitis rupestris*, the genetic tendencies of the two give Etna vines a fighting chance where surface water is hard to find and extremes in temperature with unsystematic changes in soil type and depth occur regularly.

IRRIGATION

One of the first things my students notice is the lack of drip lines in Etna's vineyards. They've seen them in almost every other wine region they've visited. In fact, irrigation lines have become so normalized that it seems strange that a vine might survive without it. While many appellations permit irrigation to support viticulture, it was written out of the 1968 law that defined what Etna wines would be. The general belief is that each vine ought to be grown sustainably, without any kind of enhancements.

Honestly, there's no need for regular irrigation. The mountain receives about 25–75 inches of rain throughout the year. Vineyards on the eastern half are on the high end of that scale. The top of the volcano receives snow between November and April. As rainwater and snowmelt trickle through the volcanic sands, surplus water is trapped in vast underground basins.

An estimated 185 billion gallons of water in Etna's aquifers are constantly receiving and releasing water, which trickles down through subsoils in the Etna DOC. Add to that the moisture evaporated from the sea and the 500,000 gallons of steam that are emitted into the atmosphere directly from the volcano, it seems superfluous to add a well and a drip line.

Winegrowers who use irrigation are relegated to making wines labeled as Sicilia DOC/DOP, IGT/IGP Terre Siciliane, and Vino da Tavola (VDT). It should not be assumed, however, that wines labeled this way are using irrigation.

ETNA'S SECRET WEAPON

In the heat of summer, people in the cities go to the coast for the cool breezes. Folks who live on the coast, on the other hand, go up the mountain, where it's cooler still. The vines make a similar retreat. They shut down all above-ground activities and search for water far beneath the vineyard floor. But in an environment that frowns on any vineyard enhancement (i.e., irrigation), the root tips find respite in allophane.

As Etna's volcanic ash is incorporated into the soil and begins to weather, aluminum silicates form andisol—a fertile, dark brown soil. As andisol weathers, the iron and silica in the soil react to create allophane. Allophane is described as a free-form sponge that attracts and retains nutrients and water. High concentrations of allophane can be found one meter or more below the vineyard floor, where organic and volcanic materials marry. It's the first reliable stop for vine roots, as they climb deeper into the mountain.

One of the best ways to discover Mount Etna is during an off-road excursion with a professional, certified guide. I love spending the morning on the mountain and the afternoon at a winery.

met Salvo Giammanco around the corner from his office, in the heart of Catania. Salvo is a veteran researcher and educator at the National Institute of Geophysics and Volcanology (INGV). We usually see each other on the mountain, but that day we were at a pastry shop, leaning over a selection of cakes and coffee.

I told Salvo, "Every time I visit Murgo winery, I find myself at the edge of the Nerello Mascalese vineyard, staring up at the mountain." It's an awe-inducing vista that reveals both the delicate beauty and ferocious power of the volcano.

Salvo smiled. He knows the spot precisely. He's been studying Etna since he was a boy. He said, "From that location, at one glance, you can see much of the evolution of the mountain."

I took notes as he unpacked the geological complexities of the volcano.

Looking south from the Murgo winery, a rolling, protracted rise stretches from the Ionian Sea to a plateau near the village of Tarderia, at about 800 meters AMSL. Along this lengthy slope, scores of spent craters follow a shallow fault line that climbs up the volcano. Just past Tarderia, however, the plateau ends at a dramatic precipice, at the southern edge of the Valle del Bove. This massive, broken caldera measures three-and-a-half miles across and a half-mile deep. In the walls and cliffs of the Valle del Bove, researchers have found evidence of at least seven unique volcanoes that layered on and pressed up against one another. As each new volcano replaced an older one, the plumbing system shifted course. Internal and external vents opened and closed. Lava poured out. Sand and rocks were scattered. Every event formed the mountain we see today.

Named for its broad, round shape, the largely effusive Ellittico volcano gave Mount Etna its circumference. Approximately 15,000 years ago, as the last ice age was receding, the Ellittico exploded with incredible force, reforming the mountain yet again. And a new volcano was born. From a distance you can see where the slope steepens, at about 1,600 meters. Here is where the Ellittico ends and Mongibello begins. In Sicilian, we say Mungibeddu. When literally translated, Mongibello means "Mountain-Mountain" or "Mountain of Mountains," a repetition of Italic and Arabic words for *mountain*: "*monte*" and "*jabal*," respectively.

Long after the Ellittico had extinguished, the young Mongibello found outlets along the western rim of the volcano. For nearly five thousand years, the new activity threw enormous quantities of lava into the environment and inside the Ellittico crater. Where rock overlaid sand, frequent flank slips occurred. One fateful day, about eight thousand years ago, part of the eastern wall of the Ellittico crater broke, and an avalanche of water, sand, mud, and rock rushed down Etna's eastern flank and into the sea. The splash was so large it sent a tsunami across the Mediterranean Basin, wiping out Neolithic villages as far east as Atlit Yam, on what is now the coast of Israel.

I don't remember my precise expression after hearing this story, but Salvo takes all of it in stride. He sipped from his mug, then smiled. "We are only now reading a page or two of Mount Etna's story. There is so much more she has to tell us."

PLATE TECTONICS

The way I think about it, a pot of water needs to come to a boil before you add pasta. Before you add the pasta, you need to add salt. When the salt enters the boiling water, it creates an excited bubbling as the gasses are agitated by its coarse surfaces. The truth is, you would get the same result if you tossed sand into the water, though I'm not sure the pasta would taste as good. Now imagine tossing sand or large pieces of the earth's crust into boiling magma.

Immediately to the south, east, and north of Mount Etna, there are shallow fault lines and fissures in the earth's crust. These breaks in the upper mantle are caused by shifting tectonic plates. Over eons, the African Plate has gradually and forcefully shifted north and west, against the southern limit of the Eurasian Plate. Where the two plates meet, the earth's mantle folds and pieces of the African Plate shift downward (subduction), crumbling into the magma below. Intense pressure is created from the trapped, sudden release of gasses and vapor, and magma moves in the direction of least resistance. Mount Etna is that direction.

The Cyclops—In Homer's *The Odyssey*, the protagonist-hero, Odysseus,[14] ransoms powerful sweet wine from Maro, a priest of ancient Thrace. After fleeing the island of the Lotus Eaters[15] (the modern-day Tunisian island of Djerba[16]) Odysseus and his men arrive on the island of Polyphemus the Cyclops (modern-day Sicily).

Over two days, Polyphemus eats several of Odysseus's men. To distract him from killing more of his crew, Odysseus offers some of Maro's wine—a nectar usually blended with water at 1:20—and the Cyclops quickly gets drunk. He is used to a lighter-style wine grown on the volcano. Polyphemus thanks Odysseus for the buzz by asking his name and offering to eat him last. Odysseus tells the giant that his name is "Outis" (literally, No One).

As Polyphemus falls asleep, Odysseus stabs him in the eye with a spear, blinding him. When Polyphemus shouts for help, he tells the other Cyclopes, "No One is hurting me." So, they don't bother helping.

The next day, the men escape. As they flee, Odysseus taunts the blind Cyclops. In a rage, Polyphemus hurls massive stones at the men and their ship.

Today, those "boulders" stand off the coastline of Aci Trezza. For Homer, it was a way to explain the large rock formations a few meters from the shore. They are, in fact, the remnants of Mount Etna's above-water birth, about 220,000 years ago.

Prior to this, all of the eruptions occurred under water, at the edge of the Eurasian and African tectonic plates. Over time, the lava that emerged from the earth's mantle formed a shield volcano, which spread out across the sea floor and rose until it broke the surface of the water and began building the mountain we see today.

A STAGGERING AMOUNT OF SAND (AND ROCK)

My father-in-law, Frank, was a Merchant Marine Captain. For more than twenty years, he traveled the world by sea. He knows the ports, depths, currents, and winds by name. (The seafaring life is a wonder to me. I get seasick in a bathtub.) Frank says that when coming back to Sicily from the east you can watch Mount Etna growing on the horizon for the last hundred miles. Seeing the volcano was a sign for him. He was almost home.

My first eruption in my new home occurred over several weeks in the spring of 2013. Day after day, Frank and I cleared the volcanic ash from the roof, terraces, and courtyard around the house. Every bag was small and heavy. We had to use a pulley system just to lower them, one by one, level by level, into the car to take them to the dump. By the end of it, a spoonful weighed a ton. Thankfully, there were no rocks. The heavier stuff stays closer to the site of the eruption. It's one of the reasons Etna is so tall. The rocks and sand just keep piling on each other.

Every time Frank and I finished the cleanup, Etna would erupt again. Night after night, we listened to the coarse ash raining down on the house, pelting the metal railings, the terra cotta roof tiles, and the car. One morning,

I went out to assess the situation. There was a new layer of sand and pumice one-inch thick. It crackled like eggshells underfoot. Everything—the roof tiles, clothesline, barbecue, potted plants—was covered in black sand and small pieces of pumice that smacked of sulfur.

I stood next to the table where we eat lunch in the summer, picked up some of the ash in my hand, and let it run out, making a small mound near the center of the table. Then I added more, sprinkling a little at a time, watching how the mound transformed with each distribution. Then I bumped the table, to represent an earthquake. The shape of the small dune changed again. Weak spots fell flat while pieces of pumice interlinked (albeit loosely) to form larger pieces of rubble. With every bit of sand, the pile grew. With every shudder, it settled. The amount of material required to form a mound that can be seen for a hundred miles is staggering.

Of course, Mount Etna is not solely made of sand. She is a hardened mountain, riddled with disfigurements, hundreds of individual lava flows, dead lateral volcanoes, faults, fissures, and collapses. Out of context, this sounds like a hellscape, but it's not. The sand settles, the rocks get covered with grasses, the boulders crumble, and the blemishes become part of a much larger picture.

Parent Material, Deconstructed—Since the young Mongibello produced its first layers of lava, thousands of eruptions have thrown igneous material in every direction. This parent material comes in many shapes and sizes with a range of compositions, but it always arrives from the core of the earth.

From there, the natural elements—wind, temperature extremes, and water—contribute to the initial erosion. As lava weathers, it fractures into boulders, rocks, pebbles, sand, and eventually silt.

Lichen and moss are the first pioneer communities to start the long process of transforming stone into soil. Complex plants with the capability to live in shallow soils are next. Grasses, sorrel, shrubs, *ginestra* (broom), and fir trees continue to fracture the cooled lava into smaller pieces as their roots explore the rock and sand for water. Where each plant thrives it also perishes, adding layers of organic matter within the stratum of Mount Etna. The same is true of local fauna.

One variable requires significant consideration: the effect of human activity. Without question, humans have modified and manipulated the planet's landscape over the last fifteen thousand years. Ironically, this is roughly the same age as Etna's current volcanic edifice, Mongibello. In that time, farms, domesticated animals, roads, villages, forests, war zones, and cemeteries have folded into the soil matrix where Etna's wine grapes are grown.

THE UNIQUE SOUTHEAST

Ash from Mount Etna's explosive eruptions are found everywhere on the mountain. However, the combination of the prevailing winds blow volcanic ash to the southeast more frequently than any other slope. The cinders and flakes of pumice that fall to the ground during a pyroclastic event are quickly adopted into the soil.

According to the INGV, an average of 700 kilograms (1543 lb.) of ash falls on Etna's eastern slope over the course of one year. Light dustings less than 0.1 centimeter begin adding beneficial nutrients to the soil in a matter of weeks. Deeper deposits from stronger eruptions can asphyxiate the roots of the vines. These sediments don't fall only around the farms. It is not uncommon to see light dustings of silica or yellow sulfur on the black lava-stone sidewalks in town.

In his book *Geography* (Book VI, Chapter 2), written at the beginning of the first millennium CE, Strabo speaks about the effects of volcanic ash in Etna's vineyards. "When the mountain is in action, the fields of the Catanaeans are covered with ash-dust to a great depth. Although the ash is an affliction at the moment, it benefits the country in later times, for it renders it fertile and suited to the vine, the rest of the country not being equally productive of good wine; therefore, just as wood-ashes nourish rue, so the ashes of Aetna, it is reasonable to suppose, have some quality that is peculiarly suited to the vine." Although the science is new, the positive effects of small quantities of ash have long been known. When folded into the soil, the porous nature of the ash promotes water drainage and increased quantities of fresh macro- and micronutrients. There is rarely the need for chemical fertilizers. Everything an Etna grapevine requires is readily available or provided for from above.

The southeast slope of Mount Etna is one of the most intriguing areas for winemaking on the mountain. Not only does this part of the volcano have more than thirty unique lateral volcanoes and a disproportionate amount of fresh soil deliveries, a series of shallow faults and fissures administer tiny amounts of carbon dioxide and sulfur into the soil and air from below. The levels of gas emissions are not typically dangerous. They are, however, higher than normal. And they contribute something to the vineyards and other plants that take root here.

Carbon dioxide is crucial for photosynthesis. Sulfur is absorbed through the roots as sulfate. Sulfur works with nitrogen to promote shoot growth and elasticity in the green material of the vine. This flexibility is particularly important on Etna, where winds and breezes are constant.

Volcanic ash from Mount Etna's pyroclastic eruptions fall on the southeast slope more frequently than any other. The cinders and flakes of pumice that scatter across the ground are quickly adopted into the soil. The ash promotes drainage and adds fresh minerals and nutrients directly into the soil.

The Best Seafood Around—The southeast flank of Mount Etna is one of the most unique landscapes in the world for wine.

While the contours and numerous lateral craters contribute to an array of fascinating soils and topographic changes, the area is regularly treated to ash emissions from the volcano's central craters.

When those ashes are captured by the trade winds they can travel hundreds of kilometers. Portions are deposited at sea. When the ash settles on the sea floor, it fertilizes the phytoplankton that are consumed by other organisms on which the local fish dine regularly. As a result of this easy-to-access diet, fish grow fat and contented.

The best fish are found at the historic Catania market. A second market is in Riposto, in front of the Porto dell'Etna. Not only are the markets a fantastic place to get fresh fish, the restaurants that surround these neighborhoods serve some of the finest seafood in the Mediterranean.

The best seafood in the Mediterranean can be found at the historic Catania market. A second market is in Riposto, in front of the Porto dell'Etna. Not only are these markets a fantastic place to get fresh fish, the restaurants that surround these neighborhoods serve some of the finest seafood in the Mediterranean. Photo by Genís Ceballos Mestres.

never gave much thought to the weather until I started making wine in California. It didn't matter if the sky was filled with sunshine or snow, weather was something we dealt with or talked about when the conversation ran dull. It was above us, out of reach, and rarely exciting. As it happens, weather is not an abstract. In some cases, it's quite manipulatable. During my first year of training in the cellar, the assistant winemaker asked me for help. He was going to all of the rooms and adjusting the climatic conditions—humidity, temperature, and ventilation.

When I asked why, he said, "We want the new wine to think it's springtime. Warming up the rooms replicates the change in season. There are bacteria in wine that come out of hibernation in the spring. When they wake up, they're hungry. They feast on the malic acid in the wine and convert it to lactic acid. The process is called malolactic fermentation—MLF for short."[17]

I must have looked like a deer in headlights. "Malo . . . what now?"

"It makes the wine better, softer, and more stable," he said.

"What happens after an MLF?"

"We turn the temperature down."

I tried to put it all together. "So, cool fermentation, then a warm period for MLF, followed by a big temperature drop?"

He's a smiley guy. "That's how we make wine. Most wines. Some wines. Yes."

It's trickery, to be sure, but these false changes in season help to stabilize wine in ways that only time and natural processes can. If we are able to make climatic, seasonal changes occur in a shorter period of time—nine months instead of one year, for example—a wine leaves the cellar relaxed and ready to face the world.

In practice, many modern wines are bottled at the end of a false winter phase, during which the temperature of the wine is dropped to near freezing, using a refrigeration system. The wines are then cold filtered and allowed to warm up before being bottled at about 16°C (60°F). Those are springtime temperatures. As it happens, it's also a good temperature for drinking most wines.

MEDITERRANEAN CLIMATE

It seems redundant to say that Mount Etna's climate is listed as "Mediterranean," considering that the mountain is in the center of the Mediterranean Sea. In truth, there are a lot of wine regions that have similar weather. What "Mediterranean" generally means is that the volcanic vineyards enjoy warm sunny summers, cool wet winters, and annual temperatures that are moderated by a large body of water.

This would be fairly standard if Etna were a series of rolling hills along the seaside. Once we consider the mass of the volcano and the nuances of her height and architecture, the Mediterranean designation skews toward the complex. Winters are cold and rainy. Spring and autumn are cool and wet, while summers can be hot and humid, even at elevation. In many ways, Etna is a hybrid. If there were a pre-alpine, subtropical Mediterranean subcategory, Etna would fit into it perfectly.

LIGHT

One of the first things people notice is the light. From the early morning sunrise hues to the colorful evening sunsets, light pummels Mount Etna 250 days of the year. Much of the luminosity is simply sunlight reflecting off of the sea and bouncing around the molecules of water in the air. Shade is often a welcome friend.

The black basalt stones absorb light and give it off as heat and are found in every town, city, and farm around the mountain. In the vineyards, the basalt can radiate heat late into the evening, keeping the vines and root zone warm as temperatures drop.

But the sun doesn't strike Mount Etna the same in all places. If we follow its arc across the sky, it favors the southern flank. The east and north slopes get ample sunlight, but for bud break and the harvest it's deflected light. As the season moves on, the sun rises higher in the sky and direct light increases. While the eastern half of the volcano is kissed by the morning light, it also falls on the windward side of the mountain where the quantity of rain can approach 1,900 millimeters per year (75 in.), while the western half of the mountain benefits from Etna's rain shadow, receiving less rainwater.

Promoter and local sage Nino Franco used to host the popular Costa d'Oro wine tasting every summer, in the Passopisciaro town square, to

Mount Etna's is on the east coast of Sicily, in the center of the Mediterranean Sea. The high elevation, volcanic vineyards enjoy warm sunny summers, cool wet winters, and annual temperatures that are moderated by their proximity to water.

celebrate the producers who make wine along the northern "Gold Coast"—between Linguaglossa and Randazzo. For Nino, who passed away in 2021, the wines grown on this twelve-mile stretch of the volcano are the best expressions of the mountain.

"Here," he said, with a thick Australian accent, "the vineyards are drier and sunnier. On average, they get an extra three weeks of sunlight. It's not direct sunlight then, during the harvest, you know, it's a little softer, but it helps the grapes reach full maturity. Every bit helps when you're this high up."

The eastern amphitheater of Mount Etna gets brilliant luminosity in the morning, but by mid-afternoon the sun breaks behind the jagged rim of the Valle del Bove. It's one of the reasons this area is a white wine mecca. The bright morning light followed by an extended cool break in the day helps to slow maturation, keeping sugars low and acidity high at harvest. Red varieties planted on the eastern half of Etna often take advantage of a southern exposure.

Flank collapses, lateral craters, striations and *sciare* (hardened lava flows), create multiple exposures to the changing path of the sun. The peaks, valleys, and berms of decomposing rock can capture or block periods of light. While many vineyards are laid bare beneath the sun and cooled by natural breezes, others are planted at the edge of woodlands that block hours of light per week. In the pastoral valley floors, residual heat in the soil can last hours after the sun has fallen behind the mountain. As the angle and intensity of the sun changes during the growing season, Etna's contours begin to have an effect on sunlight, the flow of wind, and the ripening of grapes.

Similarly, every cloud that passes between the vines and the sun makes a difference. Large clouds that collect on the top of the volcano can diminish the light a vine receives by minutes, hours, days, or even weeks. New plantings take advantage of any additional hours of available sunshine or work is adapted in the vineyard and cantina to adjust for subtle changes in vintage.

The moon has attracted our attention since the beginning. In some moments, it illuminates the sky. In others, it seems to vanish.

As a child, I was told the moon and the sun have an ongoing game of hide and seek, each one chasing the other until they both appear in the sky together. It was a story that kept me looking up, but I never considered what this game might mean to the earth under my feet.

On Etna, the moon is less of a competitor and more of a guide. Following the lunar cycles informs farmers when to do particular types of work.

In the waxing phase, when the moon is illuminated, liquids in the plant are attracted outward, toward the light. This is a good time to plant new vines. However, new plantings should also be made when the moon is descending toward the horizon—waxing and descending. The vine's primordial attraction to the light tells it to reach for the moon, while the liquids follow the gravitational pull toward the horizon, into the soil. When planted in this moment, when the light is bright and all of the energy in the plant is focused on root growth, the vine's connection with its precise location in the universe becomes much more profound.

In the waning phase, when the illuminated moon grows dark, liquids in the plant turn inward. This is when seeds should be planted and vines should be pruned. Vines can also be planted in this moment but the aforementioned strategy (waxing-descending) is considered better. The waning-descending moon is the perfect time to till the soil, because the earth will be breathing in the nutrients.

Harvest is the unique moment when farmers look for the combination phase of waxing-ascending, when the moon is at its apex in the sky and fully illuminated. In this instant, all of the energy in the earth and vine is moving outward and directly into the grape clusters.

The entire process of waxing, ascending, waning, and descending takes about twenty-eight days. In this protracted 655-hour day, the full moon acts as a stand-in for the high-noon sun. If we consider the behavior of plants during a solar day, we can think of them within the scope of a lunar day—closed when it's dark and open when it's bright. What we call one month is not a lot of time, but it's a schedule that makes sense. All you have to do is watch the sky.

When you look up, you'll notice that the moon is not alone. Circling, in the distance, are constellations of stars that have played an integral part in every ancient agricultural calendar. They are still in use on Etna today.

During a new-descending moon, liquids are calm. The lees is packed. Fermentations and MLFs are slower. It's the perfect time to move or rack the wine. On the opposite side of the spectrum, the full-ascending moon activates liquids. Lees moves more easily. Fermentations and MLFs are active. This is a good time to do bâttonage or make additions. The wine is open to suggestions, in a way. Sunny and rainy weather can aid or inhibit the flow of winemaking practices too. One is open. The other is closed. The wines react to this ambient climate.

You may be able to change the temperature and humidity of your cellar, but the systems outside are far more powerful than an oscillating heater or chiller. Yet, by pairing the rhythms we see on Earth with those repeated patterns in the sky, and annual seasons, we begin to make connections to the processes and expressions of a wine. It goes a bit further, in fact.

This relationship between a liquid made from the fruit of a plant is particularly interesting in the way it manifests in wine. Have you ever wondered why your favorite wine tastes good one day and awful on another? It's possible that the earth's alignment with and proximity to the moon and its movement have something to do with it. There are periods in the cosmic calendar when aromas and flavors are likely to reflect the earthy, vinous, floral, or fruit characters of a given plant.

According to Matthias Thun's book *When Wine Tastes Best: A Biodynamic*

Calendar For Wine Drinkers,[18] wines tend to smell and taste better on "fruit" and "flower" days, as opposed to "root" or "leaf" days. At its most basic, Thun's system associates the behavior of a grapevine with the location and phase of the moon. As an extension of the grapevine, the wine in your glass continues to behave in a similar manner.

For some professionals in the wine trade, the calendar works. They arrange tastings only when the stars and moon are aligned with a fruit or flower day. Who wants to taste a wine that features the leafy or subterranean qualities? For biodynamic wines and wines made using celestial schedules, it is of increasing importance to follow through on the vineyard and cellar work and present the wines when the moon is waxing-ascending.

CLOUDS

Mount Etna spends 115 days per year (on average) under stratus clouds that are low hanging, gray, and wet. Due to various winds, humidity, and changes in atmospheric pressure, the density of clouds fluctuates from delicate to cumulonimbus, which can generate tremendous thunderstorms.

One of the most intriguing cloud formations gathers moisture over the peak of Mount Etna in convex layers that resemble the lens of the human eye or a soft linen hat. These lenticular clouds are so perfectly round and otherworldly—sometimes stacks of them appear on top of one another— they have been compared to UFOs.

At a distance, it's curious, but living on Etna we see these clouds often. Usually when the skies are a clear and brilliant cerulean blue.

WIND

You get used to catching your hat on Etna. Sometimes it's right when the wind takes it, so grabbing the hat looks like a trick you've been practicing for just such an occasion. Other times you've got to run after it.

As the quantity of water can be too little, just perfect, or too much, the wind has a reputation for being both benevolent and disastrous. To be clear, it's not the wind necessarily. It's what it can carry—from African sands to heavy pieces of jagged ash and baseball-size hail stones. Apart from the rare occurrences of damage, wind is one of Mount Etna's greatest assets.

The grecale (a.k.a. the Bora) wind carries cool breezes from the surface of the deep Ionian Sea against the sunbaked eastern face of the mountain. Winds entering the Alcantara Valley, between Mount Etna, Peloritani, and the Nebrodi Mountains, mix with the cool tramontana winds that arrive from the north. Those that skirt around Etna's southern flank, into the Valley of Catania, meet with the ostro and libeccio winds, which arrive from the south and southwest. The confusion these winds create keeps the vineyards aerated, dry, and cool.

Arriving from the south, the sirocco winds carry warm air from North Africa. Though it is technically a wind, it's the laziest wind I've ever experienced. It just kind of languishes, coating everything with enough humidity that the red and yellow sands in its wake can turn a white car orange.

The ponente (westerly) winds roll over Mount Etna, compounding and pushing apart cloud systems that get bogged down at higher elevations.

Without all of this fast-moving air, Mount Etna would be a hot, humid place, not unlike a subtropical jungle. But because it stands approximately two miles high, thermal excursions can lower the average temperature in a mountain vineyard by 10°–20°C. There's a fine balance, however. Variations in velocity and temperature (hot or cold) can shut down a vine's ability to respire.

Have you ever tried sticking your head out the passenger window of a moving car and opening your mouth? It's impossible to capture all of the air. The same thing happens in a sauna. The heat makes it difficult to breathe. Grapevines are just as sensitive to the environmental changes as we are.

Although, just like dogs, I imagine some vines actually like a bit of wind in their face from time to time.

WATER

I strapped into my snowboard and rode the rope tow to the top of Piano Provenzana. It hadn't snowed like this on Mount Etna in fifteen to forty years (depending on who you talked to). Either way, it was a lot of snow. Every run and lift was open. There were impromptu jumps and new lines of fresh powder everywhere, but there was also another cloud coming over the mountain, throwing snow like a sandstorm. Downslope, they were likely to see rain. At sea, it was just more water.

By the time all that snow melted and started making its way to the coastline, it would be springtime, precisely when the vines need water most. Well into summer, however, the trickle diminishes. The soil is dry, but the subsoil withholds water. It's the allophane. The clay-like mineraloid is like a leaky spoon. Whatever it can't hold, it lets go of.

Freshwater springs are everywhere. I keep bottles in the car just to try the different springs around the mountain. I particularly like one on SS120, in Montelaguardia, but my favorite natural springs are in Giarre. The water downslope has more mineral content and more flavor. The water up mountain is pure and crystalline, almost flavorless.

I bet the vines have a preference too. It's why their roots follow one path but not another. A recent study done by the University of Western Australia's Center for Evolutionary Biology showed that plant roots emit sound waves in the search for water. Where the waves bounce back, confirming the density and form of water, the plant directs its roots.[19] Where water finds a way through the volcanic rock and sand, so too the vines go, searching for the vibrations of rain and snowmelt.

Umbrellas and white chairs stretch across a sandy beach at Capo Schisò, where Greek colonies were established in the eighth century BCE. This fertile area in the lower Alcantara Valley, below Monte Tauro and the city of Taormina, are ideal for vineyards.

PART TWO

Our dog, Blu, leads the way up Monte Castello. He scales the sandy hill, passes the Church of the Holy Cross, where the statue of Saint Phillip of Syria is housed, and continues up to Castello Calatabiano. Photo by Benjamin Spencer.

THE HISTORY IN YOUR GLASS

Our dog, Blu, leads the way. We've done the hike up Monte Castello before. He scales the sandy hill and pauses in the shade of the Church of the Holy Cross, where the statue of Saint Phillip of Syria is housed. The wide stone staircase I have to climb is worn smooth by centuries of foot traffic. Every third Saturday of May, the statue of Saint Phillip is carried down from the church to the city below, in a procession that dates back to 1766.

The pageant starts a weeklong celebration of Phillip, Calatabiano's patron saint, before the statue is carried back up the mountain on the fourth Sunday of May. Each leg is a precarious and colorful scene, as men dressed in white and red carry the ornate sculpture bathed in flowers down and back up Monte Castello on their shoulders. It's one of the oldest religious events in the area.

One hundred meters upslope from the church is Castello di Calatabiano. Much like the volcano, Castello di Calatabiano is a stratification of human history. Nearly every culture that called this area home left something here. These days, the castle is a museum and conference center. Restoration of the site, including a reclined elevator that carries guests between the castle and the parking lot, was completed in 2009.

Blu gave me a thirsty look. I poured some water into a cup for him. We weren't going any farther. We sat on the edge of the promontory below the church and took in the view. From that one location, it's possible to see the rolling hills of terraces of long-defunct vineyards, the southern reach of Reggio Calabria, the rise of Monte Tauro and Taormina, the Port of Riposto, Mount Etna, and twenty miles out to sea. I don't have to wonder why this part of Sicily has been home to hundreds of generations. The plains and hills are fertile. The forests and rises are ideal for defense. And the coastline is ready for trade. It is the definition of a promised land.

THE GREEKS

After nearly three centuries of drought in their homeland,[20] Greek settlers—Chalcidians, who took a chance on Sicily—discovered that the cool volcanic sands south of Mount Tauro made for easy farming. The stones and rocks in the area also made for quick construction material. With every success, word of Sicily's potential spread. As more Greeks arrived, they migrated up the northeast and eastern slopes of Mount Etna. After first fighting with the Greek settlers,[21] the Sicels welcomed and even coupled with them, joining the new Greek culture with their own.[22] Others moved up the Alcantara Valley and into the Nebrodi mountain range. In 729 BCE, an additional port was built at Katane (Catania). Within ten years of their arrival, the city of Catania was founded, and the thirty-mile stretch of coastline at the base of Mount Etna was considered one of the most fertile landscapes in the classical world. It's one of the reasons the name Naxos evolved to Giardini Naxos (the gardens of Naxos). For those who lived there, and those who arrived, Etna was a sacred place, where the natural and mythological congregated to create a new reality for all Greco-Sicilian citizens.

By the sixth century BCE, the eastern half of Sicily and select areas in the lower Italian Peninsula were being populated by Greek Sicilians. The bigger the communities grew, the more powerful and alluring the island was to the rest of the ancient world. As populations and ideas mingled, the Etna community was inseminated with a devotion to viticulture, wine, and the gods who made these things possible. Soon, Southern Italy had the nickname "Oenotria"—the land of staked vines.[23]

Sounds bucolic, right? It was also a time when many things were very tentative. Settlements on Etna were frequently sacked by neighboring tribes, and in 403 BCE, Naxos and the cities south of Naxos were destroyed by the tyrant Dionysius I. In times of trouble, early Etneans sought comfort and mercy from their gods. The local Sicel population worshipped the god of fire, Adranus, who lived under Mount Etna.[24] The Greeks deified the entire volcano, naming her Aitna, and adopting Uranus (god of the sky) and Gaea (goddess of the earth) as her parents. Sure, you could pray to or celebrate these gods, but Dionysus was the only god you could depend on.[25] Not only was he the god of wine, the grapevine, the harvest, fertility, struggle, and re-birth, his connection to Etna was written into his origin story.

Born of a god and a human—Zeus and Princess Semele—Dionysus connected the magical and the real. In the prelude to his birth, Semele is tricked into asking her lover, Zeus, to reveal his true self. When he does, Semele perishes in a fiery death. Zeus saves baby Dionysus by carrying him to term in his thigh. After Dionysus is born, he's whisked away to be reared by the nymphs of Nysa, the Hyades who bring the rain.[26] Born of fire and raised by rain, just like a volcano. Throughout his own life Dionysus is de-stroyed and restored. This repeated demise and rebirth are metaphors for the cycles of nature and the rhythms of the mountain. More importantly, they are a constant reminder to live life to its fullest. For the devout followers of Dionysus, life was often lived in excess.

Wine on Mount Etna symbolized more than the euphoria we get from drinking alcohol. Through wine, men could find work. Good viticulture and winemaking required laborers. Artisans were needed to make storage and shipping vessels, rope and nets, oars, and sails. Merchants sought horses and boats and skilled sailors to transport their products. In very short order, wine had become the great comfort of the world. It kept the elements at bay, doubled as medicine, curbed depression, and offered inspiration and promise.

Even the standard Greek currency, the drachma, was forged in silver with a relief of Dionysus on one side and a grape cluster on the other. With its likeness on the national currency,[27] wine had officially pervaded every corner of Etnean life.

At homes, in taverns, and during Greek symposia, wines from Etna were consumed regularly alongside rustic and elegant dishes. The plump, fresh fish from Siracusa to Naxos were considered delicacies. Fishermen recognized then, as they do today, that the best tasting fish in the Mediterranean fed there. Vegetables, fruits, and oils from the volcano made it to market too. Merchants may have had a road to travel, but the best chefs in the ancient and modern world depended on the flavors that produce from the volcano could contribute to a meal. Wine was no exception. In fact, the oldest written use of the word *wine* in Italy— "Nunustentimimarustainamiemitomestiduromnaniposduromiemitomestiveliomnedemponitantomeredes*viino*brtom"—comes from an amphora dated to the fifth century BCE, which was found in Centorbi,[28] approximately ten miles from Adrano, on the volcano's southern flank.

The volcano had become such an integral icon of Greek Sicilian culture that, in 474 BCE, the Siracusan tyrant Hieron pushed the existing population of Catania out to make room for thousands of new Greek settlers. To mark the event, he renamed the city Ætna, struck new coins, and invited the famed playwright Æschylus to perform. During the festivities, Æschylus presented a new play about Thaleia, a nymph who lived on Mount Etna.[29] It was a prosperous time for the mountain and her new colonies. In the poet Pindar's Nemean Odes, he praises the winner of the chariot race during the Nemean Games—precursors to the Olympics—in Peloponnese, Greece.[30] The winning driver and horses hailed from Ætna.[31]

It was a good run, but after Alexander the Great died, in 323 BCE, Greek influence on the island diminished. Over the next century, cities and settlements fractured, and fighting was more common than a good glass of wine, whether you had food or not.

THE ROMANS

The Mamertines were the worst. The loose-knit mercenary army crushed the city of Zancle (Messina) in a bloody and demoralizing assault that stunned the Greek-Sicilian population. From Zancle, they plundered the Italian Peninsula and sacked the Etna coastline. The thing is, they weren't very organized. The locals kept them on their heels, using the contours and forests of the mountain for safety and defense. After one-too-many losses, the Mamertines sent messengers to Rome to ask for help.

Rome had been buying wheat from Sicily for a long time. The way they saw it, it would be easier if they owned the farm, so they launched a land war for the island—The Punic Wars, between Greeks, Carthaginians, and Romans. Once the Greek colonies fell, Roman Sicilians reworked everything Greek Sicilians had standardized. Techniques and best practices were revised to improve, track, and quantify every part of winemaking. Defining weights and measures were of particular importance if the Roman Empire was going to receive its weight in taxes. For example, a staked vineyard of alberelli was expected to produce about three *cullei* (*culleus*, a cattle-skin bag), or about 500 liters from a *jugera* (quarter hectare, or 1.25 ac.).[32] Grapes and solid goods were traded using the *libbra* or *libra*, which was equal to 317 grams, or a pound weight that could be reduced further to 12 *unciae* (ounces), an alternate measure of weight.[33] It wasn't all economics, however. Before long, grape names and unique sites around Etna were of increasing significance, for the quality of the wines that grew there.

One of the grapes used most frequently was Aminea or Aminnia (likely a relative of Greco di Tufo[34]). These vines were low yielding and produced fine wines capable of some aging. It's the other varieties—Aminnia Minuscula, Aminnia Maior, Gemina Minor, Gemina Maior, Singularis, Lanata, and Aminnia Nigra—that give us a clue as to how varied Etna vineyards were.[35] Adrumenitanum (grown around Adrano) and Catiniensis (from vineyards surrounding the city of Catania) were also popular on the mountain, the former being preferred over the latter. Old vines that the Greeks had planted around the volcano were still disseminated, though with less frequency as tastes changed.[36] Popular varieties of Roman record include Eugenia (possibly an ancestor of Ugni Blanc/Trebbiano); Graecula (a black grape); and Murgentina,[37] especially when it was planted in volcanic soils. Eugenia was so popular in Rome that cuttings of vines from around Taormina were introduced in the Alban Hills, near the eternal city.[38]

By the mid first century BCE, wine had captured the heart of Etnean society. As much as the Greeks had done to improve viticulture, the Romans eclipsed their efforts in every way. By adopting knowledge and technology from around the empire, Roman Etneans were making multiple wines from a single harvest. The best and most expensive wines were made by the first juice released from the grapes, what we call the *primo fiore* (first flower), or free-run. Wines were also made from grape skins in contact with the juice. Others came from pressed grape skins. When all the wine had been squeezed from the grapes, *acqua tina* (water from the vat) was made.[39]

A Recipe for Acqua Tina—This low-alcohol wine-water is still made on Etna today, though less frequently than it was in the past.

The recipe is simple enough. After the final pressing—while the grapes are still held in the press—a small amount of water is added and allowed to soak overnight.

In the morning, the grapes are pressed again. The pigmented and flavored water has a small amount of alcohol (less than 5%) and some acidity. By adding acqua tina to water, the small change in chemistry helped to keep water potable for longer periods of time.

Most of the acqua tina that I have tasted, from fermented and pressed grapes, isn't very good for very long. Acqua tina made from fresh grapes that have been pressed can be interesting because the water and sugar ferment together.

There is no reference to acqua tina in the Etna DOC rules.

THE VANDALS & GOTHS

We had a saying at the winery in California: "It takes a lot of beer to make good wine." I'm sure it's not original, but I like to think the Vandals and Goths might have used a similar turn of phrase, after the Western Roman Empire succumbed to their advances, and fields of grain and barley were repurposed, along with fruit, honey, and grape must, to make increasing quantities of ale and mead.

By most accounts, these "barbarians" had an ephemeral interest in Etna wine, but they had no long-term goals for Sicily. The Goths stayed on the island a little longer than the Vandals, playing with their newfound power, arranging marriages, and swimming in politics. But for the redistribution of grain fields into the hands of the church and a staggering increase in illiteracy, between the years 476 and 553, most Etna communities experienced relatively little change to their daily lives.[40]

Beer remained a part of the diet, if only loosely so. Fifteen hundred years on, artisan producers are once again using grain, barley, hops, local fruit, honey, and grape musts for an emerging craft beer culture in Sicily.

Birra Vulcano

Birrificio dell'Etna

Birrificio di Catania

Birrificio Namasté

Birrificio Timilia

La Caverna del Mastro Birraio

Officina Brassicola Siciliana (OBS)

San Bull

THE EASTERN ROMAN EMPIRE

When I think of the Byzantines, I think of color. The mosaics and paintings from this period in Sicily's history are vivid and inviting. All the flash was intentional. Christianity had become the religion for the Eastern Roman Empire. Color and luminescence were a way of portraying Christ as a guiding light. Something beautiful in a world of blandness and struggle. This was the message they spread when they took Sicily from the Goths in a massive show of force. Glorious, colorful salvation.

However, after two decades of fighting, the mountain was scattered with empty houses and abandoned estates and farms. Land that wasn't claimed or sold following the Gothic War was given to the church, who leased parcels to paying tenants. All the real estate made the Christian Church and the government extremely wealthy. They spread the money around, of course. In particular, they built schools. A lot of them. Free men and boys were offered an education steeped in Christianity.

It seemed like everything was going in a good direction, but the government monopoly on grain and, in particular, silk effectively strangled the local wine industry.

Vineyards were converted to mulberry farms by the dozens. Silk worms like mulberry leaves. In fact, it's almost all they eat. Vineyards weren't the only farms converted. Food was also at a premium. In the mind of the Byzantines, a little asceticism purified the soul.[41] Through the silk industry and religious acculturation, the Etna community came to see the joy of bread and wine as a religious rite instead of a human right. It was a shame, in the moment—there are stories of Christians plundering boats at the seaside—but it prepared everyone for what came next.

ISLAMIC SICILY

The first attacks came at night. In June 827, one hundred Muslim ships laden with 11,000 men and a cavalry with 700 horses landed at Mazar,[42] on Sicily's southwest coast. One month later, they were using the elaborate system of roads, built centuries earlier by the Romans, to lay waste to the countryside and anyone who challenged them. In truth, it wasn't the Sicilians who resisted. As one historian puts it, "They were frightened by Muslim fanaticism, but they'd had enough of Byzantine fanaticism."[43] It took fifty years and a malaria epidemic to cross Sicily and conquer Siracusa and the better part of a century spent fighting around Mount Etna before the Byzantine capital in Taormina was leveled, and the population slaughtered. But in 902, Sicily yielded to its new landlords, a mix of Berbers, Arabs, and Moors.[44]

In the prescripts of the Koran, the central religious text of Islam, alcohol consumption is a no-no. For the first few years under Muslim control, Etna's vineyards were uprooted and the vines burned. For those who continued to sell wine after the drink was banned in public, the penalties were severe. How high must the plumes of smoke have billowed? What ancient varieties did we lose? Just thinking about it still makes me want a drink. It was a way to encourage people to convert their grape production to food, one thing that Etna lacked under the Byzantines. The charred vineyards made great fertilizer for an abundance of farmland for dates and citrus, almonds and pistachios, melon, eggplant, and spices, cotton for simple clothing, sumac for tanning and dying, and hemp for clothing, rope, and sails. Irrigation and animal husbandry also took a leap forward. In a very short time, Etna and her eastern seaboard found economic stability[45] and another kind of wealth in the food that she could produce. Wine just wasn't on the menu.

As close as the Muslims were to wiping out wine on the mountain, they didn't go all the way. Practitioners of Christianity and Judaism were respected members of the *dhimmis* (protected "communities under Muslim rule"), so some vineyards and wine consumption was tolerated, as part of the religious rite. You couldn't worship in public, and dhimmis were forbidden from celebrating in any way that piqued the interest of a practitioner of Islam, but wine as part of a religious ceremony was okay behind closed doors.[46] It was just enough wine to keep the faithful away from the edge of provocation.

Despite this bad rap, it didn't make sense to "throw out the alcohol." It wasn't all bad. Alcohol has been a large part of Mediterranean culture for millennia, as a medicine, a direct treatment for wounds, and as a distillate used in the production of perfumes. Wine can be converted to vinegar. But since about 640 BCE—ten years after the death of Muhammad and the publication of the Koran—consumption of alcohol was banned throughout the Islamic world.

That said, in sura 47:15 of the Koran, Paradise is described as having rivers of delicious wine. For some, there were too many similarities between Mount Etna and depictions of "Paradise." Was it possible? Some tested the waters. "As always, it was the ruling class that took the most liberties, both in drinking and in selling wine (or in having the right to sell wine) to others.

Even caliphs—the highest rank of ruler—showed a desire to participate in the Promised Land of the Koran."[47]

They weren't the only ones. The popular Muslim poets Omar Khayyam and Ibn Hamdis wrote about wine as a part of life rather than an award given in the afterlife. It was important to know a wine's qualities (*khamar malsa* [soft wine][48]), the colors (red, white, yellow, and black), as well as the development of each vintage, the appearance of a wine (cloudy, clear), and ways to improve wine through the addition of honey, spices, drugs, water,[49] or salt water. In fact, there are more than 350 Arabic words and phrases dedicated solely to the description of wine.[50]

It wasn't all campfires and sing-alongs, I'm afraid. Some of the parties must have been fantastic, but more than a few of them got out of control. Maybe some words were said or rumors were started. Whatever happened, political, economic, and religious rivalries began to affect more than the administration of the citizenry. Ultimately, the tension and infighting sewed enough discord to design the elaborate backdrop of a bloody invasion.

This time, however, it was Wine that had the last word.

Saint Agatha—Nadine and I made our way into Catania at dusk for the annual procession of wax, one of the largest religious festivals on the planet. Every year, hundreds of thousands of devotees descend on the city to celebrate their patron, Saint Agatha. Throughout four days in February, masses, dedications, lectures, prayer sessions, music, jugglers, amusements, and an obscene amount of food are offered in Agatha's name.

The feast of Saint Agatha begins three straight days of celebration with an early morning mass on February 3, after which a twenty-ton carriage of Agatha's relics is pulled up Via San Giuliano by thousands of faithful followers. Festivities continue until February 5 and resume again for a single day on the twelfth. A fifth day is held on August 17. The August feast day corresponds to the day, in 1126, when her relics were returned to Catania after being stolen by General George Maniace and transported to Constantinople, in 1040. Over the centuries, Agatha has become the patron saint of women, rape victims, breast cancer patients, wet nurses, bell founders, incorruptibility, earthquakes and eruptions on Mount Etna, and for anyone who works around fire or suffers from contact with it. In the countryside, statues in her likeness appear most often at the edge of lava flows, where the rolling liquefied rock stopped.

The procession of wax follows the theme of a metaphorical destruction of the darkness. So, things really get going at sundown, when the framed lights hanging over Via San Giuliano and Via Etnea light up, and the crowd sprawling out from the Cathedral of Sant'Agata roars with adulation. Almost immediately, young men in the ceremonial *sacco agatino*—a white long-sleeve tunic tied together with a woven belt, a black chechia hat, sturdy gloves, and a handkerchief—walk through the crowd, carrying enormous lighted candles on their shoulders. Behind them, another wave of young men in costume carry burdensome white candles, and following that is yet another group of candle bearers, all of them forming a long illuminated path of light and flame up Via Etnea.

Moments later, the heavy *cerei* (decorative carriages) follow the candle bearers. These elaborate carved wood *cerei* are ensconced in gold and decorated to resemble a candle and flame bringing light to the darkness. Each of the thirteen *cerei* is carried and cared for by a local guild and the church. Some have small paintings, ornate sculptures, bright lights and angels, fresh flowers, spun columns and flags, or a combination of these. And they aren't small. The bakers' *cereo*, "A Momma," weighs about a ton. As many as twelve men, yoked like animals of burden, are needed to carry it. The good thing is, this isn't a sprint. Every few steps, the procession pauses, the carriages are set down, and other young men and candles flood by, illuminating and clearing the course ahead.

The charge, for Agatha's followers, is to celebrate her strength and share her burden along the proverbial road of life. This procession is as much a show as it is an opportunity to reconnect with other followers while celebrating the message of Saint Agatha. This is not a solemn procession, mind you. The *cerei* are surrounded by thousands, in various phases of prayer and wonder. For the faithful, who make it to the end of the procession, the view back toward the beginning resembles the road to Paradise, illuminated, as it were, by the light of an honest and chaste life. For those who stop part way, they can see the beauty of the road ahead.

It's a sentiment that arrived through incredible brutality. Agatha's short life came to a violent end on February 5, 251 CE. After denying a life of leisure and the affections of a powerful Roman, her illegal Christian faith was put on trial, and she was imprisoned in a brothel. When she again refused to recant her faith, her breasts were cut off. Her ferocious torture did not end there. Through all of it, she prayed to God. Nothing could deter her from her faith. Even the pain of being raked over coals and shards of glass steered her to prayer. At the moment of her death, an earthquake rocked the city. One year later, on the anniversary of her martyrdom, Mount Etna had a massive eruption. When Agatha's name was invoked, the eruption subdued. It was just enough reality and magic to make sense. The pagan community of the city and foothills around Mount Etna gave rise to her piety, as they folded into the Christian faith with Agatha's message as their guide.

One of the first things Norman Count Roger I of Sicily did for the Etna community was donate an enormous sum of money for construction of the Monastery of Saint Agatha, in the heart of Catania. It sounds easy enough, but after more than two centuries of Muslim control, the island wasn't easily won. After a series of fierce battles, the Varangian Guard (Norsemen hired by the Byzantine Empire) was stranded near Nicosia, in the plains west of Mount Etna.[51] They had wounded soldiers. It was snowing. They were exhausted, out of supplies, and completely surrounded by the Muslim army. In a moment of dramatic irony, the winds changed direction and the drunken voices of the Muslim soldiers could be heard in the Norman camp. The Norman Army took advantage of their inebriation and attacked, trapping and slaying their foes in the midst of their own paradox.[52]

The Normans immediately saw the potential of Mount Etna, but maintaining control of the landscape meant pleasing the population. Coming out of a war, no one wanted a revolution. Roger knew that if he gave land to the nobles who assisted in the overthrow of Sicily, the land grab would evolve into a power struggle.[53] Instead, he handed the Bishop of Catania, Ansgarius, the abbacy of Saint Agatha and complete reign over the visible landscape.[54] It was a bold move, turning your kingdom over to God, but it was also a boon to Christianity. It also gave Christian armies a military base from which they could launch Crusades.

The development of the hospital and church of the Knights Hospitaller and Christian monasteries around Catania and on the south slope of the volcano effectively stole Etna's wine industry from the clutches of ruin.[55] The construction and dedication of small churches and abbeys established new routes and communities around the mountain.

The Salma and the Mudd—Weights and measures changed frequently on Mount Etna. What the Greeks had called a *modion*, the Romans changed to *modius*, and the Muslims called a *mudd*, which translates to *salma* in Latin. All of them corresponded to an area of land that amounted to 4.3 acres (1.75 ha). The Normans adopted the "*mudd*" throughout Sicily.[56]

The modion, modius, mudd, and salma were used for area, dry measures of weight—grain, nuts, and beans—as well as grape must and wine. *Salma* sounds a lot like the Arabic word and name for "peaceful."[57] For the Sicilians, however, *salma* means "corpse."

It's a curious choice, but salma stuck for goods that were traded on a daily basis. It was used for the next 850 years—along with countless other weights and measures—until it was replaced by the metric system in 1861. For some, it was just as easy to keep using salma as a system of measures, well into the twentieth century. Why change something if it works, right?

When salma was applied to dry weights, its application varied based on what was being measured (i.e., grain, manure, or marble). One salma of grape must was equal to 86 liters (22 gal.). A salma of wine equaled 68.8 liters (18 gal.), or two small *barili* of 34.4 liters each, which could easily be carried on a mule in one load (*carico*).

The word *calata* was used to mean three *salme* (3 hl.), in Adrano and villages along the southern slope of the mountain.[58]

THE FIRST BEST VINEYARDS

Shortly after the island was rebranded as the Kingdom of Sicily, in 1130, King Roger II hired a Muslim geographer named Abu Abdullah Muhammad al-Idrisi al-Qurtubi al-Hasani as-Sabti (known as al-Idrisi) to draw a map of the known world. From that rendering, he was asked to write a directory of each place that he included. By then, the Knights Hospitaller had developed vineyards and winemaking practices around Paternò into a cru on the mountain. In his notes, al-Idrisi writes that the wines from these vineyards—where there is an intricate mix of ancient alluvial and volcanic soils and good exposure to sunlight and wind—were the best in the area.[59]

The wine grapes included Giustalisi, Pitrusa Nera, Pitrusa Bianca, Nocellara, Muscadine, Vispalora, Mantonico Bianco and Mantonico Nero, Greco, two types of Inzolia, white and red Guarnaccia, the Hospitaller's own clone of Gerosolimitana Bianca and Nera, Calavrisi, Barbarossa, Cataratto, Chimmunite, Durache, Malvagie, Verdiso, and Mandilaria. What we immediately notice is that the modern varieties included in the Etna DOC legislation are missing.[60] Either they weren't good enough to plant or, as I've come to realize, the Nerello Mascalese and Carricante varieties were not yet born. According to DNA research referenced in the first part of this book, one of Nerello's parents is missing from the list of grapes above. For that matter, al-Idrisi only mentions Mascali in passing, for its quality timber[61] and fertility, instead of the wine it would become known for seven centuries later.

The completion of the map was a defining moment for the Norman government. Not only were they in cahoots with the Byzantine Empire and in control of the largest strategic outpost in the Mediterranean, they had a map of the world they wanted to conquer.

All these quick successes were hushed on February 4, 1169—the eve of the celebration of Saint Agatha—when an earthquake registering seven on the moment magnitude scale (MMS) caused a tsunami that wiped out Etna's eastern seaboard,[62] followed by a near-simultaneous eruption of the volcano. These two events claimed 15,000 lives. The natural disasters were a devastating blow that also inadvertently forced migration inland and up the mountain for years to come. When students ask why the Etna DOC is so far from the coastline, I mention this and a second tsunami that followed anoth-

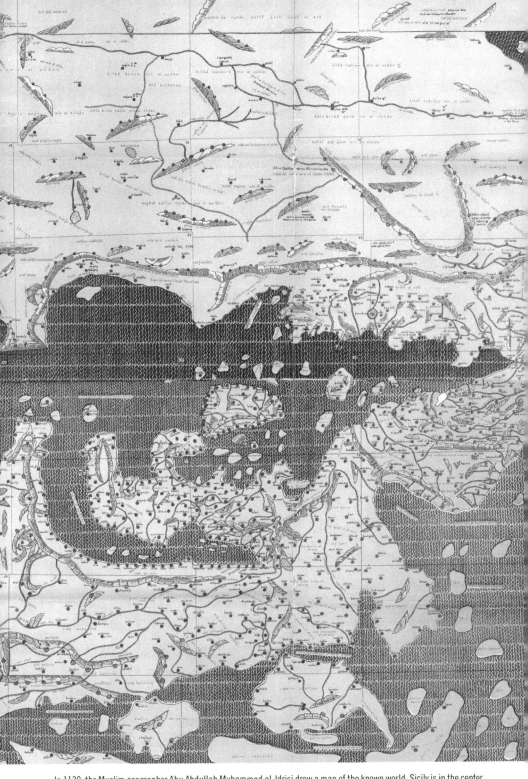

In 1130, the Muslim geographer Abu Abdullah Muhammad al-Idrisi drew a map of the known world. Sicily is in the center. Back then, Mount Etna was called *gebel al nar* and the religious elite were making the best wines on the mountain.

er earthquake in 1693. Both events pushed communities and their vineyards up the volcano. It's this migration that inadvertently jump-started one of the most significant viticultural epochs in Etna's history.

Al-Idrisi's Map of Sicily—When the map was drawn onto the fabric panels and sewn together into a massive colorful tapestry, the known world included Eurasia, Europe, and North Africa.

It's an interesting map. All the names of places are written to be read looking south. The map is, essentially, upside down.

There are also seven additional islands between Sicily and Tunisia, and three more islands in the Aeolian Archipelago.

Catania's name isn't included but Acis is. Only, it's called Liag (*gazair* Liag, the islands of Akis). Mount Etna is called *gebel al nar* (the black mountain, or the mountain of fire).

LAWS & DISORDER

I had to file an incredible amount of paperwork when I moved to Sicily. Nothing got easier as I went. Italian bureaucracy is an obstacle course of signposts that point in every possible direction. Rarely did I get anything done on the first or second attempt, yet inevitably, I was almost always successful on the third. When I wasn't able to get something done after a third attempt, the clock reset. Some forms or stamps or applications took six visits to get right. It was infuriating, but I was learning as I went. When I tried to use simple A-to-B logic, the more things went off the rails. I found that the only way to get past the insanity of creating ten problems out of one was to go limp. Like a dummy in a car crash. Let the absurdity of being thrown into unexpected chaos pass. It almost always does.

Over months, Nadine and I began to call it "the rule of three." Reading between the lines, translating chronic systematic miscommunication, and waiting patiently became survival skills. In Sicily, persistence is often rewarded. Other times, it is mocked.

It's nothing new. One of the most public displays of bureaucratic assault happened after the Normans were ousted by a line of German kings (the Svevi).[63] Suddenly, land holdings that had been kept in families for generations were no longer guaranteed by birth. Leases were torn up. Imagine having to apply, and reapply, for the right to work and live on your own land and then being denied because someone with power sought to take it. The Svevi were terrible, but the Angevins (French), who took the island in 1268, also bent the laws to gobble up even more land than their predecessors. By the time the Aragonese (Spanish) took control in 1282, any semblance of bureaucratic order on Mount Etna was a joke. The only things you could depend on were confusion and deception.

It all came to a head in the War of the Sicilian Vespers.[64] Over the next twenty years, it was easy enough to find intrigue in the cities and ports of Catania, Naxos, Acis or Giarre—most of the fighting took place at sea—but Etna's vineyards were left intact.[65]

I like to think the mountain communities consumed copious amounts of local wine when Frederick III of Sicily (Spanish) and Eleanor of Anjou (French) married in 1303. Their houses were the reason for all of the fighting. And now, they had made up. The marriage was good for a few years of peace—followed by many decades of war—but the relationships they cultivated had a hand in changing the face of Etna's viticultural landscape forever. As with many things on Mount Etna, part of that story took place offstage.

Eighty years earlier, while Saint Francis of Assisi was writing his *testament*, he openly encouraged his brethren to criticize corruption and any priest who did not adhere to the monkish qualities of Christ. He was so adamant about the importance of living a humble life that he submitted his manuscript for papal approval.

If Francis's testament was accepted as is, under the umbrella of Christian doctrine, it would have created a lot of problems for Pope Innocent III and the high cardinals. They were the wealthiest Christians in the world. Every time I tell this story, I think of them all laughing maniacally as they discussed "poor Francis" from their stacks of money and gold. Needless to say, his first draft was rejected. A revised document eventually got the okay. The pope and his entourage were safe. At least until 1226, when, on his deathbed, Francis publicly recanted the edited version of his testament in favor of the original.

After his death, Franciscan friars multiplied like stars on a clear night. A few decades on, they were involved in every facet of life throughout the Italian Peninsula and, to a lesser extent, Sicily. Pilgrimage was required as a part of monastic life. Wherever pilgrims traveled, they communicated in the culture of wine. Seeds and cuttings of favored grape varieties from the north—Calabria, Northern Italy, France, Germany, and Spain—found their way into local Etna vineyards. Other times, they arrived in bundles, carried by wandering scholars, who often drank far more than they taught.[66]

When on pilgrimage, friars stayed as long as was helpful. They kept things simple, lived honestly, gave generously, and left a small wake behind them. Their monasteries were modest, but they also held expansive vineyards and land, with barns for storage of water, wheat, vegetables, fruits, wine, and the tools necessary to work the land. They were expert farmers. They took farming cues from Palladius,[67] the *Liber de vinis*, by Arnaldus de Villanova;[68] and the *Liber ruralium commodorum*, by Petrus de Crescentiis. The Crescentiis treatise was widely circulated among Christian monastics. It includes twelve books that focus on selecting a vineyard site, the practical matters of cultivation, the work of agriculture, the harvest, vines and the methods of wine production, fruiting trees, vegetable gardens, as well as a detailed calendar of tasks based on the agricultural year.[69]

The friars weren't wealthy. Their treasure was in the land they worked and the communities they served. Instead of increasing the riches of the pope, however, surpluses were bartered or used wherever there was need. As a result, the friars and monasteries grew more self-sufficient and influential. Though the Franciscans thought of their lifestyle as independent living,[70] the pope called their lack of investment in the Vatican coffers heresy. When the trouble boiled over in 1296, friars were excommunicated, defrocked, and even executed. As the Vatican continued to persecute the friars, scores of Franciscan mendicants and lay churchmen sought refuge in Sicily, under the protection of Frederick III and Queen Eleanor.

Shortly after their wedding, in 1303, Eleanor was given the Camera Reginale (Queen's Chamber), a fiefdom that included a board of administrators to help oversee much of Etna's developing countryside, including parts of Paternò, Castiglione di Sicilia, and Francavilla di Sicilia.[71] She invested heavily in local churches and monasteries, hospitals and schools, and she took a liking to the local Benedictine monks. They were feisty, hardworking, humble, and smart.

Word that Mount Etna had become one contiguous farm of interconnected and independent monasteries spread like wildfire. Queen Eleanor was a good Christian. When the Franciscan friars begged for safety, she opened the countryside to them. At first, it was a small group. Then, they came en masse. Books on religious matters and farming arrived with them.

Many more brought tools, initiative, and vine cuttings. Of particular value was an as yet unnamed red grape variety that had been growing in the monastic vineyards around Umbria, Tuscany, and Emilia-Romagna. The friars were originally given safe haven near Paternò[72] and Santa Maria di Licodia, but eventually there were too many friars to hide, so they donned the habits of the Benedictines and folded into Etna's monastic community.

For the better part of three decades, the monks worked to improve daily life on the mountain. But during sunset, on June 28, 1329, Etna had a spectacular lateral eruption lasting two weeks and claiming twenty-four square kilometers of agricultural land along the eastern slope. In a seemingly apocalyptic occurrence, a solar eclipse punctuated the eruption on July 15. As it reached for the historic cities of Acireale, Aci Catena, and Aci Sant'Antonio, Queen Eleanor led a procession of monks, friars, and able-bodied parishioners with Saint Agatha's relics ahead of the lava, effectively stopping the molten rock before it reached the population centers.[73] In exchange for their prayers, Eleanor dedicated a substantial amount of property in the area around Santa Maria di Licodia for tax-free use.

It's difficult to say, with certainty, exactly how much land the church owned in the fourteenth century, but almost all of the agricultural land between Adrano, Catania, Taormina and Randazzo,[74] including thousands of acres of vineyards, fell under the protective eye of God. It was an incredible gift, but there was too much land to manage. As they had done in the past, the diocese of Santa Maria di Licodia began leasing parcels of land in emphyteusis. The initiative offered religious families small and large farms at a nominal rent, with a contract that typically lasted three generations. The emphyteuta (renter) was given all the rights of the landowner without actually holding the deed to the property. These were not palaces nor large estates with villas and a staff. Most were in dire need of attention. New farms were started from favored seeds and plant material—vegetables, spices, olives, fruits, nuts, wheat, corn, and vines—which could be traced back to donations from the monasteries. This kind of turnkey thinking attracted migration up and around the mountain. Not only did emphyteusis offer a way of life to those who could manage it, the program invited curiosity, experimentation, and biodiversity into Etna agriculture.[75] Even the smallest farm could be turned into a perpetual source of food, wine, and currency, especially if you followed a monastic model. Though emphyteusis was eventually done away with, the seeds of systematic, sustainable permaculture were planted.

Your Own Pet Crater—In 1859, author Helen Lowe published her memoir *Unprotected Females in Sicily, Calabria, and on the Top of Mount Ætna*[76] following an adventurous vacation in southern Italy and Sicily.

On walking atop Monte Rosso, Lowe writes, "The higher of two craters thrown up the last time Catania was destroyed . . . [Monterosso is] a brilliant red, save where the vines clothe the steep sides. Arrived at the top, on looking down the concave crater, beautiful trees are seen to grow from whence the consuming fire once issued. Looking around, endless other volcanic hills appear crowding together over Ætna's sides, to the number, it is said, of more than a hundred, which peculiarity makes her so different to other mountains. They are turned into vineyards, and everybody in the neighborhood who can afford it, has his own pet crater, and drinks the wine."

While vines have grown among these craters for millennia, it remains one of the most beautiful and exciting viticultural areas on the mountain.

Wineries Among the Southeast Craters

Barone Beneventano / Monte Ilice

Benanti / Monte Serra

Biondi / Monte San Nicolò

Cantina Malopasso / Monte Ilice

Cantine di Nessuno / Monte Ilice

Eudes / Monte Gorna

LatoSud / Monte Gorna

Monterosso / Monte Rosso

Nicosia / Monte Gorna

Santa Maria La Nave / Monte Ilice

Tenuta Monte Gorna / Monte Gorna

Tenuta Monte Ilice / Monte Ilice

Tenute Mannino di Plachi / Monte Serra

Terra Costantino / Monte San Nicolò

THE LATE MIDDLE AGES

If you want good fish, go to the Catania fish market. If you want the fattest, tastiest fish in the Mediterranean, get there early. They begin calling out the catch at seven o'clock, every day except Sunday. *Sepia! Alice! Polpo!* From there, it gets louder. Calls teasing fresh *orato*, *spigola*, *neonati*, *gamberi*, and *gamberone* merge with the sounds of sharp cleavers cutting away at swordfish. The best vendors get personal, drawing onlookers with enthusiastic one-liners about family and food, or teasing about the poor quality of his neighbor's catch. The shouting and haggling are all in good fun. The market is a spectacle, but it's because people have *always* come to the center of Catania for food. It says a lot about the character of a place, when the vendors can claim an eternal history with the local cuisine.

In the fall of 1347, the first thing vendors noticed was a change in the din, as the crowds at the market started thinning out. One day after another, the sounds of the city shifted tone. Genovese merchants importing goods from the east unknowingly spread the disease. First introduced in Messina, the plague quickly spread from there. Over the course of the next twenty years, up to two-thirds of the population of Europe died in a painful, skin-blackening pandemic. Some villages and cities were completely decimated. All that migration and community building that occurred through emphyteusis only spread the plague and disorder faster.[77] All the vines could do was keep growing.

One century later, the Etna community was still making some of the finest wine on the island. King Alfonso, in Naples, had a taste for wine. Some of his favorites came from the areas around Taormina and Aci, which he bought in quantities of young, aged, and "the oldest [wines] you can find."[78] Not only did this purchase signify the qualitative importance of viticulture on Etna, it heralded the birth of a second cru on the mountain, centered around Aci—including nine separate villages whose names all begin with Aci.[79] Alfonso's wine purchase went one step further. It helped to stimulate the local wine economy. Vineyards that were abandoned during the plague were revived. Palmenti were cleaned and reopened. The ceremonial carriages used to move the must between palmenti and clients were repainted. Reviving the agricultural sector was a genius solution to a list of growing troubles. But it wasn't enough.

THE NEW WORLD

In 1469, the Spanish King Ferdinand II married Isabella of Castile, fortifying Sicily's connections to Spain. Shortly after their ten-year wedding anniversary, the couple kicked off their own version of the Inquisition—a religious pogrom aimed at eradicating their lands of non-Christians.

An incident in Castiglione di Sicilia, on Mount Etna's north slope, inspired the local community to move ahead with the idea. A religious procession turned violent when a Jewish resident threw rocks at an effigy of Christ, breaking the arm. The crowd became enraged. Two brothers killed the attacker, and when the perpetrators got in front of a judge, they pled for forgiveness, adding that they would prefer it if all non-Christians would be expelled, because if the victim's bloodline was Christian instead of Jewish, the entire violent incident never would have happened.[80] It must have been one hell of a lawyer arguing on their behalf. The judge was sold. He banged his gavel and the road to mass deportation of non-Christians got very slippery. The chaos it created in every corner of the mountain had a devastating effect on the farming and merchant communities, which had been multicultural for centuries.

It was the proverbial shot in the foot. When stories about the New World reached Etna, they found the mountain sealed in a vacuum of Christian purity and economic desperation. Agriculture and viticulture around the volcano had slipped into lazy habits. A farm or a vineyard was no longer the place to make money. Spanish gold was buying timber now. The Crown needed boats for additional expeditions to the New World. Once again, the collective attention turned toward the volcano, and the deforestation of Etna began in earnest. It was an incredible amount of work, bringing the trees from the mountain to the sea. But all the activity between Catania and Naxos attracted Barbary pirates. These were not nice folks. One of their primary trades was slavery. It didn't matter if you were a fisherman, a twiddler, or you had one shot in your foot. If they wanted you, they were coming for you. On a volcano that reaches the sea, there aren't a lot of directions to go or places to hide, especially now that many forests were removed. When the pirates attacked, you either ran, stood your ground, or laid down in it.

THE BIRTH OF MASCALI

Nerello Mascalese (nayr-rehl-lō mas-ca-lay-zay) is a hard name to say. When it's translated from Italian to English, it means the "pale black grape from

Mascali" (literally, "little black from Mascali"). "Little" because the "black" variety doesn't produce a wine of deep color. "Mascali" because that's the town the grape calls home. I know it sounds like an overly practical origin story, but a name is not a story.

By the time the battlements along the coastline were built to defend against pirate attacks, the dominant red grapes in Etna's monastic vineyards included scores of new upstarts, including Niuridduni and Niuriddu ordinariu. If we translate these names through the centuries, we arrive at "Nerello" and "Ordinary Nerello." The black grape and the ordinary black grape. At best, these only made up a portion of a vineyard. At the time, the common practice was to grow, harvest, and ferment several grapes together. The palmento system—an open fermentation house with no temperature control—made it impossible to get the most out of a single grape. The vineyard had to grow several hearty cultivars with strong characters that could withstand the rough treatment and heat of the palmento process. I have no doubt that Niuridduni added something to a blend, but why was the Niuridduni grown in Mascali so special?

Credit for the "Mascalese" surname goes to the Bishop of Catania at the time, Nicola Caracciolo. Caracciolo was a powerful and contemplative man. He didn't enjoy watching his congregation suffer. Between the plague, the poverty, and the pirates, he knew something needed to be done. Over the course of several days, he penned a letter to King Charles V—also known as the Duke of Burgundy, the Holy Roman Emperor, the Ruler of Spain, and King of Italy—asking for assistance. On March 12, 1540, with the wave of a quill, a few signatures, and stamps, the *feudo* of Mascali was elevated to a *comune* (municipality) and Bishop Caracciolo was appointed Count of Mascali.[81]

These sound like simple administrative changes but the bishop had a plan. It took some time to manifest—daily civil unrest and church politics distracted him from completing a use strategy for the countryside around

Mascali—but in October 1558, he held a town meeting in a small church to announce that land around the village of Mascali (*Masculum*) would be leased in emphyteusis. A collective sigh fell over the crowd. Mascali was a mess. There was very little arable land. Entire forests needed to be felled. Swamps had to be drained and filled too. Countless steep slopes required terracing. Roads and transportation routes had to be conceived. Those who saw the promise also knew that turning a forest into farmland was going to be a colossal undertaking. But, for the cost of developing the land and a modest rent—to be paid in fees or in measures of wheat, fruit, wine, etc.—it was more than a fair deal.[82]

Those who leased land hired those who couldn't afford to. Skilled laborers went to work for enterprising families. Nobles with an eye for business and the coffers to lease large pieces of land also sublet parcels to long-term tenants.[83] Loggers cut trees for timber. Shipbuilders built skiffs and larger crafts. Master coopers bought chestnut wood to make barili and botti. Fields of hemp were farmed for rope and sails. Mascali gave Etna a clean slate. It was the mountain's first planned community. For those who invested, Mascali was somewhere something new could happen. It was a place with a future. Looking up at it all from the seaside, I'm willing to bet a lot of people wondered, What are we going to do with all of that land?

Enter the merchants. They wanted a say too, about the wines, in particular. There was nothing savvy about it. Business is business. Clients in the north liked Etna wines for several reasons. Most importantly, the warm Mediterranean weather and bright sunlight guaranteed ripe grapes every vintage. But the Etna wines also produced flavors that were eerily similar to those in other places. If the merchants could get the grapes they wanted into the new vineyards, they would be very wealthy men. Vine material that didn't come directly from the church on the south slope of Etna, Aci, or Taormina was imported from Calabria, Messina, Noto, and Palermo.

By the time the initial work was complete, a portion of the seaside and the foothills immediately south of Naxos had been transformed into an intentional cru, where the black grapes all had a similar style and often the same name.[84]

ETNA ERUPTS

A few months before we left California for Sicily, Eric Asimov published an article in the *New York Times* about Etna wines. I thought the lede was funny, and more than a little apropos.

He opened the article this way: "I can't imagine what it's like to live next to a volcano, much less root my family and my hopes for its future within spewing distance of one."[85] I literally laughed out loud. It was exactly what we were planning.

The thing I neglected to consider before moving to Europe's largest and most active volcano is that she didn't get this way by sitting around. In my short seven years on the mountain, there have been more than 3000 small earthquakes and multiple eruptions. You get used to it. It fades into the background, like the tremor of a subway for someone living in New York City.

The sixteenth and seventeenth centuries were particularly busy times for Etna. The first big eruption in the series emerged from a lateral fissure, northwest of Randazzo, four years before Mascali became a comune. This was no ordinary lava flow. The molten rock blocked a portion of the Flascio River, forming Lake Gurrida. The tremors were so powerful that a second fissure opened on the opposite side of the mountain, destroying a portion of Nicolosi. One year later, the façade cracked again, in the hills above Nicolosi at Monte Nero, spilling enough lava to consume 182 vineyards and 200 homes in the countryside, plus seventy more homes in the city.[86]

Ten years later, a second emission at Monte Spagnolo neutered hundreds of acres in the hills east of Randazzo. Like clockwork, in 1566, a lateral eruption sent lava lumbering toward Passopisciaro. Within hours, spectators watched in horror as a massive rolling tongue of molten rock unfurled on houses and stables and precious farmland along the border of Contrade Arcuria and Feudo di Mezzo. Another dozen eruptions over fifty years flooded the western slope, rendering most of it unsuitable for vineyards—but ideal for pistachios—for centuries to come.

The decade-long discharge from 1614 to 1624 tops the list of single eruptions in Etna's modern history. This contiguous event could have built a wall of stone standing ten feet wide, fifty feet tall, and a mile-and-a-half long.[87] As lava, it melted into the hills above Montelaguardia, between Passopisciaro and Randazzo, covering roughly eight square miles of forest, farms, and vineyards. After such an enormous emission, Etna took a ten-year sabbatical before going back to work—part-time—from 1634 to 1638. Over 850 days, she spread lava and pyroclastic material down the east slope. Three years later, Santa Venera and Portosalvo, two small villages north of Mascali, were consumed.

All of these small events were merely the warm-up acts for the historic eruption that started in the second week of March 1669. Multiple strong earthquakes resulted in a collapse of the central crater, which caused a crack in the mountain between the summit and Nicolosi. The lava consumed more than ten miles of the southeast flank, destroying parts of Nicolosi, Camporeale, Mascalucia, San Pietro Clarenza, San Giovanni Galermo and the southern neighborhoods of Catania, before rolling into the sea.

Whole houses and sections of vineyards were seen riding the slow-moving lava as it rolled downhill. It's a picturesque description. It almost makes you wonder why it comes up at all. Shouldn't people be running, instead of gazing in wide wonder at one of Etna's natural disasters? It was a massive depressurization of the magma chamber; the activity continued for months.

People had time to watch it. Some of them were artists. This eruption, more than any in Etna's history, has been rendered with such beauty that the devastation is more alluring than frightening.

The volcano was quiet for decades after that, but it wasn't the end of the destruction. In January 1693, an earthquake measuring more than 7.4 on the MMS shook seventy communities on Sicily's eastern coastline to the ground. The quake was so powerful, Malta and the Aeolian island of Lipari felt the shock wave. A short earthquake two days before scared people just enough that they ran into the countryside. Those who stayed among the unstable walls in urban centers witnessed the ugliest side of nature's awesome power. In one account, "the broken earth swallowed people, animals, and [entire] rivers. Etna erupted violently and immense waves swept coastal towns into the sea."[88]

The waves were, in fact, a tsunami. Mascali was hit the worst. The gigantic surf reached more than one mile inland, washing away a century of work and urban planning.[89] Buildings previously damaged during the 1669 events, as well as new construction, were reduced to rubble.[90] Though rare deaths were recorded in communities on the volcano, tens of thousands were killed in southeast Sicily and along Etna's coastline. Few periods of record have so thoroughly glazed the mountain with this much suffering. It begs the question, why stay? Or why come at all? I've wondered these things myself, many times, for an array of reasons. Regardless of how I come to an answer—the food and wine, the lifestyle, the weather, the history—the reply is always the same. We are here because we want to be and because the mountain allows us to stay. For as long as she'll have us, Etna is home.

LATE-MODERN ETNA

I think about the tsunami every time I go to the beach in Fondachello. In the summer the expanse of pebbles and deep-sea silts are covered with pop-up lidos. It's a good place to get away from the heat, or bathe in it. From the end of the seventeenth century, merchant ships arriving in Riposto[91] and Fondachello[92] simply slid up onto the beach and anchored, or they sent skiffs that did the same. A few minutes on foot or in the back of a cart and they were in the heart of town.

The seaside around Mascali had become famous for its culinary delights. Anything and everything grown on the mountain made it downslope to the markets. Wine and must too. In Francesco Cupani's dissertation *Hortus Catholicus*, about the agriculture of Sicily, he names forty-eight different varieties grown around Etna.[93] It's a dizzying array of grapes to have in such a small space, but field blends and blends of field blends had previously satisfied the market. Cupani, a Franciscan monk, had unique access to the diaspora of cultivars in the vineyards of every Etna monastery. Now, merchants were influencing trends in Mascali farms with their buying power. Cupani's list, published in 1696, is the last time we see so many native grapes on the Etna menu.

By the time Tuscan scientist Domenico Sestini turned his pen on Mascali, in 1774, the comune was producing between 170 and 200 salme per year, or approximately 420,000 gallons of wine[94]—slightly less than the total production of Etna DOC wines today. At that time, it amounted to half the production of the entire mountain, but the number of marketable grapes had reduced to a dozen. The wines Sestini focused on were Etna's new blends. In particular, those grown in the cru of Mascali.

The Nigrello was the grape with the most potential for red wines. He favored Catarratto over Carricante for white wines. Both the Nigrello and the Catarratto, he notes, are "generous, strong, durable, and perfect for shipping [overseas]"[95] Sestini says Carricante has "good fruit but mediocre quality,"[96] adding that extended lees contact and MLF reduced the natural acidity in the wine,[97] making it more sturdy and palatable. A century before, different grapes would have been included in a blend to shift the profile of a wine.

Now, winemakers were using simple enology. Sestini takes time to note that while old vines only produce a quarter of the quantity of young vines, "*Vigna vecchia fa buon vino* (old vines make good wine)."[98] I tend to agree with him.

Rumor has it that Queen Marie Antoinette was a kind lady. That callous comment she's credited with about giving cake to French peasants to calm the revolution is baloney. In 1793, as she approached the guillotine at the Place de la Révolution, Marie Antoinette accidentally stepped on the boot of the executioner and apologized. She had no reason to be nice—her husband, King Louis XVI, was killed the exact same way ten months earlier—but that's the kind of person she was. When word of their deaths reached the royal family in Naples—King Ferdinand IV and Queen Marie Caroline, sister to Marie Antoinette—they were devastated. Six years later, they too were faced with the potential of a similar fate, as Napoléon Bonaparte punctured Italian defenses and made his way to their city.

With help from the British Navy's Admiral Horatio Nelson, they escaped to Sicily. En route, Nelson ordered the fleet to block any further French incursion south. As a thank-you for this and additional duties, in autumn 1799, Nelson was rewarded for his heroism with the title Duca di Bronte (Duke of Bronte). His nobility came with an estimated 22,000 acres of property on Mount Etna's northwest flank, near Bronte.[99] The title was an honor, but Nelson saw the *ducea* (duchy) as a backhanded gift. The estate, like much of Bronte, had deteriorated to a figment of its former glory. In the thirteenth century, the castle and main structures were part of the opulent Benedictine Maniace Abbey. Now it was in shambles. Whatever his reasons, Nelson never lived on the estate, despite the amount of treasure he invested to revive it.[100]

A few years earlier, another Englishman by the name of John Woodhouse started a business in Marsala based on a Sicilian recipe for strong, sweet wine from local grapes. Though the recipe was an adaptation on perpetual, fractional blending, it reminded Nelson of Caribbean rum, a cane spirit he took a liking to while he was in command of a British fleet in the Americas. One of his first orders was for 500 pipes[101] of Woodhouse & Co. Marsala. He wanted the order shipped to the English fleet in Malta. Going forward, Woodhouse branded Nelson's product Bronte Madeira, Bronti Madiera, Bronti, Marsala, and even Bronte Bronte.[102] It was a way to leverage Nelson's fame, but Marsala didn't need any promotion.

The fortified, sweet wine was so popular in the United Kingdom that it helped forge an alliance between Sicilian royalty and the English. It was a political friendship almost completely built on wine. This led to expansive investments in the island's viticultural heritage and, by default, its economic stability. By 1812, more than 17,000 English soldiers and thirty British administrators were managing the island's affairs.[103] From Riposto, the British Navy was making regular trips to Malta with wine from Etna, as well as timber, cattle, and grain.[104] With Napoléon's army behind the British naval blockade, transport of Etna wines was safe. The local economy took off.[105]

The Brontë Sisters—Admiral Horatio Nelson was so admired in his time that several communities and memorials were attributed with his name in New Zealand, Egypt, England, Wales, Canada, and the United States. Most interesting is the naming of the Brontë family in honor of the admiral.

As the story goes, the Brontë family was born of an old Irish clan called Ó Pronntaigh. When the name was Anglicized, it became Prunty and then Brunty. According to a biography, Patrick Brunty, the father of authors Charlotte, Emily, and Anne, changed the family name to Brontë in a show of support for Admiral Nelson, although no relation.

The Brontë sisters have been recognized for their literary fame and the writing of several influential books, including Jane Eyre (Charlotte), Wuthering Heights (Emily), and The Tenant of Wildfell Hall (Anne).[106]

THE NINETEENTH CENTURY

William H. Smyth was a ready sailor. Though he had no education to speak of, he had circled the globe by the age of twenty. As much as Smyth loved the open waters, he was fascinated by the places where water met land. When he received a post with the British Royal Navy's Sicilian fleet he fell in love with the seaside and the cities in the volcano's embrace. It fascinated him.[107]

Smyth spent a fair amount of time studying and writing about the vineyards between Mascali and Riposto. He paints it as a semi-contiguous vineyard area of 90 million vines, producing 90,000 pipes of wine per year[108] (14,670,000 US gallons), roughly thirty-five times what the comune was re-

By the mid 1800s, the Port of Riposto, at the base of Mount Etna in eastern Sicily, had a fully-functioning wine economy. Master coopers, wine merchants, and boat makers worked together to ship countless wood barrels of Etna wine throughout Europe.

porting one century earlier. Other areas around the mountain were eclipsed in comparison.[109] "Mascali is an exuberantly-fertile spot," Smyth writes. "The wine is high-flavored, but universally polluted with an infusion of burnt gypsum (sulfur); for, owing to the too free admission of atmospheric air, and mismanagement in the fermentation, it would otherwise become acid [vinegar]."

Based on his description, this isn't a wine I would buy, but knowing how strong-smelling even small amounts of sulfur can be, and how miniscule quantities of it can protect a wine from oxidation and spoilage, his tasting note makes a lot of sense. Riposto was a marketplace, after all. The merchants were using sulfur to stabilize the wines and barrels for shipment. Most wineries do the same thing today. Before bottling, a small amount of sulfur is added to postpone the inevitable shift to vinegar. With approximately 40,000 botticelli[110] being shipped from Riposto each year, wines were expected to arrive at their destination "intact." Sulfur was the key.[111]

It seemed to be working. The wines being shipped from Riposto in the nineteenth century assumed a reputation for being good blending wines (*vino da taglio*), with a diversity of organoleptic qualities. They were used to cut or blend up lighter or lesser wines in foreign markets. In some regions of northern Europe, where the days are shorter and cooler, it can be difficult for *Vitis vinifera* to reach full maturity. In Sicily, the sunlight and warm climate increase the potential for alcohol, color, and flavor. Vineyards on Etna have an added advantage in that mature grapes grown at higher elevations also retain a healthy amount of natural acidity. Vineyards at lower elevations benefitted from warmer weather and fertile volcanic soils, and the wines were headier. The most skilled blenders could build a wine that impersonated or improved almost any wine in Continental Europe.

By the time Captain Smyth published his memoir, in 1824, Riposto was the primary port for the English fleet. Etna wines were being shipped to

Malta en masse. A depot there had been constructed solely to supply English excursions throughout the Mediterranean and the Americas. Nearly all the new ships in the port were being built by local craftsmen for local merchants and financed by local investors.[112] Ten years after Smyth's memoir was published, Riposto was exporting 54 percent of the island's wine and drinkable alcohol.[113] Royal records from a decade later accounted for 63,000 acres of vines on the mountain, encompassing more than 50 percent of all the arable land.[114] Thanks in large part to the timber business, which shipped out of the Casa Cottone, between the Alcantara River and Riposto,[115] farmable land on Etna expanded exponentially.

The communities between Acireale and Mascali had become the wealthiest in all of Sicily. Everyone one on the mountain was contributing to colossal quantities of wine, brandy, grappa, essences of exotic spices, pistachios, almonds, olives and oil, figs, raisins, anchovies, wheat, rice, and silk.[116] In Viagrande, on the southeast slope of the volcano, more than 1,000 acres were under vine, with an emphasis on brandy production at four independent distilleries, and four factories were processing tartaric acid.[117] Virtually every shipment of wine from Riposto was complemented by Etna's other products. Even ice, stored in caves on the higher flanks of the volcano, was such a regular product that one pound of it could be bought for a few pennies.

The Ice Business—One of Mount Etna's most intriguing histories is partially hidden in the contours of the mountain. During the formation of the volcano, layers of lava formed numerous lava tubes and subsequent *grotte* (caves). According to the Parco Dell'Etna, many of Etna's caves were used during the Bronze Age as dwellings, animal shelters, and burial sites, in particular at lower elevations. Through the ages, the grotte were used by pirates, bandits, and even as a site for meditation. Some of the caves are small or shallow while others are spacious, delving deep into the mountain.

The deeper the *grotta*, the cooler the temperature can be. Historically, since the time of Muslim occupation of Sicily (if not longer), as the first snows arrived on Etna, teams of workers would climb the mountain to pack the grotte full of snow; the snow would freeze into blocks of ice. As the snow was piled into the grotte, it was separated into layers using ferns, making it possible to harvest portions of the ice during the spring and summer.

Ice was used for several reasons: keeping fish and other animal products cool in area markets; protecting medicine; keeping wine shipments cool during summer travel; and making flavored, icy drinks and granita (frozen sweet juice).

Between the seventeenth and nineteenth centuries, ice from Mount Etna also became an important export commodity. After citrus and wine, ice was Etna's third-most exported product during the spring and summer months. In fact, ice was such an important export that it was often shipped with "bandits" who protected the product.

Important communities where ice was harvested included Pedara, Trecastagni, and Zafferana Etnea. Important ports for ice included Aci Trezza, Ognina (the mythical port of Odysseus), Riposto, and Santa Maria La Scala.

During World War II, Etna's grotte served the local population as hiding places, in particular through the battles that followed the allied invasion of Sicily, in 1943.[118]

It was a prolific time in Etna's wine history, but it wasn't without its struggles. Eruptions and a cholera epidemic in Catania added a heaping teaspoon of disorder. Newspaper headlines spread unrest around Europe. The potato blights of 1843 and 1845 and a terrible grain harvest in 1846 contributed to the failure of banks, which fanned the fires of distrust between the "haves" and an incongruent group of "have-nots" in virtually every nation of Europe. When word of a riot in Palermo arrived on Etna, peasants gathered in the piazza of Viagrande, and local revolutionaries waved *il tricolore* (Italy's three-colored flag) in solidarity. It didn't do them a lot of good. They were all arrested. Some were deported. As much as the western half of Sicily and the western half of Mount Etna wanted independence from the Bourbon king, Etna's wealthy businessmen weren't willing to trade economic stability for theoretical aspirations of freedom.

As it so often happens on Mount Etna, life outplayed politics, effectively refocusing everyone's attentions back to the vineyards. This time, all it took was a little fungus. A curious mildew settled in the bunches, stems, and leaves of Etna vineyards. The vines shut down. What was thought to be a parasitic attack came to be known as oidium (a.k.a. *Oidium tuckeri, Uncinula necator*, or powdery mildew).

I hate oidium. It's a pernicious fungus, if left untreated. All it needs is a moderate temperature, a little humidity, and a breeze to spread. Vineyards in Mascali were the most affected. It didn't matter if the vine spacing was one pace or four. Until it was discovered that spraying or dusting with sulfur killed and prevented the fungus, oidium continued to spread. Some botanists believed, incorrectly as it turns out, that the cure rested in planting and grafting American vines, which remained unaltered by the fungus.[119]

Unfortunately, oidium was only the latest disaster to strike the historic vineyards on the south slope of the mountain. Eleven of thirty vintages between 1821 and 1850 were decimated by hail or other weather problems, reducing the crop to one-third or less of its potential. In 1825 and 1846, there was no grape harvest at all. In Biancavilla, the problems went beyond the weather. Emphyteutic tenants had sublet their lands until farms were so small they produced only enough food and wine to sustain the leaseholder. Palmenti all along the south slope were understaffed. In some cases they simply closed their doors.[120]

Not everyone on Etna's southern flank was hurting. After centuries of family investments in sulfur mining, cotton, wheat, silk, tuna, and other businesses, Barone Antonino Spitaleri, of Feudo Muglia, converted nearly 150 acres of his family's 740-acre estate to vineyards. Work began outside of Adrano in 1848. Stones recovered from digging and strategic explosions of gunpowder he arranged into terraces and *rasole* (walkways) spanning hundreds of kilometers around the estate, at elevations of 600 to 1,200 meters AMSL. What lava stones remained after the construction of the vineyards and the excavation of wine caves were amassed for a medieval castle, designed by the famed architect Carlo Sada. It was as much a statement of wealth as it was a show of Spitaleri's intentions.

His first ten years in production were dedicated almost exclusively to research. He kept copious notes and applied repetitious methods as a way of understanding the terroir, the aspect and elevation of the vines, ideal cellar practices, and the best use of chemistry in stabilizing wines. Over sixty experiments were completed using Barolo (Nebbiolo), Bordò Nero (Merlot), Cabernet Franc, Cabernet Sauvignon, Calabrese Nero, Canaiolo, Grignolino, Catarratto, Carricante, Chardonnay, Freisa, Gerosolimitana Bianca, Greco Nero, Guarnaccia Nera, Mantonico Nero, Nigrello, Nigrello Etneo, Pinot Blanc, Pinot Grigio, Pinot Noir, Pitrusa Nera, Riesling Renano, Ruchè, Sangiovetto Grosso, Sauvignon, Semillon, Sirrah dell'Hermitage, Verdot, and Viognier.[121] These varieties were, for Spitaleri, the best chance Etna had to compete in the fine wine market. His long-term goal was not only to make high-quality wines, he also hoped to inspire his fellow countrymen to give it a try too. Unfortunately, history had other plans.[122]

THE RISORGIMENTO

For some Sicilians, the name Giuseppe Garibaldi invokes images of the freedom fighter who took on the establishment and a unified Italia. For others,

Garibaldi was a mercenary hired by a bankrupt class of elites to "liberate" Sicilians from their treasure and land. In Sicily, where news was slow to arrive and often unreliable, much of what people heard about Garibaldi was the hyperbolic prose of journalists that had been passed along the grapevine. As for "L'Italia," that was the name of a woman.[123] Who fights a war over a woman? Didn't we learn anything from *The Iliad* and *The Odyssey*?

Oddly, things were different in the vineyards on the mountain, for it was Garibaldi who allegedly solved the problem of oidium. Stories like these added tertiary layers of mystique to Garibaldi, even before he arrived in Sicily. Whether it was his recipe or not, it seemed to be working, and it was simple enough to administer: powdered copper sulfate and lime were mixed with water and sprayed on the vines during periods of intense humidity. Unknowingly, by sharing a common procedure for combating oidium in France with winegrowers in Piemonte and Liguria, in 1856, he became a bridge between those in politics and those in the fields.[124]

When Garibaldi and a volunteer army of 1,089 men landed in Marsala, in May 1860, they were met with little resistance from the Bourbon army or navy.[125] For two days, they marched through the city, calling out for additional men to join his ranks. A lot of people were hesitant. They had seen armed hordes before. It rarely turned out the way anyone hoped it would. In the countryside around Marsala, Garibaldi found hundreds of willing volunteers. After a brief pause in Salemi, where he recognized himself as dictator of Sicily, Garibaldi and his growing army marched north. By the first of June, Palermo was in ruins—largely due to shelling from Neapolitan ships anchored offshore. Ultimately, the city folded, the Bourbon administration and army left, and civilian revolts broke out in communities around the island.

On Mount Etna, news of Garibaldi's victories was tied to promises of land for any male who fought with him against the Bourbons.[126] Have you ever played a game of *passaparola* or telephone? By the time Garibaldi's invitation arrived on the volcano, the message was twisted. The common belief that Garibaldi invaded Sicily to fight with the peasantry for independence and the democratic distribution of land and wealth was a bit off the mark. He had no intentions of agitating the nobility or staying on the island. His goal was to gain enough steam and support to roll into Naples with a passionate army at his back.

In advance of his approach on Messina, Garibaldi sent a team of guerillas, the Cacciatori dell'Etna, to disrupt Bourbon control on the volcano and in Catania by cutting telegraph wires and generally disturbing civil infrastructure.[127] Following behind the Cacciatori dell'Etna was a brigade of *garibaldini,* led by Colonel Nino Bixio. On the northwest slope of the mountain, in Bronte, Bixio found a peasant uprising had already taken place. One of the areas that had been hardest hit was the Ducea di Nelson, Admiral Nelson's family estate. Their vineyards in Porta Bigliardo were burned during the uprising. On August 2, 1860, one of the inciters broke into a church in Bronte and climbed the bell tower. Looking out over the piazza below, he grabbed the rope and sounded the funeral peal. Chaos took over the town. Sixteen local nobles were slaughtered, forty-six houses and the local theater were torched along with the municipal archive and a local gentlemen's club. Things were so bad that "the smell of death attracted lawless elements" from as far away as Adrano, Biancavilla, and Pedara.[128]

Peasants believed they were aiding Garibaldi's cause, and they would be rewarded for their "service." Instead, Bixio violently suppressed the revolt and executed its leaders, adding another layer of confusion to the anarchy. Then Bixio published a death threat "to all insurgents," which was amplified by the administrators of Catania. Anyone caught looting or involved in a murder would be killed. Garibaldi couldn't have lawlessness while the rest of L'Italia was watching.

As Garibaldi and his army moved north into the Italian Peninsula, the Etna community was left reeling. Shipments of wine from the mountain to Riposto all but stopped. Blends and botti laid in wait. The vineyards were in shambles. Those who had joined Garibaldi's fight for independence were aghast. After Bronte, some *garibaldini* took off their uniforms, wandered home, or joined brigand armies or mercenaries who worked for wealthy landowners.[129] Others followed the hero dictator onward into history. Of those who went, three young *garibaldini* joined the parade on Etna's southeast slope, in Viagrande, carrying in their cart 26 salme (470 gal.) of Etna wine and other provisions[130] to share with the 30,000 troops now in Garibaldi's ranks.

As the harvest on Etna began in 1860, Sicily was annexed by the House of Savoy and the Kingdom of Sardegna, under the auspices of "fear and ambition rather than the will of the Sicilian people."[131] The following spring, Sicily, Sardegna, and the Italian Peninsula were unified under Victor Emmanuel II. By 1862, administrators in Turin and Rome were looking at Sicily like they hadn't eaten in a week. The church's significant landholdings made the Etna countryside gainful prey, and monasteries and lands held in emphyteusis were the first to be confiscated and auctioned off to the wealthy. Riches found on any abandoned property, including animals, machinery, or agricultural products were either co-opted, sold, or left to decay. A general might call these the spoils of war, but for the eastern half of Etna, it was a very personal attack. For years, the House of Savoy had been writing IOUs instead of checks. Looting Sicily was an easy way for the new Kingdom of Italy to make some quick cash. Needless to say, the immediate results were devastating. On top of the demoralizing land and power grabs, Sicilians were taxed wherever possible, and all young men were drafted into the new Italian army. If they didn't go willingly, they were arrested and forced into service. Deserters were put in front of a firing squad. Any work in the fields and palmenti were performed under incredible duress. Vineyards were left untended. Entire stocks went sour. All anyone could do was continue making wine for buyers who were much too slow to come.

PHYLLOXERA—THE STOWAWAY

Lucky for Etna, someone really messed up. I like shining the light on French vigneron Léo Laliman. Five years before Garibaldi set foot in Sicily, Laliman was importing American grapevines into France and passing them around to friends across Europe. He believed that grafting the European *Vitis vinifera* to the American *Vitis rupestris* or *berlandieri* could produce a hybrid vine, possibly serving as a final cure for oidium.[132] So far, the copper sulfate and lime mixture was working to abate the fungus, but Laliman and others were convinced that American grapevines could be a lasting cure, and the import of American grapevines into Europe grew.

No one realized it at the time, but there was a tiny louse stowed away on those American vines: *Phylloxera vitifoliae*.[133] The name really doesn't do the bug justice. It's a nasty little thing. Once the American vines were planted, the phylloxera multiplied, attacking *Vitis vinifera* leaves and roots. They have no defense or resistance to phylloxera. American varieties do.[134] Within about two years of an infection, a vine is dead. In very short order, phylloxera spread through continental Europe, killing millions of acres of *Vitis vinifera* and devastating the wine economy.[135]

The merchants in Riposto and the winemakers on the mountain were ready. As phylloxera spread and demand increased, estate owners and exporters expanded vineyard plantings to compensate for Europe's sudden insatiable demand. Farms planted to grain, hazelnuts, and fruit were converted to vineyards. With more wine, additional production facilities were required, existing palmenti were put back into service, new barili, botti, and ships were built, laborers arrived, and public squares and taverns buzzed with business.

The vineyard area in the hills northwest of Catania, along the southeast slope of the mountain, made prolific quantities of wine during this moment.

In Viagrande, vineyards were producing 35,000 hectoliters (924,600 gal.) of wine in a given year, from 648 hectares (1,600 ac.) trained in alberello with tight spacing. In the lull following Italian unification, distilleries in Viagrande created Zambu—an inexpensive anise-flavored liqueur made to resemble absinthe—which became a popular add-on for wine shipments north.

Wines produced on the extinct crater Monte Serra, in Viagrande, were at the top of many clients' lists.[136] The Benanti family makes two wines from Monte Serra today. The *Contrada Monte Serra* and *Serra della Contessa* are Nerello Mascalese blends. Both wines are grown on the slope of the crater. While the former is produced from young vines and the lower half of the vineyard, the latter comes from old vines trained in alberello.

A few kilometers upslope from Viagrande, the hills were alive with tendrils. Pedara counted more than 530 hectares (1,300 ac.) planted to alberello, with a production of 30,000 hectoliters (792,500 gal.) of wine, plus *liquori* and *distillati*. The village of Nicolosi had 465 hectares (1,150 ac.), also in alberello. Trecastagni took the award for having the largest area under vine. The comune tallied 674 hectares (1,665 ac.) with mixed training systems.

Away from the eastern slope and the commercial center of Mascali and Riposto, two wineries—Barone Antonino Spitaleri and the Ducea di Nelson—were attempting to change the conversation from blending wine to something *finer*.

Barone Antonino Spitaleri and his son Felice were researching blends grown at elevation around Castello Solicchiata, in Adrano, plus recipes for an Etna Bianco, Etna Cognac, and a sparkling wine made using the classic method. Despite the scores of varieties that the Spitaleri family had access to, the final recipe for their Etna Bianco was based on six parts Chardonnay, three parts Catarratto, and one part Pinot Blanc.[137] The cognac was assembled from distillates of Carricante, Catarratto and Pinot Blanc. The spirit was aged in three- to thirty-hectoliter vats of French oak, Etna chestnut, and Etna cherry wood made by a live-in master barrel maker from Bordeaux.[138]

Spitaleri bottled his first metodo classico sparkling wine based on Pinot Noir, which he called *Champagne Etna*. His first pure Pinot Noir table wine was labeled *Etna Rosso*. The Bordeaux blends, which took the name of the castle, were from Cabernet Franc, Cabernet Sauvignon, and Merlot. Spitaleri took awards in London, Palermo, Vienna, Berlin, Brussels, Zurich, and Milan,[139] creating a buzz about Etna and the fineness of the mountain wines.

Like Spitaleri, the Ducea di Nelson trusted French methods over those being used in Mascali. They hired French enologist Louis Fabre to head the estate's wine production. Fabre's primary focus was on the performance of the vineyards to improve the quality of grapes entering the winery. In the cellar he used a simple vacuum pump that could move 1,000 gallons of wine per hour with minimal oxidation.

Most of the vines had been planted in degraded sandstone and limestone, in the valleys and alluvial, undulating plains north of Bronte. He trialed Nerello Mascalese as well as Bordeaux and Madeira varieties; Grenache Noir from Roussillon, in Southeastern France; Syrah from Hermitage, in the Rhône valley; and Tinto Nero, Palomino, Xarel-lo, Macabeo, Parellada, and Pedro Ximénez from Spain. After years of experimentation, he settled on planting the greatest percentage of the estate to Grenache Noir.[140] He also made two cognacs for the Ducea. The first, destined for the Italian market, was light in color. The second, made for the English market, was darker.[141]

By 1880, Mount Etna was the most-planted wine region in Sicily, with 123,000 acres under vine. When phylloxera arrived in Sicily that spring, the devastation seen across Europe began to take hold on the island. Ten years after it first appeared, Sicily was host to 50 percent of the Italian phylloxera infection. Strangely, while vineyards at lower elevations and in the valleys adjoining Etna withered and died, vineyards on the slopes of the mountain continued producing. The phylloxera just wasn't attacking those vines. It couldn't. Phylloxera hate volcanic sand.

THE TWENTIETH CENTURY—DAL MARE AL MARE

Riposto remained a bustling port and naval yard, but merchants were buying less wine and more food. Urban populations throughout Europe needed a constant supply of vegetables, cotton, fruit, pistachios and hazelnuts, honey, spices, meat, timber, fish, and ice. Unfortunately, transportation of fresh goods was slow, and it often arrived in bad condition or it was unripe, as farmers tried and failed to choose the perfect harvesting moment. There was a faster and better way.

The first trains began working around Palermo in 1863. Four years later, the central station at Catania opened. Shortly thereafter, the Messina to Catania line was completed. Compared to the trains in the north, which were regulated and organized by the state for the transport of people and goods, Sicilian trains quickly devolved to a transportation network that often satisfied powerful landowners instead of citizens. It didn't take long to read the writing on the wall. The communities around Etna needed reliable haulage beyond the rustic capabilities of a donkey and cart. If the state wouldn't provide the assistance, the Etna community was going to build it themselves.

On New Year's Eve 1883, a provincial association formed to do just that.[142] Seventeen communities on the mountain drafted plans for a train that would circumnavigate the volcano. They called it the Ferrovia Circumetnea. Though an Etna train had been discussed for decades, it never fully capitalized. Now, every community in the association was ready to pay for a single narrow-gauge track that would traverse the south, west, and north slopes of the volcano—from Catania to Riposto—assuming the form of a *C*. It would not, however, link to itself on the east. In Giarre and Catania one could easily find connections to the major railway that followed the coastline.

Merchants immediately got behind the idea. The Ducea di Nelson invested heavily in the construction of the Maletto station. However, the community in nearby Bronte resisted the idea of a train. It was largely a problem of easements. The path of the Circumetnea cut through too many farms. Land was purchased from owners whose property, vineyards, orchards, and brush were needed to join each segment of the track. Those who could not settle on a price had their land confiscated. The English engineer Robert Trewhella was hired to design the track and the stations of the Circumetnea. The cost to build the seventy-mile railway was shared by the communities it would serve. Investors, who might benefit from its completion, subsidized the rest.[143]

The stony and sandy terrain was difficult to manipulate. Tons of dynamite and hundreds of men and mules cleared the way as the initial demolition cut a circuitous route around the mountain. Local masons were hired to build walls, bridges, and tunnels, and *carusi* (boys) were employed to do the dirtiest work for pennies.

The first trains started running in March 1895, between neighborhoods in Catania. By June, the western line between Adrano and Bronte opened, and one month later, the steep, snaking route up the north slope, from Giarre to Castiglione di Sicilia, was operating on a daily schedule. The next section, from Bronte to Castiglione was completed in time for the harvest. The short line from Giarre to Riposto was finished last, just as the first snows were falling on the mountain. It took three more years for track switches, rail yards, and stations to be completed, and years more to teach everyone about train safety, but the Circumetnea provided what it promised: a boost to the local economy and the soft urbanization of the farming community. Within the first year of full operation, thirty-seven trains were serving 640,000 Etna inhabitants.[144]

For wine merchants, the Circumetnea was a godsend. Must and wine arrived in Riposto and Catania faster, cheaper, and fresher than they ever had. The train also introduced new concepts of civil engineering and architecture to the rural community. "Smart growth" neighborhoods in Piedimonte Etneo, Linguaglossa, Rovittello, and Passopisciaro sprouted up around each new station. Artisans, cellars, and master blenders established workshops and offices at ground level and homes on the floors above. Taverns, blending houses, and palmenti were built along the tracks by and for grape growers, grower-producers, and blenders.

On the eve of the twentieth century, the City of Catania started encouraging tourism on the Circumetnea. In one travel guide, the "Giro dell'Etna Experience" invokes "views of forests, olive groves, almond trees and vineyards, the snows of Etna, and panoramas of the Ionian Sea and Taormina."[145] Those who bought a ticket were not disappointed. The raw beauty of the

The Circumetnea train turns into Passopisciaro, on Mount Etna's north slope. Passopisciaro is a reliable stop, with the greatest number of wineries within walking or cycling distance.

landscape was as breathtaking as it is today, but Mount Etna's pastoral luster was starting to appear a little . . . *che dire* . . . overgrown.

Traveling the countryside in the early twenty-first century, it's much the same. Only, there are many more farmhouses and country roads with inviting signs that read "Agriturismo." These country houses and estates offer guests comfortable rooms, generous board, and plenty of local wine. Riding the Circumetnea is a trip. The old train car goes through some of the most important terrain on the mountain. Though the railway is primarily used by students and commuters, local tourism bureaus have begun promoting the train as an "experience." Recent investments are helping to maintain and improve the infrastructure of the track, for the arrival of a heftier, more modern locomotive.[146] The current train, though quaint, is a little burly.

There are a handful of special events that use the Circumetnea in the high season (April through September), but don't expect to find a daily schedule between the train stations and the wineries. At least, not yet. You have to get around by foot or bicycle, and country roads generally don't have shoulders or sidewalks. Taxis are virtually nonexistent on the mountain, and there can be great distances between the Circumetnea stations and some wineries (i.e., not walking distance). Passopisciaro is the most reliable stop, with the greatest number of wineries within walking or cycling distance. Be sure to make reservations and confirm distances and train schedule before setting out.

Passopisciaro wineries worth the effort (2 miles or less)

Antichi Vinai	Irene Badalà	Siciliano
Calcagno	Palmento Costanzo	SRC
Camarda	Passopisciaro	Tascante
Filippo Grasso	Patria	Tenuta delle Terre Nere
Frank Cornelissen	Pietradolce	Valenti
Girolamo Russo	Planeta	Vini Scirto
Graci	Sciara	Wiegner

Rovittello is worth a stop on the north slope. Benanti and Tenuta Pietro Caciorgna have vineyards and visiting areas there. Tenuta di Fessina, a combination winery and inn, is only a few steps from the Rovittello stop.

Randazzo is the last city on the northern line, coming from Riposto or Catania. You can change trains here and continue on or stay a while. The medieval city is a fun destination for a few hours or a day.

Places to visit in Randazzo*

Archaeological Museum Paolo Vagliasindi

Enoteca Il Buongustaio dell'Etna

Pasticceria Santo Musumeci

Ristorante San Giorgio e Il Drago

Ristorante Veneziano

*Accessible on foot or bicycle. Confirm distances, appointments, and train schedule in advance.

THE SPECIALISTS

It doesn't matter what time or day it is. The *edicola* (newsstand) around the corner from our house is always astir with conversations of parochial intrigue, *calcio* (soccer), and food, as people come in for cigarettes, *caramelle* (candies), or lottery tickets and join the conversation or leave it. Off to the side, there's a wall of newspapers, crossword puzzles, and glossy lifestyle magazines, but there's not a single publication about wine. This wasn't always the case.

In the 1920s, journals like *Enologia*—published by Francesco Battiato—were available at newsstands from Catania to Riposto. Battiato edited multiple manuals about viticulture, winemaking, distillation, and vinegar production.[147] They included how-to sections dedicated to winemaking tools and equipment, commercial advice for selling wines, the international market, the nuances of chemistry in must and wine adjustments, instructions for grafting Etna varieties to American rootstocks, and essays by enological writers. Unquestionably, the availability of these booklets helped to change practices for the better, but it was the exporters who were deciding the ultimate fate of Etna's wines.

In the years leading up to and following the Great War, the port of Riposto became a bazaar of specialist wine brokers with a talent for nicknaming the mountain communities based on the wines they produced. In the *Annuario vinicolo d'Italia*—a national publication dedicated to the alcoholic beverage industry—wines from Etna were largely promoted using the names of producers and merchants, a list of the neighborhoods and contrade where they had clients, the currencies they worked in, means of transport (train or boat or both), and the names of local or foreign banks that were willing to finance contracts. To pay for the publication, advertisements for enological services, wine storage, brokerage, and exportation filled the margins.[148] The listings sorted wines based on geography, color, and organoleptics.

Etnea red wines, from the villages of Randazzo, Solicchiata, Castiglione, Linguaglossa, Piedimonte Etneo, Mascali, Acireale, and Giarre, were known for their bright ruby color, robust flavors, fruitiness, fragrance, and some bitterness.

The Forest of Catania (Vini del Bosco [Wines from the Forest]) was considered the best area on the mountain for red wines. Though they resembled Etnea wines, these had better color and no bitterness. Vineyards within the municipalities of Zafferana Etnea, Viagrande, Trecastagni, Pedara, Nicolosi, Belpasso, and Mascalucia were included. This was also the primary location to source white wines, although the descriptions—tasty, with a pale straw color, greenish highlights and a *correct* alcohol content—leave much to the imagination.

The *Vino da Taglio* category was for blended and blending wines. They had good aromas and elusive flavors while also being the heaviest style on the mountain. Most of the vino da taglio arrived at Riposto via the "Mascali Plain"—a low and rolling plateau that runs through Mascali, Riposto, Giarre, and Acireale.

The *Feudo Plain* produced the biggest and clumsiest wines. They lacked acidity, but they were easy to find in the low-lying areas from Riposto to Fiumefreddo.

Supple wines with a little sweetness were often found in the foothills west of Capo Schisò, around the *Calatabiano Plain*, a large swath of land around Calatabiano, between Fiumefreddo, near the sea, and Piedimonte Etneo and Gaggi, in the hills.

Wines from the plains and high ground west of Catania[149] were called *Terre Forti* (strong lands). They were known for their alcoholic power and a dour color.

The red wines from *Alta Montagna* (high mountain), produced from the highest vineyards. had the lowest average alcohol levels and a brackish acidity.

Moscato Liqueur and *Amaro* (sweet and bittersweet digestives) were cordoned off into a separate but important category that avoided description.[150]

The edicola (newsstand) around the corner from our house is always busy. There's a wall of newspapers, crossword puzzles, and glossy magazines, but there are no publications about wine. This wasn't always the case. In the 1920s, journals like *Enologia* and *Annuario Vinicolo d'Italia* were available from Catania to Riposto.

Both red and white wines were being styled as table wines, but they could also resemble Marsala (strong, sweet, partially oxidized, and aged), if the client wished.[151]

END OF AN ERA—THE DEATH OF MASCALI

Etna is a trickster. She likes to divert our attention from what's really happening. A little steam over there, a light show during the night. But then comes the sleight of hand.

The earthquakes started as the 1928 harvest came to a close. The eruption released lava above Piano Provenzana, far enough from the population that everyone went back to doing what they were doing. But Etna wasn't done yet. The central crater collapsed on itself and arrested the eruption, but it blocked the release of pressure from inside the mountain. On November 2, Etna's northeast slope ripped open in a terrifying pyroclastic display. Just days before the festival of San Martino—the annual celebration and first tasting of the new vintage—nearly two thousand acres of historic vineyards and agricultural space,[152] roads, forests, creeks, small parishes, a portion of the Circumetnea train track, and most of the village of Mascali were buried under an avalanche of molten rock.

As the lava started to cool, a freefall in the United States stock market instigated a global depression. Italian industry in the north was hit particularly hard. Etna producers continued making wine, but the specialists who worked to develop a market for smaller appellations around the mountain were back to buying vino da taglio. With every repackaged downsale, Etna's prices and reputation weakened, jobs were lost, and palmenti doors closed. It was difficult for such an active community to be so reduced.

Between 1929 and 1934, the national unemployment numbers doubled. It was a problem, but the Italian Prime Minister, Benito Mussolini, had an idea:

invade Ethiopia[153] and give the land to those who were out of work. In Mussolini's defense, he wasn't thinking about the impoverished conditions on Etna. He was dreaming of a new Italian empire. His invasion of Ethiopia made front-page news as the aromas of the 1935 vintage were filling the local palmenti. Four years later, radios crackled with the announcement of Fascist Italy's Pact of Steel with Nazi Germany. When Mussolini signed his name at the bottom of the document, he placed Etna squarely in the path of World War II.

I spend a lot of time on the mountain. It's hard to imagine battleships in the bay, warplanes bombing the fields, panzer tanks in the streets, barbed-wire barricades, armed soldiers in the markets and cafés, or how that must have changed the local atmosphere. In the early years of the war, the fighting took place away from Mount Etna but wine exports stopped all the same.[154] Food was rationed, due to an air and sea blockade, and a black market for just about anything thrived.[155]

Despite the lockdown, international bulletins suggested Sicilian "spirits were high," adding that 300,000 soldiers were prepared to fight "to the last drop of blood" for *l'Italia*.[156] It was pure propaganda. Etneans hated the Fascists and the Nazis, but people were also scared. When the bombings started, the only real safe places were churches, the arched tini of palmenti, and the numerous lava tubes and snow caves in the countryside. While Axis[157] troops (German and Italian) fortified the coastline and the mountain villages against an invasion from the Allies,[158] the Americans were working behind the scenes with Sicilian Separatists and the Mafia (both US and Sicilian) to plan a surgical assault on the island.[159] They hoped it would turn the war in the Allies' favor and give the Sicilian people some relief.[160] The Mafia saw it as a way to regain control of land and assets they lost when Mussolini came to power.[161]

On July 10, 1943, the Allies invaded Gela, on the southeast coast of Sicily. The all-out offensive, Operation Husky, delivered a massive blow to the Axis armies, forcing them to retreat north, toward Messina. The Allies bombed and then invaded Catania on August 5, but the next few weeks proved difficult. Axis forces had regrouped in the hills and villages of Mount Etna. The higher perch gave local and German fighters an advantage as the Allies ascended the mountain, cautious of tight valleys, stooping through vineyards, olive groves, and arenas of thorny brambles. Despite their defensive efforts, the Allies overwhelmed the mountain and the Germans were forced out of one shattered village after another.

To a trained German soldier, it must have seemed like the Italian infantry were missing their targets intentionally. You could hardly blame them. When the Sicilians looked in their scopes, they saw their plainclothes countrymen alongside the Allies. What they hadn't realized was that, as the island's cities were liberated, American soldiers opened the prisons, releasing members of the Mafia, Sicilian Separatists, and anti-Fascists into the countryside.[162] It was a decision that would have negative consequences for the social and economic development of the island for generations to come.

After the war, life on the mountain went into slow motion. Roads that had been reduced to rubble were repaired. Villages trounced in the fighting got back to work. But almost everything everyone had worked for was fubar.

SICILY'S FIRST DOC

It took years before the wines resembled those made before the war. Barone di Villagrande was one of the first to get a bottled Etna Rosso into the market, in 1948. And even that was on a small scale.[163] Enopolio Etneo was another. The company exported *Vino Umbra Santonocito*, which arrived in red, rosé, and gold colors. The Stivis winery offered a rosato called *Castelriccio*. Their two reds were called *San Salvador* and *Val di Lupo*. Two white wines from Carricante were called *Ciclopi*.

Other cantinas, like Torrisi, Torresi & Rosario, released a Vino Commune Rosso from the hills around Aci Sant'Antonio and Santa Maria La Scala. They called the wine *Kalliston*, which they adopted from the Greek belief that beautiful and inspiring things come through sacrifice.[164] Cantine Russo was established by the Russo family, who has been farming on Etna for generations. The first wines from the cantina were grown on the mountain and bottled in Giarre, close to the port of Riposto where the wines were traded. Wine that wasn't bottled was sold sfuso.[165] Growers who did not have a facility of their own brought their grapes to cooperative cellars. Many wines were sold in bulk, at the cellar door. But things were improving. In 1960, the Alleanza Viticultori Etnei (A.V.E.) Cantina Sociale, along SS120 in Linguaglossa, released a bottled and labeled red wine, called *Ràgabo Extra*, from a selection of local grapes.

When Carlo Nicolosi-Asmundo, professor of Enology at the University of Catania and the winemaker at Barone di Villagrande, sat down with his colleagues in 1965 to define a historical area of wine production on the mountain, it was unclear what condition Etna's vineyards were actually in. Jobs in the cities had lured able-bodied workers away from the fields. Vines were producing but fewer people knew how to manage a vineyard or a fermentation in a good way. While some palmenti continued to operate, others were used for storage or looted until they disintegrated. Only a few short months into their research—meeting farmers, examining vines, tasting and analyzing a multitude of wines—one thing was infinitely apparent. If Mount Etna was going to apply for Sicily's first Denominazione di Origine Controllata (DOC) it would have to offer a clear and realistic path forward.

Defining an Etna DOC in those challenging conditions was audacious. To start, the research team considered where vines were growing, what grapes were planted, vinification methods, the resulting chemistry, and, ultimately, how the wines tasted.[166] Month after month, the consistencies and

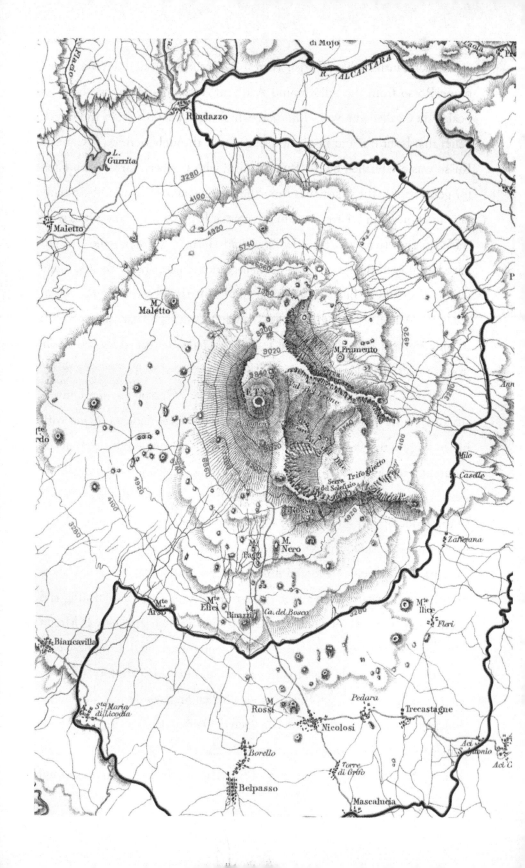

irregularities among samples were plotted on an illustration of the mountain. When they finally took a step back to look at the map, that persistent Etna charisma had assumed a shape. From the existing pool of data, they reverse engineered the wines that appeared repeatedly in the survey.

Their notes read like a cookbook—which grapes to buy and where, followed by a diagnostic representation of the final product. Apart from the percentages of grapes that could be used in a blend, the recipes for each wine were written without any instructions. It was a diplomatic way to approach a sensitive situation. Few families had capital to invest in new vineyard or cellar equipment. The authors of the Etna DOC knew this. They legalized a system that gave structure to the realities on the ground. The guidelines could be followed again and again, *almost* without effort.

Carlo Nicolosi-Asmundo is the ninth generation of his family to manage the winemaking at Barone di Villagrande. He has a sense of Etna that very few people do. One summer afternoon, he and I were sitting on the veranda at the winery and small resort in Milo. "It wasn't perfect," he said. "Defining the wines took [three] years of deliberation. In the end, some people were upset that their vineyards were not included in the DOC. Some vineyards were dead or abandoned or the wines were [terrible]. Others showed heart, but they weren't using traditional Etna grapes. If the vineyards were too high or too low [in elevation], or too far to the west, the wines . . ." he made a gesture implying that something wasn't right, ". . . they changed."

In the end, the team proposed a menu of four wines—Etna Bianco, Etna Bianco Superiore, Etna Rosato, and Etna Rosso—from a semicircle around the lower third of the mountain, between 400 and 1000 meters AMSL,

---

The Etna DOC assumes the shape of a semi-circle, from about 400–1000 meters AMSL. Within this space are ancient soils, spent volcanic craters, and a mosaic of volcanic material in various phases of erosion. When we wrap these qualities over a sloped landscape, the commonalities and differences between each vineyard site matter even more.

which crossed portions of twenty communities.[167] A thirty-three kilometer stretch of the western flank wasn't included in their proposal. Many wineries continue to explore vineyards outside the defined DOC boundary with delicious results, they merely elude the scope of idiosyncrasies in ways that other wines on the mountain can't. This is important to note, because all wines that wish to have the word Etna on the label have to be approved through tasting and laboratory analysis.

It was enough. The legislation was approved on August 11, 1968, and published later that month, just in time for the harvest.

LEVELING THE TERRACES

When the Etna DOC legislation was published, rural flight was still on the rise. It was a matter of economics. Field work didn't pay the wages a job in Acireale or Catania could. With every laborer who walked away, the work in the fields became more difficult or impossible. The troubles weren't isolated to the volcano.

By 1973, European financial systems were in steep decline. With every new ripple of the depression, mountain communities throughout Europe depopulated. Bureaucrats pointed to the difficult terrain as a catalyst for some of the problems and reasoned that if they could make it easier for farmers to work, they could thwart further neglect of the continent's agricultural patrimony. In April 1975, the European Council, the European Parliament, and the European Economic and Social Committee approved a directive to arrest the abandonment of "unfavourable" agricultural communities and rejuvenate the whole of Europe.[168]

It was a tall order, but allowances were offered to permanent farmers who were struggling because of the form or slope of their land.[169] Those who took advantage of the initiative broke down their terraces, grubbed up vines, and leveled the land. Production levels from alberello vineyards planted in quincunx were reduced by 40 percent or more, as every other row was grubbed up to make room for tractors or rototillers. Driving around the mountain, it's easy to see which properties took advantage of the subsidies. The old three-dimensional bush vines have been manicured into oblique bilateral cordons, with shoots trained upward on tension wires strung between concrete posts. Optics aside, it was one of the first political moves in 500 years that was specifically designed to improve the agrarian way of life on Etna. Those who pressed on started to see the value in sticking together.

In 1971, the Torrepalino cooperative winery opened its doors to anyone who needed assistance. The cantina took the name from an old Spanish tower that served as a signpost for pilgrims traveling on the north slope of the volcano. Scores of farmers and technicians flocked to the facility. For those who wanted to make Etna DOC wines, the co-op offered solutions—some temperature control, stainless steel vats, large Slavonian casks, expansive fermentation areas, sophisticated aging rooms, and bottling options. Most grapes were relegated to simple Vino da Tavola or sold in sfuso for drinking or blending. Torrepalino bottled wines from a selection of grapes, which they sold under the name of the cantina and the new Etna DOC scheme, which drew the attention of the *New York Times*.[170]

Another cooperative, La Cantina Sociale Vigne dell'Etna, produced a wine called *Etna Nibbio*. Andre Simon's *Wines of the World* listed it as one of Sicily's best non-DOC red wines. While the wine was made from Nerello, the name suggested it tasted more like a Barolo or Barbaresco. It was a clever promotional ploy to sell wine by attracting the affections of Nebbiolo admirers.

Not everything was an attempt to attract attention. When the Raciti Gambino family planted their first vines in the foothills above Linguaglossa and Piedimonte Etneo, in 1979, the small vineyard was an amenity attached to the family chalet. They drank the wine they made with their meals. Vittorio Raciti and his wife, Maria Gambino, thought it tasted good, so he planted another broad terrace of vines. And another. Today, the family-run Gambino winery and hospitality center in Contrada Petto Dragone (Breast of the Dragon) is not only one of the most popular wineries on the mountain, the location provides an unparalleled view of the Alcantara Valley, the Nebrodi Mountains, and the Ionian Sea.

"We had no preconceptions," Francesco Raciti Gambino tells me. "We loved coming here. It was nice to be out of the city, surrounded by nature. My father did all of the work himself, when he had the time and the money. Everything we have came with time." The realization of a winery only occurred in 2002.

Many others were working in a similar way, if only for a small income or a personal connection to the land. But in 1986, the Italian wine market was stopped in its tracks when thirty wineries in northwest Italy were closed for adding methyl alcohol (methanol) to their basic wines. Twenty-six people who drank the wines were killed. Eight more went blind. No products from Etna were implicated, nor were they a part of the scandal, but the humiliation took the Italian wine industry out at the knees.

Exports dropped by one third in only a few months. Shipments of wine were confiscated, whether they were tainted or not. If the wines arrived at their destination, they were scrutinized. News and government agencies alerted citizens against drinking *any* wines from Italy until further notice, while restaurants and retailers around the world posted notices of corrupted Italian wines.[171] Those wines that did make it to a table, any table, had a long tradition of doing so. For most of Etna, that meant wine sold by the liter for the table, *vino da pasto*. When stocks didn't sell and went bad, they were sent to the distilleries.[172]

As the sun set on the methanol scandal, Dr. Giuseppe Benanti went to lunch with colleagues at a trattoria on the north slope of the volcano. During the meal, he ordered a local wine to share with his guests.

After a sip, Dr. Benanti confronted the server. "What is this?"

"It's the wine from this village. As you asked," the server replied. "It's good, no?"

"No," he said. "It isn't."

Dr. Benanti is a proud and exuberant man. He loves Mount Etna and Sicily with a magical kind of energy. It was heartbreaking for him that this might be the best wine that Etna could offer. He raised the wine glass and looked at his guests. "I remember drinking much better wine than this when I was younger. If, in my life, I could know one good enologist, I would make better wines for my family and my friends."

An enologist is essentially a doctor of wine. Dr. Benanti is a chemist, like his father and his grandfather before him. "I'm not a wine connoisseur," Dr. Benanti tells me. "But I've traveled and tasted enough to know there was obviously something wrong with that stuff." He just couldn't diagnose it.

A few months after the lunch, Dr. Benanti was introduced to a young and as-yet-untested enologist by the name of Salvatore Foti. Foti had received training at the university level in Catania, followed by a period working at the Donnafugata winery, in Marsala. The two became quick friends.

"The coast was unclear," Dr. Benanti tells me, "but there was inspiration and guidance in the terrain. Etna's legacy of winemaking only needed someone to read it."

At forty-three years old, he felt there was no time to lose. But rather than go it alone with Foti, Benanti engaged foreign enologists—Rocco Di Stefano, of the Experimental Institute for Oenology in Asti; Jean Siegrist, of the French National Institute of Agriculture (INRA) in Beaune; and Giandomenico Negro and Alessandro Monchiero from Piedmont—to assist and supervise along the way. From the beginning, everyone was able to agree on one thing: if they were to attempt a single recipe per year, it would take an eternity to understand the true potential of the mountain. They had to come at it from every direction.

The first experiments amounted to 125 individual trials under monitored and controlled situations. They focused on different types of vineyard work, unique harvest times, wild and cultivated yeasts, acid conversion, variant temperatures, and the effects of fermentation in an array of storage containers. When the wines had settled, the team sat down to taste the results. Very quickly, the aerobic experiments were rejected. The essence of the wines had evaporated. Wines made without temperature control were also dubious. From an analytical standpoint, the *best* wines were those in which every effort was made to protect the integrity of the grapes, the purity of the must, and the resulting wine from extreme heat or oxygenation. When the wines were analyzed, they also hit the Etna DOC targets with near pinpoint accuracy.

That said, very few of the wines were drinkable. At least, not out of the gate. The organoleptics were too taut, nervous, and shy. There *was* something there, but it would take time to fully develop. The wines required aging. It was an unexpected result for a region known for wines that you could drink or put on your salad in place of vinegar. Etna wines were regularly consumed within a year of their production, not because people were thirsty but because they were made in such aerobic, hot conditions that they frequently went bad before the next vintage. These new wines couldn't be fully assessed for years.

Benanti couldn't wait to know if one strategy was better than another, so he pressed on under the guidance of Giandomenico Negro and Alessandro Monchiero, with a focus on phenolic ripeness of the grapes at harvest, gentle anaerobic treatments in the cantina, and overall wine stability prior to bottling. The new company's first bottled Etna Bianco—dubbed *Pietramarina*—was produced from the 1990 vintage.[173] The Etna Rosso, from Nerello Mascalese grown in the village of Rovittello (its namesake), was made the same year. When Dr. Benanti first presented the wines to his twin boys, Antonio and Salvino, the crisp wine labels were already in place and the name of the family winery—Tenuta di Castiglione—had been decided.

Looking back on this moment in the family's history, Antonio said, "It was very obvious to Salvino and I that my father was filled with enthusiasm and that his new hobby had become something more substantial."

In 1993, the family attended VinItaly with the *Pietramarina* and *Rovittello* wines. "When guests tasted the Carricante, oh, they were [swooning]," Dr. Benanti said, gesturing. "It was the 1990 vintage. They kept saying, 'That's a good wine, you know, but can we have the latest release?' I tried to explain that it was the latest release! They couldn't believe that a white wine tasted that fresh and young three years after it was made."

The trade hadn't quite caught on to indigenous Etna cultivars the way Benanti was making them. Consumers wanted fresh fruit aromas and flavors. Perhaps something made with grape names they recognized. At that time, the Regional Institute of Wine and Oil of Sicily was recommending the planting and use of international grape varieties across the island. Portions of Etna were planted to an assortment of different wine grapes and cultivars. Most of the grape varieties were, in fact, of French origin, with some Italian varieties added for good measure. As the vineyards began to produce, experts from around the country descended on Sicily and Etna, to gain firsthand knowledge of the successes that were being promoted.

One of those experts was Giacomo Tachis, father of Italian enology and a student of Émile Peynaud, the grandfather of modern winemaking. On Mount Etna, Tachis tasted samples of the local wines, including those from

Tenuta di Castiglione. However, wines from Carricante and Nerello Mascalese were not to his taste. He believed that Carricante required a blender like Traminer, to enhance the aromas in particular. He encouraged Benanti and other producers on the mountain to embrace more well-known varieties with a broader appeal. Instead of Nerello Mascalese, for example, Tachis preferred Pinot Noir.[174] One of the wines he tasted came from Contrada Marchese, in Dr. Rocco Siciliano's winery, between Solicchiata and Passopisciaro. The small plot of mixed Pinot Noir clones only produces a single barrel of wine every year. It was proof for Tachis that Etna could make their own world-class wines from French varieties. He went so far as to suggest that Mount Etna Pinot Noir could rival Red Burgundy. Some Etna producers still echo his sentiments, in one form or another, today.

A statement like that, from Tachis, was enough for some producers to investigate the potential of Pinot Noir, and maybe a few other varieties. Dr. Benanti was curious, like everyone else, but Tachis was too late to convert Benanti. The Carricante and Nerello had already captured his heart. While he continued to perfect the DOC wines, he took everything they had learned and, on a limited scale, applied it to a medley of international and Sicilian grapes.

Over two decades, Benanti experimented with Moscato, Minella, Chardonnay, Pinot Noir, Cabernet Sauvignon, Nero d'Avola, Nerello Cappuccio, Petit Verdot, Syrah, Tannat, and combinations of these. Each performed an important role for the new winery. Not only did they prove that Carricante or Nerello play well with other grapes, blended wines featuring Etna varieties offered an introduction to the native grapes through wines many consumers already knew. As each visitor, wine buyer, and journalist tasted through the portfolio, they were being introduced to increasing percentages of Carricante and Nerello. When they were ultimately offered the pure expressions of Etna Bianco and Etna Rosso, the thought that Mount Etna was making wine at all was outshined by the feeling that the volcanic wines were actually quite *fine*.

It was the time for experimentation. In the cellar at Murgo winery, in the hills above Santa Venerina, Michele Scammacca disgorged the first bottles of his 1989 metodo classico spumante, made from Nerello Mascalese vinified as white wine. This *bianco di nero* was the first bottle-fermented sparkling wine made on the volcano since Castello Solicchiata created *Champagne Etna*[175] in the nineteenth century. The process was the same, only the grapes and technology had changed.

Ten years earlier, the Scammacca family hired Luigi Lo Guzzo, a local enologist, to help direct their winemaking. "We weren't accustomed to the new ways back then," Scammacca said, alluding to changes in European wine laws that prohibited the use of Etna's old winemaking facilities. These days, the estate counts more than twenty-five hectares (60 ac.) of grafted vines trained in cordon. In Michele's mind, this is the better way. "Without the alberello, we find the flavors are much improved. We were alone then. Every effort was to improve the winemaking. That is why we built the [underground] cellar at the edge of the vineyard. We can process the grapes immediately after they are harvested. In the winery, the technology [temperature control systems, inert and wood containers, a bottling system] helped us achieve a good quality more often. Of course," Michele smiles, "this helped sell the wine."

Apart from Murgo's Etna DOC bottlings, their experimental plots of Pinot Noir and Cabernet Sauvignon were only allowed to produce *vino semplice* (simple wines). It made sense to label them as such, they were table wines. But something had changed. With all of the work going on in the vineyard and the improvements in the cellar, the wines were cleaner, chemically stable, and fresher. Other wineries were making similar high-quality products all over the country. Some wines were fetching unusually high prices. As the bureaucrats ran the numbers, they realized that wineries were benefitting financially from the ambiguities of Italian bureaucracy. In so many words, some cantinas were stuffing the basic wine category with luxury products. Taxes on basic wines were minuscule, leaving enormous profit margins for savvy wineries with a talent for marketing. This made the taxman incredibly uncomfortable.

In 1992, under the direction of Italian Minister of Agriculture Giovanni Goria, the Italian Parliament restructured the existing legislation to include an additional category for these "super" table wines. The new Indicazione Geografica Tipica (IGT) scheme introduced a qualitative level between Vino da Tavola and DOC or DOCG (Denominazione di Origine Controllata e Garantita), which had been in place since 1963. Attached to the law was a tax for wines entering the category.

Before this, any wines on the mountain not labeled Etna DOC were prohibited from including the vintage year, a grape variety, or the name of the estate on the label. Now, they could do everything the DOC producers were doing and they had more creative freedom. Any grapes on a growing list of approved varieties and cultivars were fair game. Only the phrasing was different. That didn't mean producers could call their wine Cabernet-Nerello from Etna. They had to use "Sicily" as their geographic location, but almost everything else about the wine inside the bottle was communicable. For those who were already making quality wines from international grape varieties—namely Dr. Benanti, Dr. Siciliano, Cantine Russo, Barone di Villagrande, Murgo, Cottanera, and Patria—it was another step in the right direction.

However, Goria's law included a nasty side effect. In a few line items about sanitary conditions the enological standards for this creative new wine category aligned with those established by the European community a decade earlier.[176] Once again, Etna's gravity-operated palmenti were barred from producing any category of wine destined for sale and consumption.

Only fifteen years earlier, the European community had financed the revival of these mountain vineyards. Now they were adding foreign grapes to the playing field, but the traditional wineries weren't permitted? For a lot of producers, it didn't make any sense. The new law was about wine, right? Wrong. It was about money. In a race to gain more of it, lawmakers disregarded everything that Etna had become in order to further commoditize wine. It's difficult for me to put the sensation of this betrayal into words. The sound of that notary stamp marking the page has echoed for decades. You can still see the frustration and dismay in the countryside. There are decrepit palmenti in and around almost every village on the volcano. In a precious few, everything remains intact. It's obvious the workers intended to return, but they never came back. They couldn't. The one tool that had made these sites sacred for millennia was now illegal.

Some palmenti were lucky. They survived by the slow conversion to restaurants, hotels, event spaces, private homes, or museums. Others use the stepped construction and gravity to pass the must and wine between inert containers but without contact with the stone surfaces. A few estates feature their own historic palmento during community programs that promote Etna's viticultural heritage. Whatever their state or design, visiting these facilities is a powerful part of any Etna experience. It's one of the first things I did when I arrived on the mountain, in 2012.

Four days after Nadine and I landed, I went up the volcano to meet a winemaker in the Santo Spirito neighborhood. After a walk through the old alberello vineyard, we entered the dark, dank palmento. The structure had seen better days, but everything required for wine production was there. The entire estate had been abandoned decades earlier. While the vineyard was under restoration, they were throwing the harvested grapes into the pista, macerating them by foot, and fermenting everything together in the tina. On my way out, he handed me an unlabeled bottle.

Marco de Grazia walks through the Don Peppino vineyard with his dogs, in Contrada Calderara Sottana, as the first buds begin to push. The rocky, sandy, and fertile vineyard stretches out from the winery, which was founded on the idea that every site on Etna has a story worth telling.

Frank Cornelissen examines his vineyard in Feudo di Mezzo at the onset of bud break. After two decades of study, he has learned to follow the lead of the vineyard and vintage for his portfolio of territorial wines.

Ciro and Stephanie Biondi discuss the potential of a new vintage in their converted palmento, in Contrada Ronzini, near Trecastagni.

Dr. Rocco Siciliano holds a bottle of 'Rossoeuphoria' in his winery in Contrada Marchesa. His vineyard includes local and international varieties, including a storied Pinot Nero and Cabernet.

Marco Nicolosi-Asmundo presents a new vintage of wines from Barone di Villagrande. He is the tenth generation of his family to make wine in Contrada Villagrande, near Milo.

The father and daughter team of Gaetano and Graziella Camarda produce wines from Contrada Feudo di Mezzo, where the family has worked for generations.

Giuseppe and Valeria Scirto repeat the same steps every day. Every ounce of work is done by hand and without the use of chemical herbicides or fertilizers.

Bruno Ferrara Sardo manages a single vineyard in Contrada Allegracore, near Randazzo, where he produces a single Etna Rosso, called 'nzemmula, which means "together."

In 2001, Signore Rosario Licciardello reorganized the family vineyard on Monte Gorna, above Trecastagni. Today, the boutique family winery is a regular destination for guests from around the world.

Laura Torrisi, Giovanni Messina, and their dog Sascha meet in their vineyard on the east slope of Monte Gorna, one of Etna's many extinct volcanic craters.

"A gift," he said. "From the last vintage. The Nerello we made in the palmento. No yeast, filters, or sulfites. Only wine."

I had my doubts that the dusty, wine-stained, lava-stone vats could produce anything of *real* quality. Wine, for me, required the kind of structures and details that Goria made into law. Basically, that meant clean, organized machinery. When I got home, I put the bottle on the counter. Every time I entered the room, I obsessed about what was inside. The next day, while Nadine and I prepared lunch, I uncorked the bottle. I didn't even have to put my nose in the glass. Aromas of cherries, plum, mulberries, and sage wafted around the rim. In the mouth, the wine was dark and brooding, lush and juicy but not sweet, with a streak of acidity and satin tannins that lingered, lazily, on the finish.

The winemaker was being facetious, I thought. This is too vibrant to have been made in that room, in those conditions, the way he suggested. There would be obvious flaws, it would taste more . . . wild. But . . . what if it *was* made the old way? How could a wine this good possibly be illegal?

In all of my academic studies, the Goria law was regarded as a positive move forward in the Italian wine industry. The IGT/IGP category it created is often raised to hero status, for organizing the soup of miscellaneous wines that entered the international market following the Second World War. But looking up at the mountain from my glass, I knew Goria was wrong to discount Etna's patrimony. Nothing so unique should ever be disregarded.

Maybe it was the timing. After a year of stressful planning, we were finally in Sicily, in our new home, with the sea serenading our view of the volcano. Perhaps it was the realization that this bottle was one of the last of its kind. Whatever the confluence of events, by the time we sat down to eat, that illegal bottle of old-vine Nerello was the most enchanting wine I'd ever tasted.[177]

Before moving to Sicily, I never really lived near the sea. It's a wonder to me. I could watch it for hours. Every wave has a beginning. It all starts with the swelling of the water, followed by a massive, unified movement forward. Throughout Etna's viticultural history, there have been countless waves of activity and calm, climbs, and crashes. The new wines of Mount Etna that we drink today had starting points too.

For the Cambria family, it started with a plateau of hazelnut orchards. Francesco Cambria bought the old trees from half a dozen families in 1961, but he wasn't interested in cultivating *nucidde*. Almost immediately he began removing the trees, leveling the ground, and preparing the soil for grapevines. Twenty years later, cases of grapes were being shipped to the A.V.E. Cantina Sociale in Linguaglossa. After a few vintages without a return on their investment, the family reached out to Tuscan winemaker Roberto Cipresso and Leonardo Valenti, professor of Agriculture at the University of Milan, for guidance. Under their supervision the farm continued its conversion and the wine production moved to the Torrepalino cooperative. At the time, the wines were being sold using the family name, but the idea of calling their effort a "winery" was still up for discussion. One vintage after another, the experimental rows of vines proved successful, and the silhouette of a business started to take shape. In 1997, Francesco's sons, Guglielmo and Enzo, opened the doors of their new winery in Contrada Cottanera.

Francesco's grandson, also named Francesco, manages the family winery—Cottanera. He could easily be a young Bob Dylan impersonator and laughs when I tell him so, but we are quickly on to the subject at hand: the birth of quality winemaking on Mount Etna. Francesco says, "We didn't talk about 'quality wine' in the beginning, at least not the way we talk about it today. Wine was . . . a part of the farm, and the farm was part of everyday life.

Of course, no one outside of Etna knew anything about [Nerello] Mascalese, either. If you offered them a bottle of Nerello or Syrah in the nineties, they'd choose the Syrah every time."

Syrah was popular at the end of the twentieth century. It made sense to try it on Etna. When grown in the right terrain—stony, cool, and sunny—Syrah makes some of the most delicious wines in the world. The day Guglielmo Cambria called the vine nursery to confirm their order for Syrah, they were 6,000 vines short. In their place, the nursery offered Mondeuse vines instead. Mondeuse—an inky, perfumed, lightly succulent and tannic red wine—was a logical choice for Etna. Its home is historically in the sandy-stony highlands of Savoie, in southeast France. Guglielmo didn't want to wait another year for the vines he was promised so he pulled the trigger. The Mondeuse was planted alongside the Syrah in Contrade Cottanera and Feudo di Mezzo, with Cabernets Franc and Sauvignon, Merlot, Viognier, and the white Sicilian variety Inzolia. It was the first concerted influx of international grape varieties that Etna had seen in almost a century.

One vintage after another, the experimental rows of vines proved successful, and the silhouette of a business started to take shape. Unfortunately, the Torrepalino facility, where they had been making most of the wines, was struggling. It wasn't always easy to create the wines they wanted from the grapes they planted. They decided to take control of their situation. In 1997, Francesco's sons, Guglielmo and Enzo, opened the doors of their new cantina in Contrada Cottanera, where they continue to make the wines today.

The following year, the Di Miceli family bought the Torrepalino company and renamed the facility Patria, for the district in west Sicily where their company began fifty years earlier. Many of the standards that Torrepalino initiated in the 1970s were continued by the Di Miceli family. For a small fee, the winery processed your grapes separately. They also fermented and aged the wine as you requested. Your own bottle and label? They did that too. If you didn't want to go through all the trouble, the foreman bought your grapes. The better the quality, the higher price the winery paid. Those who worked the vines and showed up each autumn with pristine, ripe clusters were able to make a living. Those who didn't continued to scrape by.

Everyone on the north slope could sense something was happening. The roads were a little busier. The cafés became louder. And the plumes of smoke in the landscape were rising more frequently as the brush was cleared and burned. For some, bottling and naming their effort was a tantalizing ideal. For those who were making it happen, the hardships began to leave a positive impression. In the preceding decades, nearly everything except the vines had been wiped from Etna's game board. Now, it was up to individual growers and producers which pieces, if any, they put into place.[178]

Massimo and Massimiliano Calabretta made their move in 1997, using the family's vineyards to reestablish the winery started generations before. The uncle and nephew built a cellar east of Randazzo. They brought in large Slavonian vats and smaller French casks to compliment the fiberglass and stainless steel tanks. From the vineyard through bottling, the focus was on temperature control in the cellar and minimal intervention with any natural process. Though the vineyards are trained in alberello, guyot, and espalier, old and young vineyards were often harvested together to make a single wine. They also found flexibility within the Italian labeling schemes.

Massimiliano is the sole owner today. We were in his kitchen one afternoon while workers used small jackhammers to liberate loose concrete in another room. Massimiliano watched the searing pan of Randazzo sausages get hotter as the noise grew louder. When the pan started to smoke, he doused the meat with an unlabeled bottle of red wine. "Something from the cellar! A treat!" he shouted over the din, as the liquid reduced. "This is the way we used to sell wine. You bring your bottle to Calabretta, we filled it! We knew but we didn't know how the good wine was made. It comes from the vineyard, yes, but this lunch, it doesn't only come from the market. It is a bit of everything!" With that, Massimiliano put the sausage links on our plates and carefully added the wine reduction. At the table, he filled our glasses from the unlabeled bottle. "Nerello Cappuccio!" he shouted. "The recent vintage." Calabretta is one of only five cantinas on the mountain to bottle a pure Nerello Cappuccio.

I asked him why he chose to bottle the wine on its own. It's most often used as a blender for Nerello Mascalese, but on its own the wine can shine.

Massimiliano shouted through the jackhammering. "In 2003 and 2004, I began experimenting with a small quantity of Carricante. It was a way to understand how wine was made. I was curious about always trying new things after that. But I also wanted to know how to make *my* wine. Not someone else's wine. Someone else's wine is not my wine. My wine is my wine!"

One of the grapes he fell for was the white Minella. He remains the only producer on the mountain making a pure Minella. These choices and others were not based on a business plan. They were guided by pure curiosity. In every corner of the mountain, wine assumed a new kind of novelty. In most cases, it was immediate and unplanned.

In the spring of 1998, when Giuseppe Mannino, a fifth-generation wine producer from Viagrande, drove to the north slope to visit a friend, he was so overcome by the aromas and the beauty of the farm that he rented the land to make his own wine for the next few years. "I couldn't explain it," Mannino said, in the garden of his estate at the base of Monte Serra, in Contrada Sciarelle. "It was a feeling I could not disregard. I knew immediately that I had to spend time there."

Time is an operative word here. Not everyone could make wine for a

Mount Etna is a sloped terrain. Many vineyards have been sculpted into terraces, like these in Ciro and Stephanie Biondi's Chianta vineyard, in Contrada Ronzini, outside Trecastagni, on the volcano's southeast slope. The vineyard climbs the slope of a spent crater and must be worked completely by hand.

living. Many producers had jobs during the week so they could work the vineyard on the weekend. This was the story for Ciro and Stephanie Biondi when they turned their attention to the family winery in 1999. During the week, Ciro was an architect, and Stephanie was as an English-language assistant at a local school. Each weekend, in the valley south of Monte San Nicolò, they hauled their tools up the lava-stone terraces to cut back the brambles, uproot bushes, and chop down trees that had encroached on the vineyards over decades.

Ciro's father, Turi, wasn't happy about his son's decision to revitalize the vineyards. Turi knew the work that went into a bottle of wine. The Biondis have worked in Contrada Ronzini for generations, but the market for Etna's products had taken a steep downturn over the course of Turi's life. He wanted something easier for Ciro and Stephanie, and he urged them to focus on their careers. They both knew Turi was right. The work was hard. Stopping was a sometimes-attractive option. But with every terrace they exposed, the compacted soil began to soften, and they started to believe that making a high-quality wine from the family vineyards was possible.

What they didn't know was how to make wine the new way. To get started, they enlisted the help of a consulting winemaker and the facilities at Benanti. Over the next few years, they trialed a Cabernet Sauvignon with Nero d'Avola and an experimental Pinot Nero, in addition to the local varieties already planted in the vineyards. Some of the wines were good, others were not.

"It was the winemaking as much as the grapes in this terrain," Ciro recalls over dinner at Frumento one evening, in the historic center of Acireale. "The [international varieties] didn't grow up on Etna. They taste awkward, out of place because of that."

"The better wines always came from the Etna varieties," Stephanie adds. "To be honest, we were a little surprised."

The Grasso family had a similar feeling about the influence of the terrain on the flavors of a wine. The contrada name "Calderara" refers to the broad lava fields that dominate the mountain in this area. "Sottana" suggests the edge of the rocky lava flow. The Grassos felt that the part of the vineyard that extended into the lower area of Calderara Sottana was too fertile for the wines they wanted to make. During the purchase in 1999, the lower vineyard was separated from the higher and drier terraces.

The Grasso family had produced wine on the fertile eastern slope for almost a century. In the late 1990s, they sold their vineyards in Dagala del Re, near Milo, and moved to the north slope, where it was sunnier and drier. The Contrada Calderara vineyard had contours, broad terraces, centuries-old olive and fruit trees, a mix of old and young vines, and a small palmento.

The soil throughout Contrade Calderara and Calderara Sottana is covered with *ripiddu*, eroded basaltic rocks the size of a child's fist. It's a consequence of where the winery is located, in the ancient eroded lava flow. When the Filippo Grasso winery finally came online, two of the wines were named for the lava stones in their vineyards—*Ripiddu*, for the Nerello blend, and *Mari di Ripiddu*, for the Carricante. It was a way of communicating something about their terrain to their customers and sommeliers who serve their wines around the globe.

When Sonia Spadaro, of Santa Maria La Nave, was introduced to Contrada Nave, on the volcano's northwest slope, there were no standard-bearers of the DOC. The contrada was at one time a part of the Ducea di Nelson, but following decades of neglect, the vines were simply swallowed up by nature. These were more than stories of ancient vines hiding in the countryside. The local farmers remembered precisely where these vines were. Beginning in 2000, inspired by a local agronomist and with the support of Etna farmers, Sonia embarked on a restoration project that sprung from a fifteen-year mass selection of Grecanico Dorato and Albanello vines found in the brambles and abandoned garden vineyards. Four years later, she purchased a few contiguous pieces of land in Contrada Nave at 1,100 meters, neighboring a young Traminer vineyard planted by Nunzio Puglisi, of Enò-Trio.

In this cool area of the mountain, the Grecanico vines began going into the ground. Rather than clear the area for a larger vineyard, the vines are surrounded by fruit, nut, and olive trees, and the spontaneous flora that impregnates the landscape every year. More than 15 percent of the vineyard is ungrafted, and much of it was propagated through layering. The first microvinifications of Grecanico Dorato began shortly after planting. Eventually, they arrived at a succulent still wine they call *Millesulmare*, and an elegant metodo classico sparkling wine called *Tempesta*, made from the same grapes.

"This line of tall trees," Sonia says, walking through the vineyard with me. "They block most of the morning light, so this part of the vineyard does not warm up the way the other part does. The grapes have good sugar but great acidity. We thought it would be a perfect plot for a classic method sparkling wine." They were right.

The Grecanico was a good jumping off point. At the start of 2018, Sonia embarked on a research project in her vineyard on Monte Ilice. The gnarly alberelli vines climb up the steep, sandy southeast slope of the 1,000-year-old crater, which overlooks the Ionian Sea and miles of the Sicilian coastline. For more than fifty years, the vines were tended by gentleman farmer Don Alfio. Together, Sonia and Don Alfio began isolating the relic varieties among the old and prephylloxera Nerello vines that go into the Etna Rosso, *Calmarossa*.

The relics were marked and carefully moved to small plots of their own in 2018. As of this writing, researchers at the University of Catania have identified some of the plants. Two varieties are known to be ancient Etna cultivars no longer in production anywhere. But two others have no DNA comparison. Just as Sonia fostered the Casa Decima vineyard in Contrada Nave from vines once hiding in the brambles, she hopes to replicate a distant past that was once considered "traditional" on Monte Ilice.

Things were a little more mysterious for mountaineer and wine merchant Frank Cornelissen, who arrived on the mountain in December 2000. "I visited the mountain and when I went home, I kept thinking about Etna. After years of trading wine, I wanted to try making some of my own. Once I saw Etna, the idea started to come together. I never wanted an estate. I liked the idea of making a wine that reminded me of liquid stone. I had no idea what would happen."

In 2001, Cornelissen made his first wine from less than an acre of Nerello. The process was enough to pique his interest. In 2002, he made another attempt. The wines were almost as wild as the volcano, but he considered these wines "unnecessarily provocative . . . intellectual wines," but the goal wasn't to make a 96-point wine. They were attempts at understanding the grapes and the mountain terrain. He excluded modern enological practices (i.e., oak, additives, enzymes, and sulfur) from his playbook, opting for experience and knowledge that arrived over time.

"I could have studied textbooks," he told me one morning in his office. "But that's no way to understand winemaking. You don't read a book to climb a mountain. You have to climb the damn thing."

Two decades on, Azienda Agricola Frank Cornelissen produces a dozen wines from more than fifteen different sites covering twenty-seven hectares (66 ac.) on the north slope of the volcano. Each bottle either represents a single vineyard or a blend of local grapes, but no additives of any kind are ever used to chaperone the wines. Instead of cultivated yeasts, a pied de cuve or spontaneous fermentation is customary. In place of sulfur additions in the wine, he employs a labor-intensive approach to each vineyard, reductive winemaking techniques, and methodic cleanliness in the cellar. Over time, by rejecting inessential ingredients and any calculated interpretations of how they should taste, the wines began to express their true territorial merits. Sometimes they were blended together to make a better wine. In others, they were bottled as a representative of the vineyard and vintage. "With every vintage," Frank tells me, "I started to feel like I was a part of this place."

After successfully launching the Trinoro brand, in the nineties, from vineyards planted at an average of more than 500 meters AMSL in Tuscany, winemaker and marketing virtuoso Andrea Franchetti initiated a search for vines grown at higher elevations. When he first arrived on Etna, in 2000, it seemed strange to him that so many terraced vineyards had been planted so high up the mountain. Certainly, the grapes wouldn't ripen. But when he tasted the wines and put his hands into the soil beyond the reaches of the 1947 lava flow, he had a feeling he'd found what he was looking for.

Franchetti purchased the vineyards and an old farmhouse in the hills above Passopisciaro. Through his dentist, he was introduced to Vincenzo Lo Mauro. Lo Mauro had experience planting vineyards on Etna. Franchetti asked him to address each vine by hand. With a density approaching 12,000 vines per hectare[179] Lo Mauro anticipated that some of the plantlets might not survive, but virtually every plant took root.

"I had never seen anything like it," Lo Mauro quipped on a walk through the vineyard. "It felt . . . like the place was waiting for us."

As the vines and vineyards began to produce, Franchetti and Lo Mauro took notice of how the Nerello Mascalese, in particular, seemed infinitely capable of translating the elevation, aspect, and volcanic components of each vineyard site. Every lot of grapes that came into the winery was being fermented separately. Eventually they started bottling them the same way, as representative samples of Nerello grown in a single contrada and vintage. Today, the Passopisciaro wines continue to follow this model, adding an opulent single-vineyard Petit Verdot, an appellation blend of Nerello, and a single-vineyard Chardonnay to their lineup of wines.

In a wine shop, the portfolio offers options. Franchetti's project is more than a reliable house. They have amassed one of the most important modern wine libraries on the mountain. Not for the volume, mind you, but for what the wines can tell us about Etna.

Marc de Grazia has a kindred interest in the way Etna communicates through Nerello. His winery, Tenuta delle Terre Nere, holds an archive of wines from small vineyards planted at elevation on the edge or in the embrace of violent eruptions that reshaped the volcano. Each wine presents the tension of these places as aromas, flavors, and textures. The effects of the terrain weren't always so obvious for de Grazia. His first couple of vintages on Etna were difficult and unconvincing, but de Grazia had help.

His vineyard manager, Don Peppino, was of primary importance. "At every obstacle, he urged me on," de Grazia told me one morning as we walked through the old gnarly Nerello vineyard in sight of the winery in Contrada Calderara Sottana. "If it wasn't for him, I don't think any of this would have happened. This vineyard and the wine that we make from it carry his name."

Dr. Benanti helped de Grazia make his first wines. Their combined efforts and constant critical experimentation not only convinced each of them of Etna's potential as an appellation, it divined a future based on wines from individual vineyard sites. By the time de Grazia moved out of the Benanti cantina and into his own, his comparison of Etna and Burgundy was catching on. The connection sounded a lot like the one Giacomo Tachis made ten years earlier, only de Grazia took it several steps further. Instead of focusing on the potential of Pinot Noir, as Tachis had, de Grazia likened Burgundy's cool climate to the low temperatures in Etna's high-elevation vineyards, and the ability of every vineyard site to speak through the wines in profound ways. While much of Etna had been relegated to Etna Bianco and Etna Rosso blends, it seemed more appropriate to de Grazia that his wines should carry the name of the place where the vines grow. Since the 2002 vintage, he has used contrada names to highlight the differences among his wines.

Fifty years after Professor Nicolosi-Asmundo and his colleagues delimited the mountain into areas where the wines had a common typicity, producers were testing their own subtle variations on this theme. No one knew a vineyard's peculiarities better than the people who managed them. With each successful attempt, it became clear how the aspect, elevation, soil type, and age of the soil play crucial roles that can change the wine in our glass. When those wines began to show up in the market, with the names of contrade where the wines were raised, the image of Etna pixelated into a medley of interconnected neighborhoods with their own volcanic history and a spice rack of inviting possibilities.

The Portale family's vineyards, near Biancavilla on Etna's southern flank, had been dedicated to making wine for the bulk market since the nineteenth century. Piero Portale grew up making simple country wine with his father and selling off what they didn't use. But by the turn of the twenty-first century he saw something more in the landscape.

Portale had an idea but he also knew he needed a hand. He asked local agronomist Giovanni Marletta to help him expand the vineyard to about thirteen hectares. It was a tall order, but the southern flank of the volcano had proven its potential before. The *azienda* Masseria Setteporte was founded in 2002, as Marletta was isolating and planting clones with drought-resistant American rootstocks that could limit vigor in favor of flavor in this warm and blustery part of the mountain. For the reds, they focused exclusively on Nerello Mascalese. The white blend included Carricante with one-third Catarratto. The vines responded almost exactly as they hoped. For the first several vintages, they used a consulting cantina to guide the wine into full production.

A parallel narrative was developing a few miles up the road at the Platania d'Antoni farm, in Contrada Cavaliere. As a child, Margherita Platania played among the old alberelli and terraces that surround the thirteenth-century Benedictine abbey-turned-palmento, in which the family forged their wine business in 1880. More than a century later, the vineyards were still producing, and new vines were planted, but the buildings had fallen to disrepair.

I went to visit Margherita on a warm summer day during the restoration. The enormous chestnut botti had been moved outside to make room for new stainless steel tanks. There was a litter of puppies in the shade of two wood vats, pining for their mother's attention. "We're bringing new life to this old place," Margherita tells me, adding a smile. "It was difficult watching time take its toll on the estate. It has an incredible history. Restoring the vineyards and now the buildings . . . it's taken time, but I couldn't allow so many moments to be forgotten."

It was hard in the beginning. Without a proper winemaking facility, she turned her grapes over to Cantine Nicosia for vinification. The first bottles under the Feudo Cavaliere label were from the 2008 harvest. The quality of the wine was good, but they were made by someone else. It made sense to move ahead, one step at a time. As the wines found their footing, they also found markets to sell them. Eight years after the family winery was relaunched, Margherita moved the production to the renovated palmento permanently.

To the west of Feudo Cavaliere, Arnaldo Spitaleri di Muglia was experimenting with clones of Pinot Nero in the family's old vineyards at Castello Solicchiata, in Adrano, for a series he would call *Pinetna*—a play on the Pinot Nero and Etna. In his memoir about the wines of the mountain, Spitaleri writes about the work that he began in 2001. "It was obvious that the [Pinot Nero] vines had undergone uniquely positive genetic mutations since they were planted in the 1850s. In particular, there were three distinct clones with low yields, small bunches, and darker grapes." Spitaleri named the clones AS1, AS2, and AS3, using his initials. The first bottles arrived from the 2010 vintage only two years after the new plants had gone in the ground. Since then, the portfolio has diversified to include a range of wines from Pinot Nero planted at high elevations.[180]

Another line in the portfolio was named for the castle, just as it had more than a century before. It follows recipes based on Cabernet Franc, Cabernet Sauvignon, and Merlot. Because the vineyards fall outside of the Etna DOC boundaries and the grapes are not on the list of approved varieties, the wines being produced—though of significant historic importance—are labeled Indicazione Geografica Protetta (IGP) or IGT. Considering that Castello Solicchiata makes about 400,000 bottles per year, it is currently the largest strictly non-DOC winery on the mountain.

On the other side of the mountain, in Contrada Marchesa, Peter Wiegner was talking with his neighbor Dr. Rocco Siciliano, whose Pinot Nero, *Rossoeuphoria*, had stoked the comparisons between Mount Etna and Burgundy years earlier. Alongside the Pinot vines, Dr. Siciliano grows Cabernets Franc and Sauvignon, Chardonnay, Nerello Mascalese, and Carricante. The Nerello Mascalese Wiegner planted in 2002 was still in its first leaf, but he didn't want to depend on Nerello to fill out the estate. Already an established professional in the wine trade, he still wasn't convinced that Carricante was the right white wine for Etna. In its place he chose Fiano—a white wine grape with an affinity for volcanic soil—plus Aglianico and Cabernet Franc for the reds.

As Wiegner's vines were taking root, Alberto Aiello Graci drove past their estate, in awe of the mountain vista. He had read about the work that Cornelissen and Franchetti were doing on the north slope and wanted to take a look around. During his first visits to the mountain he could tell they were on to something; his family once made wine from their holdings in Enna. For the next two years, he studied the landscape and kept an eye open for vineyards. The new wines entering the market were motivation enough, but that's not what captured Graci's attention.

"There is a kind of ceremony that went into every decision," he tells me, on our way up to his vineyard at 1000 m AMSL, in Contrada Barbabecchi. "Everywhere you look, you see it. The people who organized the vineyards of Etna took great pride in their work. They had an ambition for the territory, but their sacrifices also required great humility."

Graci sold the family land near Enna to purchase a vineyard in Contrada Arcurìa and one of the largest palmenti on the north slope of Mount Etna, in the heart of Feudo di Mezzo. His first wines were guided by Donato Lanati, but he also sought the advice of other grower-producers, in particular Frank Cornelissen, Giuseppe Russo, Andrea Franchetti, Ciro Biondi, and Marco de Grazia. Everyone was tasting each other's wines, learning from their mistakes and successes, and growing together as a community.

"Sometimes," Graci said, "I think we judge ourselves more harshly than others judge us."

He's right. Every producer has a goal in mind. When we hit that mark, we celebrate (a little), but then we're always on to the next vintage, the next wine. When we miss the mark, after a year of hard work, it hurts. As Graci progressed, he adapted ideas from each of his confidants—harvesting for elegance, using a pied de cuve instead of selected yeasts, avoiding temperature control during fermentation, implementing the use of large casks and concrete tanks, and bottling with natural cork. Graci adds, "But I have only one strategy for working in the vineyards. I call it total and constant intervention." By continuously working the vines, the extra effort assures that only the best grapes make it into the cantina at harvest.

The Costantino family applies a similar approach for their vineyards in Contrada Blandano, in the embrace of Etna's southeast craters. Blandano has been known for its structured white wines and soft reds for centuries. When Dino Costantino purchased the 27-acre estate in the 1970s, it was a weekend getaway for the family. The farm was interplanted with olive and fruit trees, prickly pear cactus, and intermixed vineyards of white and black grapes growing side by side, however, there had never been chemical pesticides, herbicides, or fertilizers of any kind used anywhere on the farm. Twenty-five vintages after buying the property, the family turned their hobby into something more.

Fabio Costantino manages Terra Costantino with his father, Dino, today. "We felt this was the right way," Fabio tells me, rocking back on a simple chair in the shade of the new winery. "Without chemical controls we work more in the vineyard. A lot more! But, when you are always in the vineyard, you realize you don't have to fight nature. We wouldn't win. Instead of telling the farm what we wanted it to do, the farm showed us what it does."

I hear this sentiment a lot. Especially when it comes to old vineyards. When Michele Faro initially conceived of a wine company, "We knew we didn't want to start with new plantings. I preferred instead to find older vines with at least forty vintages behind them," Faro said, walking into a vineyard behind their destination winery, Pietradolce, in Solicchiata. Forty was a good minimum average for Faro, but he didn't set an age limit. Some of the vines he works with were planted before oidium or phylloxera reached Europe. "These vines have already found an equilibrium with the environment and the volcano," Faro adds. "The monuments [vines] we started with, that became our way forward."

This was another step in the right direction for some Etna wineries. To grub up an existing site of established vines to suit a modern concept of viticulture in other places would have erased a chunk of the mountain's history. There were, of course, winegrowers who did this for the simple reason of animating what they saw as an idle landscape. Where there is quiet, however, we often find wisdom.

Paolo Caciorgna is a Tuscan winemaker with decades of experience. He's planted multiple vineyards over the years. "It's nice to see young vines take to a place, and how the wines taste as they get older and become a part of the terrain," Caciorgna said, parking the car outside a gate on a bumpy road in Contrada Marchesa. "Occasionally, I used to come to Etna to see Marco [de Grazia]. One day he showed me this."

Caciorgna led me along a short path to the edge of a prephylloxera vineyard in the embrace of the 1566 and 1646 lava flows. It was the first place on Etna where I ever got goose bumps. The old and ornate alberelli assumed elaborate postures, their young shoots reaching into the fog that was rolling among the vines from up mountain. Caciorgna quietly walked through the vines, speaking softly, as though he didn't want to bother them. I didn't either. It was enough to be among them. "This is a very special place," Caciorgna says, climbing up the skirt of the 1646 lava flow for a better view. "It's an honor, taking care of these vines."

His first Etna wine, *N'Anticchia* (a little)—a Nerello from the 2005 harvest—arrived from a selection of that vineyard. After two successful vintages, he bought the property. A second Nerello, which Caciorgna calls *Guardoilvento* (I watch the wind) came from old vines in Contrada Santo Spirito. A third wine, *Ciauria*, a pure Nerello Mascalese, arrived later from a selection of small vineyards on the north slope.

Chiara Vigo had recently completed her doctorate studies with a thesis on the subject of wine labels. As Caciorgna's first wines were entering the market, Chiara Vigo was attending Vinitaly, in Verona. Upon visiting the Sicily pavilion, she said, "I couldn't help but admire what Etna producers were doing. They were smiling when they talked about their wines. They were really proud of the work they were doing. I had never seen this kind of energy about Etna before."

As a girl, a portion of the Vigo family farm was erased by the March 1981 eruption, which decimated an area between Randazzo and Montelaguardia, claiming over sixty acres of the Vigo estate in Contrada Allegracore. It was a disaster the family had not completely recovered from. "Our family history on Etna is deep. It made sense to try again." Vigo started working on the farm that summer, with a plan to produce her first wines from her family's remaining vines of Nerello. She hired Benanti to help.

That same spring, Guido Coffa went for a bike ride in the countryside. He needed to clear his head. It was a beautiful day, he remembers. The clouds in the sky were creating fingers of sunlight that played on a hillside. He stopped the bike and watched how the light struck the undulating terraces built into the knuckles of the 1634 lava flow.

"It was an immediate sensation," Coffa said over lunch at the estate. "I saw what I wanted to dedicate my life to. In that moment, I was thinking of returning to the United States for work. After seeing this property, I knew I needed to stay." Coffa purchased the property in parcels and began to explore and restore the estate. In the process, he discovered it had been maintained by monks of the Order of Saint Anne.[181] When he opened his luxury resort on the property, he called it Monaci delle Terre Nere (Monks of the Black Land). Today, the estate includes a hotel, restaurant, vineyards, and an organic farm.

It was obvious to the producers that a sense of intrigue and possibility had fallen over the mountain, and it was spreading.

In the fall of 2007, I Custodi delle vigne dell'Etna made their first wine, *Aetneus*, from old vines on the north flank. The wine is made up of 80 percent Nerello Mascalese, 10 percent Nerello Cappuccio, and 10 percent Alicante. The owners, Mario and Manuela Paoluzi, were inspired by the results, and they have since purchased, planted, and leased vineyards in Contrade Puntalazzo, Nave, Moganazzi, Feudo di Mezzo, Sant'Alfio, and Milo. The heart of the company is located around the modern winery in Contrada Moganazzi.

In Montelaguardia, Antonio Destro was testing the vineyards he found abandoned only a few years earlier. Transitioning between the vineyard and his career in rough-hewn marble, Destro released their first production of a pure Nerello Mascalese from the 2007 vintage. The wine is called *Sciarakè*, a play on the local word for a lava flow. The vineyards, nineteenth-century palmento, and modern winery are neatly positioned in the embrace of a massive prehistoric eruption. Like many modern Etna producers, Destro was drawn to Etna by chance. He was hunting for mushrooms when he stumbled out of the forest above the vineyard and cantina where he now produces his wines.

When I ask him about this moment, Destro smiles and wraps his arms around his chest. "Imagine finding a jewel that very few people knew existed. That was me."

For Silvia Maestrelli, the owner of Tenuta di Fessina, in Rovittello, the jewel was a glass of wine she drank in 2007. Precisely, Tenuta delle Terre Nere's 2004 Etna Rosso, from Contrada Guardiola. The wine that would change her life. Until that moment, Maestrelli was working on her family's estate, Villa Petriolo, in Tuscany. Her agronomist was Federico Curtaz, who was managing and replanting vineyards in Tuscany with Maestrelli when the glass of de Grazia's *Guardiola* shifted their focus to the volcano.

On a trip to Etna, they saw a seven-hectare (17 ac.) estate for sale along the Circumetnea train line, in Rovittello, on the volcano's north slope. The owner was selling a palmento and his old vines, which were planted along the eastern edge of the 1911 lava flow. Maestrelli was sold on the idea, but there was an obstacle. The vineyard in play was part of a larger vineyard that was owned by at least fifteen different families. Buying the vines took time—as of this writing, there is still one family who manages a small plot in the center of the vineyard—but the protracted process of securing each parcel to create a continuous vineyard, Silvia contends, was worth it.

"Signore Musmeci was vital to the negotiations and for our understanding of this vineyard," Silvia tells me over dinner at Villa Neri, a luxury resort in the hills above Linguaglossa. "Without him, we would still be working it all out."

Tenuta di Fessina's first wine—2007 *Musmeci*, Etna Rosso—received broad critical praise. The wine is still made from the oldest vines in the vineyard and named after the previous owner of the palmento. Curtaz put a Barolo spin on the wines at first—oak *élevage* with bold tannins and extracted flavors—but as the team merged with the vineyard, so too did their understanding of the mountain. Curtaz left Fessina in 2015 to launch his consulting company and a line of Etna wines under his own name. Today,

Benedetto Alessandro[182] guides the winemaking, which requires a profound understanding of the variables of the volcanic terrain. Tenuta di Fessina features three of Etna's aspects—in Rovittello on the north, Biancavilla on the south slope, and Milo on the east.

As Maestrelli's first vintage on Etna was going through veraison, Nadine and I were at the end of our first vacation on the mountain. I didn't realize it at the time, but things were changing fast for Etna. In fact, a lot of the important changes had already taken place. I was in the Catania airport reading *Italian Wines 2007: A Guide to the World of Italian Wine for Experts and Wine Lovers* by Gambero Rosso and Slow Food Editore as I waited to board our flight back to California. Benanti had been named by the publisher as the Italian Winery of the Year. It was an incredible coup, to win out over much bigger estates from elsewhere in Italy or Sicily, but the work Benanti had been doing was finally paying off for everyone on Etna. Not only did a small winery from the volcano win the year's top prize, the award gave visibility and credence to the work that everyone was doing.

It's difficult to look up when you're working hard; you want to get the job done, move on to the next thing. There were echoes of others in the countryside and proof of their efforts in the press and local wine shops, but only a handful of producers knew exactly what their colleagues were doing. Working on Etna in the early aughts was a lot like maneuvering through the dark. Then someone strikes a match and everyone can suddenly see everything.

Andrea Franchetti was the person who lit it. He arranged what amounted to the first public tasting of Etna wines, at the Passopisciaro winery. The inaugural Contrade dell'Etna was held on Sunday, March 16, 2008, and included more than sixty wines from thirty-eight cantinas and *anteprima* (preview) samples of the 2007 vintage.

Apart from the importers and distributors who were already promoting Etna with private tastings and special events, there was very little marketing of any scale. The Consorzio per la Tutela dei Vini Etna, a local agency designed to control and regulate wine production within the Etna DOC, didn't have the finances for a multi-million-dollar advertising push. Their activities were funded by the wineries, with barely enough money to hire a staff. In truth, any kind of artificial publicity (full-page advertisements, commercials) wouldn't have helped. The wines had too many personalities to convey the kind of prevailing commercial typicity that other regions claim as a part of their appeal.

What's more, some winemakers openly admitted their ignorance. There just wasn't enough evidence to know how the trajectory might track. It was this collective shrugging of shoulders that drew so much interest. For many who attended the tasting, the experience was a mixed bag. There were good wines and bad wines. Believers and skeptics. One thing was certain, the new wines of Mount Etna provoked a response. Producers who had developed a sensibility for their role as an interpreter of the volcanic terroir were the ones who drew the most attention. Those who came unprepared were left out of the conversation.

Since that first Contrade dell'Etna tasting, the number of registered wine producers has more than quadrupled. Not because of the event, or the exposure in the press, but because winemakers were doubling down on their own curiosities and personal insights about the grapes, the mountain, and themselves. With every new vintage they began to speak with the level of authority that comes from experience and risk. The media, critics, sommeliers, importers, and consumers seemed to like what they were hearing and tasting. Consequently, the Contrade dell'Etna has become one of the most exciting and well-attended wine events in Sicily.

Changes to the Etna DOC—Things were happening faster now. When amendments to the DOC regulations were proposed in 2009 it was in response to enthusiastic work being done by Etna producers.

The recommended revisions included subtle clarifications[183] plus two new categories—Etna Spumante and Etna Rosso Riserva—and permission for producers to identify a contrada of the vineyard where the grapes were grown on the label.

Etna Spumante was based on the traditional method—which employs a second bottle fermentation to sparkle the wines. The recipe was almost exclusively based on the work that Michele Scammacca was doing at Murgo. The sparkling wines could be white or rosé, but they had to be made from a minimum 60 percent Nerello Mascalese, with the rest of the blend composed of Sicilian grape varieties. In practice, the proportion of Nerello approaches purity. They must also be aged in their bottle, on lees, for a minimum of eighteen months. After disgorgement, the bottles are closed with a high-pressure cork that is secured with a muselet (the cage that connects the cork to the bottle).

The Etna Rosso classification was tweaked ever so slightly to include wines made from 100 percent Nerello Mascalese.

The concept for Etna Rosso Riserva springs from the basic Etna Rosso, but the yields per plant are reduced (a maximum of 3.5 tons/ac. or 80 quintali/ha) to ensure better flavors. In the cantina the wines are raised in wood for a minimum of one year, with at least of four years aging within the DOC before release to the public. Many producers stretch the élevage in wood to two, four, or even seven years, depending on the vintage and the quality of the wine through extended aging.

Wineries were also permitted to feature the name of a contrada on their labels. Today, the Etna DOC includes 133 individual contrade shared among twenty communities (see Appendix). Nearly all bottles that carry the name of a contrada are single-vineyard wines.

In 2021, the Etna DOC proposed modifications to some of its rules once again.

For the region, producers can now refer to Sicily on the label; a minimum number of vines per hectare were established at 4,600; and "flat closures" like natural cork are obligatory for Etna Rosso Riserva and Etna Bianco Superiore only, opening the door for screw caps and other seals to be used for all other still wines.

For Etna Rosato, the color and hue of the wine shifted away from pink-ruby toward pink-orange, reflecting both the tradition of *pistamutta* and the styles of pale red wines being made with Nerello Mascalese.

For Etna Spumante, less intense colors are now customary; the minimum alcohol level was reduced to 10.5 percent; the minimum percentage of Nerello Mascalese was increased to 80 percent; and the Classic Method was named (rather than referred to) as the only way of producing this quality, bottle-fermented sparkling wine.

Our trip back to Etna in 2010 could have been longer, but I had business in Romania and wine to tend to back in California. Pointing the car north from Riposto, I thought about my meetings with Ciro Biondi and Frank Cornelissen over the previous week.

At the Biondi winery in Trecastagni, Ciro led Nadine and I through the cellar. His nephew and cellar master, Manfredi, was busy hand label-ing a single-vineyard Nerello they called *M.I.*, for Monte Ilice—a massive, unterraced pyroclastic crater on the southeast slope of the mountain. I asked Ciro how the *M.I.* compared to their appellation blend, *Outis*, which I had tasted in the States. Instead of responding with a theoretical treatise on the differences between the wines, Ciro walked over to two stainless steel vats and drafted a sample of each.

He handed me the two glasses. "You tell me."

The vineyards were only a few kilometers apart, and both the vines and the wines were managed by the same team, but I might as well have been tasting different grape varieties and regions. My face probably said as much.

"This is Etna," Ciro said.

The next afternoon, I met Frank at Cave Ox, in Solicchiata. On our way to his apartment, we stopped at his old cantina—where for years he fermented some of his wines in buried amphora—for a conversation and a glass or two of wine. He presented a clear glass bottle with a ruddy-pink liquid inside and pointed at the name on the label.

"'*Contadino*' is farmer," he said, "This is a kind of peasant wine." He opened the bottle and poured a glass for each of us, explaining that the wine was born from Nerello with other white and black varieties that were allowed to ferment together without intervention. "I like this wine. It makes me feel easy," he said, smiling. "We had so much rain last year and so many grapes coming into the winery all at once. It was impossible to manage everything. So, with the *Contadino*, we know we can let the grapes and the vinification be what they are. That's a good feeling, to know your vines and grapes enough to trust them."

The 2009 vintage was a bear. The rain began on the first of September and didn't let up for a month. The bad weather reached a crescendo during a regional storm on September 16. One week later, hillsides began slipping, roads and terraces eroded, and the grapes were swollen or bursting.[184] Many producers simply dropped the fruit on the ground or declassified the grapes when they came in. Those who did make wine harvested before any serious damage could be done.

As we ferried from Messina to Calabria, I leaned on the railing and looked back at the eastern Sicilian coastline. If my first trip to Sicily ignited my interest in wine, this trip poured gasoline on the flame. By the time we reached Bari, to catch our second ferry to Greece, it was obvious to me just how much we were dressing the wines in California to attract attention in a room full of other wines competing for the same thing. As we waited for border security to check our passports, crossing from Bulgaria into Romania, I leaned against the car and said, "I think Etna's on to something."

Nine years after I said those words, I still believe them. Not because of the success that Etna has found or the number of producers stamping the name of the volcano on their labels, but because of the way producers continue to experiment so that they might refine the process of discovery. Sometimes a chance experiment pays off. In others, the result points in an alternative direction.

Terrazze dell'Etna is a keen example of this. When Nino Bevilacqua purchased the centuries-old terraces of Nerello in Contrada Bocca d'Orzo, in 2008, he hardly imagined the course the project would take. What started with a single wine—*Cirneco*, made from the oldest part of the vineyard—has blossomed into a portfolio that explores Etna's traditions with a curiosity for the possible. Today, the estate includes thirty-six contiguous hectares of vineyards, orchards, chestnut forests, stables, a restored palmento, and a modern winery that operates under the guidance of Riccardo Cotarella, one of Italy's leading enologists.

Forty-four properties in total were purchased when the last agreements were signed. As the team was going through the existing vines of each small farm, they found a lot of Nerello and some Petit Verdot, but no Carricante. Taking this as a sign, they planted Chardonnay, but instead of making a still wine, they duplicated Castello Solicchiata's nineteenth-century project to produce *Champagne Etna*, which was composed of French varieties. A second sparkler is based on Pinot Nero with some Nerello, for a brut rosato. The rest of the Pinot vineyard went toward an opulent Pinot Nero that spends several months in toasted French tonneaux, like most of the company's red wines. That small percentage of Petit Verdot they found is used to blend up a bold Mascalese. Another Nerello blend and a rosato follow the Etna DOC lead. All of this comes from Etna, but each wine, every vintage, is made with intention.

The Fischetti winery goes in the opposite direction, choosing minimal intervention over experimentation. "When we bought the house in Contrada Moscamento, the old alberelli in the yard were a bit of a mystery," Michela Fischetti told me, as we walked through the alberello vineyard. "There were grapes, but the vines were being managed simply. Some of these were in pretty bad shape. We weren't interested in changing things around. We were very curious about what was here."

In 2008, they sought assistance from Andrea Marletta, who consults for several estates around the mountain. They immediately got to work addressing the vines. For three vintages, they sold a portion of the grapes and produced a little wine to understand the direction ahead. By 2011, the vines and winery equipment were ready. The vintage had progressed beautifully. It was the opportune moment to start.

As the bubbles of gas filled the must in the Fischetti fermenters, I lay awake in California, staring at the ceiling and freaking out about our move to Etna the following year. After a frustrating and sleepless couple of hours, going in circles about the thousands of things that had to happen, I went downstairs and got on the internet. By the time the sun came up, I had saved scores of links to Etna wineries, vintages, critical reviews, and articles.

For the next few months, I downloaded and bookmarked everything I could about the volcano and wines. I sent emails with my résumé to wineries, asking about work on the mountain, mentioning that I would be in Verona in April, for Vinitaly, if they would like to meet. I received many dispassionate responses, but Ciro Biondi responded with an invitation to their stand. "Let's meet there. We can taste some wine and talk about your plans."

Weeks later, after a flight from California to New York and another from New York to Milan and a train to Verona, I arrived at the Biondi booth in the Sicilia pavilion, and found a hand-written note on the counter.

Torno subito. Be right back.

The wait was to be expected—few stories ever go as effortlessly as we think they should—but I was too nervous to mull around. Up the row, I met Francesco Calcagno and tasted the fabulous Calcagno Etna Rosso from vineyards in contrade Feudo di Mezzo and Arcurìa. Then I stopped to speak with Sebastiano Licciardello about the wines and jams Tenuta Monte Gorna makes from Nerello and Carricante grown on the shoulder of Monte Gorna, a spent volcanic crater. When I stopped back around to see Ciro, he was standing beside his booth, dressed casually to the nines. Our entire conversation lasted a few short minutes.

In the end, Ciro said, "If you can give us a hand in September when you arrive, we would be happy to have you."

Ciro and I communicated by email and Skype. He kept me up to date on the construction of their new vinification area, deals he and Stephanie were making with importers in foreign markets, and articles being written about the winery.

The day I arrived at the cantina, I could smell the intoxicating aromas of carbon dioxide emanating from the fermenters and the pomace pile beneath the eucalyptus trees. Manfredi was preparing the horizontal bladder press to receive the fermented grapes designated for the *Outis* Etna Rosso.

"La fermentazione è finita?" The wine is finished fermenting?

"Il clima era veramente caldo ad agosto, dovevamo raccogliere l'uva tre settimane prima del normale. Dammi un mano? Voglio attaccare questo tubo alla pressa." The weather was really hot in August, we had to harvest the grapes

three weeks earlier than normal. Give me a hand? I want to attach this hose to the press.

It was a strange feeling, arriving in the middle of a harvest, but no one could have anticipated the heat. In a way, 2012 was a hallmark year. The heat contributed to an uncharacteristic maturity in the grapes, which in turn helped sell a lot of wine. Arriving on the heels of the classic 2011 vintage, the warmer weather gave new wineries entering the community another strong vintage to stand on.

The 2013 growing season was cool, with a wet spring and a tepid summer. The grapes reached physiological ripeness only at the moment of harvest. The 2014 *vendemmia* was flawless all across the island. While the Italian Peninsula endured floods and hail, Etna saw one of the best vintages in a decade. The following year, the weather was a real mixed bag. The awkward growing season produced wines with exceptional balance and complexity—and very low yields.

The 2016 vintage was cool in the beginning and hot in the middle. Shoot growth in the spring was slow to moderate, but then a heat spike forced the vines into overdrive. By mid-August, temperatures were dropping. Growers defoliated the fruit zone of their vines to expose the grape clusters to more sunlight. The rain started in the first few days of September. Every morning was beautiful and sunny, and every afternoon the rain clouds gathered around the mountain. Portions of Etna were under a nagging siege of light rain. Some vineyards were devastated by hail. The Carricante was harvested at the end of September, but almost everyone waited until the last possible moment before bringing in the Nerello. The berries were swollen, but unbroken. A few days later, the scent of healthy fermentation filled the wineries.

The following vintage saw a six-month drought. Thankfully, the snow that blanketed the mountain over the winter was enough to maintain the plants. Yields were low and flavors were so good that some producers have made comparisons between 2017 and other great years. The 2018 season was a contrast to the previous vintage. Scattered showers and storms, cool temperatures, and one month of sun in July seemed to keep the vintage on track for a decent harvest. But the rains started back up in August. Virtually everyone harvested in between the rains.

When I ask friends about their 2018s, almost everyone says the same thing: It was hard won . . . a good year for Etna Bianco, Rosato, and Spumante, but the reds are lighter and more elegant. Kind of like the 2013s.

The 2019 vintage was slow to start, it was hot through the summer months, but by the time of harvest everything had cooled off, leading to balanced acidity and ripe flavors.

In 2020, due to the limitations and stress of the Covid-19 pandemic, winemakers spent a lot of time in their vineyards and cellars. Rains led to an earlier harvest for some, resulting in wines with a light fresh style throughout the appellation.

We had approximately 60 eruptions and the hottest summer ever recorded in Europe in 2021. Yields at harvest were low, but flavors are excellent with soft acidity in the still wines and ripe fruit in the blossoming Etna Spumante category.

We are optimistic about the 2022 vintage, which started out with a dry winter, intermittent spring rains, and a protracted spike in the heat from the beginning of June through the end of August.

I know some of this is marketing. Everyone's promoting the positives of the growing season. But part of me realizes that something far more important is happening.

Producers are recognizing patterns and similarities between vintages.

The old and new mingle in every Etna neighborhood and town. Here, young vines grow around a centuries-old palmento in Contrada Blandano, on the mountain's east slope.

They are also learning how to manage the vines and the wines based on their personal experience with Etna's predictably unpredictable weather, and how to communicate those variables in the glass, during a tasting, or in a class. Producers that don't have the experience are taking notes from those who do. Their success is what's created so much excitement, after all. One twist is that new investors are developing the viticultural arena at a speed that many local families cannot. In fact, some of the wineries responsible for Etna's current reputation are being bought out, sometimes quite happily since the value of viticultural land has tripled in a decade. The question is, how will newcomers treat the place that so many others have reverently nourished back to health?

Everyone on Etna remembers the days when selling wine by the liter at low prices to the community was the norm. Only a few short decades ago, it was almost the only way to buy local wine. Now, we are seeing the price of a bottle rise to €20 or even €250. Certainly, the amount of work that goes into a bottle of wine should be recuperated, and people need to make a living, but here, a liter of wine still costs an average of two euros.

I visit my sfuso vendor almost every week. He is at a loss to explain the prices of bottled wine on the mountain. He's been growing grapes and making wine on Etna his entire life, just as his father and grandfather did. When I ask him why he thinks there's such a disparity between the prices he charges and those of his neighbors, he throws up his hands and shouts, "People *want* to pay too much! Is there gold in there? They should come here. One liter, €1.70. They could have ten or twenty of mine for *one* of those bottles!"

This is, of course, one of the reasons I return to his place. He has good wine at a great price. To his palate, there's no difference between the wine he makes and the "fancy" bottles he sees entering the market. To my taste, there is a distinction. The new wines of Mount Etna are managed, from the vineyard to service. At every opportunity a choice is made. Vineyards and projects dedicated to anything other than fine wine simply make fewer choices or choose to do less to manage the wine away from its natural process. *Fresh ingredients prepared with care inevitably taste better than something you walk away from.* For decades following the Second World War, going to the vineyards each morning was an act of inertia. What's turned these wines from bulk wine to fine wine are those who, with a scrupulous amount of spite, actually return to work in the vineyards and the cellars after they've had lunch.

Every year, a little more of the Etna landscape is rediscovered and developed. While we are all betting on the future, the conversation about what Etna does best is still very much a conversation in process. We can debate the vibrant, nervy, and savory wines, the volcanic soils, the importance of aspect and altitude or clonal selections, but the reasons the wines taste the way they do add as many questions as they provide answers. This is part of what makes Mount Etna wines and this mountain so much fun to explore. It often defies our expectations. Nowhere else is this more true than in the company of the people who live and work on the mountain.

Vini Gambino Winery, in Contrada Petto Dragone, above Linguaglossa, also presents an in-depth educational tour of the winery. Many Etna wineries offer a range of hospitality options, including wine tastings, food pairings, and walking tours. In the following section, we offer contact details for scores of Etna wineries.

PART THREE

On Mount Etna, we do things differently. No one serves you crackers and expects you to be happy about it. On Etna, you're a guest. No doubt, by the end of the visit, you'll also be a friend.

QUICK TIPS FOR TASTING

We've all saddled up to a bar in a tasting room, chosen a flight from the menu, and nibbled on a few crackers between sips of wine. Sure, the guy or gal behind the counter might know a good anecdote about the winemaker and something about the vineyard soil, but they repeat the exact same script to a young couple a few feet away. Almost as soon as your crackers and wine are gone, they present you with a bill, you hand over some cash, and someone else takes your place at the bar. This is not a wine tasting. It's voluntary robbery. Unfortunately, this is what many people expect, because it's what gets offered. On Mount Etna, we do things differently. No one serves you crackers and expects you to be happy about it. We don't show you pictures of the vines, we walk through them. We won't point at a poster and say, "That's the winery." We'll bring you there, open a few bottles, have a conversation, and enjoy a leisurely meal. On Etna, you're a guest. No doubt, by the end of the visit, you'll also be a friend.

PLACES TO STAY

There are countless options for lodging on and around the mountain. Basic and luxury hotels are everywhere, as are long-term apartments and villas. The *agriturismi* (rural farms) offer comfortable accommodations at an affordable price, with the added bonus of being closer to the natural splendor of Etna.

My suggestion: rent a car, get out of the cities and away from the bright lights. Find a place in the countryside that looks comfortable and offers the amenities you like.

If you prefer to stay closer to a town and you don't have wheels, look along the main thoroughfares (A18, SS120, SS114, SP59) and within walking distance of the Ferrovia train lines. Otherwise, you can look for a local car service or taxi to get around.

PLANNING YOUR VISIT

I can drive through the Etna DOC, from one end to the other, in two hours. I know the back roads, the short cuts, the distances between wineries. But I always allow for extra time to get where I'm going. It doesn't matter how good the weather is. Road conditions change. You never know what kind of traffic you might encounter (cyclists, a funeral procession, a herd of sheep).

Mapping apps and GPS systems are helpful for getting around the mountain, but they fail sometimes, and service in several areas is still spotty. It's a good idea to have a map and plan out where you're going.

Knowing how to get to a winery is almost as important as making a reservation. Only a handful of producers offer walk-in guests the same opportunities as those who call ahead. You can call to make a reservation, but email and social media work too. Some cantinas make it possible to make a booking through their website. The most important thing is that you get a response, confirming your visit. In my experience, it's a good idea to reconfirm too.

During the conversation, ask what kind of experiences they offer, and tell your potential host something about yourself, including any preferences you might have—dietary or otherwise. If the winery can't help you, for whatever reason, they'll introduce you to someone who can. Where some cantinas only produce one or two wines, others can create vertical tastings of their best vineyards and vintages, if you like. More than one winemaker offers a tasting directly from their vats, and several more will cook you a rousing Sicilian lunch. Everyone does visits differently.

When you reach out to someone, give them time to respond. Many producers split their time between jobs, the fields, the cellar, and travel. They have private lives too. Hospitality is an important part of many businesses, but it's also a fairly recent phenomenon for Etna producers.

Keep in mind that not everyone speaks English. Some wineries have educators who speak different languages and know the territory, just don't bet your house on it. Instead, try learning a little Italian before you arrive, or find a robust app for your phone or tablet that can help you communicate in real time.

That brings us to your coverage. I'm not talking about insurance for the rental car (though it's a good idea to get the bonus package). I'm talking about your service plan for your phone. While you're in Sicily, you're going to need it to contact people, receive messages, emails, and follow a map. It's a priceless add-on for any trip.

When you head out, I suggest dressing in layers. Have a hat, a small pack for carrying your personal effects, water, sunscreen, and an umbrella. While summers in Sicily are hot and sunny, the weather can change fast on the mountain. Flash thunderstorms are not uncommon, and the volcano does erupt from time to time. It's a good idea to wear sneakers or hiking shoes. Bring a battery pack or charging cables for any electronics, and make sure there's space available on your camera. The views on Mount Etna are stunning. Before snapping off photographs or videos in the winery, ask your guide if it's okay.

TASTINGS AND ETIQUETTE

When you get in front of a few glasses of Etna Bianco and Etna Rosso, take your time. What do you see, smell, and taste? If you don't know, don't be shy. Ask questions.

Most wineries offer one pour of each wine that you are scheduled to taste. If you like it, you might be offered more, but don't expect your glass to be refilled time and again. Italians like to drink but they don't like to get drunk. Nor do they want to be responsible for you getting inebriated. Being jovial is one thing. Public drunkenness is quite another.

Drinking and driving or drunk driving can get you in serious trouble. For seasoned drivers, the blood alcohol limit is 0.5 g/l. If you are the designated driver, don't feel like you have to drink every glass you're presented with. Seeing and smelling a wine are great ways to get to know it. You can also spit and buy a bottle or two of the wine you like for later.

You are able to buy bottles at some wineries, and many of them can ship it to your home. Prices vary, based on the wine and the logistics company responsible for getting it overseas, through customs, and to your door. For now, prices are reasonable for the service. Don't be shocked if the cantina doesn't sell wine from their cellar door. Some only work with retailers and restaurants. If you ask, they'll be happy to tell you exactly where to find their bottles.

Tipping is an oddity. As an American, I add a gratuity without thinking. On Etna, it's not expected, but it is appreciated. In restaurants, a small tax is usually added to the bill for service. If you feel like adding something more, go for it.

GETTING SOCIAL

It's not hard to find Etna wineries and wines. All we have to do is pick up our smartphones or jump on the computer and search. In 2007, on our first visit to Etna, there were no apps. Social media was barely a thing. Now, nearly every winery on the mountain has adopted one or more communications strategies to attract attention, share their lives, and make a few sales.

Not only is it a way to promote the business, it serves as a free space for owners, sommeliers, and consumers to communicate about the brand. Those who publish photographs, stories, and videos tend to garner more attention than those who don't. Unfortunately, the swagger of one's social media account doesn't necessarily correlate to the quality of a product and vice versa. It is a way of reaching out, however. A way for producers to bridge the distance between the winery and the rest of the wide world.

"The approach is simple," Antonio Benanti tells me in the dining room at the company's Viagrande estate. "Of course we want to sell wine. But it's much better for all of us if we create Etna ambassadors. Etna cannot survive on bottle sales alone. We are building a community, one exchange at a time."

Cultivating a community is priceless in this moment. There was nothing glorious about the mountain wines at the turn of the twenty-first century. Two decades on, Etna has name recognition among wine lovers, journalists, and those in the trade. As much as this is due to the availability of Etna wines in the international market, the advent of digital communications has paralleled Etna's rebirth. Producers are using social media to document this moment for the rest of the world to see. What's more, they're inviting us to join them.

The following list of Mount Etna wineries* is organized by slope, in this order:

- South, Page 227
- East, Page 233
- North, Page 259

* Only wineries that contributed information are listed.

Private tasting rooms, like Terrazze dell'Etna's wine cellar near Randazzo, are available on request. Many Etna wineries offer local delicacies, pairings, and even full meals with their wines. Every visit is unique to that winery. Don't be shy about asking questions when arranging a visit.

In Tenute Bosco's Vigne Vico, in Passopisciaro, we see the potential complexity of a single vineyard site. The terraces of old Nerello vines follow a cascade of Mongibello eruptions, changing in elevation 50 meters over a very short distance. The hills that flank and separate the terraces are from the 1566 (left) and 1897 (right) eruptions.

Tenuta Monte Gorna's Carricante vineyard is on Monte Gorna, a spent volcanic crater. This is a great place to experience Mount Etna's unique southeast slope. In the near distance is Monte Ilice, Monte Gorna's sister crater. In the background, steam from the central craters, at the top of the mountain, is carried by the wind.

Every year, the vineyard at Gurrida fills with water, submerging the Alicante vines planted here at the end of the nineteenth century. The location of the vineyard—between two lava flows (1273 and 1536)—encourages flooding.

WINERIES ON THE SOUTH SLOPE

Azienda Falcone

Feudo Cavaliere

Reale Vini Etna

Tenuta Masseria Setteporte

* For an updated selection of wineries present on the volcano, you can refer to *The Newest New Wines of Etna* on page 327

AZIENDA FALCONE

Contrada Cavaliere
Santa Maria di Licodia, CT
95038
www.aziendafalcone.it
info@aziendafalcone.it
+39 349-303-6652,
+39 348-726-4350
Founded: 2008
Find the Winery On:
Facebook, Instagram
Contrada: Cavaliere
Hectares: 4
Vine Training: Cordon
Etna DOC Wines: Etna
Bianco, Etna Rosato, Etna
Rosso
Other Wines: IGT/IGP Terre
Siciliane
Bottles Produced: 5,000

Visits: Only by request
Hospitality: Vineyard Tour,
Wine Tasting
Amenities: Small Groups
(<15), Family Friendly, Pet
Friendly
Languages Spoken: Italian,
English, Spanish

Wines to try—
Aitho Etna Rosso
Aitho Etna Bianco
Aton Vino Bianco

High in the hills above Santa Maria di Licodia, the Falcone family looked at the old vines in their vineyard and decided to take the risk. In 1990 there were so few producers on Mount Etna that a move in any one direction was a gamble. Replanting, retraining, and reorganizing the old vines and terraces was only the first part of the work. In an effort to avoid mistakes, they sought advice from Giovanni Marletta, a skilled agronomist who has worked on Etna for years. As the vineyard came back to life and the vines began to produce quality fruit, trials were made with the traditional Etna DOC varieties and blends, as a way of understanding the potential of the site. As the health of the vineyard improved and yields increased, they sought assistance from a consulting winery to begin making, aging, and bottling the wines in a modern way. It was *piano piano* (little by little) at first, but the pure Nerello Mascalese named *Aitho*—an ancient nickname for Mount Etna—began rolling off the line. Today, the company has expanded their portfolio to include an Etna Rosato, Etna Bianco, and a Nerello Mascalese vinified in white. Any grapes they don't use are sold to other Etna producers.

I can imagine the Benedictine monks working the fields that stretch out from Feudo Cavaliere. For nearly a millennium the foothills above Santa Maria di Licodia were some of the most fertile and manicured on the mountain. Here, the democratization of the Etna landscape began in earnest through emphyteusis, a program which gave long-term leases to lay parishioners of the church. Margherita Platania's family has been making wine at this site since 1880. Business lulled during the twentieth century, but she relaunched Feudo Cavaliere in 2008, each year restoring more of the ancient labyrinthine palmento and dispensa. While she restored the vineyards, she sold grapes to the local winemaking community. Eight years later, the wine production returned to this sacred site. The new equipment, large wood vats, and stainless steel tanks add a level of awe as you enter the winery, not for their shine, necessarily, but for how they honor the space. With each new vintage, the musts bypass the open lava-stone vats of the palmento to vinify in temperature-controlled stainless steel tanks and fine-grain botte. The sorting table and peristaltic pumps are magic, compared to the ancient ways that relied on moon cycles and gravity, but the intention remains the same. Make a sacred wine, not for what you do to it, but for where the work is done.

Strada Cavaliere Bosco
Santa Maria di Licodia, CT 95038
www.feudocavaliere.it
feudocavaliere@gmail.com
+39 348-734-8377
Founded: 1880
Find the Winery On:
Facebook, Twitter, Pinterest, LinkedIn
Contrada: Cavaliere
Hectares: 15
Vine Training: Alberello, Cordon
Etna DOC Wines: Etna Bianco, Etna Rosato, Etna Rosso, Etna Rosso Riserva
Other Wines: DOC Sicilia
Bottles Produced: 40,000

Visits: Only by request
Hospitality: Vineyard Tour, Winery Tour, Palmento Tour, Wine Tasting
Amenities: Small Groups (<15), Large Groups (15+), Family Friendly
Languages Spoken: Italian, English

Wines to try—
Millemetri Etna Bianco
Don Blasco Etna Rosso
Millemetri Etna Rosso

REALE VINI ETNA

Biancavilla, CT 95033
realevini@libero.it
+39 331-210-5948
Find the Winery On:
Facebook, Twitter, LinkedIn,
YouTube
Contrada: Biancavilla
Hectares: 12
Vine Training: Cordon
Etna DOC Wines: Etna
Bianco, Etna Bianco
Superiore, Etna Rosso, Etna
Rosso Riserva
Other Wines: IGT/IGP Terre
Siciliane
Bottles Produced: 20,000

Visits: Only by request
Hospitality: Vineyard Tour,
Wine Tasting
Amenities: Small Groups
(<15), Family Friendly, Pet
Friendly
Languages Spoken: Italian,
English, French, German,
Mandarin, Portuguese

Wines to try—
Bètula Carricante
Gold (Tierra) Nerello blend
Nerello Mascalese

Did you hear the story about the boy who finds a golden ticket attached to his favorite candy and gets invited to the factory where the candy is made? Reale Vini Etna decided they'd do something similar, but with wine. Two rounds of winners were announced at the end of 2018. All you had to do, as a loyal Reale Vini Etna customer, was buy the wine. Several corks were printed with a winning message, *Hai Vinto* (You Won). If that's the cork you saw when you opened the bottle, you were encouraged to take a selfie with the wine and share it on the Reale Vini Etna Facebook page. That picture went into a raffle at the end of the year. One lucky winner received five cases of wine. What the organizers don't tell you is that these wines come from old alberelli planted at 700 meters AMSL in the hallowed soils around Biancavilla. The technicalities may be important to some, but Reale Vini Etna trusts that you love the wines because you know the wines. They're in the local bars, restaurants, and wine shops. The last bottle you opened, did you see the message? Even if you didn't, you win.

I get excited when I see Masseria Setteporte's wines. Their vineyards, located around Biancavilla, on Etna's southern flank, are renowned for their opulence. It's not the barrels or the treatments. The Portale family has been growing wine here for generations. They know the landscape like the backs of their hands. In the nineteenth century, the estate was dedicated to bulk wines for the local and export market. Piero Portale grew up making simple wines with his father and selling off what they didn't use, but with every passing year, he saw more potential in the landscape. Masseria Setteporte was founded on a selection from their own vines. Drought- and disease-resistant rootstocks were chosen to limit vigor in favor of flavor in this warm and blustery part of the volcano. For the reds, they focused on Nerello Mascalese, with a small quantity of Nerello Cappuccio. The white wine arrived at Carricante with one-third Catarratto. For the first several vintages, they used a consulting cantina to guide the wine into full production. Now, the wine production has moved back to the estate. With every vintage, Piero seems to get one step closer to perfecting a modern version of what the family has always done on this sacred slope of the mountain.

Contrada Setteporte
Biancavilla, CT
95030
masseriasetteporte@email.it
+39-335-533-8152
Founded: 2002
Find the Winery On: Facebook
Contrade: Spadatrappo, Setteporte
Hectares: 10
Vine Training: Alberello, Cordon
Etna DOC Wines: Etna Bianco, Etna Rosso
Other Wines: DOC/DOP Sicilia
Bottles Produced: 30,000

Visits: Only by request
Hospitality: Vineyard Tour, Palmento Tour, Winery Tour, Wine Tasting, Lunch
Amenities: Small Groups (<15)
Languages Spoken: Italian, English, Spanish

Wines to try—
N'Ettaro Etna Bianco
Etna Rosso
Nerello Mascalese

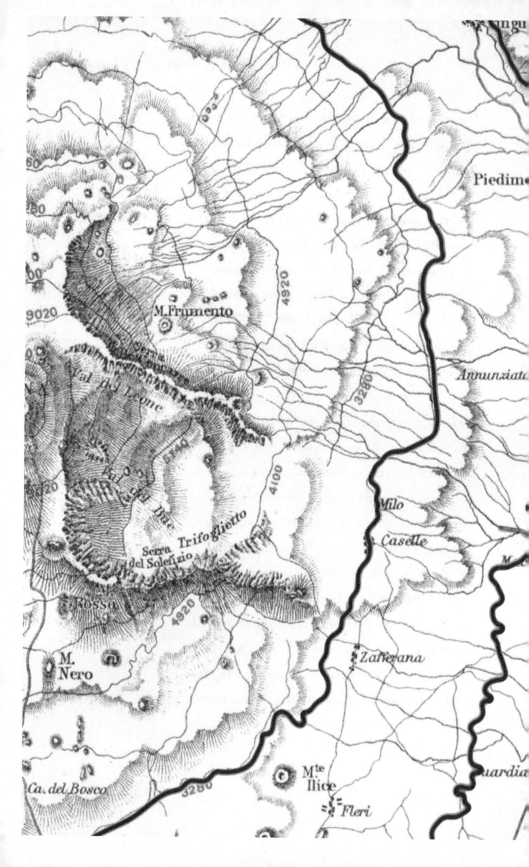

WINERIES ON THE EAST SLOPE

Aeris

Antichi Vini di Sicilia

Antonio Di Mauro

Azienda Agricola Monterosso

Barone Di Villagrande

Benanti

Biondi

Cantine Edomé

Cantine Nicosia

Conte Uvaggio

Etnella

Eudes

Guido Coffa

La Gelsomina

Grottafumata

Murgo

Santa Maria La Nave

Tenuta Monte Gorna

Tenuta Monte Ilice

Tenute Donna Elia

Tenute Mannino di Plachi

Terra Costantino

Terre di Nuna

* For an updated selection of wineries present on the volcano, you can refer to *The Newest New Wines of Etna* on page 327

11715 Skyline Blvd
Los Gatos, CA 95033
www.aeriswines.com
info@aeriswines.com
+1 650-419-2050
Founded: 2010
Find the Winery On: Twitter
Contrade: Caselle,
Montelaguardia
Hectares: 5
Etna DOC Wines: Etna
Bianco Superiore, Etna Rosso
Vine Training: Alberello
Bottles Produced: *

Visits: Only by request

Wine to try—
Etna Bianco Superiore

Kevin Harvey follows his instincts. For the venture capitalist turned California winemaker, a tasting of Benanti's *Pietra Marina* Carricante in 2001 turned his attention to Mount Etna. For Harvey, the Etna Bianco Superiore reminded him of "Grand Cru whites from Burgundy and Alsace. The red wines from Nerello Mascalese also had a streak of magic. They resemble great Pinot Noir." It was a correlation that was being made by others, but it was curiosity and a chance meeting with Etna enologist Salvo Foti that led to the eventual purchase of a vineyard in the hills above Milo, on the volcano's eastern slope. There, they focused exclusively on Carricante. A second vineyard in Montelaguardia, on the volcano's north slope, is dedicated to three biotypes of Nerello Mascalese. Recent vintages have been dedicated to restoring old vines, new plantings and study. Based on the wines being made nearby, the bar for quality is set high. Harvey realizes this. "My intention is not to make an Etna wine just to say 'I have Etna.' I refuse to make a mediocre wine. It has to be special or I won't release it." So far, Harvey likes the results. So much, in fact, that he planted a vineyard at Centennial Mountain, in California, with cuttings of Carricante and Nerello.

* The producer did not respond to requests for comment.

Antonio and Dino Lizzio grew up in the vines. Their family had a small vineyard on the northeast slope outside the historic center of Piedimonte Etneo. Over the years, the brothers followed in their footsteps, working in the vineyard, making the harvest, and producing the wine. While they worked, the stories played out like an echo—the Greeks, the Romans, the myths—but the wines were made in a modern way, with minimal interference in the winery and hundreds of hours in the vineyard. There were no flavored wines. No amphorae. And very little experimentation. When Antonio and Dino decided to make a go of producing their own wine, they wanted to include recipes and techniques of Etna's past. The Etna Bianco and Etna Rosso follow the contemporary blends of Carricante and Nerello, but the other products they introduced include a sweetened almond wine popular with the Moors, an aromatic off-dry Moscato that brought fame to Etna at the turn of the twentieth century, an amphora-aged Nerello, and a passito wine from Nerello Mascalese. It's a lot of different wine to produce when you're only making a few thousand bottles, but the project speaks of a past on the mountain that is rarely a part of today's dialogue.

Via Ragonesi 66
Frazione Presa, Piedimonte
Etneo, CT 95017
www.antichivinidisicilia.it
info@antichivinidisicilia.it
+39 328-056-7257;
+39 340-236-3478
Founded: 2004
Find the Winery On:
Facebook
Contrade: Friera, Terremorte
Hectares: 1.5
Vine Training: Alberello, Cordon
Etna DOC Wines: Etna Bianco, Etna Rosso, Etna Spumante
Other Wines: IGT/IGP Terre Siciliane
Bottles Produced: 5,000

Visits: Only by request
Hospitality: Winery Tour, Wine Tasting
Amenities: Small Groups (<15), Large Groups (15+), Family Friendly, Pet Friendly
Languages Spoken: Italian, English

Wines to try—
Kyathos Rosso Anfora
Mandorvin
Prima Luce Etna Rosso

ANTONIO DI MAURO

SP59 III
Vena-Piedimonte Etneo, CT
95017
www.vinidimauro.com
antonio.dimauro@
vinidimauro.com
+39 340-669-2708
Founded: 2004
Find the Winery On:
Facebook, Twitter, Instagram
Contrada: Fossazza
Hectares: 2
Vine Training: Cordon
Etna DOC Wines: Etna Rosso
Other Wines: IGT/IGP Terre
Siciliane
Bottles Produced: 3,000

Visits: Only by request
Hospitality: Vineyard Tour,
Winery Tour, Palmento Tour,
Wine Tasting, Lunch
Amenities: Small Groups
(<15), Family Friendly
Languages Spoken: Italian,
English

Wines to try—
Giretto Nerello Mascalese
Due Note Red Blend
Kephas Etna Rosso

After fighting in the First World War and laboring in Australian cane fields for a decade, Pietro Patanè returned home to Sicily, to the small farm and a palmento where the family began making wine. With each passing year, the vines produced better grapes and the wines began to sell, first in Vena then in Riposto. Generation to generation, the estate passed hands, and the vineyards continued producing. But after years of struggle, the vines and terraces were reorganized in 2004, with the intention of improving efficiency and quality. That meant simple modernizations, more time with every vine, and minimal intervention in the vinification. One afternoon, Antonio di Mauro was giving me a tour of a restored room adjacent to the family palmento. After years of selling wine in bulk at local markets and fairs, I asked him how it feels to finally have the family wine in bottle. He paused at the window and looked out. "Once you get to know this place, the more of it you sense. Every time I open a bottle it's like experiencing that vintage again. It's more than the weather and the harvest. It is another year of the family history in the glass. That feels very good."

As the sun set on June 28, 1329, Etna had a spectacular lateral eruption, originating on the southeast flank. When the lava cooled, the locals nicknamed the spent crater Monte Rosso, Red Mountain, for the oxidized iron in the soil. Three friends who grew up in the area—Giovanni Ferlito, Aurelio Marconi, and Gianluca Strano—knew the wines that came from the mountain were special. In 2015, they purchased an old, gnarly alberello vineyard on top of the crater. On a walk through the vineyard with Marconi, he says, "We recently had an official audit of our vines. Now that we know what we have, we'll study how each variety performs in this. . . ." Marconi picks up a handful of oxidized volcanic soil and lets some drain out. "The reds love it!" He's right. The reds have a rich profile that benefits directly from the age and composition of the soil, but all the wines have a nerviness that rouses the palate. Marconi leads me to an open area among the vines, with a barbecue, table, and chairs. "We created this space for our guests," he says, looking out at one of the most spectacular vistas on Etna. "The vineyard is where we grow the wine. This is where we meet friends."

Contrada Monte Rosso
Aci Sant'Antonio, CT
www.monterosso.wine
info@monterosso.wine
+39 346-313-9495
Founded: 2015
Find the Winery On:
Facebook, Twitter, Instagram
Contrada: Monte Rosso
Hectares: 1.5
Vine Training: Alberello
Etna DOC Wines: Etna Bianco, Etna Rosso
Other Wines: IGT/IGP Terre Siciliane, DOC/DOP Sicilia
Bottles Produced: 8,000

Visits: Only by request
Hospitality: Vineyard Tour, Wine Tasting
Amenities: Small Groups (<15), Family Friendly, Pet Friendly
Languages Spoken: Italian, English

Wines to try—
Crater Etna Bianco
Sisma Nerello Mascalese
Volcano Etna Rosato

BARONE DI VILLAGRANDE

Via Del Bosco, 25
Milo, CT 95010
www.villagrande.it
info@villagrande.it
+39 095-708-2175
Founded: 1727
Find the Winery On:
Facebook, Twitter, Instagram
Contrade: Villagrande; Monte
Ilice
Hectares: 18
Vine Training: Guyot, Cordon
Etna DOC Wines: Etna
Bianco Superiore, Etna
Rosato, Etna Rosso
Other Wines: IGP Terre
Siciliane; DOC Malvasia delle
Lipari Passito; IGP Salina
Bianco DOC
Bottles Produced: 95,000

Visits: Only by request
Hospitality: Vineyard Tour,
Winery Tour, Palmento Tour,
Wine Tasting, Lunch, Dinner
Amenities: Small Groups
(<15), Large Groups (15+),
Event Space, Wi-Fi, Family
Friendly, Pet Friendly
Languages Spoken: Italian,
English, French

Wines to Try—
Etna Bianco Superiore
Etna Bianco Superiore
Contrada Villagrande
Etna Rosso
Etna Rosso *Contrada
Villagrande*

Long before the Nicolosi-Asmundo family was given the noble title for their viti-vinicultural work in 1726, they had a reputation for making some of the finest wines on the mountain. By 1869, the family was committed to separate vinifications of white and black grapes—instead of fermenting the two together, as was customary for centuries. One hundred years later, while working as professor of enology at the University of Catania, Carlo Nicolosi-Asmundo and colleagues began defining the borders and traditions of what would become the Etna DOC, Sicily's first delimited historic area of production. One of the notable supplements was the creation of Etna's only cru for wine. Wines made from Carricante grown in Milo could be labeled Etna Bianco Superiore. Barone di Villagrande did the initial research that launched the category. Marco Nicolosi-Asmundo leads the winemaking today. The estate includes two sites on Etna, in Contrade Villagrande and Monte Ilice, and on the Aeolian island of Salina. After three-hundred years, the wines continue to attract a worldwide audience. Guests arrive regularly to visit the nineteenth-century modern-traditional winery, lunch in their salon, or vacation at the Etna hotel. Many things have changed over the centuries, but Barone di Villagrande has become more than a beacon for wine. It has become a destination.

Somewhere in the Benanti records is a royal
document asking the "Benati" family of Bologna to
move to Sicily and flourish. Two hundred fifty years
later, Dr. Giuseppe Benanti, a successful pharmacist,
began making fine wines using Carricante, Nerello,
and other varieties. Two decades of unimpeachable
trial and error culminated in 2012, when Giuseppe's
twin sons, Salvino and Antonio, joined the family
wine business. The company immediately doubled
and focused Giuseppe's efforts. "My father did an
incredible amount of research," Salvino Benanti
told my guests in the shade of two persimmon trees
in their Monte Serra vineyard. "What it showed
us was something we already knew. We wanted
to focus only on Etna." To that end, the team
completed a decade-long study of indigenous Etna
yeasts to use in their wines. In the countryside,
they identified and planted sites for small-batch
productions of Carricante, Nerello Mascalese and
Nerello Cappuccio. Their estate in Viagrande, at the
base of Monte Serra, is the best place to find these
limited production wines in one place. Looking over
their archive of awards and articles written about
the winery, it's easy to admire their dedication to
the Etna community. But if we take a step back, it's
rather easily explained as the fulfillment of a promise
made to the King of Sardegna a long, long time ago.

Contrada Monte Serra
Via Giuseppe Garibaldi 361
Viagrande, CT 95029
www.benanti.it
info@benanti.it
+39 095-789-0928
(Wine Tastings);
+39 095-789-3399 (Office)
Founded: 1988
Find the Winery On:
Facebook, Twitter, Instagram
Contrade: Calderara
Sottana, Cavaliere, Dafara
Galluzzo, Monte Serra,
Rinazzo
Hectares: 30
Vine Training: Alberello,
Cordon
Etna DOC Wines: Etna
Bianco, Etna Bianco
Superiore, Etna Rosato, Etna
Rosso, Etna Rosso Riserva,
Etna Spumante
Other Wines: IGT/IGP Terre
Siciliane
Bottles Produced: 200,000

Visits: Only by request
Hospitality: Vineyard Tour,
Winery Tour, Palmento Tour,
Wine Tasting, Lunch, Dinner
Amenities: Small Groups
(<15), Large Groups (15+),
Wi-Fi, Family Friendly, Pet
Friendly
Languages Spoken: Italian,
English, French, Portuguese,
Spanish

Wines to try—
Pietra Marina Etna Bianco
Superiore
Serra della Contessa Etna
Rosso
Nerello Cappuccio
Noblesse Metodo Classico

BIONDI

Via Ronzini 55a
Trecastagni, CT 95039
www.levignebiondi.it
ciro@levignebiondi.it; stef@
levignebiondi.it
+39 392-117-9746
Founded: Early 1900s
Find the Winery On:
Facebook, Twitter, YouTube,
Instagram
Contrada: Ronzini
Hectares: 7
Vine Training: Alberello
Etna DOC Wines: Etna
Bianco, Etna Rosso
Bottles Produced: 27,000

Visits: Seven days a week
Hospitality: Vineyard Tour,
Winery Tour, Wine Tasting,
Lunch
Amenities: Small Groups
(<15), Wi-Fi, Family Friendly
Languages Spoken: Italian,
English

Wines to Try—
Pianta Etna Bianco
Cisterna Fuori Etna Rosso
San Nicolò Etna Rosso

Ciro Biondi's father, Turi, warned him about restarting the family wine business. Turi had seen the weeds and trees and brambles encroach upon their vineyards until the vines were nearly concealed. But as hard as his father pressed, Ciro's attention returned to the vines. "I was curious," he says over dinner one night. "Someone tells you not to do something, it's natural that you want to do it. The family made wine for centuries. A lot of it was sold in bulk. I wondered what we might achieve if we aimed for something better." In 1999, Ciro and Stephanie, his wife and partner, began clearing and replanting the family vineyards. Over the following decade the project took its hits—tough vintages, changing enologists, and continued revitalization—but it kept Ciro and Stephanie coming back to the vineyards and the cellar. Today, the winery, in Contrada Ronzini, is a touchstone for anyone visiting Etna. One recent afternoon, Ciro brought Turi to Chianta, the family vineyard planted in 1860. He was curious what people were coming to see. When Turi saw the lush manicured terraces and vines blushing with ripe fruit leaning against vertical chestnut stakes, he looked at his son and said, "I wish I could have shown this to my father." Ciro responded, "I am the lucky one. I get to share it with you."

It's not easy starting from scratch, unless you know what it takes. Shortly after the Cianci family purchased a plot of alberelli in Contrada Feudo di Mezzo, they planted thousands of Nerello vines. Now, the father and daughter team of Antonio and Paola Cianci are watching over their Carricante vineyard in Contrada Salice, below the main square of Milo. This vineyard was a lucky find. The young alberelli are planted without irrigation in a weathered volcanic sand brindled with lapilli and ripiddu—deposits of the landslide that created the Valle dell Bove. "I don't worry about these vines taking root. It rains in Milo. They'll find the water they need," Antonio says, walking along the edge of the vineyard. "When we planted the vines on the north slope, I worried. It's much drier there. But the vines survived." When I ask him if there's a secret to dry farming on Etna, he says, "You've got to give the vines a good start, but then you stand back. They almost always make a connection with their environment." After years of experimentation, the family started bottling the wines based on the age of the vines and the contrade where they grow, Paola tells me. "This new vineyard will be treated the same way. We're excited to see what the wine will taste like."

Piazza Nettuno 4
Catania, CT 95126
www.cantinedome.com
info@cantinedome.com
+39 328-633-6277
Founded: 2005
Contrade: Feudo Di Mezzo, Salice
Hectares: 4
Vine Training: Alberello
Etna DOC Wines: Etna Bianco Superiore, Etna Rosato, Etna Rosso
Bottles Produced: 17,000

Visits: No services offered

Wines to try—
Aitna Etna Bianco
Aitna Etna Rosso
Vigna Nica Etna Rosso

CANTINE NICOSIA

Via Luigi Capuana 65
Trecastagni, CT 95039
www.cantinenicosia.it
info@cantinenicosia.it
+39 095-780-6767
+39 095-780-9238
Founded: 1898
Find the Winery On:
Facebook, Twitter, Instagram,
YouTube
Contrade: Cancelliere-
Spuligni, Eremo Santa
Emilia, Monte Gorna, Monte
San Nicolò, Ronzini
Hectares: 40
Vine Training: Alberello,
Cordon
Etna DOC Wines: Etna
Bianco, Etna Rosso, Etna
Rosso Riserva, Etna
Spumante
Bottles Produced: 270,000

Visits: Seven days a week
Hospitality: Vineyard Tour,
Winery Tour, Palmento Tour,
Wine Tasting, Lunch, Dinner
Amenities: Small Groups
(<15), Large Groups (15+),
Event Space, Wi-Fi, Family
Friendly, Pet Friendly
Languages Spoken: Italian,
English, Dutch, French,
German, Russian

Wines to try—
Tenute Nicosia Etna Bianco
Sosta Tre Santi Etna Brut
Spumante
Sosta Tre Santi Nerello
Mascalese

By the end of the nineteenth century, the wine bubble on Mount Etna was sagging. There was a lot of fantastic wine available, but fewer merchants were buying it. A young entrepreneur named Francesco Nicosia knew the vineyards and how good the wine was in the Forest of Catania. The town of Trecastagni was, for a time, the hottest producer on the mountain. It was there, in 1898, that he opened a shop to sell wine. Soon, they were blending and making their own vino da pasto from select sites among the southeast craters. The family carried on the tradition for five generations, expanding to Catania and Vittoria until the end of the twentieth century, when the business underwent a massive renovation that included construction of a modern winery and broad improvements in the vineyards at Monte Gorna. Today, Carmelo Nicosia works side by side with his two sons Francesco and Graziano, to bring the work of winemaker Maria Carella and the Etna name to an ever-broader audience. To that end, the new Nicosia winery offers a warm and inviting lounge bar, restaurant, educational tours, and a wine shop that serves and sells every wine the company makes. It's the kind of place Francesco only dreamed of, the moment he opened his doors to the world.

Our family decided to drive up the mountain to Sant'Alfio for dinner one night. Instead of reading the menu, looking down at my plate and the table, I turned around to take in the view. The valley below opens to a stunning vista of the Eastern Sicilian coastline. For many new restaurants, it's important to have an array of Etna wines to choose from. The wine list I was looking at only offered one, Conte Uvaggio. The cantina takes its name from an old Etna ideal—the work of a master blender, who could compose a single wine from disparate or complementary parts. Conte Uvaggio plays with the potential of monovarietal wines as well, opting to feature Carricante and Nerello Mascalese in purity alongside its DOC and IGT blends. The vineyard sites in Linguaglossa and Castiglione di Sicilia contribute to the discussion of potential when sites are combined or kept separate. Theoretically, the potential of each wine comes not only from the site or the mixture of grapes but also from the expertise of the blender. In addition to its line of playful Etna wines, the company promotes a portfolio of jams made from local Etna grapes.

Via John Fitzgerald Kennedy 62A
Acireale, CT 95024
www.conteuvaggio.it
info@conteuvaggio.it
+39 095-293-5423;
+39 328-080-9166
Founded: 2011
Find the Winery On:
Facebook, Twitter, Instagram
Contrade: Piano dei Daini, Arrigo
Hectares: 5
Vine Training: Alberello, Cordon
Etna DOC Wines: Etna Bianco, Etna Rosato, Etna Rosso
Other Wines: IGT/IGP Terre Siciliane, DOC Sicilia
Bottles Produced: 9,000

Visits: Only by request
Hospitality: Vineyard Tour, Winery Tour, Palmento Tour, Wine Tasting, Lunch
Amenities: Small Groups (<15), Large Groups (15+), Wi-Fi, Family Friendly, Pet Friendly
Languages Spoken: Italian, English

Wines to try—
Il Carricante del Conte Etna Bianco
Il Rosato del Conte Etna Rosato
Il Nerello del Conte Etna Rosso

SP 7iii, Contrada Bonanno
Passopisciaro, CT 95012
www.etnella.com
info@etnella.com
+39 338-636-5933
Founded: 2008
Find the Winery On:
Facebook, Twitter, Instagram
Contrade: Nave, Savina,
Pino, Santo Spirito, Feudo di
Mezzo-Porcaria, Crasà, Monte
Dolce, Malpasso, Galfina
Hectares: 7
Vine Training: Alberello,
Cordon
Etna DOC Wines: Etna
Bianco, Etna Rosso
Other Wines: IGT/IGP Terre
Siciliane
Bottles Produced: 18,000

Visits: Only by request
Hospitality: Vineyard Tour,
Wine Tasting, Lunch
Amenities: Small Groups (up
to 15), Event Space, Wi-Fi,
Family Friendly, Pet Friendly,
Overnight Accommodations
Languages Spoken: Italian,
English, French

Wines to try—
Attia Vino Bianco
Kaos Vino Bianco
Kaos Vino Rosso

I remember how hot it was as I pulled off SP59, in the hills above Linguaglossa, and drove higher into Contrada Valle Galfina. When the trees cleared, a series of terraces opened up on the side of the road. Davide Bentivegna was working the vines with his team. This rugged terrain was once the stomping grounds of pioneers, loggers, and monastics. Davide, not strangely, fits the mold for all three. His wines tend to suggest that they are of another time, when *Wine* was wine, the mountain was the mountain, and man worked in unison with them. Taking his lead, the vineyard workers stopped for lunch. We were sitting along a short lava-stone wall and a log in the middle of the vineyard, as Davide's partner in crime, Paolo, gathered everyone's lunch and offered it in communion. An old plastic water bottle was passed around to fill every small cup. There was no explanation or academic analysis of the red wine as we ate and talked, the wine connecting new friends. During a momentary pause in the conversation, I raised my glass and said, "It must have been this way all the time, in the old days. Cheers." Davide translated for his team. Paolo cocked his head a little and smiled. "It's still this way!" On that we toasted.

There are very few people with the enthusiasm and drive of Giovanni Messina. When we first met at the family estate in 2013, the vines planted by his father, Dr. Salvatore Messina—after purchasing the property in 1989—were finally capable of the quality of wine they wanted for a family label. Laura, Giovanni's wife, was translating our conversation. Giovanni talks and moves fast. He showed me the new plantings of Carricante, explaining the plan ahead and up. The Eudes estate rests on a small plateau of the spent volcanic crater Monte Gorna. "Up?" I asked. "Up," Giovanni said, in perfect English. Together, we looked toward the top of the crater. Laura explained, "The property climbs the southeast slope of Monte Gorna to its summit," at 850 meters. I took the information to mean they would get around to it eventually, but five years later the terraces and plantings have been on a continuous procession up the crater toward an old palmento. From this vantage point, halfway up the side of Monte Gorna, it seemed redundant to suggest that the work would be arduous. It's the kind of effort that would wear down the strongest of those who would even try, but every time I see Giovanni his smile is bigger and brighter, and the wines are singing from ever new heights.

Strada Vicinale Minnoliti 14
Trecastagni, CT 95039
www.eudes.it
vini@eudes.it
+39 348-950-6533
Founded: 1989
Find the Winery On:
Facebook, Twitter,
Instagram, Flicker,
Foursquare
Contrada: Monte Gorna
Hectares: 3.5
Vine Training: Alberello,
Cordon
Etna DOC Wines: Etna
Bianco, Etna Rosso, Etna
Rosso Riserva
Bottles Produced: 10,000

Visits: Only by request
Hospitality: Vineyard Tour,
Palmento Tour, Wine Tasting,
Lunch, Dinner
Amenities: Small Groups
(<15), Large Groups (15+),
Wi-Fi, Family Friendly, Pet
Friendly
Languages Spoken: Italian,
English, Spanish

Wines to try—
Bianco di Monte Etna Bianco
Monte Etna Bianco
Milleottocentoquaranta

GUIDO COFFA

Via Monaci Snc
Zafferana Etnea, CT 95019
www.guidocoffa.com
info@monacidelleterrenere.it
amm@monacidelleterrenere.it
+39 095-708-3638
Founded: 2008
Find the Winery On:
Facebook, Instagram,
Pinterest
Contrada: Monaci
Hectares: 25
Vine Training: Alberello,
Cordon
Etna DOC Wines: Etna
Bianco, Etna Rosato, Etna
Rosso
Other Wines: IGT/IGP Terre
Siciliane
Bottles Produced: 9,000

Visits: Only by request
Hospitality: Vineyard Tour,
Palmento Tour, Wine Tasting,
Cocktail Bar, Lunch, Dinner
Amenities: Small Groups
(<15), Large Groups (15+),
Event Space, Wi-Fi, Family
Friendly, Pet Friendly,
Overnight Accommodations,
Helipad
Languages Spoken: Italian,
English

Wines to try—
Etna Bianco
U' Ranaci Grenache Noir
Etna Rosso
Le Viti di Minico Nerello Blend

A few months after arriving on Mount Etna, I was introduced to Guido Coffa in the *bottaia* of his palmento. The large barrels had been substituted with a fireplace, elegant furniture, and a bar, for the guests of his country hotel, Monaci delle Terre Nere. The palmenti and buildings around the property have been restored and then converted to elegant private cottages at the edge of the 1634 lava flow. Guido is a meditative man. He speaks quietly and slowly. "You never know, in life. When I saw this place, it was an immediate sensation. In a second I saw what I wanted to dedicate my time to." Since he bought the estate, in 2007, he has transformed it into a full-service luxury property and an organic farm, but the first plants that took root were vines. The name *Monaci* translates to "monks." For centuries, the monasteries around Zafferana Etnea served the parish and pilgrims. For a time, the grounds were managed under the auspices of the church. In the nineteenth century, the property was reallocated and eventually abandoned. "It was a lot of work," Coffa reminisces, "but everything we do, from the first time I put my shovel into the ground to now, is an attempt to share the living history of this hallowed place."

Every autumn, ripe bunches of Moscato Bianco grapes are laid in broad, shallow boxes to raisin in the sun for a sweet wine. Up the hill from the drying racks the olive, fruit, and nut trees mark every open space. At the top of the hill, finely organized terraces of Carricante, Catarratto, and Nerello Mascalese begin to step down toward a small house that has been restored for visitors. From this vantage point, we can see for miles. Here also, the steep terraces of Moscato vines descend seventy meters, forming a snug amphitheater with a pond at the bottom. According to local legend, the La Gelsomina estate has always been a stop for migrating herons. When the property was abandoned in the twentieth century, the water dried up and the herons stopped coming. Recently, the pond was reconceived. Herons have begun circling and landing again. Now that the cantina is open for visitors, the only problem you have to anticipate is which wine to pair with this impeccable vista.

Via Presa 48
Mascali, CT 95016
www.tenuteorestiadi.it
lagelsomina@tenuteorestiadi.it;
enoturismo@tenuteorestiadi.it
+39 366-684-4071
Founded: 1986
Find the Winery
On: Facebook and Instagram (Tenute Orestiadi)
Contrada: Presa
Hectares: 15
Vine Training: Alberello, Cordon
Etna DOC Wines: Etna Bianco, Etna Rosso, Etna Spumante
Other Wines: IGT/IGP Terre Siciliane
Bottles Produced: 30,000

Visits: On request, Wednesday to Sunday
Hospitality: Vineyard Tour, Winery Tour, Wine Tasting, Lunch, Dinner
Amenities: Groups, Event Space, Family Friendly, Pet Friendly, Overnight Accommodations
Languages Spoken: Italian, English

Wines to try—
Etna Bianco
Etna Rosso
Metodo Classico
Moscato Passito

GROTTAFUMATA

Contrada Monte Ilice
Trecastagni, CT 95039
www.oliogrottafumata.it
aziendagrottafumata@
gmail.com
+39 328-822-6100;
+39 380-302-2789
Founded: 2017
Find the Winery On:
Facebook, Instagram
Contrade: Civita, Guardia
Maio, Monte Gorna, Carpene
Hectares: 4
Vine Training: Alberello
Etna DOC Wines: Etna
Bianco, Etna Rosso
Bottles Produced: 10,000

Visits: Only by request
Hospitality: Vineyard Tour,
Wine Tasting
Amenities: Small Groups
(<15)
Languages Spoken: Italian,
English, French

Wines to try—
Lato Sud Etna Bianco
Lato Sud Etna Rosso

"Growing up in Zafferana Etnea," Mauro Cutuli says, opening a creaky gate and walking into a vineyard on Monte Ilice, "when I looked out my bedroom window, I could see this vineyard." It both inspired and informed him. The old alberelli are spotted with fruit, nut, and olive trees. The volcanic sand crumbles with every step, but there are no terraces. The only thing that anchors here are the vines and other plants. Cutuli points to an old cableway that used to carry tools, water, and grapes up and down the vineyard. "This hasn't worked in years. We have to carry everything by hand." This is a different kind of work than he's used to. After years in finance and working as a sommelier, he returned to Etna and the family farm in Contrada Grotta Fumata, where he produces olive oil (from the local Nocellara Etnea) and a selection of honeys. Tasting his 2017s from the bottling vats, Cutuli confides in me how important this vintage is. "The company was founded by my grandfather in 1977. We made wine until 1995. Now, I'm starting it again, forty years after we began. It's humbling . . . to have this history, and to finally taste this [wine]."

The Scammacca family has been making wine around Mount Etna for a very long time, but the modern winery took a new step forward in 1969, when broad terraces of new vines were planted in the hills above Santa Venerina, on the volcano's eastern flank. Michele Scammacca is Murgo's winemaker. "I remember watching the Moon landing on television and hearing my family talking about the new vines. These were not the Etna alberelli; they were cordon. Without the alberello, we find the flavors of Nerello are much improved," Scammacca says, leading me through the aging room for their metodo classico. Through the seventies and eighties Murgo focused on producing premium quality wines from Sicilian and international varieties. By 1989, they also had a recipe for a bottle-fermented Nerello—in bianco and rosato. Two decades later, the Etna DOC added the Etna Spumante category to their bylaws, based on Scammacca's work. [The Murgo *Brut* was the first Nerello Mascalese I ever tasted.] These days, Murgo (*Tenuta San Michele*) offers in-depth educational tours, guided wine tastings and family-style lunches that feature wines from their estate. Just up the hill from the restaurant, the estate's agriturismo boasts an impressive view of the Valle del Bove and the southeast slope of the volcano. It's one of the most beautiful places on the mountain.

Via Zafferana 13
Santa Venerina, CT 95010
www.murgo.it
info@murgo.it
+39 095-950520
Founded: 1860
Find the Winery On:
Facebook, Instagram, Flickr
Contrada: Cancelliere, San Michele
Hectares: 55
Vine Training: Cordon
Etna DOC Wines: Etna Bianco, Etna Rosato, Etna Rosso, Etna Spumante
Other Wines: IGT/IGP Terre Siciliane, Vino Locale / Sfuso
Bottles Produced: 230,000

Visits: Seven days a week
Hospitality: Vineyard Tour, Winery Tour, Palmento Tour, Wine Tasting, Lunch, Dinner
Amenities: Small Groups (<15), Large Groups (15+), Event Space, Wi-Fi, Family Friendly, Pet Friendly, Overnight Accommodations
Languages Spoken: Italian, English, French, German

Wines to try—
Etna Bianco
Brut Metodo Classico
Pinot Nero
Cabernet Sauvignon

SANTA MARIA LA NAVE

Via Sebastiano Catania, 137
Catania, CT 95123
www.santamarialanave.com
sonia@santamarialanave.com
+39 346-222-7606
Founded: 2009
Find the Winery On:
Facebook, Twitter, Instagram,
Pinterest
Contrade: Nave, Monte Ilice
Hectares: 5
Vine Training: Alberello,
Guyot, Cordon
Etna DOC Wines: Etna Rosso
Other Wines: IGT/IGP Terre
Siciliane, DOC Sicilia
Bottles Produced: 10,000

Visits: Only by request
Hospitality: Vineyard Tour,
Palmento Tour, Wine Tasting,
Lunch, Dinner
Amenities: Small Groups
(<15), Wi-Fi, Family Friendly,
Pet Friendly
Languages Spoken: Italian,
English

Wines to try—
Millesulmare Grecanico
Dorato
Calmarossa Etna Rosso
Tempesta Classic Method
Spumante

Sonia Spadaro and Riccardo Mulone met for the first time during a dinner with their two families. Almost twenty years later, not remembering that they had shared the previous encounter, they once again sat across the table from one another. This time, there was a bottle of wine between them. Riccardo's family had been making wine since they moved to Etna from Enna, in the 1950s. In the 1980s they began experimenting with their own grapes. Sonia didn't drink wine, but she was curious. Six years after their meeting, she is a trained sommelier and her company, Santa Maria La Nave, is one of Etna's exciting young wineries. The first vines were planted in Contrada Nave, at 1,100 meters AMSL. Here, outside of the Etna DOC, a selection of Grecanico Dorato produces the savory *Millesulmare*. A vibrant metodo classico sparkler comes from a cooler part of the same vineyard. From the spent volcanic crater Monte Ilice, on the southeast slope of the mountain, Sonia makes a single-vineyard Etna Rosso from prephylloxera and old-vine Nerello. While working in this vineyard with the previous owner, Don Alfio, they discovered relic varieties among the Nerello. Slowly, she has begun propagating the plants. "Sonia's excitement is contagious," Riccardo says, during a tasting in the vineyard. "I might have introduced her to wine, but she has shown me the wonder of it."

Signore Rosario Licciardello and his wife, Santina Cipolla, grew up in a post-World War II Etna, hearing stories about another, better time. Rosario and Santina's children—Arianna, Sebastiano, and Stefania—were raised with stories about their grandfather, a *capu* (boss) at one of the local palmenti. Wine was in their blood, but by the 1990s, the family just didn't make wine anymore. A chance came to sell the property or do something with it. "Sometimes," Sebastiano says, "passion comes to you." In 2001, Rosario began by replanting and organizing the family's vines in the high valley behind Monte Gorna, a lateral volcanic crater from an eruption in 396 BCE. After years of making various decisions about the vines, wines, and the business, it seemed to Rosario that you could change your mind about everything except the terroir. "We could do one thing or another," he says, sitting across from me in the winery's new tasting room. "But the wines always taste like this place." Tenuta Monte Gorna's vines of Carricante, Catarratto, Nerello Mascalese, and Nerello Cappuccio are planted in fertile volcanic sands, surrounded by a pine forest, ginestra, olive and fruit trees, and fields of wild flowers. You cannot fake the bucolic charm of these wines. They are reminiscent of a younger, softer Etna, when the seasons rather than clocks set the pace.

Contrada Monte Gorna/Carpene
Trecastagni, CT 95039
www.tenutamontegorna.it
info@tenutamontegorna.it
+39 328-778-8989;
+39 327-424-1853
Founded: 1998
Find the Winery On:
Facebook, Twitter, Instagram
Contrada: Monte Gorna/Carpene
Hectares: 4.5
Vine Training: Alberello, Cordon
Etna DOC Wines: Etna Bianco, Etna Rosso, Etna Rosso Riserva
Other Wines: DOC Sicilia
Bottles Produced: 20,000

Visits: Only by request
Hospitality: Vineyard Tour, Winery Tour, Wine Tasting, Lunch, Dinner
Amenities: Small Groups (<15), Large Groups (15+), Family Friendly, Pet Friendly
Languages Spoken: Italian, English, Spanish

Wines to try—
Etna Bianco
Etna Rosato
Etna Rosso

Via Ronzini 154
Trecastagni, CT 95039
www.tenutamonteilice.com
info@tenutamonteilice.com
+39 095-780-1477;
+39 346-303-0250
Founded: 2005
Find the Winery On:
Facebook
Contrada: Ronzini
Hectares: 6
Vine Training: Alberello,
Cordon
Etna DOC Wines: Etna
Bianco, Etna Rosato, Etna
Rosso
Other Wines: IGT/IGP Terre
Siciliane
Bottles Produced: 25,000

Visits: Only by request
Hospitality: Vineyard Tour,
Palmento Tour, Wine Tasting
Amenities: Small Groups
(<15), Large Groups (15+),
Event Space, Wi-Fi, Family
Friendly, Pet Friendly,
Overnight Accommodations
Languages Spoken: Italian,
English

Wines to try—
Asia Catarratto
Etna Bianco
Etna Rosso

Giacinto and Pina were looking to buy a property for the family. They considered it good fortune that the keystone over the door of the palmento featured the letters of their surnames, Romeo and Leone. They bought the original 12-acre (5 ha) property in 2004 and enjoyed one of the most arresting views on Etna for the next two years. But it was an awful lot of land to keep for themselves. In 2006, they began developing the property. It started with a series of terraces planted to Catarratto, Carricante, and Nerello Mascalese. Then the terraces started to multiply. As the vines began producing, the Romeos turned their attention to the restoration of the buildings, roads, and walkways, with the long-term goal of opening the estate to visitors. The first wines were made from the 2010 vintage. Today, the Romeo family offers their line of Etna DOC and IGT/IGP Terre Siciliane wines paired with a breathtaking view of the eastern flank of the volcano and the Ionian Sea. Giacinto and Pina's son, Salvo, helps manage the estate. He's also a jazz musician. Leading me to an overlook, he says, "It's been a busy period, but when you're up here, you forget about everything. You feel Etna's rhythm. Wine is nature's way of adding a little harmony."

I was introduced to the Donna Elia wines just as the winery was releasing their first bottles. They were looking for representation, a twenty-first century salesman, someone to introduce the portfolio to a broader market. Tasting the wines, one thing was clear. These are not wines of the times. They are, however, a wine of a moment, a particular part of the day, in fact, when the sun rises to an apex in the sky and its celestial movement seems to be arrested. On Etna, everything and everyone, everywhere, slows down with it. Even the breezes seem to take a break. The leaves and tendrils cease to flicker about. The workmen put down their tools. The dogs stop barking to find a cool bit of shade. And the plumes of smoke rising from homes across the countryside rise from their chimneys. The following hours of warm, intense sunlight are consumed by the vines, almost in private. If not for the harvest and vinification, we might not otherwise be privy to the number of these moments in a growing season. The estate—located in the hills between Piedimonte Etneo Linguaglossa—gets plenty of them. But once the sun gets moving again, it tucks behind the shoulder of the mountain rather quickly, giving the grapes a long phase in which to cool down, relax, and prepare for another day in the sun.

Via Bardazzi Chiuse del Signore 1
Piedimonte Etneo, CT 95017
info@donnaelia.it
+39 328-406-3963;
+39 328-406-3964
Founded: 2012
Contrada: Chiuse del Signore
Hectares: 2
Vine Training: Alberello, Cordon
Etna DOC Wines: Etna Bianco, Etna Rosso
Other Wines: DOC/DOP Sicilia
Bottles Produced: 7,000

Visits: Only by request
Hospitality: Vineyard Tour, Winery Tour, Palmento Tour, Wine Tasting
Amenities: Small Groups (<15), Wi-Fi, Family Friendly, Pet Friendly
Languages Spoken: Italian, English, French

Wines to try—
Etna Bianco
Etna Rosso

Via Sciarelle 32
Viagrande, CT 95029
www.tenutemannino.com
info@tenutemannino.com
+39 095-316849;
+39 348-260-6259
Founded: 1863
Find the Winery On:
Facebook, Twitter, Instagram
Contrade: Pietramarina/
Bragaseggi, Le Sciarelle
Hectares: 9
Vine Training: Alberello,
Cordon
Etna DOC Wines: Etna
Bianco, Etna Rosso, Etna
Spumante
Other Wines: IGT/IGP Terre
Siciliane
Bottles Produced: 30,000

Visits: Seven days a week
Hospitality: Vineyard Tour,
Palmento Tour, Wine Tasting,
Lunch, Dinner
Amenities: Small Groups
(<15), Large Groups (15+),
Event Space, Wi-Fi, Family
Friendly, Pet Friendly,
Overnight Accommodations
Languages Spoken: Italian,
English, French

Wines to try—
Caterina di Plachi Etna
Spumante
Tenuta Mannino di Plachi
Etna Bianco
Tenuta Mannino di Plachi
Etna Rosso

The Mannino family was one of the earliest producers to receive international acclaim for their bottled wines, back in the 1870s. Since then, the three family estates have seen several shifts of political and economic changes, and the evolution of the Etna DOC as one of Italy's most important terroirs. Giuseppe Mannino was the president of the Etna DOC for more than a decade. During that time he watched the restoration of the countryside. He was also managing his own estates, two white wines from Carricante, three red wines from Nerello, including an occasional Etna Riserva, a vintage Etna Spumante from Nerello, and a 160-acre (65 ha) citrus and olive farm that produces oil and marmalades. It's the kind of work three or four people might handle. There are always more expectations in the wings. Mannino handles it all with poise. He grins when asked about the successes that Etna has seen in the international market over the last several years. He pauses before speaking. In that pause, he receives and handles a short business call, then answers my question without missing a beat. "It's not that something has changed. Etna has always been this way. We have always farmed the mountain and made these wines. People are simply paying attention again."

Fabio Costantino smiles when he remembers making wine as a child. "I remember the aromas of the fermentation the most. Every year was similar and different," he tells me one afternoon. The Costantino family began working in Contrada Blandano in the seventies, but wine has been made on this site dating back to the seventeenth century. In the beginning, Fabio recalls, "We made everything in the palmento, by hand, and we sold the wine by the liter from the cellar door." A portion of their production is still sold this way. The family invested in technology as they went, completing a modern subterranean winery in time for the 2015 harvest. In the vineyards, the Nerello, Carricante, and indigenous Sicilian varieties are grown *maritato*—with black and white grapes side by side—using certified organic practices. This is not a fad or innovation. These are Etna's oldest viticultural traditions. Though the grapes are grown together, Fabio harvests them separately, handles them delicately, and only releases the wines when they are ready. "When we started making wine," Fabio says, "we were drinking it ourselves and sharing it with friends. Now we are more curious. What else can the farm tell us?" Tasting the wines, it's hard not to agree with the process. Sometimes, you really do just need to follow your nose.

Via Garibaldi 417
Viagrande, CT 95029
www.terracostantino.it
info@terracostantino.it
+39 095-434288
Founded: 1978
Find the Winery On:
Facebook, Twitter, Instagram
Contrada: Blandano
Hectares: 10
Vine Training: Alberello, Cordon
Etna DOC Wines: Etna Bianco, Etna Rosato, Etna Rosso
Other Wines: DOC Sicilia
Bottles Produced: 40,000

Visits: Only by request
Hospitality: Vineyard Tour, Winery Tour, Palmento Tour, Wine Tasting
Amenities: Small Groups (<15), Large Groups (15+), Event Space, Wi-Fi, Family Friendly, Pet Friendly
Languages Spoken: Italian, English

Wines to try—
Contrada Blandano Etna Bianco
deAetna Etna Rosato
deAetna Etna Rosso
Rasola Vino Rosato

TERRE DI NUNA

SP59 3
Sant'Alfio CT, 95010
nunatra@virgilio.it
+39 333-335-9060
Founded: 2010
Find the Winery On:
Facebook
Contrada: Cavagrande
Hectares: 3.5
Vine Training: Spaliera,
Guyot
Bottles Produced: 5,000
Etna DOC Wine: Etna Bianco

Visits: On request
Hospitality: Vineyard Tour,
Wine Tasting
Amenities: Small Groups
(<15), Family Friendly, Pet
Friendly
Languages Spoken: Italian,
English

Wine to try—
Etna Bianco

The dinner was at the home of local wine expert Brandon Tokash and his bride, filmmaker Lidia Rizzo. In attendance were Fabio Percolla and Maria 'Nuna' Novella. Halfway through the meal Brandon mentioned the new Carricante vineyard that Fabio and Maria had planted. Little did I know that the vineyard, positioned along the 1971 lava flow, where I had been stopping with guests for years, was theirs. For me, the location is an ideal example of beauty and adaptation on Etna. The rows of vines literally hug the hardened lava flow beneath the dramatic cliffs of the Valle del Bove. Listening to Fabio talk about the farm and the vines over dinner that night, I couldn't help feel that all the effort was a romantic gesture to his wife, for whom the wine was eventually named. I was finally able to taste the first wine during a recent Contrade dell'Etna event, which features Etna wines in *anteprima*. A sketch of a cat on the Terre di Nuna label seemed to suggest a playful, or less-serious wine. To the contrary, it has a lot of stuffing. I told Fabio, "This is good. What's up with the label?" He smiled and said, "Everyone's always so serious when it comes to wine. We've put so much work into this. We wanted to lighten things up a bit."

Terraces of young Carricante vines climb toward the Valle del Bove in Contrada Rinazzo, in Milo, on the eastern slope of the volcano. This is Etna Bianco Superiore territory, but it is also one of the most intricate crossroads for fine wine in the world. Photo courtesy of Benanti Viticoltori.

WINERIES ON THE NORTH SLOPE

Aitala

Al-Cantàra

Alta Mora

Antichi Vinai 1877

Azienda Agricola Francesco Modica

Azienda Agricola Siciliano

Azienda Agricola Sciara

Calabretta

Calcagno

Camarda

Cantine Russo

Cantine Valenti

Contrada Santo Spirito di Passopisciaro

Cottanera

Destro

Don Michele

Donnafugata

Duca di Salaparuta

Eduardo Torres Acosta

Enò-Trio

Etna Wine – Fratelli Grasso

Fattorie Romeo del Castello

Feudo Arcurìa

Feudo Vagliasindi

Federico Graziani

Filippo Grasso

Firriato–Cavanera

Fischetti

Frank Cornelissen

Giovanni Rosso

Girolamo Russo

Graci

Gurrida

I Custodi dell e vigne dell 'Etna

Irene Badalà

Masseria del Pino

Nicola Gumina

Palmento Costanzo

Passopisciaro

Patria

Pietradolce

Planeta

Quantico

Scilio

SRC

Stanzaterrena

Tenuta Di Aglaea

Tenuta Benedetta

Tenuta Delle Terre Nere

Tenuta Di Fessina

Tenuta Pietro Caciorgna

Tenuta Tascante

Tenute Bosco

Tenuta Paratore

Terrazze Dell'Etna

Terre Di Trente

Theresa Eccher

Tornatore

Torre Mora

Vini Ferrara Sardo

Vini Gambino

Vini Scirto

Vino Nibali

Vivera

Wiegner

* For an updated selection of wineries present on the volcano, you can refer to *The Newest New Wines of Etna* on page 327

AITALA

Via Domenico Gagini 13
Linguaglossa, CT 95015
www.aitalavini.it
info@aitalavini.it; aitala@
hotmail.it
+39 095-777-4113;
+39 333-906-9834
Founded: 2002
Find the Winery On:
Facebook
Contrade: Martinella,
Pomiciaro, Terremorte
Hectares: 3
Vine Training: Cordon
Etna DOC Wines: Etna
Bianco, Etna Rosso
Other Wines: DOC/DOP
Sicilia
Bottles Produced: 8,000

Visits: Only by request
Hospitality: Vineyard Tour,
Palmento Tour, Wine Tasting
Amenities: Small Groups
(<15), Family Friendly, Pet
Friendly
Languages Spoken: Italian,
English

Wine to try—
Etna Bianco
Etna Rosso

At the beginning of the nineteenth century, the Trefiletti family was one of thousands immigrating to America. They quickly realized that the United States was not Sicily and returned to their mountain home. Shortly after arriving on Mount Etna, Carmine Trefiletti planted vineyards around Castiglione, on the north flank of the volcano. He wasn't after fame or fortune. He was carrying on the tradition of his family. Every year, the new wines were shipped from the Port of Riposto to locations around the Mediterranean. The family winery is continued today by Rocco Trefiletti, with vineyards located on the breezy northeast slope around Piedimonte Etneo and Linguaglossa. The vines are managed organically, in cordon, at variable elevations between 500 and 700 meters AMSL. The arms of the vines are kept short and close to the trunk to concentrate flavors and the energy of each plant. A manual harvest delivers clean ripe grapes to the cantina, where the wines are vinified at cool temperatures and stored until release, but only if it's a good vintage and the grapes reach full maturity. If they do not arrive at an optimum level of quality, the wines are declassified or sold in bulk. It's a tough decision some years, but Trefiletti is confident that it's the right decision. A wine with *Etna* on the label has to be good.

This winery takes its name from the Alcantara River, which borders the estate. The Al-Cantàra vineyards span a broad plateau along the Etna DOC's northernmost border. Their playful labels, and the names of the wines, draw connections between wine and Sicilian culture. The imagery extends to the estate, a place with its own history. In the early twentieth century, the farm was part of one of the largest properties between Randazzo and Passopisciaro. Some of these vines are still in production. During WWII, the farm was used as a campsite for a military hospital. Soldiers found respite in the shade of the old trees, olive groves, and in the spaces between the Nerello vines. Forty years later, many of those old, ornate alberelli were grubbed up and burned. The remaining vines were reorganized into rows, to make the farming easier. You can't blame them. Much of the vineyard is composed of ripiddu (fist-size basalt stones) from an eruption of the Ellittico volcano. Holding one of those stones in my hand, the message these wines convey is clear: one needs a fair amount of humor and humility to live and work on an active volcano.

Contrada Feudo S. Anastasia, SP89
Randazzo, CT 95036
www.al-cantara.it
info@al-cantara.it
+39 095-339430;
+39 339-339-2350
Founded: 2005
Find the Winery On: Facebook, Instagram, Pinterest
Contrada: Feudo Sant'Anastasia
Hectares: 15
Vine Training: Alberello, Guyot, Cordon
Etna DOC Wines: Etna Bianco, Etna Rosato, Etna Rosso, Etna Rosso Riserva
Other Wines: IGT/IGP Terre Siciliane, DOC/DOP Sicilia
Bottles Produced: 100,000

Visits: Only by request
Hospitality: Vineyard Tour, Winery Tour, Wine Tasting, Lunch
Amenities: Small Groups (<15), Large Groups (15+), Family Friendly, Pet Friendly
Languages Spoken: Italian, English

Wines to try—
O'Scuru O'Scuru Etna Rosso
Amuri di Fimmina e Amuri di Matri Etna Rosato
Lu Disìu Nerello Mascalese Passito

Contrada Verzella
Castiglione Di Sicilia, CT
95012
www.altamora.it
info@cusumano.it
+39 091-890-8713
Founded: 2013
Find the Winery On:
Facebook, Twitter, Instagram,
YouTube
Contrade: Guardiola, Feudo
Di Mezzo, Pietramarina,
Verzella, Solicchiata, Arrigo.
Hectares: 33
Vine Training: Alberello,
Guyot
Etna DOC Wines: Etna
Bianco, Etna Rosato, Etna
Rosso, Etna Rosso Riserva
Sicilia
Bottles Produced: 100,000

Visits: Only by request
Hospitality: Vineyard Tour,
Winery Tour, Palmento Tour,
Wine Tasting
Amenities: Small Groups
(<15), Wi-Fi, Family Friendly,
Pet Friendly
Languages Spoken: Italian,
English

Wines to try—
Etna Bianco
Feudo di Mezzo Etna Rosso
Guardiola Etna Rosso

After visiting Mount Etna on multiple occasions over eight years, in search of a site for the company's expanding portfolio of wines, Alberto Cusumano was shown a terraced vineyard in the hills above Passopisciaro, at the edge of an old forest perched above the 1879 lava flow in Contrada Guardiola. It was love at first "site." Other vineyards, in coveted districts on the volcano's north slope, were also available. In February 2013, Cusumano bought each property. That fall, in preparation for the harvest, Alberto transported the necessary tools, machines, and tanks from Palermo to Etna, but the only space the consulting cantina could offer them was outside the winery. The 2013 vintage presented one challenge after another. It was cold and rainy, and problems with the grapes and logistics made everything slow going. When the electricity went out one night, Alberto used the headlights of his car to continue working. "In Palermo, the harvest goes easy," he says. "It was the most difficult vintage I had ever experienced." The following year, the company's eco-conscious, subterranean, gravity-operated winery was built to anticipate every potential setback that Etna could present. No expense was spared. When they finally tasted and released the finished Carricante and Nerello from the 2013 vintage, it became obvious that every ounce of the struggle was worth the wine.

The Gangemi family has been trading wine on Etna since 1877, in the beginning as winegrowers and merchants and later as a family-operated winery. Today, the fourth generation manages a modern cantina in the heart of Passopisciaro, on Etna's north slope. At the seaside, in the historic port town of Riposto, the company has a modern wine shop—once a proper *scanno*, where patrons could rest and drink their wine. As fashionable as Etna has become, Antichi Vinai remains a staunch advocate for the longstanding local traditions. Apart from being one of the only wineries on the mountain to use chestnut as a regular part of their aging scheme, the cellar also acts as an incubator for new wineries. Many of them have gone on to have their own cantinas. Marco Gangemi pours two glasses of Etna Rosso Riserva and sits across from me in their hospitality area, in Passopisciaro. When I ask what it's like to be the fourth generation in his family to make wine, he pauses. "We've gotten very good at adapting. Every couple of years the focus changes," Gangemi says. "First, it was 'quality.' Then everyone was talking about how to market your wine better. Now, it's 'tourism.' You leave all of that aside, we have always had wine."

Via Castiglione 49
Passopisciaro, Castiglione di
Sicilia, CT 95012
www.antichivinai.it
info@antichivinai.it
+39 094-298-3232
Founded: 1877
Find the Winery On:
Facebook, Instagram
Contrade: Feudo di Mezzo,
San Lorenzo
Hectares: 49
Vine Training: Alberello,
Cordon
Etna DOC Wines: Etna
Bianco, Etna Rosato, Etna
Rosso, Etna Rosso Riserva,
Etna Spumante
Other Wines: IGT Terre
Siciliane, DOC Sicilia
Bottles Produced: 350,000

Visits: Only by request
Hospitality: Vineyard Tour,
Winery Tour, Wine Tasting,
Lunch
Amenities: Small Groups
(<15), Large Groups (15+),
Event Space, Wi-Fi, Family
Friendly, Pet Friendly
Languages Spoken: Italian,
English, French

Wines to try—
Koinè Etna Rosso Riserva
Petralava Etna Rosso
1877 Etna Metodo Classico
Millesimato

AZIENDA AGRICOLA FRANCESCO MODICA

Via Soldato Cavallaro, 27
Contrada Sciara Nuova
Randazzo (CT) 95036
www.aziendamodica.it
info@aziendamodica.it
+39 339-109-4260
Founded: 1968
Find the Winery On:
Facebook, Instagram
Contrada: Sciara Nuova
Hectares: 2.5
Vine Training: Alberello,
Cordon
Etna DOC Wines: Etna
Rosato, Etna Rosso
Other Wines: VDT (Vino da
Tavola)
Bottles Produced: 15,000

Visits: Only by request
Hospitality: Vineyard Tour,
Winery Tour, Palmento Tour,
Wine Tasting
Amenities: Small Groups
(<15), Family Friendly, Pet
Friendly
Languages Spoken: Italian

Wines to try—
Nonno Ciccio Etna Rosso
Sciauru Bianco
Terre dei Modica Rosso

Back in 1968, the Etna DOC was just getting started. Putting the vineyards on a legal footing gave the wines added clout. For Peppina and Francesco Modica, the idea of a family winery emerged from a far simpler plan. The stony vineyard surrounded by olive and fruit trees in Contrada Sciara Nuova was the idyllic place to raise their children. The wine they made they could sell as Vino Semplice or Etna DOC. There were no markets of interest beyond the economy of the family. Today, the bottles are sold widely, but the modesty under which the Francesco Modica winery operates remains the same. The two white wines play with traditional Carricante blends, by including 40% of Grecanico. The reds are made from Nerello Mascalese, but the *Terre dei Modica Rosso* also includes a small percentage of Grecanico. The one pure Etna DOP Nerello is named *Nonno Ciccio*, for Salvatore Modica's grandfather, the co-founder of the farm. Salvatore continues to ferment his two reds in an open lava-stone vat—before pressing to stainless steel vats and barriques for aging—making it one of the last places on the mountain to ferment this way legally. When everything else has changed so much, I like to think that this one thing contributes something special to the red wines.

As you drive through the curves of SS120 between Solicchiata and Passopisciaro, take your foot off the gas. You don't want to miss the entrance to Dr. Rocco Siciliano's estate, an unassuming plateau of vines in Contrada Marchesa. This small plot of local and international varieties, including mixed Pinot Nero clones, was used to buttress the idea that Etna could challenge Burgundy to a wine-off and win. It's an easy comparison on some levels, but his single-barrel Pinot Nero takes up far less space in the cellar than the Cabernets Franc and Sauvignon, two Etna Rossos, and a savory Carricante that arrives from a three-day maceration on the skins. "By the time the farm came to full production, I realized there are a lot of roads one can choose when making wine on Mount Etna," Dr. Siciliano tells me, overlooking his vineyard from a stone tower behind the cellar. "After years of making wines by the book, I began limiting aggressive decisions in the vineyard and in the cellar. The wines are different than they were, of course. I prefer the new wines more." It's impossible to understand the amount of work that this decision requires from the road. You need to see the vines and taste the wine. You have to slow down as you enter the curve.

SS 120, Km 194.8
Castiglione di Sicilia, CT
95012
www.vinisiciliano.it
sicilianoetna@gmail.com
+39 349-818-8484
Founded: 1987
Find the Winery On: Facebook, Instagram
Contrada: Marchesa
Hectares: 2
Vine Training: Cordon
Etna DOC Wines: Etna Bianco, Etna Rosso
Other Wines: IGT/IGP Terre Siciliane, Vino Spumante
Bottles Produced: 8,000

Visits: Only by request
Hospitality: Vineyard Tour, Wine Tasting
Amenities: Small Groups (<15), Family Friendly, Pet Friendly
Languages Spoken: Italian, English

Wines to try—
Rossoeuphoria Pinot Nero
Magipirò Cabernet blend
Nonna Aurelia Etna Rosso

AZIENDA AGRICOLA SCIARA

Contrada Taccione SS120
Randazzo, CT 95036
www.sciaraetna.com
sciaravolcanicwine@gmail.com
+39 366 8232180;
+39 328 2071785
Founded: 2015
Find the Winery On:
Instagram
Contrade: Barbabecchi, Carrana, Feudo di Mezzo, Montedolce, Nave, Rampante, Sciara Nuova, Taccione, Tartaraci
Hectares: 8.3
Vine Training: Alberello
Etna DOC Wines: Etna Bianco, Etna Rosso, Etna Rosso Riserva
Other Wines: IGT/IGP Terre Siciliane; DOC/DOP Sicilia
Bottles Produced: 12,500

Visits: Only by request
Hospitality: Vineyard Tour, Winery Tour, Wine Tasting, Lunch, Dinner
Amenities: Small Groups (<15), Family Friendly, Event Space, Accommodations
Languages Spoken: Italian, English, French, Cantonese

Wines to try—
630 Etna Rosso
760 Etna Rosso
980 Etna Rosso

When I was a sommelier in training, my wine director made me watch the uncorking of a 1945 Château Léoville-Las Cases on YouTube. It was, for my boss, the model execution of a duty that I would be expected to repeat for some of our guests. Stef Yim, the managing partner of Azienda Sciara, was the sommelier who flawlessly opened a sixty-year-old bottle of wine in front of a live audience. I didn't make the connection until he and I were in the vineyard of his agriturismo, in Montelaguardia. Somewhere in his personal revelations about making wine from vineyards on Etna's north flank, I heard the contemplative voice of the sommelier from the video. After years of working as an educator and importer, "I realized something," he said. "All of the wines I fell in love with were volcanic! But when I tasted those wines against each other, Etna won. Every time." The parcels he now farms are small, as are the quantities he produces, but rather than focus on Etna's contrade system for his boutique winery, Yim features Nerello Mascalese grown at 630, 750, and 980 meters AMSL. "Elevation is where we sense the real changes in Nerello," he adds. Putting a few of his wines on the patio table, he hands me the corkscrew and says, "Let's open some bottles."

Massimiliano Calabretta is a professor of electrical power systems at the University of Genoa. In 1997, he and his father, Massimo, established a facility to begin bottling the wines from the family's vineyard holdings. "We weren't interested in reinventing a wheel," Massimiliano tells me, as we descended into the cellar where he keeps the wood vats. "We wanted to understand the volcanic terroir and the local grapes. The Minella Bianca is a good example. I started fermenting it alone, without the Carricante or Catarratto. Another winemaker asked me why I wanted to make wine with a terrible grape. I told him I want to know how *terrible* it is!" In truth, the Minella is quite good, if only made in small quantities—and it's the only pure Minella produced on the mountain, even though the grape is planted in nearly every vineyard. A Pinot Nero—from eight different clones—and a pure Nerello Cappuccio followed. Most of the wines are bottled as IGT Terre Siciliane and vino da tavola. The more the father and son team studied the vines and how the treatments and containers adjusted the lifespan of the wines, the more intimate and less invasive their strategies became. "We want to be logical, of course," Massimiliano says. "But wine is natural. We don't want to overthink it."

Via Bonaventura 178A
Randazzo, CT 95036
www.calabretta.net
info@calabretta.net
+39 328-456-5050
Founded: Early 1900s
Find the Winery On:
Facebook
Contrade: Calderara/
Calderara Sottana, Feudo di
Mezzo, Solicchiata, Battisti/
Zocconero, Taccione
Hectares: 10
Vine Training: Alberello,
Guyot, Cordon
Etna DOC Wines: Etna Rosso
Other Wines: IGT/IGP Terre
Siciliane, VDT (Vino da
Tavola)
Bottles Produced: 60,000

Visits: Only by request
Hospitality: Vineyard Tour,
Winery Tour, Palmento Tour,
Wine Tasting
Amenities: Small Groups
(<15), Family Friendly, Pet
Friendly
Languages Spoken: Italian,
English

Wines to try—
Gaio Gaio Vino Rosso
Piede Franco Vino Rosso
Pinot Nero

CALCAGNO

Via Regina Margherita 153
Passopisciaro, CT 95012
www.vinicalcagno.it
info@vinicalcagno.it
+39 338-777-2780
Founded: 2007
Find the Winery On:
Facebook, Twitter, Instagram,
LinkedIn
Contrade: Arcurìa, Feudo di
Mezzo
Hectares: 6
Vine Training: Alberello,
Cordon
Etna DOC Wines: Etna
Bianco, Etna Rosato, Etna
Rosso
Other Wines: IGT/IGP Terre
Siciliane
Bottles Produced: 25,000

Visits: Only by request
Hospitality: Vineyard Tour,
Wine Tasting
Amenities: Small Groups
(<15), Family Friendly, Pet
Friendly
Languages Spoken: Italian

Wines to try—
Ginestra Etna Bianco
Romice delle Sciare Etna
Rosato
Feudo di Mezzo Etna Rosso
Arcurìa Etna Rosso

The new Calcagno family winery, in the heart of Passopisciaro, opened just in time for the 2016 harvest. After a century of trading in bulk, the family hired a succession of consulting wineries beginning in 2007, to help them launch the Calcagno label. The first wines were good, but stylistically they had the imprint of the consulting wineries. Francesco, Gianni, and Giusy Calcagno were attempting to define a house style. Now that the wines are made in their own cantina, they speak of the Etna terroir that the family has known for generations. "When we didn't have our own place, we absolutely noticed the effects that temperature and oxygen had on the wine," Giusy tells me, leaning on their new bottling line. "It raised a question for us. "What would happen if we aged our wines at higher elevations? There's less oxygen, it's cooler, and there are a lot less germs!" A short time later, they delivered a few cases of wine to the INGV observatory, at 2813 meters AMSL. Two years later they held a public trade tasting of some bottles, side-by-side, with the same wines aged inside the DOC. It was exactly as they hoped. The wines aged near the central crater of the volcano were fresher than those resting at 750 meters AMSL. Every time I taste through their profile, I come to my own conclusions. You could age these wines at any elevation. I would drink them all.

There is no keystone with a date of foundation in the Camarda family vineyard. The vines have been cared for and passed down for at least four generations. And every day, Gaetano Camarda begins the work again. To the east and west of their estate in Feudo di Mezzo, the ornate alberelli are hemmed in by the 1566 and 1879 lava flows. It's one of the lucky places on the mountain. Not only because the site has survived two of Etna's devastating eruptions, but because the vines have been worked organically, by hand, for more than 150 years, and the own-rooted Nerello planted in the nineteenth century is still used to perpetuate the vineyard. The white wine follows the Carricante lead, with accents of Inzolia, Minella Bianca and Catarratto in the blend. A new vineyard of Carricante, planted in Contrada Sciara Nuova will follow a modern scheme. But there are no yeasts or additives used in the production of Camarda wines. The only modernizations include anaerobic vinification, and élevage for the Nerello Mascalese in neutral barriques. You don't need to add anything to make these wines delicious. There is flavor in their honesty, in particular when they are paired with the local cuisine.

Passopisciaro, Castiglione di Sicilia, CT 95012
www.camardavini.it
graziellacamarda@alice.it
+39 338-613-5549
Founded: 1965
Find the Winery On: Twitter, Facebook
Contrade: Feudo di Mezzo–Porcaria, Sciara Nuova
Hectares: 2
Vine Training: Alberello, Cordon
Wines: IGT/IGP Terre Siciliane, VDT (Vino da Tavola)
Bottles Produced: 9,500

Visits: On request

Wines to try—
Vino Bianco
Nerello Mascalese

CANTINE RUSSO

Via Corvo, SP64
Solicchiata, Contrada Crasà
Castiglione di Sicilia, CT
95012
www.cantinerusso.eu
cantinerusso@hotmail.it
+39 094-298-6271
Founded: 1950
Find the Winery On:
Facebook, Twitter, Instagram
Contrade: Crasà, Piano dei
Daini, Rampante
Hectares: 12
Vine Training: Alberello,
Cordon
Etna DOC Wines: Etna
Bianco, Etna Rosato, Etna
Rosso, Etna Rosso Riserva,
Etna Spumante
Other Wines: IGT/IGP Terre
Siciliane
Bottles Produced: 150,000

Visits: Only by request
Hospitality: Vineyard Tour,
Winery Tour, Wine Tasting,
Lunch
Amenities: Small Groups
(<15), Large Groups (15+),
Event Space, Wi-Fi, Family
Friendly, Pet Friendly
Languages Spoken: Italian,
English, French

Wines to try—
Mon Pit Brut
Pietra Lava Etna Rosso
Rampante Etna Bianco

As children, Gina and Francesco Russo used to play in the family cellar. "We would chase each other around and leap from one vat to another," Gina says. "You could smell the sulfite puff out of the empty botti every time. It is a fond memory," she adds. It was around this time that Francesco grew curious about the process of winemaking. "Everything matters," he says, showing me his photo library of every plant that grows on the mountain. "From the spontaneous vegetation in the vineyard to the person tasting the wine." There aren't many technicians like Francesco on Mount Etna. It takes experience and a trained eye to anticipate the nuances of grape-growing and winemaking here. The Russo family has worked in Castiglione since the nineteenth century. Following the Second World War, they began bottling and selling their wines from a depot in Giarre. The modern winery is located in Contrada Crasà, just north of Solicchiata. The grapes arrive from three contrade to produce still and classic method sparkling wines with local charm and an international appeal. Instead of jumping from botte to botte, these days Gina and partner Robert leap from place to place promoting the wines that Francesco makes with their father, Vincenzo. "It doesn't feel like work a lot of the time," Gina says. "It feels like maybe we're still playing."

The old palmento and distillery that Giovanni Valenti turned into a modern winery and tasting room were built across the road from the Circumetnea train station in Passopisciaro. At the end of the nineteenth century, there were so many people growing grapes and making wine that the neighborhood west of *la colonna* was a perpetual open-air convention of farmers, merchants, and curious travelers. These small streets are quieter now, but the Valenti cantina is no less busy. What started in 2004 as a family dream now includes vineyards stretching between 600 to 1000 meters AMSL in some of the most sought-after contrade on the north slope. With more than a decade of experience to look back on, the company continues to move toward noninvasive treatments in the vines and in the cantina. Giovanni says, "We see the greatest results when the plants produce less fruit. We are not concerned with generating high quantities the way they were [more than a century ago]. We want the transformation of grapes into wine to be what nature wants. We believe this is the right direction for us."

Via Roma 42
Passopisciaro, Castiglione di Sicilia, CT 95012
www.cantinevalenti.it
info@cantinevalenti.it
+39 094-298-3016;
+39 335-598-1785
Founded: 2004
Find the Winery On:
Facebook, Twitter, Instagram
Contrade: Arcuria, Bonanno, Cottanera, Guardiola, Pietramarina, Santo Spirito
Hectares: 38
Vine Training: Alberello, Guyot, Cordon
Etna DOC Wines: Etna Bianco, Etna Rosato, Etna Rosso, Etna Rosso Riserva
Other Wines: IGT/IGP Terre Siciliane, DOC/DOP Sicilia
Bottles Produced: 130,000

Visits: Only by request
Hospitality: Vineyard Tour, Winery Tour, Palmento Tour, Wine Tasting, Lunch, Dinner
Amenities: Large Groups (15+), Wi-Fi, Family Friendly, Pet Friendly
Languages Spoken: Italian, English

Wines to try—
Malavoglia Bianco
Poesia Etna Rosato
Puritani Nerello Mascalese

CONTRADA SANTO SPIRITO DI PASSOPISCIARO

Contrada Santo Spirito
Castiglione di Sicilia, CT
95012
www.feudomaccari.it
info@feudomaccari.it
+39 057-547-7857
Founded: 2011
Contrada: Santo Spirito
Hectares: 9
Vine Training: Alberello
Etna DOC Wines: Etna
Bianco, Etna Rosso
Bottles Produced: 9,000

Visits: Only by request
Hospitality: Vineyard Tour,
Wine Tasting
Amenities: Small Groups
(<15), Pet Friendly
Languages Spoken: Italian,
English

Wines to try—
Animalucente Etna Bianco
Animardente Etna Rosso

Turning left off of SS120, into Contrada Santo Spirito, the road follows several overlapping lava flows. Near the end, a little pink house overlooks rolling terraces of vines and olive trees that populate the estate. Just above the confines of the vineyard are the brush- and ginestra-covered tongues of the 1947 lava flow. There are other vineyards nearby, but this location is perfect to understand the effects of Etna's contours on sunlight, the flow of wind, and ripening grapes grown at high elevations. Here, at more than 700 meters AMSL, the Carricante and Minella Bianca ripen within a few days of one another. The Nerello Mascalese takes more time. Every cloud and shadow makes a difference. New plantings are taking advantage of nuances in hours of available sunlight. It's an important topic that seldom gets the attention it requires. Antonio Moretti Cuseri, owner of Contrada Santo Spirito di Passopisciaro, has experience studying the countryside. One of his first wine projects—Tenuta Sette Ponti, in Tuscany—takes its name from the road painted into the background of *La Gioconda* (a.k.a. the *Mona Lisa*). You almost don't see it, but it's there, just over her shoulder, in the countryside. As mysterious as Etna can be, if you can relax your gaze, it's possible to see beyond her elusive grin.

Francesco Cambria bought the old hazelnut orchards from half a dozen families in 1961, but he wasn't interested in cultivating *nucidde*. Almost immediately he began removing the trees, leveling the ground, and preparing the soil for grapevines. It quickly became more than a passion project. For guidance, the family reached out to Tuscan winemaker Roberto Cipresso and Leonardo Valenti, professor of Agriculture at the University of Milan. It was the first of many decisions that would convert this old orchard into one of the early innovators on the mountain. "No one talked about 'quality wine' in those days," Francesco Cambria says. "As we started planting [the vineyards], no one outside of Etna knew anything about [Nerello] Mascalese." Along with some Nerello and Carricante the family planted Cabernet, Merlot, Viognier, Inzolia, Syrah, and Mondeuse. Things have changed over the last twenty years. People ask for Nerello and Carricante now. When the winds of interest turned in Etna's direction, the Cambria family was ready with a range of wines that show the versatility of the mountain terrain. Tucked into the hills between Passopisciaro and the Alcantara River, the Cottanera winery offers guests a unique opportunity to taste more than a dozen blends and monovarietal bottlings of indigenous and international varieties with a single thing in common: they were all raised on Etna.

Contrada Iannazzo, SP 89
Castiglione di Sicilia, CT 95012
www.cottanera.it
staff@cottanera.it;
winetours@cottanera.it
+39 094-296-3601 (winery);
+39 391-393-9073 (tours)
Founded: 1997
Find the Winery On:
Facebook, Twitter, Instagram
Contrade: Calderara, Cottanera, Diciassette Salme, Feudo di Mezzo, Zottorinoto
Hectares: 64
Vine Training: Alberello, Guyot, Cordon
Etna DOC Wines: Etna Bianco, Etna Rosato, Etna Rosso, Etna Rosso Riserva
Other Wines: DOC/DOP Sicilia
Bottles Produced: 300,000

Visits: Only by request
Hospitality: Vineyard Tour, Winery Tour, Wine Tasting, Lunch, Dinner
Amenities: Small Groups (<15), Large Groups (15+), Event Space, Wi-Fi, Family Friendly, Pet Friendly
Languages Spoken: Italian, English

Wines to try—
Calderara Etna Bianco
L'Ardenza Mondeuse
Zottorinoto Etna Rosso Riserva

Contrada Montelaguardia
Randazzo, CT 95036
www.destrovini.com
info@destrovini.com
+39 095-921134;
+39 335-134-1118
Founded: 1897
Find the Winery On:
Facebook, Twitter
Contrada: Montelaguardia
Hectares: 10.6
Vine Training: Cordon
Etna DOC Wines: Etna
Bianco, Etna Rosato, Etna
Rosso, Etna Spumante
Other Wines: IGT/IGP Terre
Siciliane
Bottles Produced: 70,000

Visits: Only by request
Hospitality: Vineyard Tour,
Winery Tour, Palmento Tour,
Wine Tasting, Lunch
Amenities: Large Groups
(15+), Wi-Fi, Family Friendly,
Pet Friendly
Languages Spoken: Italian,
English

Wines to try—
Isolanuda Etna Bianco
Saxanigra Etna Spumante
Sciarakè Etna Rosso

Antonio Destro liked to forage for mushrooms on the mountain. One day, in 2002, he pushed through the brush at the edge of a forest in Montelaguardia, on the volcano's northern flank. Stretching out below him was a partially abandoned winery and an amphitheater of terraces that were spotted with vines and olive trees. It was an impressionable moment that would steer him directly into wine after two decades in the marble business. He bought the vineyards and old palmento that year. In 2003, he planted 45,000 vines, of which the rabbits ate 7,000. The replanting was tedious, but the young vines followed his lead. Antonio and his enologist Giovanni Rizzo made a small test run with a selection of grapes in 2006. The following year, production began in earnest with a focus on indigenous cultivars and DOC Etna blends, including a line of distinctive classic method sparkling wines from Nerello Mascalese. As much as the uniqueness of the site contributes to these wines, Antonio believes "a wine reflects the spirit of the winemaker more. [Rizzo] has been with me from the beginning. We knew everything that had to be done. It was an enormous investment. But my first taste of the 2007 *Sciarakè* [100% Nerello Mascalese] was...." Antonio gestures rhapsodically, adding a smile, "an emotional moment."

Don Michele Pennisi was a cardiologist in the area around Randazzo. Everyone knew his name, but according to his children—the owners of the property since 2006—the doctor had a *mistress*. They say this jokingly, but the reality was that he had fallen in love with a vineyard in Contrada Moganazzi. He spent all of his free time there, caring for the old vines that gave the family wine each fall. Harvests were modest in the beginning, but after 1994, when he hired a local man by the name of Vito to assist in the farming, the entire production changed. "Vito is the heart and blood of this farm," Giuseppina says of her father's decision to ask for help. "Together, they gave another life to this place." Dr. Pennisi's three children continue to care for the property with Vito's guidance. By 2012, the siblings had established a trio of wines that focus on Etna's indigenous varieties and traditions, which they released under the label Don Michele. In the beginning, they sold many of the grapes to local producers, making only 1500 bottles for themselves. "Slowly, they began to sell less. We wanted to make more wine," Giuseppina tells me, walking together along the *rasola* to their old palmento. "By then, we had our own relationship with the vines that captured our father's heart."

Contrada Moganazzi
Passopisciaro, Castiglione di
Sicilia, CT 95012
www.tenutemoganazzi.com
tenutemoganazzi@gmail.
com
+39 333-118-8706
Founded: 2006
Find the Winery On:
Facebook, Instagram
Contrada: Moganazzi
Hectares: 7
Vine Training: Alberello,
Cordon
Etna DOC Wines: Etna
Bianco, Etna Rosato, Etna
Rosso
Other Wines: DOC Sicilia
Bottles Produced: 4,000
Visits: No services offered

Wines to try—
Etna Bianco
Etna Rosato
Etna Rosso

DONNAFUGATA

Contrada Statella
Randazzo, CT 95036
www.donnafugata.it
info@donnafugata.it
+39 092-372-4206
Founded: 2016
Find the Winery On:
Facebook, Twitter, Instagram,
YouTube
Contrade: Allegracore,
Calderara, Campo Re,
Marchesa, Montelaguardia,
Statella, Verzella
Hectares: 21
Vine Training: Alberello,
Cordon
Etna DOC Wines: Etna
Bianco, Etna Rosato, Etna
Rosso
Bottles Produced: 91,000
Visits: Only by request
Hospitality: Vineyard Tour,
Winery Tour, Wine Tasting,
Brunch
Amenities: Small Groups
(<15), Large Groups (15+),
Family Friendly
Languages Spoken: Italian,
English

Wines to try—
Sul Vulcano Etna Bianco
Sul Vulcano Etna Rosso
Fragore Etna Rosso

The light arrives in the Montelaguardia vineyard a few minutes earlier than some other areas of the mountain. Over the course of a growing season, those minutes add up. Here, in the youngest Donnafugata vineyard, the soil is drier because of it. The soils are much older too. They were once part of the Ellittico volcano, on which Mongibello sits. "Our first trials came from the plot above where we just planted," winemaker Nino Santoro says, pointing to a lush green terrace above thousands of new chestnut stakes. A few miles to the east, the prephylloxera and old-vine Nerello vineyard in Contrada Marchesa is the company's highest on the mountain. These are younger Mongibello soils, surrounded on three sides by the 1566 lava flow. The mounds of cooled lava block the light for hours during the day. At an elevation near 900 meters AMSL, the fruit from these old vines is more elegant than formidable. Back at the winery, in the barrel room, Santoro pulls a sample from one of the barrels and says, "We've learned not to make any assumptions on Etna. We made wine from vineyards in other places on the mountain for years before we decided what was the right way for us. We wanted to learn from Etna, before we tried to interpret it."

My first tasting of Duca di Salaparuta's portfolio of wines from Mount Etna was a Pinot Nero. I was in my kitchen. According to my biodynamic tasting calendar, it was a "fruit" day. (When possible, I prefer not to taste on a "root" or "leaf" day.) I examined the label, made notes about the packaging, removed the foil capsule, extracted the cork, and poured the plum-dark liquid into a wineglass that had been painstakingly-designed to lift and capture the regal aromas of Pinot Nero at the rim. It was the first time I tasted a Pinot Nero from Etna instead of an Etna Pinot Nero. The *Nawàri* had somehow escaped the generalization that the red grape is destined to carry the terroir on its shoulders. Instead, Etna was making comments from the sidelines. Lucky for us, this is no game. I cross-referenced the location of the vineyard with my map of Etna's lava flows. On Etna, there's a reason for everything. This pocket of the mountain has shown an affinity for international varieties, especially Pinot Noir, for decades. The vineyard is on a rise of decomposed Mongibello soils dating between 15,000 to 4,000 years old, but the aspect of the vineyard is turned away from the morning and autumn sun. Wines grown here—straddling Cde. Moganazzi and Marchesa—can't help being elegant.

Via Nazionale 113
Casteldaccia, PA 90014
www.duca.it
info@duca.it;
visitaduca@duca.it
+39 091-945201
Founded: 2003
Find the Winery On:
Facebook, Twitter, Instagram
Blog: www.duca.it/wineroom
Contrada: Marchesa
Hectares: 11
Vine Training: Alberello, Cordon
Etna DOC Wines: None
Other Wines: IGT Terre Siciliane, DOC Sicilia
Bottles Produced: 43,000
Visits: No services offered

Wines to try—
Làvico Nerello Mascalese
Nawàri Pinot Nero
Sciaranèra Pinot Nero

EDUARDO TORRES ACOSTA

SS120 1 and Cross Street N6
Solicchiata, CT 95012
www.eduardotorresacosta.com
eduardotorres30@hotmail.com
+39 366-486-4691

Founded: 2014
Find the Winery On:
Facebook, Instagram
Contrade: Allegracore,
Capreri, Fossa Politi, Nave,
Pietramarina, Sant'Alfio,
Santo Spirito, Sciara Nuova
Hectares: 4.5
Vine Training: Alberello,
Cordon
Etna DOC Wines: No
Other Wines: IGT/IGP Terre
Siciliane
Bottles Produced: 30,000
Visits: No services offered

Wines to try—
Contrada Pirrera Blend
Versante Nord Blend

There are few people who carry themselves as quietly as Eduardo Torres Acosta. After finishing his studies in enology and viticulture, he was tapped by Andrea Franchetti to join the team at Passopisciaro. "Working on Etna," Eduardo says, "you start to get an idea of the different contrade and which soils are good or not so good. The only constant is that all the work has to be done by hand." His vineyards are all on the north slope of Mount Etna, both inside and outside of the Etna DOC. "It's windy here," he adds. "It helps keep the vines free of pathogens, but we can't only depend on the wind." Eduardo grew up in the sunny, windswept Canary Islands, southwest of Spain. "There's a lot about the volcano that reminds me of home, but the culture of wine in Sicily has always been more advanced." After four vintages with Franchetti, he launched his own wine label, focusing on single vineyards and blends of different sites. Some of the vineyards were all but forgotten when he began working with them. Slowly, they have come back to life with his guidance. "We can't fight the environment," he says. "This is almost entirely a work of observation."

If you ask Nunzio Puglisi where he and his daughters, Stefany and Désirée, make wine, he will point to the vineyard. This isn't an altogether new philosophy. What matters is how a philosophy is applied. Nunzio admits some of his thinking is a little old school, but you don't make thought-provoking wines on Etna by taking shortcuts. "Every interaction with a vine is treated as a unique collaboration with the surrounding environment," Nuzio tells me over the phone, from the vineyard. "As a vintage changes, so does the approach to the work. No two vintages on Etna are ever the same." All the vineyards are located on the north flank of Mount Etna. Over the last forty years, the family has developed an eclectic mix of cultivars that are managed completely by hand. Natural predators like ladybugs are attracted to the spontaneous vegetation that is tilled into the soil as green manure. In place of plastic ties to train young shoots, long grasses from the vineyard floor are used to organize the canopy. This isn't a seasonal job. The work is done daily. As a result, the vineyards are teeming with life. It's no surprise the wines are inviting, they come from a good home.

Contrada Calderara
Randazzo, CT 95036
www.vinienotrio.com
enotrio.vini@gmail.com
+39 388-954-2812;
+39 388-379-1422
Founded: 2013
Find the Winery On:
Facebook, Instagram, Twitter
Contrade: Calderara, Nave, Lago
Hectares: 5
Vine Training: Alberello, Cordon
Etna DOC Wines: Etna Rosso
Other Wines: IGT/IGP Terre Siciliane
Bottles Produced: 15,000

Visits: Only by request
Hospitality: Vineyard Tour, Winery Tour, Wine Tasting
Amenities: Small Groups (<15), Wi-Fi, Family Friendly, Pet Friendly
Languages Spoken: Italian, English, French

Wines to try—
Calderara Etna Rosso
Tiurema Pinot Nero
Traminer Aromatico
Dejanira Grenache Noir

FATTORIE ROMEO DEL CASTELLO

Contrada Allegracore SP 89
Randazzo, CT 95036
www.romeodelcastello.it
info@romeodelcastello.it
+39 095-799-1992;
+39 333-249-8903
Founded: 18th century
Find the Winery On:
Instagram
Contrada: Allegracore
Hectares: 12
Vine Training: Alberello,
Cordon
Etna DOC Wines: Etna
Rosato, Etna Rosso
Other Wines: DOC/DOP
Sicilia
Bottles Produced: 20,000

Visits: Only by request
Hospitality: Vineyard Tour,
Palmento Tour, Wine Tasting,
Lunch, Dinner
Amenities: Small Groups
(<15), Large Groups (15+)
Languages Spoken: Italian,
English, French

Wines and Spirits to try—
Allegracore Etna Rosso
Vigo Etna Rosso
Vigorosa Etna Rosato
Goialuce Acquavite from
Coscia Pears

The Romeo family has been a part of the greater Randazzo community for centuries. Located between Castello Romeo and the Alcantara River, the heart of the estate was constructed as a *masseria* in the seventeenth century, in Contrada Allegracore. Additional construction continued into the twentieth century. Today, the working farm also highlights a depth of Etna's history in a way that few others can. Much of the facility is being converted to a living museum that showcases the agricultural and architectural heritage of this part of the mountain, including personal effects left behind by soldiers who fought on Mount Etna during World War II, and a new exhibit curated by Chiara Vigo—co-owner of the estate—which focuses on a history of Etna's wine labels. There on the estate we see how fickle the volcano can be. The March 1981 eruption covered more than sixty acres of the farm and today embraces the old-vine Nerello vineyard. The wines connect the family to consumers in unsuspecting ways. Each label features a detail of the main house, the local lava flows, members of the family, and their endeavors on the mountain. "With these images," Chiara tells me, "the bottle contains more than wine. Every vintage, we tell another part of our story."

In the twelfth century, the popular way of communicating over long distances was by carrier pigeon. The elegant and colorful Byzantine dovecote at the edge of the Feudo Arcurìa vineyards stands as a witness to the profound history of Mount Etna, on the edge of Contrade Feudo di Mezzo and Arcurìa. For centuries, the birds flew to and fro carrying news of daily business, peace, and war. Stretching out to the north of the dovecote is where the Nerello vineyard now thrives. The exposed soil includes some of the first effusive layers of the young Mongibello edifice. The uniqueness of the site was realized by Giuseppe La Monaca and enologist Alfio D'Urso, who made their first wine from Nerello. It was the 2006 *Palummaru*, specifically, that was listed among the *Best 100 Wines in Italy*. Other awards followed. "There were no tricks to the wine," says La Monaca. "I applied the lessons I learned sitting on my grandfather's shoulders as he conducted the workers of the palmento." Over the years, La Monaca's father purchased one small vineyard at a time, until the vines and olive and cherry trees filled a hamlet on the eastern skirt of the 1566 lava flow. In 2002, the vineyards were passed down to him. He smiles at this moment in our conversation and says, "That's when I started to play."

SP7iii
Castiglione di Sicilia, CT 95012
www.feudoarcuria.it
feudoarcuria@gmail.com;
giuseppe.lamonaca@
feudoarcuria.it
+39 347-527-5075
Founded: 2003
Find the Winery On: Facebook
Contrada: Arcurìa
Hectares: 3
Vine Training: Cordon
Etna DOC Wines: Etna Rosato, Etna Rosso
Bottles Produced: 12,000

Visits: Only by request
Hospitality: Vineyard Tour, Wine Tasting, Lunch, Dinner
Amenities: Large Groups (15+), Event Space, Wi-Fi, Family Friendly, Pet Friendly
Languages Spoken: Italian only

Wine to try—
Contessa Etna Rosato
Palummaru Etna Rosso

FEUDO VAGLIASINDI

Contrada Feudo
Sant'Anastasia
Randazzo, CT 95036
www.feudovagliasindi.it
info@feudovagliasindi.it
+39 095-799-1823
Founded: 1850
Find the Winery On:
Facebook, Instagram,
TripAdvisor
Contrada: Feudo
Sant'Anastasia
Hectares: 4.5
Vine Training: Cordon
Etna DOC Wines: Etna
Bianco, Etna Rosato, Etna
Rosso, Etna Rosso Riserva
Other Wines: IGT/IGP Terre
Siciliane, DOC/DOP Sicilia
Bottles Produced: 10,000

Visits: Seven days a week
Hospitality: Vineyard Tour,
Winery Tour, Palmento Tour,
Wine Tasting, Lunch, Dinner
Amenities: Small Groups
(<15), Large Groups
(15+), Event Space,
Overnight Accommodations,
Wi-Fi, Family Friendly, Pet
Friendly
Languages Spoken: English

Wines to try—
Etna Bianco
Etna Rosato
Etna Rosso
Nerello Cappuccio

Paolo Vassallo's old palazzo stands above all other structures on this part of the mountain. When it was built, at the beginning of the twentieth century, the estate had been producing enormous quantities of wine in the basement palmento for fifty years. Ninety-three years after the first grapes were thrown into the pista, the palazzo was commandeered as a military outpost and hospital during World War II. "When we opened the home, after decades of neglect, we found medical gear everywhere," Vassallo recalls. This is one of many stories he and his brother, Corrado, tell their guests, about the history of their palazzo-palmento-turned hotel. For a deeper study, the family museum houses ancient artifacts discovered on the estate. It's profound to consider that hundreds of generations have called this a resting place. But then again, *this is Etna.* There are few things that have not happened here. Take the vineyards, for instance. Nerello Cappuccio was always included as a part of a field blend to enhance Nerello Mascalese. Now, the two black grapes are grown and vinified separately. And Carricante rarely made it this far up the mountain, but the young vines are thriving. Modernizing the vineyards may not seem like a sweeping change to their family history, but without the Vassallo brothers Feudo Vagliasindi may not have had a trajectory at all.

FEDERICO GRAZIANI

Federico Graziani walked into his first wine class at the age of fifteen. Five years later, he took his first job as a professional sommelier. In 1998, the Italian Association of Sommeliers named him Italy's sommelier of the year. Since then, he earned a degree in Enology and Viticulture from the University of Milan and started writing. A recent book about wine producers in Italy has garnered a lot of attention. For someone who could very well choose any place in the world to make wine, he selected Mount Etna. In particular, he chose Etna's north slope. Vineyard management and some of the winemaking is assisted by Salvo Foti. Federico's *Profumo di Vulcano*, a red wine from Nerello Mascalese, Nerello Cappuccio, Alicante, and Francisi, shows the grace and intensity for which Etna has long been known. Rather than focus on sugar development and extracted flavors from the fruit or oak, Graziani harvests early, relying on the volcano, natural tannins, and acidity to unify the wine as it ages in neutral oak barrels. Federico has purchased additional vineyards to make a white blend and a basic Etna Rosso. Production is small but the wines exude patience and persistence. "Over the years," Federico says, "I realized that the quality of my wines comes directly from the care of the vines. I will not do without this."

Contrada Mangani
Randazzo CT 95036
www.fedegraziani.it
info@fedegraziani.it
+39 329-022-3270
Founded: 2008
Find the Winery On:
Facebook, Instagram
Contrada: Feudo Di Mezzo, Moganazzi, Montelaguardia, Nave
Hectares: 4.5
Vine Training: Alberello
Etna DOC Wines: Etna Rosso
Other Wines: IGT/IGP Terre Siciliane
Bottles Produced: 20,000

Visits: Only by request
Hospitality: Vineyard Tour, Wine Tasting
Amenities: Small Groups (<15), Family Friendly, Pet Friendly
Languages Spoken: Italian, English

Wines to try—
Mareneve White Blend
Etna Rosso
Profumo di Vulcano Etna Rosso

Contrada Calderara
Randazzo, CT 95036
www.filippograsso.it
info@filippograsso.it
+39 320-706-1375
+39 349 75056
Founded: 2002
Find the Winery On:
Facebook, Instagram
Contrade: Calderara
Hectares: 6
Vine Training: Alberello in
Cordon, Cordon
Etna DOC Wines: Etna
Bianco, Etna Rosato, Etna
Rosso
Other Wines: IGT/IGP Terre
Siciliane, VDT (Vino da
Tavola), Vino Locale / Sfuso
Bottles Produced: 40,000

Visits: Only by request
Hospitality: Vineyard Tour,
Winery Tour, Wine Tasting
Amenities: Small Groups
(<15), Wi-Fi, Family Friendly,
Pet Friendly
Languages Spoken: Italian,
English

Wines to try—
Carrico 68.8 Bianco
Mari di Ripiddu Etna Bianco
Capu Chiurma di Ripiddu
Etna Rosso
Ripiddu DOC Etna Rosso

As everyone in cities around the world debated the potential problems of Y2K, the Grasso family was moving from their farm in Dagala del Re, on Mount Etna's fertile eastern flank, to a sunnier farm in Contrada Calderara. It was a difficult adjustment at first. The family was immediately thrown into the work of clearing brambles from the fields and salvaging the old house. Mariarita Grasso leads me through the oldest part of the vineyard. Nearing an almond tree, she pauses and says, "My father grew and sold vegetables and citrus around Giarre, but the market for wine was better. And up here the quality of the wine is always good. After we moved, we worked for years, exposing and retraining vines, pruning the olive and fruit trees, and building a new life. When the area was finally clear, we couldn't believe it. It was all rocks! We said, 'Why did we move here?' Of course, my father knew then what we know now." This is one of the most coveted viticultural areas on the mountain. Not only does the family make a portfolio of remarkable wines based on Etna varieties, they grow about 90% of the food they eat. It sounds inconceivable to many of us, to know and work the land where we live. Somehow, the Grasso family makes it all look easy.

There are many ways to get things done, but there are far fewer ways to do it right. When the Firriato company first set its sights on the vineyards around Mount Etna, in Contrada Verzella, they were only looking for wine grapes. Federico Lombardo di Monte Iato, son-in-law of founders Salvatore and Vinzia di Gaetano, considers the initial decision to make wine from grapes grown on Etna as a trial. Twenty years after the first crates were filled, the vineyards that track the northern edge of an ancient lava flow are now part of their Cavanera estate. "We were looking for high-elevation vineyards, but the more we understood the property, the more grapes we bought," he tells me, walking the circumference of the vineyards. "We were curious why one soil made the wine taste one way when another soil five meters away had another result." The soils change frequently between deep volcanic sands spiced with iron, white quartz, and volcanic scree. If you like, you can walk around the vineyards yourself, then taste the wines at the resort's wine bar that overlooks the pool and the vineyard, or in the ultramodern welcome center, which houses the new winery. What started as a trial has, in fact, become a destination.

Contrada Verzella
Castiglione di Sicilia, CT 95012
www.cavanera.it
cavanera@firriatohospitality.it
+39 094-298-6182
Founded: 1999
Find the Winery On: Facebook, Twitter, Instagram, YouTube, LinkedIn
Contrade: Cottanera, Marchesa, Montedolce, Pettinociarelle, Santo Spirito, Verzella, Zottorinoto, Zucconero
Hectares: 42
Vine Training: Alberello, Cordon
Etna DOC Wines: Etna Bianco, Etna Rosato, Etna Rosso, Etna Spumante
Other Wines: IGT/IGP Terre Siciliane, DOC/DOP Sicilia
Bottles Produced: 120,000

Visits: Seven days a week, seasonal
Hospitality: Winery Tour, Wine Tasting, Lunch, Dinner
Amenities: Small Groups (<15), Large Groups (15+), Overnight Accommodations, Family Friendly
Languages Spoken: Italian, English, French

Wines to try—
Gaudensius Brut Etna Spumante
Ripa di Scorciavacca Etna Bianco
Rovo delle Coturnie Etna Rosso
Signum Ætnæ Etna Rosso Riserva

FISCHETTI

SS120 2
Contrada Moscamento,
Castiglione di Sicilia, CT
95012
www.fischettiwine.it
info@fischettiwine.it
+39 334-127-2527
Founded: 2008
Find the Winery On:
Facebook, Twitter, LinkedIn,
Instagram
Contrada: Moscamento
Hectares: 2
Vine Training: Alberello
Etna DOC Wines: Etna
Bianco, Etna Rosato, Etna
Rosso, Etna Rosso Riserva
Bottles Produced: 5,000

Visits: Seven days a week
Hospitality: Vineyard Tour,
Winery Tour, Palmento Tour,
Wine Tasting
Amenities: Small Groups
(<15), Large Groups (15+),
Event Space, Family Friendly,
Pet Friendly
Languages Spoken: Italian,
English

Wines to try –
Muscamento Etna Bianco
Muscamento Etna Rosato
Muscamento Etna Rosso

Sitting around the table under the ancient *torchio* of the Fischetti palmento, you wouldn't imagine that the table was also the *orbis* once used to press the grapes. The wood is tidy, restored, and dressed with food and glasses of wine. In two of the glasses, the aromas of the Etna Bianco and Etna Rosato remind me of the flowers and herbs Michela Fischetti stopped to smell as we walked through the vineyard. "When we found the property, everything was growing here, but it was in pretty bad shape," Michela says, showing me a sorbo tree. "We didn't want to change anything. We wanted to save what was here and make wines that are true to the place." For Michela and Fischetti's wine consultant, Andrea Marletta, that means following the rhythms of the farm in that vintage. The three Etna Rossos in the glasses couldn't be more different. The first year they began producing the *Muscamento* Etna Rosso was in 2011, one of Etna's classic vintages. The next year, the vintage was hot. The bunches of grapes matured quickly, making a stronger wine with a mature fruit profile. The 2013 vintage was cool and rainy. As a result, the wine is pale and the flavors are lighter. "We don't want to make designer wines," Michela says. "We want to respect the place we love."

When Frank Cornelissen arrived on Mount Etna in December 2000, he could hardly have imagined the position he would be in today. "In many ways," he says over a glass of wine one Saturday morning, "those first few years I was only gardening. I knew I wanted to produce something that focused on territory instead of fruit, but the wines were almost non-vinified." Today, the peristaltic pumps, epoxy tanks, hoses, clamps, gaskets, floors, and walls are all "ridiculously clean, every lot of grapes is fermented separately, and the winery operates under a kind of enlightened despotism." It has to. Cornelissen works without a safety net of additives or sulfites in any of the eighteen wines he makes from vineyards along the north slope of the volcano. As things progressed, one vintage after another, his choices fused with a growing body of experiences at each site. As a result, the execution of each wine evolved to reflect the subtleties of the vineyard and how the grapes communicate these locations in the glass. "The changes to the details were small," Cornelissen says. "What containers to use, how to work the vines, when to harvest or bottle. These would not amount to much on their own but when you put them all together they make a big difference."

Via Canonico Zumbo 1
Passopisciaro, Castiglione di
Sicilia, CT 95012
www.frankcornelissen.it
info@frankcornelissen.it
(office);
pr@frankcornelissen.it
(visits)
+39 094-239-5440
Blog: www.tachu.net/frank/
blog/
Founded: 2001
Find the Winery On:
Facebook, Instagram
Contrade: Barbabecchi,
Calderara Sottana, Campo
Re, Crasà, Feudo di Mezzo,
Malpasso, Moganazzi,
Monte Colla, Montedolce,
Pettinociarelle, Pietramarina,
Picciolo, Pontale Palino,
Rampante,Tartaraci,
Zacchino Pietre, Zottorinoto,
Zucconero
Hectares: 24
Vine Training: Alberello,
Cordon
Etna DOC Wines: Etna
Bianco, Etna Rosso
Other Wines: IGT/IGP Terre
Siciliane, DOC/DOP Sicilia
Bottles Produced: 120,000

Visits: Only by request
Hospitality: Vineyard Tour,
Winery Tour, Wine Tasting
Amenities: Small Groups
(<15), Large Groups (<40)
Languages Spoken: Italian,
English, French, German,
Dutch, Japanese

Wines to Try—
MunJebel Bianco
Susucaru Rosato
MunJebel Rosso "Classico"
MunJebel Rosso VA, Cuvée
Vigne Alte

GIOVANNI ROSSO

Via Roddino 10/1
Serralunga d'Alba, CN 12050
www.giovannirosso.com
info@giovannirosso.com
+39 017-361-3340
Founded: 2016
Find the Winery On:
Facebook, YouTube,
Instagram
Contrada: Montedolce
Hectares: 6.5
Vine Training: Alberello,
Cordon
Etna DOC Wines: Etna
Bianco, Etna Rosso
Bottles Produced: 20,000

Visits: Only by request
Hospitality: Vineyard Tour,
Winery Tour, Wine Tasting
Amenities: Small Groups
(<15), Family Friendly, Pet
Friendly
Languages Spoken: Italian,
English

Wines to try—
Etna Bianco
Etna Rosso

The eruption that formed Monte Dolce—an extinct parasitic volcano on Mount Etna's north slope—was so powerful that it flexed the surface of the mountain before it cracked, spreading molten basalt with high concentrations of iron into the hills west of Solicchiata. The broad terraces roll out from Monte Dolce with different shades of oxidized iron, concentrations of ripiddu, lapilli, and soft volcanic sands. "The soil is only part of this place," Davide Rosso says. "Etna is not a book, or a university. Here, we must have the deeper sensibility of the farmers. They are the ones that gave value to this place. This terrain, these vines, the weather, it's a gift to learn from these things." Davide is not a novice. The company's first wines, under the same label, were launched from Nebbiolo vineyards in Serralunga d'Alba, in Piedmont. Etna is the company's second terroir. As one of the mountain's newest wine producers, each successive harvest adds another level of understanding. "We understand the changes in weather can shift the profile of a wine from year to year, but there is one thing we won't let the mountain dictate. The wines must have finesse and a very high quality," he says, leaning back in a chair at Cave Ox, in Solicchiata. "Quality is not something we will be flexible about."

The old cantina and blending house was so close to the Passopisciaro Circumetnea station that the back yard opened to the track. If there was wine or must destined for Riposto, the barili, botticelli, and sacks of wine and grape must could be loaded directly from the cellar. It was a popular place to buy and sell wine. Girolamo Russo makes and bottles their wines here now. The company is run by Giuseppe Russo, a classically trained pianist. After studying and working abroad for several years, a family emergency brought him home to Etna. Two years later, he was retraining the vineyards with a focus on making quality wine. Whether it was a conscious or unconscious decision, he was a young adopter of the theory that elevation is as equally important as the consistency of the soil. Gentle practices in the cellar feature smooth tones and longer refrains. Grapes like Coda di Volpe, Grecanico, Minella, and Inzolia are still used to add character to the Etna Bianco, while the reds are all Nerello. The Etna Rossi from single vineyards—Feudo, San Lorenzo, Feudo di Mezzo—are planted in Mongibello and Ellittico soils. These are not loud wines, however. You want to savor them, like listening to a song written by someone who knows precisely what they're doing.

Via Regina Margherita 78
Passopisciaro, Castiglione di Sicilia, CT 95012
www.girolamorusso.it
info@girolamorusso.it
+39 328-384-0247;
+39 338-483-7359
Founded: 2005
Find the Winery On: Facebook
Contrade: Feudo Di Mezzo, Feudo, San Lorenzo, Calderara Sottana
Hectares: 18
Vine Training: Alberello, Guyot, Cordon
Etna DOC Wines: Etna Bianco, Etna Rosato, Etna Rosso
Bottles Produced: 75,000

Visits: Only by request
Hospitality: Vineyard Tour, Winery Tour, Palmento Tour, Wine Tasting
Amenities: Small Groups (4+), Large Groups (15+), Event Space, Wi-Fi, Family Friendly, Pet Friendly
Languages Spoken: Italian, English

Wines to try—
Nerina Etna Bianco
Feudo di Mezzo Etna Rosso
San Lorenzo Etna Rosso

Contrada Arcurìa
Passopisciaro, Castiglione Di
Sicilia, CT 95012
www.graci.eu
info@graci.eu
+39 348-701-6773
Founded: 2004
Find the Winery On:
Facebook, Twitter, Instagram
Contrade: Arcurìa,
Barbabecchi, Feudo Di Mezzo,
Muganazzi
Hectares: 28
Vine Training: Alberello,
Cordon
Etna DOC Wines: Etna
Bianco, Etna Rosato, Etna
Rosso
Other Wines: IGT/IGP Terre
Siciliane
Bottles Produced: 100,000

Visits: Only by request
Hospitality: Vineyard Tour,
Winery Tour, Palmento Tour,
Wine Tasting, Lunch, Dinner
Amenities: Small Groups
(<15), Large Groups (15+),
Wi-Fi, Family Friendly, Pet
Friendly
Languages Spoken: Italian,
English, French

Wines to try—
Arcurìa Etna Bianco
Arcurìa Etna Rosso
Etna Rosso
Quota 1000 Barbabecchi
Nerello blend

Many people come to Etna for a slice of adventure. But it was curiosity that first drew Alberto Aiello Graci to the mountain. "My family made wine for a long time," he says, driving along the *quota mille* in his old white jeep. "I read about some of the wineries here. It was interesting, but when I saw it with my eyes, it was the honorable history [that] made me want to stay." In 2004, he bought a vineyard and a palmento. Though the two properties are only across the street (SP7iii) from one another, they are in two different contrade—Arcurìa and Feudo di Mezzo, respectively. Vineyards in Contrade Feudo di Mezzo, Barbabecchi, and Moganazzi followed. The quantities weren't high, but the quality was. In the cantina—one of Etna's largest and historically significant palmenti—the wines are basket-pressed and fermented in conical wood vats or concrete.

Alberto gets out of the truck to open the gate of his highest vineyard. When he gets back in, he shifts the truck into gear, and we rustle up the last hill to an opening with a vista of the Alcantara Valley. Walking into the vineyard, he says, "We made wines from different elevations in the beginning. Now we concentrate on all the variables that Etna presents us. I think this is where we will stay."

You never forget your first Etna winery visit. Mine was Gurrida, in 2007, the last vintage the winery ever harvested grapes. The following year, in the first week of July, softball- and baseball-size hail stones bombarded the vineyard. The vines were broken, the vintage destroyed. It didn't help that an international economic crisis was contributing to diminishing sales. For Gurrida, the future was unforeseeable. As we walked around the old Grenache Noir vineyard, which gets swallowed under rainwater and snowmelt each spring, and through the old palmento, where German soldiers drunkenly fired their pistols into chestnut botti during World War II, no one could have known that the company would come to a full stop. The vines had been in continuous production for 150 years. Back then, French enologist Louis Fabre chose this recess, beside the 1536 lava flow, to expand the Ducea di Nelson's plantings. The current owners had produced wine at Gurrida for forty years by the time I visited. Though no wines are currently being produced—the family offers nature experiences on the estate—there are still bottles in the market. And they are well worth finding.

SS 120, Km 181
Randazzo, CT 95036
www.gurrida.it
aziendagurrida@gmail.com
+39 347-617-2116
Founded: 1968
Find the Winery On:
Facebook, WhatsApp,
Twitter, Instagram
Contrada: Gurrida
Hectares: 14
Vine Training: Cordon
Etna DOC Wines: None
Other Wines: IGT/IGP Terre
Siciliane
Bottles Produced: 0.00
(since 2008)

Visits: Occasional events
Services: Wildlife sanctuary,
Hiking

Wines to try—
Triumph Grenache Noir blend
Victory Grenache Noir blend

Contrada Moganazzi
Solicchiata, Castiglione di
Sicilia, CT 95012
www.icustodi.it
info@icustodi.it
+39 393-189-8430;
+39 094-289-0523
Founded: 2007
Find the Winery On:
Facebook, Instagram, Twitter
Contrade: Feudo di Mezzo,
Milo, Moganazzi, Sant'Alfio
Hectares: 13
Vine Training: Alberello
Etna DOC Wines: Etna
Bianco, Etna Rosato, Etna
Rosso
Bottles Produced: 50,000

Visits: Only by request
Hospitality: Vineyard Tour,
Winery Tour, Palmento Tour,
Wine Tasting, Lunch, Dinner
Amenities: Small Groups
(<15), Family Friendly, Pet
Friendly
Languages Spoken: Italian,
English, French

Wines to try—
Ante Etna Bianco
Aetneus Etna Rosso
Pistus Etna Rosso

I was in Rome with my sister and brother-in-law a few years ago. We stopped in at a local enoteca with an incredible wine list. My sister handed me the wine list. It was more of a book. "You decide." They made a gesture and I started flipping through the pages. I could have chosen many of them, but I asked the sommelier for the *Aetneus* from I Custodi delle vigne dell'Etna. When he returned to the table with the bottle, my sister asked why I chose this one bottle. I could have told them about the cuvée, the history of the Alicante in the blend, the vinification and élevage, the old alberelli and stone tower in the vineyard, or the innovative new winery. I thought about telling them how, since 2007, I Custodi delle vigne dell'Etna has been meticulously restoring old vineyards throughout the northern valley of the mountain. Or how the new plantings behind the winery are managed to arrive at full sustainability, and when the grapes arrive in the cellar they are treated gently, fermented slowly, and raised without a heavy hand. Instead of flooding them with details, when the wine arrived at the table, I gave it to them straight. "None of these wines have ever let me down."

Irene Badalà was two years old the first time she visited the family vineyard in Contrada Santo Spirito. "It was cold," she says, leading me toward the vineyard. "The snow was [knee-high]." The following year, and every vintage for years to come, the family made the long drive up the mountain from Acireale to Passopisciaro. One side of the family had been making wine since the 1600s, the other since 1725. Eventually, the vineyard became more than her family could handle. There was talk of selling but Irene refused to give up on the farm. For the first few vintages, she and her husband, Matteo, sold the grapes. One year, a representative from the winery buying their Nerello Mascalese gave them a sample of the wine he made from their grapes. "It was remarkable," Irene admits. "He offered to help us get started. We were intrigued, but we also have jobs and a family to support. We couldn't do it overnight. It was something we could do over time, though." Within a few years they were able to release small batches of single-vineyard Carricante and Nerello from Contrada Santo Spirito. Irene pauses as we enter the vines she now cultivates, and gestures toward her feet. "This is where I first touched the ground. This is where the whole adventure began."

Contrada Santo Spirito
Passopisciaro, Castglione di Sicilia, CT 95012
irenebadala@gmail.com
+39 393-106-8378
Founded: 1778
Contrada: Santo Spirito
Hectares: 3
Vine Training: Albarello in Cordon
Etna DOC Wines: Etna Bianco, Etna Rosato, Etna Rosso
Bottles Produced: 6,300

Visits: Only by request
Hospitality: Vineyard Tour, Wine Tasting
Amenities: Small Groups (<15), Family Friendly, Pet Friendly
Languages Spoken: Italian, English

Wines to try—
Etna Bianco
Etna Rosato
Etna Rosso

MASSERIA DEL PINO

Contrada Pino
Randazzo, CT 95036
www.masseriadelpino.it
info@masseriadelpino.it
+39 349-713-7772;
+39 347-639-8826
Founded: 2005
Find the Winery On:
Facebook
Contrada: Pino
Hectares: 2
Vine Training: Alberello
Wines: Vino Bianco, Vino
Rosato, Vino Rosso
Bottles Produced: 4,000
Visits: No services offered

Wines to try—
Caravan Petrol Bianco
Super Luna Rosato
I Nove Fratelli Rosso

The supermoon of September 2015 was so large and bright that Federica Turillo and Cesare Fulvio could see past the edges of their vineyard, where the alberelli merge with the forest and the vines once again grow wild. They grabbed a few baskets and began picking. The entire rosato harvest was completed in moonlight. To remember and honor the moment, they named the pale red wine *Super Luna*—it was the tenth year they had been living at the masseria. "We never worked like this before 2005," Cesare says. He is a pilot. Federica is an archer. Cesare smokes the stub of a cigar and explains, "We learned from the previous owner, not only how to farm this land, but how to live here." Instead of pesticides or herbicides to control the agriculture, they depend on hand work and observation to support the health of the entire masseria. Federica says, "We want every vine to be strong. When they are weak, pests and diseases attack. If you kill the pest or the disease, you have not done anything to support the plant, or the farm." Cesare shoos one of their animals and adds, "Killing things is not the answer. We want to dissuade and include. We make the wines in a similar way. They are part of our life here, not separate from it."

I met Nicola Gumina at a wine tasting. When I stopped by his table, the conversation quickly turned to winegrowing on the volcano. There were no talking points in his banter, but every time he spoke about Etna he smiled. When I asked about the wine he poured in my glass, Gumina was more interested in talking about the things that wine connects. The countryside, his family, Etna's history. Wine tastings on Etna are often more engaging than simple socialized sipping. When I asked about his vineyards, Gumina made a face. I thought I'd changed the subject too quickly, or offended him, but he went right into it. He bought the old vineyard, west of Linguaglossa and Monte Santo, in Contrada Piano Filici, in the nineties. Unfortunately, the alberelli were too much to handle alone. The quality of the grapes began to suffer. It was a difficult decision, but he knew he had to replant the vineyard. That's what the face was about. No one likes replanting thousands of vines, but Gumina stuck to the plan. Others saw the work and hired him to help them. These days, the family farm and vineyard consultancy are managed with his son, Marco. Whenever I see their wines, run into them in the vineyards, or hear about their projects, I'm reminded that there is more to Mount Etna than the wine in my glass. Then I smile too.

Contrada Piano Filici
Castiglione di Sicilia, CT
95040
www.nicolagumina.it
info@nicolagumina.it
+39 095-751-1189;
+39 368-776-5957
Founded: 2001
Find the Winery On:
Facebook, Instagram
Contrada: Piano Filici
Hectares: 3.0
Vine Training: Alberello, Cordon
Etna DOC Wines: Etna Bianco, Etna Rosso, Etna Spumante
Bottles Produced: 10,000

Visits: No services offered

Wines to try—
Filici Etna Bianco
Filici Etna Rosso
Filici Etna Spumante

PALMENTO COSTANZO

Contrada Santo Spirito
Passopisciaro, Castiglione Di
Sicilia, CT 95012
www.palmentocostanzo.com
info@palmentocostanzo.com
(general);
hospitality@
palmentocostanzo.com
(visits)
+39 094-298-3239;
+39 340-992-5306
Founded: 2011
Find the Winery On:
Facebook, Twitter, Instagram,
YouTube, LinkedIn
Contrade: Cavaliere, Santo
Spirito
Hectares: 18
Vine Training: Alberello
Etna DOC Wines: Etna
Bianco, Etna Rosato, Etna
Rosso, Etna Rosso Riserva,
Etna Spumante
Bottles Produced: 100,000

Visits: Only by request
Hospitality: Vineyard Tour,
Winery Tour, Palmento Tour,
Wine Tasting, Lunch
Amenities: Large Groups
(15+), Wi-Fi, Family Friendly,
Pet Friendly
Languages Spoken: Italian,
English

Wines to try—
Bianco di Sei Etna Bianco
Contrada Cavaliere Etna
Bianco
Contrada Santo Spirito Etna
Rosso
Mofete Etna Rosato
Nero di Sei Etna Rosso

A few days after arriving on Mount Etna, I found my way to the palmento in Contrada Santo Spirito. I'll never forget the aroma of neglect as I entered the old building, and the sense of awe that over came me. It was unlike any winery I'd ever seen. The facility has been painstakingly restored and transformed since. The work didn't begin with the palmento, however. The entire vineyard had to be reclaimed from the mountain first. Then the lazy alberelli had to stand back up so they could produce high-quality fruit again. Owners Mimmo and Valeria Costanzo approached the project with a long-term view. "We were not trying to do things quickly," Valeria says. "Things can break if you go too fast. We had a vision, but we also changed our minds along the way." Nicola Centonze follows the winemaking. Everything about the palmento operates on gravity, but the pista has been replaced by gentle modern equipment, and the tini have been fitted with horizontal stainless steel tanks. Instead of chestnut, the wine rests in large French oak vats. Every level and tank has a purpose. You can taste how meticulous the process is. Yet, there are no hard edges. The wines are comfortable and welcoming, just like their new tasting room, across from the old palmento.

Looking down from the Strada Regionale Mareneve, a finger of the 1947 lava flow points at Passopisciaro's Chardonnay vineyard in Contrada Guardiola, as if to say, "Plant your vines here." Beyond the rolling terraces of flickering leaves and tendrils, the Nebrodi Mountains rise above the Alcantara Valley. "It is pastoral, ventilated, and sunny, but it's a crazy place to make wine," owner Andrea Franchetti wrote in a personal letter to visitors on the company website. *"There isn't Mother Nature here. You are conducting your viticulture on stuff that comes out of the terrible below."* After two decades of nurturing vineyards between 550 and 1,000 meters AMSL, Franchetti's team has an intuitive sense about the ways Nerello interprets the tantrums of Etna's past. The company portfolio includes Nerellos from dramatically different epochs and elevations on the north slope. For anyone studying the wines of Etna, Passopisciaro is a great place to dive in. Sadly, Franchetti passed away in 2021. The baton of his adventurous dream—to rediscover the magic of Etna wines and populate the tables of world with them—has been passed to an eager and capable generation of winemakers. On a recent visit to the winery, it occurred to me. Maybe what that finger of lava from the 1947 eruption is saying isn't "Plant here," but "Start here."

Contrada Guardiola
Passopisciaro, Castiglione di Sicilia, CT 95012
www.vinifranchetti.com
info@vinifranchetti.com
+39 094-239-5449
Founded: 2001
Find the Winery On: Facebook, Twitter, Instagram, Vimeo
Contrade: Guardiola, Rampante, Porcaria, Sciara Nuova, Chiappemacine
Hectares: 26
Vine Training: Alberello, Guyot
Etna DOC Wines: Passorosso
Other Wines: IGT/IGP Terre Siciliane
Bottles Produced: 95,000

Visits: Only by request
Hospitality: Vineyard Tour, Winery Tour, Wine Tasting
Amenities: Small Groups (<15), Wi-Fi, Family Friendly, Pet Friendly
Languages Spoken: Italian, English

Wines to try—
Passobianco Chardonnay
Passorosso Nerello Blend
Contrada Guardiola
Contrada Chiappemacine
Franchetti Petit Verdot Blend

PATRIA

SS 120, Km 194.5
Solicchiata, Castiglione di
Sicilia, CT 95012
www.vinipatria.it
info@vinipatria.it
+39 094-298-6072
Founded:-1994
Find the Winery On:
Facebook, Twitter, Instagram,
YouTube, Pinterest,
TripAdvisor
Contrade: Allegracore,
Moganazzi, Zottorinoto
Hectares: 30
Vine Training: Alberello,
Cordon
Etna DOC Wines: Etna
Bianco, Etna Rosato, Etna
Rosso, Etna Rosso Riserva,
Etna Spumante
Other Wines: IGT/IGP Terre
Siciliane, DOC/DOP Sicilia,
Vino Locale / Sfuso,
Bottles Produced: 100,000

Visits: Only by request
Hospitality: Vineyard Tour,
Winery Tour, Wine Tasting,
Lunch, Dinner
Amenities: Small Groups
(<15), Large Groups (15+),
Event Space, Wi-Fi, Family
Friendly, Pet Friendly
Languages Spoken: Italian,
English

Wines to try—
Etna Bianco
Pàlici Brut Etna Spumante
Etna Rosso Riserva
Allegracuore Vino Nobile
Riserva Speciale

There is an exposed wall in the Patria cellar where two lava flows meet, one over the top of the other. It's an interesting educational point during a tour, but in a lot of ways it's a metaphor for the way the cantina brings the winemaking community together, for the layers of consulting services it provides small producers, and the hospitality it offers its guests. This wasn't always Patria, however. The cooperative and winery used to be known as Torrepalino. Torrepalino was so revered, until it closed its doors at the end of the 1980s, that there are still signs along SS120 announcing its location. The new winery, owned and operated by the Di Miceli family, keeps the old signs up. "We don't tear things down," Bernardo Di Miceli says. "We try to build them up." From their own vineyards and the grapes they buy from farmers, the company produces wines from international and indigenous Sicilian varieties, grown on Etna and around Corleone. Patria also makes their tanks, aging rooms, and bottling line available to new producers while they get their businesses started. Di Miceli smiles when I make the connection between the Torrepalino cooperative and Patria's efforts to help their neighbors. "This is our community. We're always stronger and better when we work side by side."

Michele Faro remembers the handful of *edera* (green ivy) his grandfather would put in front of the house. "Everyone knew the ivy meant the new wine was ready. This was very basic wine, recently finished with alcoholic fermentation," Michele says. "One, or twenty, liters at a time he sold to his friends and the family. My father also focused on agriculture, but we didn't make wine for a long time. I wanted to reconnect with that part of our story." Michele loves plants. The family owns Piante Faro, a nursery near the seaside. On Etna, he's become a hunter, restorer, and promoter of old and abandoned vineyards. Vineyards that Pietradolce farms are also aged, and predominantly alberelli. The old vines that haven't been pushed in years are allowed to produce the grapes they can. "It is very relaxed," Michele says. "We do not make a lot of wine, but what we do make is of the highest possible quality. The new cellar in Solicchiata makes it easier to work better." Stainless steel and concrete vats and French oak botti give the wines an inviting style that parallels the beauty of their destination winery. Michele no longer produces or sells the effervescent sfuso like his grandfather, but every time I pass the winery during the harvest I catch myself looking for a tuft of ivy.

SS 120 174
Solicchiata, Castiglione di
Sicilia, CT 95012
www.pietradolce.it
info@pietradolce.it
+39 344-064-0839
Founded: 2005
Find the Winery On:
Facebook, Instagram
Contrade: Caselle, Feudo
di Mezzo, Rampante, Santo
Spirito
Hectares: 25
Vine Training: Alberello,
Cordon
Etna DOC Wines: Etna
Bianco, Etna Rosato, Etna
Rosso
Bottles Produced: 80,000

Visits: Only by Request
Hospitality: Vineyard Tour,
Winery Tour, Wine Tasting,
Lunch
Amenities: Small
Groups (<15), Large Groups
(15+), Event Space
Languages Spoken: Italian,
English

Wines to try—
Archineri Etna Bianco
Archineri Etna Rosso
Rampante Etna Rosso
V. Barbagalli Etna Rosso

Contrada Sciara Nuova
Via Guardiola
Passopisciaro, Castiglione di
Sicilia, CT 95012
www.planeta.it
reservation@planeta.it
+39 092-519-55460
Founded: 2008
Find the Winery On:
Facebook, Instagram, Twitter
Contrade: Pietramarina,
Rampante, Sciara Nuova,
Taccione
Hectares: 34
Vine Training: Alberello,
Guyot, Cordon
Etna DOC Wines: Etna
Bianco, Etna Rosso
Other Wines: DOC/DOP
Sicilia
Bottles Produced: 190,000

Visits: Only by Request
Hospitality: Vineyard Tour,
Winery Tour, Palmento Tour,
Wine Tasting, Lunch, Dinner
Amenities: Small Groups
(<15), Large Groups (15+),
Event Space, Wi-Fi, Family
Friendly, Pet Friendly
Languages Spoken: Italian,
English

Wines to try—
Contrada Taccione Etna
Bianco
Brut Metodo Classico
Carricante
Eruzione 1614 Nerello
Mascalese
Eruzione 1614 Pinot Nero

There is a long pile of volcanic rubble that runs alongside Planeta's vineyard and cultural center, in Contrada Sciara Nuova, high above Passopisciaro, at about 800 meters AMSL. "This is where the new research and development began," Planeta's winemaker, Patricia Tóth, tells me in the shade of a ginestra tree outside their winery in Feudo di Mezzo. "We fell in love with the exposition, elevation, and dimension of the property." Since 2008, they have gone on to explore and plant in three other contrade on the north flank. Originally inspired by Carricante, the team began looking at Nerello. After trials from vineyard sites at different elevations, it was obvious that every harvest required a maniacal selection in the vineyard, during the harvest, and again when the grapes arrive at the winery. "After ten vintages on Etna, we want the Planeta wines to be recognizable," Tóth says. "To do that we need to pay attention to the details, vibrations, and rhythms of each site. It's imperative that we give voice to the local varieties and terroir, but our classic behavior is to season it with a little provocation. That's why we dedicated a small corner of the property to Riesling, Pinot Nero, and Furmint. Everyone on Etna has a different method," she adds. "The one focus we all share is putting the territory in pole position."

Following the last eruption of the Ellittico volcano, which effectively ripped the top half of the mountain from its base in a massive event, the Mongibello volcano began laying down large swathes of the modern edifice we see today. In Contrada Sciaranuova, it's easy to see where the knuckles of lava stopped moving downslope, leaving older debris exposed. Primaterra's Nerello vines are planted here, at 850 meters AMSL, in both Ripiddu stones and older volcanic sands. Choosing spurred cordon for ease of farming and a focus on small quantities, Camillo Privaterra and Tiziana Gandolfo—both esteemed members of the Association of Italian Sommeliers (A.I.S.) in Sicily—have set a manageable pace for their boutique winery. With the help of local viti-vinicultural consultant Andrea Marletta, the company focused on making a single Etna Rosato and Etna Rosso from the Mascalese and Cappuccio in their vineyard. The last few years have allowed for an expansion of their portfolio to include an Etna Bianco and an Etna Spumante. They have also created a destination for events on the estate. Primaterra regularly hosts wine tasting and cultural events, featuring their wines and a breathtaking view of Etna's northern valley and the Nebrodi Mountains.

Contrada Sciaranova
Randazzo, CT 95036
www.viniprimaterra.it
info@viniprimaterra.it
+39 339-664-8951;
+39 333-581-5102
Founded: 2003
Find The Winery On:
Facebook
Contrade: Montedolce,
Sciaranuova
Hectares: 2.5
Etna DOC Wines: Etna
Bianco, Etna Rosato, Etna
Rosso, Etna Rosso Riserva,
Etna Spumante
Vine Training: Cordon
Bottles Produced: 5000

Visits: Only by Request
Hospitality: Vineyard Tour,
Winery Tour, Wine Tasting,
Lunch, Dinner
Amenities: Small Groups
(<15), Large Groups (15+),
Family Friendly, Pet Friendly
Languages Spoken: Italian,
English, Spanish

Wines to try—
Etna Bianco
Etna Rosso
Metodo Classico

QUANTICO VINI

Via A. Manzoni 89
Linguaglossa, CT 95015
www.vinoquantico.com
raiti.giovanni@gmail.com
+39 345-158-1395;
+39 348-276-8463
Founded: 2008
Find the Winery On:
Facebook, Instagram
Contrada: Lavina
Hectares: 2
Etna DOC Wines: Etna
Bianco, Etna Rosso
Vine Training: Alberello,
Cordon
Bottles Produced: 11,000

Visits: Only by request
Hospitality: Vineyard Tour,
Wine Tasting, Dinner
Amenities: Small Groups
(<15)
Languages Spoken: Italian,
English

Wines to try—
Etna Bianco
Etna Rosso

"The vines are flowering," Giovanni Raiti shouts from farther down the row, as he examines the plants and adjusts the canopy. I suggest that the vineyard is a little behind others around the mountain, which have already arrived at fruitset. Raiti explains, "Three years ago, I decided to let the spontaneous plants grow between the vines, instead of seeding [with nitrogen-fixing plants]. I don't have to till in March or even April, and the vineyard stays a little cooler. Flowering is a little later, but I am content. Look how healthy and happy they are." The vineyard was certified organic a few years back. During the process, Raiti managed the vineyard floor in different ways to understand how to balance the vegetation and fruit, reduce hydric stress, and improve the quality of the grapes at harvest. The vines are young, but Contrada Lavina is a fertile area in the hills above Linguaglossa. Knowing exactly how to organize the various parcels of the vineyard makes it possible for Raiti and winemaker Pietro di Giovanni to reduce their interventions in the cellar. The name *Quantico* evokes quantum measurements used in physics. Even the smallest changes can influence the result. By slowing and adjusting the process from one year to the next the wines have developed a profile that suggests they were guided instead of made.

The Scilio family has been making wine in the quiet hills outside Linguaglossa for five generations. The modern estate, positioned in the Valle Galfina on the volcano's northeast slope, includes an inn, restaurant, and event center. The estate wasn't always conceived to be the destination it is today. The original gravity-operated palmento was built in 1815. The wine was made here, in the traditional way, but the Carricante and Nerello were almost always sold in bulk, with a portion set aside for the family. At the end of the twentieth century, the family decided to pursue a modern course. The conversion began with the vineyards. The old alberelli were reorganized into filare and trained on tension wires. New plantings followed suit. The palmento too was transformed into a modern winery with the inclusion of new equipment, a cooling system, bottling line, and a subterranean barrel room for aging. The current portfolio includes Etna DOC wines, a Nero d'Avola, and a red passito, called *Sikèlios*, which is made from an unknown black grape variety planted generations ago. It would be easy to analyze the DNA of these plants today but, for Salvatore Scilio, not knowing adds a layer to the story. He says, "Every time I drink this, I wonder what it is. This is part of what wine should be, a glass of curiosity."

Contrada Valle Galfina
Linguaglossa, CT 95015
www.scilio.it
info@scilio.com
+39 095-932822;
+39 348-862-9754
Founded: 1815
Find the Winery On:
Facebook, Twitter,
Instagram, Pinterest,
YouTube
Contrada: Valle Galfina
Hectares: 22
Vine Training: Cordon
Etna DOC Wines: Etna Bianco, Etna Rosato, Etna Rosso
Other Wines: IGT/IGP Terre Siciliane
Bottles Produced: 80,000

Visits: Seven days a week
Hospitality: Vineyard Tour, Winery Tour, Palmento Tour, Wine Tasting, Lunch, Dinner
Amenities: Small Groups (<15), Large Groups (15+), Event Space, Wi-Fi, Family Friendly, Pet Friendly, Overnight Accommodations
Languages Spoken: Italian, English, French, Spanish

Wines to try—
1815 Etna Bianco
Alta Quota Etna Rosso
Sikèlios Passito

Contrada Calderara
http://srcvini.it
info@srcvini.it
+39 349-189-9361
Founded: 2012
Find the Winery On:
Facebook, Instagram
Contrade: Barbabecchi,
Calderara, Crasà, Pirao,
Rivaggi
Hectares: 11
Vine Training: Alberello
Etna DOC Wines: Etna
Bianco, Etna Rosso
Other Wines: VDT (Vino da
Tavola)
Bottles Produced: 23,000

Visits: Only by request
Hospitality: Vineyard Tour,
Winery Tour, Wine Tasting
Amenities: Small Groups
(<15)
Languages Spoken: Italian,
English, French

Wines to try—
Etna Bianco
Rosato
Alberello Rosso
Rivaggi Rosso

SRC began as an unnamed project of the Parasiliti family, in a rolling vineyard of gnarly old vines in Contrada Crasà, between Solicchiata and the medieval town of Castiglione di Sicilia. "The first vintage was rough," Rori Parasiliti says. "Working the vines and the soil, converting the garage into a small winery, harvesting the grapes, and managing the fermentations . . . everything was a challenge." But there was a common thread that tied the work together. In a way, it also softened the blow of the labor. "When the family worked as a unit, it wasn't so hard." Being together became a unifying theme. *Esser ci* (eh-sare•chee: to be there) became the new motto. By following every part of the process, the family produced their wines without the use of any additives, using only fresh grapes, concrete tanks, and large wood vats. Today, additional small vineyards in Contrade Barbabecchi, Calderara, and Rivaggi plus a new winery are contributing to SRC's growing portfolio of Nerello blends. A single Carricante is made from a high-elevation vineyard in Contrada Pirao. As I suggest in the winemaking section of this book, it is not difficult to make wine, but if you are going to make a good wine without using any enological tricks, the team absolutely must be there to guide it along.

The Grasso family has been making wine in Contrada Santo Spirito, on the volcano's north slope, for the better part of two centuries. At the height of the company's prowess they owned the two largest palmenti on the mountain and a sprawling landscape of vineyards. They are one of very few families to stay the course. Between the two world wars, a member of the family traveled to the United States and returned with a novel idea to build a service station and wine shop, modeled on the soda fountains he saw in America. The Etna Wine enoteca still operates today, across from the historic port of Riposto and a few doors down from the nautical school. There, you can fill up on gas, buy bottled wines and wine in *sfuso* (bring your own bottle). The old palmento and winery are located along the Circumetnea train track, west of Passopisciaro. There, you can find overnight accommodations, camping, a restaurant, and one of the largest wood wine vats in the world. What you won't find is a modern chateau. The winery does what it's always done—make, blend, and sell wine—although far less than they used to.

SS120, 192 km
Passopisciaro, Castiglione di Sicilia, CT 95012
www.stanzaterrena.com
info@etnawineagriturismo.com
+39 095-931548;
+39 329-032-5184
Founded: 1870
Find the Winery On: Instagram
Contrada: Santo Spirito
Hectares: 6
Vine Training: Alberello, Guyot, Cordon
Etna DOC Wines: Etna Bianco, Etna Rosato, Etna Rosso
Other Wines: IGT/IGP Terre Siciliane, VDT (Vino da Tavola)
Bottles Produced: 15,000

Visits: Seven days a week
Hospitality: Vineyard Tour, Winery Tour, Palmento Tour, Wine Tasting, Lunch, Dinner
Amenities: Small Groups (<15), Large Groups (15+), Event Space, Wi-Fi, Family Friendly, Pet Friendly, Accommodations
Languages Spoken: Italian, English, Spanish

Wines to try—
Citirinitas Bianco
Camelie Rosato
La Vie Fuille Nerello Mascalese

TENUTA BENEDETTA

Via della Resistenza 36a
Foiano Della Chiana, AR
52045
www.tenutabenedetta.it
info@tenutabenedetta.it
+39 392-140-7691;
+39 334-272-0047
Founded: 2013
Find the Winery On:
Facebook, Instagram
Contrade: Feudo Di Mezzo,
Verzella, Milo
Hectares: 2.5
Vine Training: Alberello
Etna DOC Wines: Etna
Bianco, Etna Rosso
Other Wines: IGT/IGP Terre
Siciliane
Bottles Produced: 11,000

Visits: No services offered

Wines to try—
Bianco di Mariagrazia Etna
Bianco
Rosso di Laura Etna Rosso
Unico di Benedetta
Sangiovese

It's hard to hide feelings of excitement. Happiness alights the eyes, softens the brow, and relaxes the muscles in the body. It's a feeling that permits us to let our guard down and opens us up to new ideas. This couldn't be truer for Daniele Noli and Laura Davide, the husband and wife team who fashioned their new boutique wine business with the joy and imagination of their daughter, Benedetta, at the heart of it. Daniele is a chemist and Tenuta Benedetta's wine director. The white wine—a mix of Carricante with Catarratto—and a Nerello blend are both exciting versions of artisanal Etna DOC wines, but the reverie at the core of this Tuscan family's portfolio is its flagship Sangiovese. "Everyone kept telling me it was a different clone of Nerello," Daniele says. "But they ripen three weeks earlier, and the bunches and leaves are different. I had them DNA tested. It's Sangiovese. So, we started treating it like Sangiovese." All of their vines are planted at altitude and trained in alberello. The wines show elegance and concentration, but what catches your attention first is Benedetta's playful gaze. On two of the labels, her eyes are looking out from the bottle with anticipation. It doesn't matter if I'm in an enoteca or a restaurant, it's the one label that catches my attention every time.

Looking up at Vigne Vico, the bold green leaves of the prephylloxera Nerello vines pour down into a pool of alberelli in a torrent of undulating terraces. From the top down, the vines are hemmed in by two lava flows—1566 and 1879—and planted in a cascade of decomposed lava from two earlier epochs. The vines are on their own roots, or they have been propagated through *propaggine* (layering) and selections of cuttings. I was with Concetto Bosco the first time I visited the vineyard. I'd never seen anything like it. Bosco is a tall man. He speaks quickly. "We felt the same way when we first saw it." He and his partner, Sofia, bought the four-hectare farm from the Vico family in 2012. The grapes produce a single cru named for the vineyard. The new winery, a few miles down the road, is built into the hillside, enclosed in long slabs of basalt. Looking out at the northern valley from the top deck, he tells me about the agronomist and the new vines planted around the modern cantina below us. It's a gigantic show of faith in Mount Etna. Bosco sees my reaction. He knows what goes on beyond the scenes. "It's a work in progress," he says. Tasting the wines, I realize, it's already much more than that.

SP64, 8
Solicchiata, Castiglione di
Sicilia, CT 95012
info@tenutebosco.com
Founded: 2010
Find the Winery On:
Facebook, Instagram
Contrade: Santo Spirito,
Piano dei Daini
Hectares: 10
Vine Training: Alberello,
Cordon
Etna DOC Wines: Etna
Bianco, Etna Rosato, Etna
Rosso
Other Wines: DOC/DOP
Sicilia
Bottles Produced: 50,000

Visits: Only by request
Hospitality: Vineyard Tour,
Wine Tasting
Amenities: Small Groups
(<15), Family Friendly, Pet
Friendly
Languages Spoken: Italian,
English, Spanish

Wines to try—
Piano dei Daini Etna Bianco
Piano dei Daini Etna Rosso
Vigne Vico Etna Rosso
Brut Metodo Classico

Contrada Calderara
Randazzo, CT 95036
www.tenutaterrenere.com
info@tenutaterrenere.com
+39 095-924002
Founded: 2002
Find the Winery On:
Facebook, Twitter, Instagram,
LinkedIn, Wine-is, Pinterest
Contrade: Bocca d'Orzo,
Calderara Sottana, Feudo di
Mezzo, Guardiola, Moganazzi,
San Lorenzo, Santo Spirito
Hectares: 42
Vine Training: Alberello,
Cordon
Etna DOC Wines: Etna
Bianco, Etna Rosato, Etna
Rosso
Bottles Produced: 250,000

Visits: Only by request
Hospitality: Vineyard Tour,
Winery Tour, Wine Tasting
Amenities: Small Groups
(<15), Large Groups (15+),
Wi-Fi, Family Friendly, Pet
Friendly
Languages Spoken: Italian,
English, French, German,
Spanish

Wines to try—
Cuvée delle Vigne Niche Etna
Bianco
Guardiola Etna Rosso
San Lorenzo Etna Rosso
Santo Spirito Etna Rosso

It's impossible to quantify Marco de Grazia's influence on Etna. Tenuta delle Terre Nere has drawn international attention to Etna's potential while fostering scores of new wineries through their startup phase. From the beginning, the wines focused on the variables of the mountain—cuvée, age of the vines, soils, aspects, elevations. This work provoked others to consider making their own studies. This is a nice lens to view one of Etna's iconic wineries through, but it's the side project Le Vigne di Eli, which dedicates its profits to the Meyer Pediatric Hospital, in Florence, that solidifies de Grazia's reputation of generosity. It's unimaginable to think all of this almost never happened. After only a few vintages, de Grazia was unsure whether to continue making wine on Etna. The credit for encouraging him to press on came from Don Peppino, who was managing the prephylloxera vineyard in Contrada Calderara Sottana, where the Tenuta delle Terre Nere winery was built. After a lifetime spent working the vines, Don Peppino had a unique outlook for how best to make a life on Etna. Those of us who live here know that the volcano isn't the place to plan world domination through vinification. With some luck and a lot of hard work, however, you may find a friend willing to carry some of the weight with you.

Anne-Louise Mikkelsen grew up sipping Bordeaux with her father in Denmark. As a young woman, her deeper interests in wine were aroused during an apprenticeship with a Burgundy importer, and as an apprentice in Meursault, in 2002. It was sometime during the weekend trips through France that she realized Wine was going to be "it" from then on. Over the next few years, she travelled through the US and Italy, and fell in love with the wines of Spain and, ultimately, the wines of Etna. Long after tasting them, the Etna wines seemed to occupy a unique space in her memory, and she eventually tried her hand at making them herself. In 2018, construction on the winery in Solicchiata was finished. The portfolio of Aglaea wines includes four reds and a single white to represent several small vineyards on the volcano's north slope. Three of the reds are bottled as Etna DOC with the remaining labeled as DOC Sicilia. "You need to be a bit of a risk taker on Etna," Mikkelsen says, "but you also have to realize that you're learning to trust the mountain as you go. Mercy is Etna's greatest gift. These grapes, these vines, they're like children. They may seem difficult and complicated sometimes, but if you get under the surface, they show you how special and talented they are."

SS120 168
Solicchiata, Castiglione di Sicilia, CT 95012
www.tenutadiaglaea.com
info@tenutadiaglaea.com
Founded: 2013
Find the Winery On:
Facebook, Instagram, Twitter
Contrade: Santo Spirito, Marchesa, Piano d'Ario/ Bocca d'Orzo, Chiusa Politi, Chiusa Monica, Nave
Hectares: 3.6
Vine Training: Alberello, Guyot, Cordon
Etna DOC Wines: Etna Bianco, Etna Rosato, Etna Rosso
Other Wines: IGT/IGP Terre Siciliane, DOC/DOP Sicilia
Bottles Produced: 18,000

Visits: Only by request

Wines to try—
Bianco Sicilia Carricante
Aglaea Nerello Mascalese
Santo Spirito Etna Rosso

TENUTA DI FESSINA

Via Nazionale 120
Rovittello, Castiglione di
Sicilia, CT 95012
www.tenutadifessina.com
fessina@tenutadifessina.com
+39 094-239-5300
Founded: 2007
Find the Winery On:
Facebook, Twitter, Instagram
Contrade: Manzudda,
Caselle, Rinazzo, Volpare,
Moscamento
Hectares: 14
Vine Training: Alberello
Etna DOC Wines: Etna
Bianco, Etna Bianco
Superiore, Etna Rosato, Etna
Rosso, Etna Rosso Riserva
Other Wines: IGT/IGP Terre
Siciliane, DOC/DOP Sicilia
Bottles Produced: 70,000

Visits: Seven days a week,
Seasonally
Hospitality: Vineyard Tour,
Winery Tour, Palmento Tour,
Wine Tasting, Lunch, Dinner
Amenities: Small Groups
(<15), Large Groups
(15+), Event Space, Wi-Fi,
Family Friendly, Overnight
Accommodations
Languages Spoken: Italian,
Dutch, English, French,
German

Wines to try—
A' Puddara Etna Bianco
Erse Etna Rosso
Laeneo Nerello Cappuccio
Il Musmeci Etna Rosso
Riserva

In 2007, Silvia Maestrelli was offered a glass of Etna Rosso. Until that moment, she had been managing her family's estate, Villa Petriolo, in Tuscany. From that one glass, her interest was piqued. She and her business partner hopped on a plane to Catania and drove up the mountain. Months later, she began the work of combining more than a dozen small vineyards with multiple owners into a single property in the heart of Rovittello, on the Circumetnea line. The first wine, an Etna Rosso named *Il Musmeci* in honor of the previous owner, was made that same year, from the oldest vines on the property. Other wines followed, from different aspects and elevations of the volcano, as the estate underwent an intensive conversion from *masseria* to luxury *locanda*. During the restoration, work in the vineyards evolved to include hundreds of hours of hand labor. In the cellar, cool anaerobic fermentations became the norm. Any MLF and aging happens in stainless steel, tonneaux or large French oak casks. Now the team is isolating smaller parcels of the Rovittello vineyard for wines that feature the contours and soils of the field. Regrettably, Silvia Maestrelli passed away in January 2022. After more than a decade on Etna, she showed the world that success may arrive from the details, but it is also important how those details are organized.

I knew then, as we tasted from a single barrique of Nerello, that Tenute Paratore was ready to enter their wines into the market. The wine we were tasting had been stored in a little garage for half a decade. It had been cared for, but by the time I tasted it, it had also seen the spikes of summer heat and the cold of Etna winters. All of that said, the wine seemed younger, was more stable, and far less delicate than other reds from other cantinas. I suppose you get to understand the potential of a place and what a wine needs, when your family has been making wine since 1864. For generations, the Lombardo di Villalonga family has been growing grapes and selling them to local producers. In 2013, they began working their old vines in Contrade Taccione and Nave with the intention of producing wine from their favored vineyards and bringing them to market. In 2016, they went for it. A recent tasting of that vintage feature the strong connections they have forged between the mountain and their vines. It wasn't a fluke that the wines were good. According to the Lombardo di Villalonga family, the Paratore name is derived from the Latin word for "ready," or as they like to say, ready for anything!

SS 120 205
Solicchiata, CT 95012
Randazzo, CT 95036
www.tenuteparatore.com
info@tenuteparatore.com
+39 338-392-6475
Founded: 2013
Find the Winery On:
Facebook
Blog: www.reteimprese.it/tenuteparatore
Contrade: Taccione, Nave
Hectares: 10
Vine Training: Alberello, Cordon
Etna DOC Wines: Etna Bianco, Etna Rosato, Etna Rosso, Etna Rosso Riserva, Etna Spumante
Other Wines: IGT/IGP Terre Siciliane, DOC Sicilia

Visits: Only by request
Hospitality: Vineyard Tour, Wine Tasting
Amenities: Small Groups (<15), Large Groups (15+), Family Friendly, Pet Friendly
Languages Spoken: Italian, English

Wines to try—
Etna Bianco
1864 Etna Rosso
Giovanni Paratore Etna Rosso Riserva

Contrada Marchesa
Castiglione di Sicilia, CT
95012
www.tenutepietrocaciorgna.com
paolocaciorgna@libero.it
+39 348-790-3804
Founded: 2006
Find the Winery On:
Facebook, Instagram
Contrade: Marchesa, Santo
Spirito, Bocca d'Orzo
Hectares: 2.5
Vine Training: Alberello,
Alberello in Cordon
Etna DOC Wines: Etna Rosso
Bottles Produced: 25,000

Visits: No services offered

Wines to try—
Ciaurìa Etna Rosso
Guardoilvento Etna Rosso
N'Anticchia Etna Rosso

The day Paolo Caciorgna bought his first vineyard on Etna, he remembers how relaxed he felt. In a handshake he owned 4,000 prephylloxera vines in the embrace of the 1646 lava flow, in Contrada Marchesa. He had visited many small vineyards during visits to the mountain, but this one is impressionably tranquil, even as its terraces line the hardened lava flow. After more than 150 years, the heavy trunks and contorted arms of the alberelli have found smart, albeit casual, postures. From these vines, Paolo makes an elegant and commanding DOC Etna Rosso, called *N'Anticchia*. A second DOC Etna Rosso, called *Guardoilvento*, is a youthful expression of Nerello from vineyards in Santo Spirito and Bocca d'Orzo. Walking among his old vines in Contrada Marchesa-Passocannone, Paolo slowly examines a vine. "They are flowering," he says, looking at the clouds overhead. "If it rains . . ." He doesn't have to say anything more. I know. Too much rain during flowering can reduce the yield at harvest. For decades, Paolo has been making wine in Tuscany at Tenute delle Macchie and as a consultant for internationally celebrated wine projects. Challenges come with every territory. "Making wine on Etna is a little different," he says. "It's paradise, but you have to let yourself relax. If you can give yourself some flexibility, you will always know what to do."

The Tasca family has been making wine in Sicily for centuries. Like many Etna stories, the inspiration for Tenuta Tascante was found through the local wine. While on holiday, Alberto Tasca was driving around Etna. He stopped on the side of the road to buy some of the local sfuso. Though only a basic *vino locale*, there was something more to it. In 2006, Alberto bought Nerello grapes from the south slope and made wine. Again, there was something there, but something was also missing. The following year, he made wine from Nerello grown on the north slope. This time, the wine was elusive and austere. This was the wine he remembered. One year later, the company bought and began restoring and replanting ninety-nine terraces in Piano Dario, which had been left to nature for decades. It took two years to organize and another four years to establish a jubilant house style, but that too took some experimentation. The first micro-fermentations were focused on the effects of soil type on vigor, the aspect of the vineyard, and the age of vines in multiple vineyards on the north, south, and east slopes of the volcano. In the end, what they've discovered works. In 2016, they settled on the north slope of the volcano, with a purchase of additional vineyards and a winery in the lower part of Contrada Rampante. Here is where you find the Tascante flag.

SS 120, Km 194.7
Passopisciaro, CT 95036
www.tascadalmerita.it
tenutatascante@
tascadalmerita.it
+39 091-645-9711
Founded: 2007
Find the Winery On:
Facebook, Twitter, Instagram, YouTube
Contrade: Crasà, Piano Dario, Rampante, Sciara Nuova
Hectares: 14
Vine Training: Alberello, Cordon
Etna DOC Wines: Etna Bianco, Etna Rosato, Etna Rosso
Other Wines: DOC/DOP Sicilia
Bottles Produced: 80,000

Visits: Only by request

Wines to try—
Buonora Etna Bianco
Tascante Etna Rosso
Sciaranuova Etna Rosso
Pianodario Etna Rosso

TERRAZZE DELL'ETNA

Contrada Bocca d'Orzo
Randazzo, CT 95036
www.terrazzedelletna.it
info@terrazzedelletna.it
(General);
tour@terrazzedelletna.it
(Tour)
+39 328-617-5952
Founded: 2008
Find the Winery On:
Facebook, Twitter, Pinterest
Contrada: Bocca d'Orzo
Hectares: 36
Vine Training: Alberello,
Guyot, Cordon
Etna DOC Wines: Etna
Bianco, Etna Rosato, Etna
Rosso
Other Wines: IGT/IGP Terre
Siciliane, DOC/DOP Sicilia
Bottles Produced: 120,000

Visits: Only by request
Hospitality: Vineyard Tour,
Winery Tour, Palmento Tour,
Wine Tasting
Amenities: Small Groups
(<15), Large Groups (15+),
Wi-Fi, Family Friendly, Pet
Friendly
Languages Spoken: Italian,
English

Wines to try—
Cuvée Brut Spumante
Pinot Nero
Cratere Nerello blend
Cirneco Etna Rosso

In 2007 and 2008, Nino Bevilacqua identified, bought, and merged forty-four continuous derelict vineyards over eighty-nine acres (36 ha) in Contrada Bocca d'Orzo. The estate, affectionately named after the numerous terraces, spans a 1,000 ft. vertical climb following the eastern edge of the 1981 lava flow. A winding path through an old forest connects all the vineyards. It's not the kind of place you tend to find on Etna. Everything is in place. The fully restored modern-rustic estate puts both feet firmly in the camp of new wineries. As if to emphasize this, Bevilacqua hired the famed Italian enologist Riccardo Cotarella to oversee the winemaking. "Without question, Terrazze dell'Etna wants to stand out," says Alessia Bevilaqua, Nino's daughter, as we walk through the old vine vineyard. "But we are all working to build something amazing here. This is our home. All of us would do anything for it." Two red wines based on Nerello are dark, rich, and extracted. A third blends Nerello Mascalese and Petit Verdot. There's also a pure Pinot Nero. Traditional method sparkling wines from Chardonnay and Pinot Nero, and a Nerello Mascalese vinified as a white wine fill out the portfolio. These are bold wines. The closer you look, however, the more you notice how much fun they're having.

Serendipity makes all the curves in the road seem a little straighter. I can think of no word that better describes the way Trente Hargrave met Filip Kesteloot, and how they came to live and make wine on Mount Etna. The keynotes of the story involve the Italian Embassy in Pakistan, an art gallery in Belgium, and an impromptu cup of tea while they were vacationing in Sicily. The first time they visited the Etna estate that they own today, it was shrouded in rain clouds. It was the same the second time, but there was a momentary break in the mist, and the ascent of terraces and vines appeared from the fog. The amphitheater, planted to old Nerello vines in Contrada Mollarella, is a rare jewel on the mountain. Few producers have ventured outside of the DOC's volcanic borders to explore the potential of Nerello grown in this white clay. The cool, moist soils result in a darker, fruitier, and softer Nerello Mascalese. After years of making wines under the supervision of other wineries, they opened their own small winery in Linguaglossa. Filip built the winery over several years while restoring buildings around Etna, and Trente just published a memoir. They admit they never planned to make wine on a volcano, but they shrug it off. Fate has a habit of getting its way.

Via Etna 38
Linguaglossa, CT 95015
www.terreditrente.com
info@terreditrente.com
+39 340-307-5433
Founded: 2007
Find the Winery On: Facebook
Contrade: Mollarella, Arcuria, Verzella
Hectares: 3.5
Vine Training: Alberello, Cordon
Etna DOC Wines: Etna Bianco, Etna Rosso
Other Wines: IGT/IGP Terre Siciliane
Bottles Produced: 4,000

Visits: Only by request
Hospitality: Vineyard Tour, Winery Tour, Wine Tasting
Amenities: Small Groups (<15), Wi-Fi
Languages Spoken: Italian, Dutch, English, French, German

Wine to try—
Dayini Bianco Carricante
Nerello Mascalese Rosso

THERESA ECCHER

Via Angelo Musco 1
Aci Castello, CT 95021
www.theresa-eccher.com
info@theresa-eccher.com
+39 094-243-6320;
+39 348-261-6935
Founded: 2010
Find the Winery On:
Facebook
Contrada: Pontale Palino
Hectares: 6
Vine Training: Alberello,
Cordon
Etna DOC Wines: Etna
Bianco, Etna Rosato, Etna
Rosso
Bottles Produced: 35,000

Visits: Only by request

Wines to try—
Alizée Etna Bianco
Ariél Etna Rosato
Altero Etna Rosso

Theresa Eccher was a tempestuous matriarch. Daniela Conta, Theresa's granddaughter, says that she spoke often of the family's estate in Trentino's Non Valley, but the tradition of winemaking had faded. Andrea Panozzo, Daniela's husband, is a seasoned journalist. He was enamored with Mount Etna. When Daniela expressed her desire to reignite the family wine business in the image of her grandmother, Etna was the region of choice. "For me," Daniela says, over lunch in Linguaglossa, "the mountain and my memories of my grandmother share several similarities. They are both wild, brazen, and welcoming." In 2011, Theresa Eccher was reimagined in the form of a Nerello Mascalese from a single vineyard on Mount Etna's northern flank, between Solicchiata and Castiglione di Sicilia. In subsequent vintages, additional wines reflecting strong Etna traditions were added to the portfolio: a supple Etna Bianco that includes 30% Catarratto; an easy-drinking Etna Rosato in the tradition of a *pistamutta*; a young-vine Etna Rosso that includes 20% Nerello Cappuccio; and an old-vine Nerello Mascalese, which includes 2% Nerello Cappuccio found among the gnarled alberelli. There is something formidable and comforting about this portfolio. Part of me can't help but wonder if these might be exactly the kind of wines that Nonna Theresa would drink.

More than 150 years ago, Giuseppe Tornatore turned two hectares of vineyards into a functioning winery in the hills above Linguaglossa. Shortly thereafter, an additional two hectares were added high on the north slope around Contrada Filici. Today, the family-owned company has been reimagined as one of the largest wine estates on the mountain. Farming in four different contrade in the comune of Castiglione di Sicilia, no expense has been spared to define a bold path forward. Nearly every vine on the sixty-hectare property has been restored, or planted on drought-resistant rootstock. Vines are trained in cordon along tension wires fixed to fiberglass posts. In the cellar, winemaker Angelo di Grazia uses an array of concrete and stainless steel vats adorned with all the latest technology. Wood botti and tonneaux are used to refine and elevate the wines. Bottling happens on site. There is no recipe to achieve absolute consistency among Etna's variable vintages, but no corners are cut, no shortcuts can be taken. However, Cantine Tornatore has shown that stone and sand can be sculpted. In the end they've created a straight road in a place where few thoroughfares ever run square for long. Through wine, the mountain can change.

Via Pietramarina, 8A
Castiglione di Sicilia, CT
95012
www.tornatorewine.com
info@tornatorewine.com
+39 095-713-1576;
+39 338-641-0271
Founded: 1865
Contrade: Bragaseggi, Malpasso, Piano Dei Daini, Pietramarina, Torre Guarino, Pietrarizzo, Trimarchisa, Verzella, Zottorinoto
Hectares: 70
Vine Training: Alberello, Cordon
Etna DOC Wines: Etna Bianco, Etna Rosato, Etna Rosso, Etna Rosso Riserva
Other Wines: DOC/DOP Sicilia
Bottles Produced: 350,000

Visits: Only by request
Hospitality: Vineyard Tour, Winery Tour, Palmento Tour, Wine Tasting, Lunch, Dinner
Amenities: Small Groups (<15), Large Groups (15+), Event Space, Wi-Fi, Family Friendly, Pet Friendly
Languages Spoken: Italian, English, French, Russian

Wines to try—
Etna Bianco
Etna Rosso
Pietrarizzo Etna Bianco
Trimarchisa Etna Rosso

TORRE MORA

SS120
Rovittello, CT 95012
www.piccini1882.it
info@torremora.it
+39 392-933-1956
Founded: 2013
Find The Winery On:
Facebook, Instagram
Contrade: Dafara Galluzzo,
Alboretto-Chiuse del Signore
Hectares: 15
Etna DOC Wines: Etna
Bianco, Etna Rosato, Etna
Rosso
Vine Training: Alberello,
Cordon
Bottles Produced: 120,000

Visits: Only by request
Hospitality: Vineyard Tour,
Palmento Tour, Winery Tour,
Wine Tasting, Lunch
Amenities: Small groups
(<15), Wi-Fi, Family Friendly,
Pet Friendly
Languages Spoken: Italian,
English

Wines to Try —
Scalunera Etna Bianco
Cauru Etna Rosso
Scalunera Etna Rosso

Walking through the Torre Mora estate above the hamlet of Rovittello, it's difficult to understand how anyone could abandon the old palmento and villa to the wild fertility of Mount Etna, but that is how the Piccini family found it in 2013. The terraces and rolling terrain east of the 1911 lava flow that separates Rovittello and Solicchiata have now been restored. After years of planting and training the vineyard, the entirety of Torre Mora's wines and olive oil received organic certification in 2018. The warm sun and constant breezes on this northeast corner of the volcano make organic processes easier. In fact, this is where the cool, wet weather of the eastern slope gives way and the sweet spot of Mount Etna's northern valley begins. Torre Mora is not alone here. Other estates have invested in Contrada Dafara Galluzzo as well. It's easy to see why. Torre Mora's wines are elegant, textured and mineral. The red wines lean into a profile of spiced black fruit and wild herbs. These are precisely the flavors I expect from vines grown at the exposed edge of a mountain forest. As the Piccini family knows, these flavors are well worth the investment.

Like so many winegrowers on Etna, Bruno Ferrara Sardo knows the work that goes into each bottle of wine. His family has been farming on the volcano's northern slope for generations. Today, he manages a single vineyard that produces a single Etna Rosso, called *'nzemmula*, which means "together." This is not a wine made by the numbers. For Sardo, it's a wine made through the sounds of work in the vineyard. As a child, he studied his grandfather's movements and listened carefully to the rhythms of the laborers. Back then, the wine was always sold in sfuso. When Sardo opted to begin bottling his own wine, the sounds and memories were what guided him through his first vintages. The forty- and fifty-year-old Nerello vines are trained in tall alberello that have been reorganized into filare. New plants are grafted to drought-resistant American rootstocks. It isn't hard to grow grapes here. The fine and fertile sands are capable of producing healthy yields. The work comes from balancing the canopy, limiting overproduction, and moderating the influence of the spontaneous flora. It's possible that the trajectory of the wine may vary from vintage to vintage, but the sounds of Bruno's vineyard remain unchanged.

Contrada Allegracore
Randazzo, CT 95036
www.viniferrarasardo.com
info@viniferrarasardo.com
+39 329-547-7782
Founded: Nineteenth century
Find the Winery On:
Facebook, Instagram
Contrada: Allegracore
Hectares: 1.2
Vine Training: Alberello in Cordon
Etna DOC Wines: Etna Rosso
Other Wines: DOC Sicilia
Bottles Produced: 4,000

Visits: Only by request
Hospitality: Vineyard Tour, Wine Tasting
Amenities: Small Groups (<15), Family Friendly, Pet Friendly
Languages Spoken: Italian, English, Spanish

Wine o try—
'nzemmula Nerello blend

Contrada Petto Dragone
Linguaglossa, CT 95015
www.vinigambino.it
info@vinigambino.it
+39 348-822-0130;
+39 389-852-5100
Founded: 1978
Find the Winery On:
Facebook, Instagram,
Pinterest, Twitter, TripAdvisor
Contrada: Petto Dragone
Hectares: 13
Vine Training: Alberello,
Cordon
Etna DOC Wines: Etna
Bianco, Etna Rosato, Etna
Rosso, Etna Spumante
Other Wines: IGT/IGP Terre
Siciliane, DOC/DOP Sicilia
Bottles Produced: 150,000

Visits: Seven days a week
Hospitality: Vineyard Tour,
Winery Tour, Wine Tasting
Amenities: Small Groups
(<15), Large Groups (15+),
Event Space, Wi-Fi, Family
Friendly, Pet Friendly
Languages Spoken: Italian,
English, French, Polish,
Russian, Spanish

Wines to try—
Tifeo Etna Bianco
Tifeo Etna Rosso
Petto Dragone Etna Rosso

Maria Gambino and Vittorio Raciti grew up on Etna's eastern flank, in Zafferana Etnea and Acireale. Vittorio engineered cement fabrications for large-scale construction jobs during the week. The natural ambiance of Etna offered a peaceful getaway on the weekends. In 1979, they decided to build on a piece of land in Contrada Petto Dragone (the breast of the dragon) in the hills above Linguaglossa, and to plant a small vineyard. The wine was decent, but it went quickly. So, Vittorio expanded, building one broad terrace after another. In 2000, their children, Maria Grazia, Delfo, and Francesco joined the company. They had grown up in the vineyards, on the northeast slope of the volcano. From their perch at 800 meters AMSL, you can see northeast Sicily, the mountains, Calabria, and the sea. It was a view the children wanted to share. The modern winery welcomes thousands of visitors each year to enjoy a broad range of wines and engaging educational tours of the cellar. The line of Etna wines is named for the mythological dragon Tifeo.[185] Though the company plays into the mysticism of the volcano, Gambino's wines aren't as ferocious as the stories make Etna out to be, but they do resemble the safety of her embrace.

It's hard to think of two more-dedicated winegrowers than Giuseppe and Valeria Scirto. Both of their families have been making wine for generations. Giuseppe and Valeria repeat these steps every day. Every ounce of work is done by hand and without the use of chemical herbicides or fertilizers. "The only way to make our wine is to work organically and give constant attention to the vines," Giuseppe says, walking through their vineyard, in Feudo di Mezzo. Valeria stops to remove a ripe fig from one of their trees and hands it to me, "This is not a vineyard, this is our home. We do everything to encourage the biodiversity of the farm." Wild greens, asparagus, fennel, and flowers occur spontaneously amid the fruit, nut, and olive trees that grow among the vines. Giuseppe began bottling under the family name for the first time in 2010. The production was modest, but quality was high. Since then, the range of wines has evolved to include a savory Carricante blend made using extended skin contact, a succulent Etna Rosato, and Nerello blends from old vines that they've been restoring since 2018. Prior to the 2016 vintage, the couple finished restoration of their winery in the heart of Passopisciaro. It hasn't been easy, they contend, but the wines remain honest expressions of the places they love.

Via Panebianco 13
Passopisciaro, Castiglione di
Sicilia, CT 95012
www.viniscirto.com
viniscirto@gmail.com
+39 328-361-1270
Founded: 2010
Find the Winery On:
Facebook, Twitter,
Instagram, Pinterest, Path
Contrade: Feudo, Feudo di
Mezzo-Porcaria, Pirao
Hectares: 5
Vine Training: Alberello,
Cordon
Etna DOC Wines: Etna
Rosso, Etna Rosato
Other Wines: IGT/IGP Terre
Siciliane
Bottles Produced: 15,000

Visits: Only by request
Hospitality: Vineyard Tour,
Wine Tasting, Lunch, Dinner
Amenities: Small Groups
(<15), Family Friendly, Pet
Friendly
Languages Spoken: Italian,
English, Spanish

Wines to try—
Don Pippinu Carricante
blend
All'Antica Etna Rosato
A'Culonna Etna Rosso

Via Regina Margherita 42
Passopisciaro, Castiglione di
Sicilia, CT 95030
www.vinonibali.com
mail@vinonibali.com
+39-366-413-5405 (Italian);
+39 338-786-2265 (English)
Founded: 2002
Find the Winery On:
Facebook
Contrada: Feudo Di Mezzo,
Moganazzi
Hectares: 5
Vine Training: Alberello,
Cordon
Etna DOC Wines: Etna Rosso
Other Wines: IGT/IGP Terre
Siciliane, DOC/DOP Sicilia,
Vino Locale / Sfuso
Bottles Produced: 12,000

Visits: Only by request
Hospitality: Vineyard Tour,
Winery Tour, Wine Tasting,
Lunch
Amenities: Small Groups
(<15), Large Groups (15+),
Family Friendly, Pet Friendly
Languages Spoken: Italian,
English

Wines to try—
Butterfly Carricante blend
Kirnào Etna Rosso
Vinazzu Late Harvest Nerello

The afternoon sun cut across the ancient terraces in Moganazzi like a razor. "In October, the weather teases us," Riccardo Nibali says, leading us into the company's palmento in Contrada Moganazzi. "A few weeks ago it was raining. People harvested, out of fear, perhaps. But now you see how warm and sunny it is." Knowing the terrain and the patterns of weather is imperative for Vino Nibali, and one of their wines in particular. The *Vinazzu* is a Nerello that goes through appassimento on the vine. This opulent wine—made only in the best years—arrives at 16% alcohol by volume or more, resulting in a healthy quantity of residual sugar. The other grapes—used to make a selection of blends and DOC wines—don't need to hang on this long. Riccardo's long-time business partner Orazio Pometti, who was laid to rest in 2021, said, "Because we work only by hand, we know how well the vines are doing, how quickly or slowly the grapes ripen, and how the wine ages [in the winery] each year." As we talk, laborers are preparing the terraces for planting. "Restoration of the palmento will come later," Riccardo says. First, they need the new vineyard to begin producing. There's little doubt that it will; for sixty years the families have been working their vineyard in Contrada Feudo di Mezzo. Now all they have to do is duplicate their efforts a little farther down the road.

Antonino and Armida Vivera started small, with an inheritance of vines. Though they lived in Catania, each autumn the family piled into the car to travel across the island for the grape harvest in Corleone. Over time, the passion of winemaking took hold. They purchased additional vineyards in Chiaramonte Gulfi and on Mount Etna in 2002. The Contrada Martinella estate is located at the mouth of the Valle Galfina, on Etna's windswept northeast shoulder. It includes thirty acres (12 ha) of vineyards and a modern, gravity-operated winery. The Carricante and Nerello blends are easily some of the most widely accepted Etna standards. It's not difficult to understand why. Gentle practices in the winery complement the fruit grown at this sunny intersection of Etna's rocky northern slope and the fertile eastern flank. Since the Middle Ages, the district has been at an important thoroughfare between the upper and lower mountain. I have always considered its precise location the point where the north and east slopes go their separate ways. For the Vivera family, this is the heart of their production. All the wine grapes arrive here in the fall. It's a busy time for Loredana Vivera, the winemaker, but it's also a lot like being at home.

Contrada Martinella, SP 59/IV
Linguaglossa, CT 95015
www.vivera.it
info@vivera.it
+39 095-643837
Founded: 2002
Find the Winery On: Facebook, Twitter, Instagram, Pinterest
Contrada: Martinella
Hectares: 14
Vine Training: Alberello, Cordon
Etna DOC Wines: Etna Bianco, Etna Rosato, Etna Rosso
Other Wines: IGT/IGP Terre Siciliane
Bottles Produced: 120,000

Visits: Only by request
Hospitality: Vineyard Tour, Winery Tour, Wine Tasting, Lunch, Dinner
Amenities: Small Groups (<15), Large Groups (15+), Event Space, Wi-Fi, Family Friendly
Languages Spoken: Italian, English, French

Wines to try—
Salisire Contrada Martinella Etna Bianco
Rosato di Martinella Etna Rosato
Martinella Etna Rosso

Contrada Marchesa 1
Castiglione di Sicilia, CT
95012
www.wiegnerwine.com
contact@wiegnerwine.com
+39 348-904-6391
Founded: 2002
Find the Winery On:
Facebook, Twitter, Instagram,
LinkedIn
Contrada: Marchesa,
Rampante
Hectares: 5.5
Vine Training: Alberello,
Guyot, Cordon
Etna DOC Wines: Etna
Bianco, Etna Rosso
Other Wines: IGT/IGP Terre
Siciliane, DOC/DOP Sicilia
Bottles Produced: 25,000

Visits: Only by request
Hospitality: Vineyard Tour,
Winery Tour, Palmento Tour,
Wine Tasting, Lunch, Dinner
Amenities: Small Groups
(<15), Wi-Fi, Pet Friendly,
Overnight Accommodations
Languages Spoken: Italian,
English, French, German

Wines to try—
Elisena Fiano
Treterre Etna Rosso
Rampante Cru Etna Rosso
Torquato Aglianico

I have the indelible image of Peter Wiegner and I standing at a bar in London drinking something strong. Some of my greatest meals and deepest laughs on Etna have been in the company of Peter, his wife, Laura Puccetti, and their son, Marco. Their estate, positioned at 700 meters AMSL on Mount Etna's north slope, is the kind of place that arouses your sensibilities and emotions. It's the food, wine, and conversation, I think. Together, the family manages one of the mountain's prototypically picturesque wine estates. The Nerello Mascalese was planted in 2002, but instead of Carricante the family chose Fiano—a white grape with an affinity for volcanic soil. By 2004, the vineyard also included Aglianico and Cabernet Franc, which are grown primarily in cordon and guyot, on the higher plateau behind the modern winery. As a result of this position, the wines are lightly styled and fresh. They resemble their environment—a breezy volcanic plateau surrounded by olive groves, fruiting cactus, ginestra, and roses—the veritable sum of their surroundings. Here, the family produces their wine and shares it with guests. You can come for tastings and meals or a short stay in their palmento-turned-cottage. It's the kind of place many of us dream to own, occasionally visit, and never forget . . . especially if Laura is cooking.

Walking through some of Etna's old palmenti, it feels as though the laborers simply finished their work, leaned their shovels along the walls, removed their boots, and walked away as if they would return the next day. But they didn't.

Mount Etna is a bastion of small holdings where practices of permaculture and perpetual farming are, and have always been, the norm. Within the confines of each small farm, it is common to find vines, orchards, and spontaneous flora working together in a natural rhythm that creates broad biodiversity throughout the Etna growing area.

THE NEWEST NEW WINES OF MOUNT ETNA

I'm on the mountain a lot. I see the scrub and bramble being pulled back. The lava-stone terraces in repair. I could count the number of old vineyards getting a new lease on life and nascent vines being planted, but the number would change tomorrow, or next week. There, it just happened again.

Mount Etna hasn't seen investments on this scale since the end of the nineteenth century. Back then, there was a need. Phylloxera was devastating Continental Europe. The more wine Etna made available, the more people came.

Cut to the beginning of the twenty-first century and Etna produces wine for a different market. The market of the individual. The days of "almost any wine will do" are gone. Consumers want something that has a story, maybe even a little romance and a bit of danger. This is part of what makes Mount Etna thrilling. Everyone is working on the edge of the world!

That, in and of itself, has helped to sell more than a few bottles. It's also attracted scores of new producers and long-time farmers to try their hand at making Etna. For some, it's what the family has always done; now, they're just giving their effort a name.

For others, it's a first effort or, in some cases, the extension of an existing brand based in another region of Sicily, or Italy.

Azienda Agricola Cannavò (www.facebook.com/vinicannavo) began making small amounts of wine from their vineyards in Contrada Feudo Di Mezzo-Porcaria, in Passopisciaro, and Contrada Montedolce, in Solicchiata. It wasn't a big project. In total, the bucolic Etna Rosso and resonant Etna Rosato that Lucio and Maria Cannavò make only now arrives at 700 and 900 bottles of each type, respectively. It's rare to find their wines in a market or on a wine list. Even the technical data sheets and website are still "in-process."

Just as some things on Etna are starting to scale at an incalculable pace, it's nice to know that other things rarely change that fast.

Azienda Agricola Sofia (www.facebook.com/AziendaAgricolaSofia) is the perfect example of a family that has lived and worked in the vineyards for generations. In the beginning, Gioacchino Sofia labored for other owners. Slowly, he began working his own vineyard, in Piano dei Daini, buying small parcels that came up for sale. Twenty years later, with his wife, Angela, and children Carmelo and Valentina, they produce stylish DOC wines in their cantina in Solicchiata using an organic scheme. Look for the three-wheeled Ape (a popular farm truck) on the label. It's the vehicle Gioacchino has used for years.

The name *Badalarc'* is given to two wines made by **Azienda Vinicola Spuches** (www.facebook.com/aziendavinicolaspuches). Both the savory Etna Bianco and medium-bodied Etna Rosso carry the same name. The vineyard reaches 800 meters AMSL in Contrada Rampante, with vines trained in filare on an undulating plateau. Today, the wines are managed by Valerio Treffiletti and veteran winemaker Pietro di Giovanni. The name "*Badalarc'*" recalls a phrase Valerio's grandfather used to tell his wife as they entered the home after a long day in the vineyard. It translates to "Watch your head on the arch of the door."

You'll find **Barone Beneventano** (www.baronebeneventano.com) on the southeast slope of Mount Etna, perched between Monte Ilice and Monte Gorna, facing the Ionian Sea. The father and son team of Roberto and Pierluca Beneventano della Corte manage the farm as a tribute to the family's noble history as winemakers and merchants, producing an Etna Bianco and a single Etna Rosso from their alberelli planted between 700 and 800 meters AMSL. While both wines are raised in stainless steel, the red wine sees time in French oak and chestnut vats.

Resting at the base of the hillside city of Castiglione di Sicilia, at the edge of the rushing Alcantara River, are the remains of a Byzantine church. Here, in sight of the dome and pendentives of the church, **Bizantino** (www. produttorietnanord.it) grows Carricante and Catarratto Lucido at 550 meters AMSL for a single Etna Bianco. Planted in 2011, the vines are organized in *filare* on alluvial and stony soils in Contrada Santa Domenica. In the winery, the grapes are macerated at cool temperatures prior to fermentation in stainless steel and aging in barrique, arriving at a wine with a pleasant floral and zesty profile.

For **Mirella Buscemi**, whose boutique label assumes her surname, the shift from pharmacology to wine was an easy one. Growing up in southeast Sicily, her family made wine regularly. Through her spouse, Alberto Aiello Graci, she was introduced to Mount Etna, but it was a small old-vine alberello vineyard of little more than a hectare that made the conversion complete. The Nerello in the vineyard is spiced with Alicante (Etna's version of Grenache Noir). The Carricante is supported by Grecanico. She named these beautiful territorial wines *Tartaraci*, for the neighborhood on Etna's northwest slope where the vineyard is located, at 980 meters AMSL, once a part of the Ducea di Nelson.

Campione Vini (www.campionevini.com) carries the name of Giuseppe Campione, who produces an Etna Rosso from a small vineyard in one of the most coveted areas of the north slope, Contrada Crasà in the municipality of Castiglione di Sicilia. The old alberelli vines have been worked by the family for more than a century, for their own wine and others. Today, Giuseppe calls his single-vineyard, ruby Nerello Mascalese *Sua Maestà*, meaning "Her Majesty," a reference to Mount Etna and the generations who have dedicated their lives to working in her vineyards.

Cantina del Malandrino (www.cantinadelmalandrino.it) can be found in the sunny, fertile hills above the historic town of Mascali, on Etna's northeast slope. The terraced, organic farm benefits from bright morning light and brisk winds that contribute to a portfolio of still wines, beers, olive oil, and vinegars. Each wine is assembled from micro harvests and spontaneous fermentations, with aging in amphora and wood. No clarification or filtration is used, but everything from the vineyard through the packaging is managed by hand. The company recently began offering curated educational tastings at their estate, which includes a typical palmento constructed in the early nineteenth century.

Don't let the name fool you. As much as **Cantine di Nessuno** (www. cantinadinessuno.it) is a nod to Homer's hero, Odysseus/Ulysses, Seby Costanzo's passion project takes its cues from the mountain that *no one (Nessuno)* will ever truly own. Costanzo—an interior designer, author, and entrepreneur—owns three alberello vineyards located between 700 and 900 meters AMSL among the vertiginous, sandy slopes and pastoral valleys of Mount Etna's southeast craters, in Contrade Monte Ilice, Carpene, and Monte Gorna. Visiting the company palmento feels like you're traveling back in time, but the modern wines are an extension of Costanzo's enthusiasm for bringing the Etna community and the mountain to the table.

Floriana and Pasquale at **Cantina Malopasso** (www.cantinamalopasso. it) produce one Etna Bianco, Etna Rosato, and Etna Rosso from old alberelli in Contrada Pietralunga, downslope from the spent volcanic crater Monte Ilice, on the southeast flank of the mountain. A second old-vine vineyard sits high above the village of Poggiofelice (Happy Hill) at 750 meters AMSL. This is a fantastic area to grow grapes. Monte Ilice has a history of interplanting relic varieties throughout the vineyards—Bracaù (Pampanuto/ Verdeca), Grecanico, Minella, Zu Matteo, along with Nerello, Carricante, and Catarratto lend a refreshing zest to these wines.

Skirting the eastern edge of Milo, the Cacocciola Creek cuts a valley in the mountain, establishing two unique contrade—Praino and Volpare— where **Cantina Maugeri** (www.cantinamaugeri.it) grows Carricante and

Nerello Mascalese for their portfolio of Etna wines. The 7-hectare vineyard, which has been in the Maugeri family for generations, is sculpted on terraces filled of sandy debris with mugearitic pebbles next to the 1689 lava flow. Two brackish Etna Biancos arrive from select parcels while the company grows only a small quantity of Nerello for a savory rosato. "This is white wine territory," Carla Maugeri says, walking through the chestnut posts supporting their vines. "We want to celebrate that."

The **Iuppa** family (www.cantineiuppa.it) first set their sights on Contrada Salice, in the hills below Milo, in 2002. By 2016, the undulating contours of the mountain were being planted with on terraces that now assume a pyramidal form leading up to a nineteenth-century palmento at the peak. As the vines took root and began to produce fruit, trials began in the cellar. Today, the breathtaking estate produces a savory Etna Bianco, spry Etna Rosato, zesty Etna Rosso, and an attractive Etna Spumante from established and young Nerello Mascalese vines growing in ancient landslide deposits from the opening of the Valle del Bove.

In the early twentieth century, merchants from Riposto knew the best *Vino da Taglio* and *Vino da Pasto* came from the plain that stretches between Mascali and Acireale, between 350-400 meters AMSL. From this perch, overlooking Giarre and Riposto, **Cantine Scudero** (www.cantinescudero. it) produces Catarratto Lucido and Sauvignon Blanc. Carlo and Martino Scudero, decedents of the Scudero Barons, gave new life to the centuries-old estate in San Giovanni Montebello in 2016. Today, the winery produces small quantities of each international variety on their own and one fascinating blend of the two, called *Sedicidieci*.

Cédric Perraud produces one wine, *Goccia*, from a small Nerello vineyard in Montelaguardia, between Passopisciaro and Randazzo. The forty-year-old vines are trained in alberello with tight spacing and 10% autochthonous white Sicilian varieties mixed in. In the cellar, the grapes are destemmed and fermented in plastic vats for one week. The wine rests for a few months before going into bottle prior to the following harvest. This lively field blend is currently labeled as an IGT Terre Siciliane.

I see Pietro di Giovanni frequently—at wine tastings, lectures, food events, wine shops. He has become one of the most important enogastronomic VIPs on the mountain. After years of consulting for other successful projects, Pietro launched the artisanal syndicate of small wineries called *Produttori Etna Nord*, for which he acts as the leading winemaker. He also produces his own wines under the label **Cuore di Marchesa** (www.produttorietnanord. it), including a graceful Etna Bianco and vivid Etna Rosso, from 60-year-old vines planted in Contrada Marchesa at 730 meters a.s.l., which are released annually in minuscule quantities.

Emilio Sciacca (www.emiliosciaccaetnawine.it) launched a winery that carries his name with the intention of making minimal intervention wines from vineyards on the north and south slopes of the volcano. One white blend, *Biancopiglio*, and two reds, *Rossobrillo* and *Neromagno* are currently in production from a total of two hectares of owned and leased vines near Linguaglossa and Biancavilla. The heart of the company is in Contrada Martinella, in Valle Galfina.

For years, the prephylloxera Carricante grown by **Eredi Di Maio** (www. facebook.com/eredidimaio) found its way into some of the most well-known and celebrated Etna Bianco Superiores ever produced. The Patanè-Di Maio family's alberelli in Contrada Rinazzo, in the comune of Milo, grow on an outcropping directly below the Valle del Bove. As of the 2018 vintage, the family changed course, opting to produce their first Etna Bianco Superiore, called *Affiu* (Alfio), from the grapes they have grown for generations. A second vineyard in the higher Contrada Caselle adds to the blend. *Affiu* is a jovial wine but there is nothing unintended about this delicious Carricante.

Etna Barrus (www.etnabarrus.com) is another wine I have started to see a lot around Etna. The unmistakable label features a Sicilian elephant, an archetype of local myth, good luck, and strength. This small company currently produces three wines from their vines in the valley at the base of Monte Gorna, an extinct crater on Etna's southeast slope. The floral and spicy Etna Rosato is possibly the only rosé on the volcano fermented in wood. The two reds are aged in either stainless steel or wood with distinctive profiles of fruit, mountain spice, and earth that show the potential of each method for fruit grown at 600 meters AMSL.

You'll find find a wealth of information and wine at **Etna Urban Winery** (www.etnaurbanwinery.it). Situated on the lower southeast slope of Mount Etna among the remnants of the Vignagrande Forest, the young vines surrounding the company's eighteenth-century palmento are planted on fertile sand with mixtures of hawaiite and mugearite. Inside, Etna's history mixes with the present. After a tour of the grounds and family winery, guests are invited to taste estate wines and luxurious pairings with other local Etna wines, making this one stop that satisfies almost any curious traveler without having to travel far from Catania or Taormina.

Famiglia Statella (www.famigliastatella.com) bought their first vineyard in Contrada Pettinociarelle, in Etna's northern valley, in 2016. After a decade of working at Tenuta delle Terre Nere, winemaker Calogero Statella founded the company with his wife, Rita, as a way of exploring the specific variables within the mosaic of Etna's geology. Two years later, the young company purchased a vineyard of old Nerello vines planted on Ellittico soils in Contrada Pignatuni, near Randazzo. Today, their artisanal portfolio includes a smart Etna Bianco, a delicate Etna Rosato, and two single-vineyard Etna Rossos with all the appeal of Etna's potential.

Federico Curtaz (www.federicocurtaz.it) has made wine on Mount Etna since 2007, when he helped launch Tenuta di Fessina, in Rovittello. Since 2015, he has consulted for several producers on Etna. The new wines that assume his name developed from his extensive knowledge of Mount Etna and Southeastern Sicily. Two Etna DOC wines arrive from the volcano: *Gamma*, a juicy Etna Bianco from Milo; and *Il Purgatorio*, a territorial Etna Rosso from the ancient soils around Biancavilla. His second red, *Ananke*—the first wine that ever carried his name—arrives from Nero d'Avola grown around Siracusa, in calcareous clay.

Entrepreneur Michele Failla launched **Feudo Failla** (www.feudofailla.com) from a small family vineyard on Etna's north slope, in Contrada Calderara. The terrain in this part of Etna is some of the most precious on the mountain, because it includes outcroppings and basalt stones from the prehistoric Ellittico Volcano. Failla released the first wines, an Etna Rosato and one Etna Rosso at the end of 2021. The initial quantities were minuscule, but the portfolio has expanded since then to include a single Etna Bianco. "I am not under the illusion that this is big news," Failla told me during a tasting. "But we have to start somewhere."

Fifth Estate (www.fifthestate.it) was launched in 2021 with the promise of offering an intrepid interpretation of Mount Etna's potential. American entrepreneur Jennifer Kahane is focused on uniquely different sites for a portfolio of Etna wines: in Contrada Croce Monaci, on the north slope of the volcano, where the Mongibello and Ellittico soils meet; the hamlet of San Giovanni Bosco, in the eleventh-century lava flow of Monte Ilice; and the Cancellieri neighborhood, in the sandy hills around Zafferana Etnea. A barrel-fermented Etna Bianco, savory Etna Rosato, and a striking Etna Rosso are joined by two rousing Brut Metodo Classico wines—in white and rosé—from Nerello Mascalese.

Generation Alessandro (www.generazionealessandro.it) brings three cousins—Anna, Benedetto, and Benedetto Alessandro—together on a single project. The three grew up in the family vineyards around Camporeale, in Western Sicily, where the Alessandro family has made wine for generations. On Mount Etna, the three cousins launched their own winery, which currently produces *Trainara*, a savory Etna Bianco, and *Croceferro*, an exciting Etna Rosso from Contrada Piano Filici. The young company's vineyard holdings have since expanded to include old and young vines in the contrade of Crasà, Sciaramanica, and Borriglione, all on the north slope of the volcano.

After decades working in Sicily, winemaker Carlo Ferrini climbed Etna and found a small vineyard on the north slope of the volcano at 950 meters, from which he bottled the first Nerello Mascalese under the **Giodo** label (www.giodo.it). The low-yielding 80-year-old alberello vines produce *Alberelli di Giodo* and are currently bottled as DOC Sicilia. It's not hard to find comparisons to the Brunello di Montalcino that Ferrini and his daughter, Bianca, make in Tuscany under the Giodo label. The flavorful fruit of Nerello and Sangiovese feature the balance of hard work with a kiss of oak.

I first met **Giuseppe Lazzaro** (www.giuseppelazzaro.it) at a prominent Etna winery, where he worked for several years. In 2020, he launched his own project based on the knowledge he had accrued on the job. A total of 2.5 hectares (6 acres) are planted to married vineyards of Nerello Mascalese and indigenous Etna varieties, which he uses to make two red wines (from old and young vines), a still rosé, and an ancestral method sparkling rosé. By harnessing Etna's natural biodiversity in the vineyard and using manual methods through production, including spontaneous fermentations in stainless steel and amphorae, Giuseppe's way forward includes a profound reverence for the past.

I was introduced to **Le Due Tenute** (www.leduetenute.it) at an event for small wineries on Etna. They were pouring one white wine from Carricante and one red wine from Nerello Mascalese. Both carried the name Cantonè, meaning a small district and, if you're familiar with Latin, the highest voice in polyphonic choral music. Of course, I had a taste. Each wine was sophisticated and youthful, a result of the advantageous position of their vineyards at 900 meters AMSL on Etna's historic southern slope and the exclusive use of stainless steel in the winery. My notes from that tasting were simple and straightforward: Two wines from small parcels that have the potential to sing.

In 1860, as Giuseppe Garibaldi marched across Sicily in an effort to unify the regions of Italy, Francesco Rallo was joining his love of agriculture and the vine in the family's first vineyard. Today, Giacomo Rallo manages **Marchese delle Saline** (www.marchesedellesaline.com), a Marsala-based winery that carries the nickname of his great-grandfather, Francesco. The winery makes a single Etna Bianco, one Etna Rosso, and a Vino Spumante from vineyards on the volcano's north slope, using the name *Tìadi*—a reference to followers of Dionysus. A second Etna Rosso, *Longitudo15*—named for Mount Etna's longitude—arrives from old vines of Nerello Mascalese.

Massimo Lentsch (www.massimolentsch.it) specialized in export management before a sailing trip through the Mediterranean shifted his career toward wine. Starting in Lipari with Tenuta Castellaro, Mount Etna captured his attention in 2018. Farming vineyards on the north slope, in Contrade Feudo di Mezzo, Calderara Sottana, Pianodario, and Chiusa Politi, one macerated Etna Bianco, an amiable Etna Rosato, and two distinctive old-vine Etna Rossos have set an optimistic stride for the new winery. "I have been tasting Etna wines since 2004," Lentsch said. "The Etna wines we have in mind will be different, but I would love to join the ranks of producers that matter."

Mecori (www.mecorietna.it) can be found on Etna's north slope, in Contrada Muganazzi. In the vineyard, Sebastiano Vinci focuses on constant guidance to maximize the influence of biodiversity surrounding the old Nerello vines. In the cellar, Serena Guarrera uses a technical approach to maintaining the vibrant aromas and tension found in their young volcanic soils. To accent the terroir where the grapes are grown, no wood is currently being used. It's a lot of work to produce only one wine, an Etna Rosso called *Duo*, but you can feel their sentiment in the glass. *Mecori* translates to "my heart."

For the last few years, the Conti family has produced one expressive Etna Rosso, Animaecorpo (Soul and Body), for their label **Mongibello33** (www.facebook.com/mongibello33). In 2021, the father and son team of Giovanni and Carlo planted another 3000 vines in the coveted hills around Rovittello. Though it will take a few years for these vines to begin producing, the young company knows that working by hand in the vineyard and experimenting in the cellar produces results. Their flagship wine, which carries the iconic falcon on the label, has been winning awards and recognition from the London Wine Competition since 2020.

Monteleone (www.monteleonetna.com) produces wine from vineyards in one of the few places on Etna's north slope that lava has not touched in millennia. Here, in the alluvial fields below the medieval town of Castiglione di Sicilia, on the north flank of the volcano, Enrico and Giulia Monteleone (father, daughter), with winemaker Benedetto Alessandro, grow Nerello and Alicante beside the ruins of a Byzantine church—La Cuba. Two lovely Etna Rossos, one carrying the name of the church, were recently joined by a prephylloxera Nerello from Contrada Pontale Palino, below Solicchiata, and an alluring Carricante from the steep slopes of Sant'Alfio, high on the volcano's eastern skirt.

Nuzzella (www.nuzzella.com) makes still and sparkling wines from vineyards positioned on the northeast slope of Mount Etna, between Piedimonte Etneo and Linguaglossa, at about 500 meters AMSL. The company began restoring an old estate in 2014, located between the white chalky hills of the Peloritani mountains and the black sands of Mount Etna, near an area known to locals as Terremorte (dead land). The painstaking work has paid off. The sustainable vineyard of four hectares now produces an

Etna Spumante (dosaggio zero), Etna Rosato and Etna Rosso from Nerello Mascalese, and a single Etna Bianco from Carricante.

I was loading wine barrels onto a truck, when Domenico Costa, of **Oro d'Etna** (www.orodetna.it), stopped along the road to give me a hand. Domenico, a trained sommelier and grappa taster, knows that lending a hand is part of life on the mountain. With very few exceptions, everyone on Etna does more than one thing. Oro d'Etna is the perfect example. In addition to Etna DOC wines, the Costa farm produces artisanal honeys, craft olive oils, and healthcare products that the company sells at their shop in the hills above Zafferana Etnea. While you're there, be sure to taste through the wines.

I was having lunch with a friend at Paradise Alcantara restaurant, in Gaggi. He said, "You have to try my friend's new wine, **Q'Assaggia** (www. produttorietnanord.it). He only makes a few hundred bottles each year." Arriving from ten terraces of Nerello Mascalese in Contrada Crasà, below the town of Solicchiata, this micro-production Etna Rosso is made by Antonio Platania for the patrons of his restaurant, Paradise Alcantara, and anyone else who may stumble upon it. *Q'Assaggia* translates as "who's tasting," as in, who would like to taste the wine before serving it to other guests. The bottle we were presented with was more than acceptable. We drank it all.

I met Fabio Caruso in his office at an agricultural organization in the heart of Catania, by chance. I was there on another matter, but I recognized the bottle of **Rinanera** (www.carusowine.it) on his shelf immediately. Fabio's grandfather, Filippo, managed a vineyard near Nicolosi in the seventies, high on the southeast slope of the volcano at 850 meters, to make wine for the family. Today, a vineyard purchased in the nineties is in the capable hands of Fabio and his father, Antonio. "The production of Rinanera, which translates as 'black sand,' may be modest," Fabio said. "But our focus has never been so enthusiastic."

Roberto Abbate (www.facebook.com/robertotindaro) is not a wine baron; his career is in citrus. For him, making wine is a passion, something he does on the weekends and in his spare time. The wines that carry his name arrive from small vineyards of very old vines at the western edge of Contrada Feudo di Mezzo, on Etna's north slope. The few thousand bottles Abbate makes each year are direct descendants of the wines his family has made for generations from the same district and neighboring vineyards. A single Etna Rosso and Etna Rosato are honest reflections of the vintages that have been carefully fermented in infinitesimal batches each year.

At the edge of **Rupestre's** (www.instagram.com/azienda_raciti) vineyard in Contrada Pietramarina stands an ancient *palmento rupestre*—a hefty boulder carved into an ancient vinification site. This icon of the Raciti family's wines also happens to be an eternal meeting place between Man, Mamma Etna, and Mother Nature. The Raciti family is respected throughout the Northern valley for planting and managing many of Etna's famed vineyards and estates. With three generations of experience, the family is now also producing a delightful Etna Bianco from Carricante and a robust Etna Rosso from Nerello Mascalese grown in Contrade Pietramarina, Verzella, Moganazzi, and Pietrarizzo, some of the most ancient wine areas on Mount Etna.

Salvo Licciardello (www.vinilicciardello.com) farms one and a half hectares on Etna's north slope, between Randazzo and Solicchiata. He splits his time evenly between two estates and the cellar, so that the vines and the wines receive careful attention. His primary focus is on Nerello Mascalese for a still white wine, a sparkling rosato, and two red wines. Licciardello produces a single white DOC Sicilia from Carricante, Grecanico, Minella Bianca, and some Coda di Volpe. All the wines share similarities: the vines are approximately 80 years old; organic and biodynamic practices are applied in the vineyard; fermentations are spontaneous; batches are small; and every bottle comes from the care and attention of one man.

On the southeastern edge of the Valle del Bove, in Nicolosi, **Serafica** (www.serafica.it) focuses on organic practices for its wines and olive oils. Founded at the beginning of the twentieth century, the new generation of the family carries on the project of reducing the intermediate steps between producer and consumer. About 15 hectares of vineyards are cultivated between the various craters on the southeast side. The winery is located at the base of Monpilieri—site of a massive lateral eruption in 693 CE—where the company produces an inviting range of still wines in the Etnean tradition, including a 100% Nerello Cappuccio and a Catarratto.

Alluding to the provocative words of the philosopher Baruch Spinoza, Giuseppe Paoli founded **Sive Natura** (www.sivenatura.it), a reference to *"Deus Sive Natura"* (God or Nature), which suggests that God and Nature are indistinguishable. Old vines of Carricante from Contrada Caselle, above Milo, go into an age-worthy Etna Bianco Superiore called *Biancomilo*. Young vines of Carricante and Nerello Mascalese, grown in the hills above Giarre around San Giovanni Montebello, are made into amiable monovarietal IGT wines. For Paoli, a patient, soft-spoken agronomist, each wine and vintage provides another opportunity to showcase the profound connections between Nature and his own subtle influence on what arrives in the bottle.

Dario **Stagnitta** (www.instagram.com/stagnitta_wine/) makes one Nerello Mascalese from a small vineyard in Contrada Santo Spirito, above the town of Passopisciaro, on the knuckle of an early Mongibello lava flow. Spatter ramparts and pyroclastic deposits from the post-Ellitico flank eruption that created this hallowed ground can be found throughout the contrada. The Etna Rosso that assumes the winery's name is hand harvested, fermented in temperature-controlled vats, and raised in French oak tonneaux for sixteen months before going to bottle. The only enhancements are the young terrain, high elevation, and deflected light found in this rare vineyard site.

Davide Di Bella and his family farm five hectares of vineyards at 600 meters AMSL on Etna's north slope, a stone's throw from the rushing

Alcantara River, where they run **Tenuta Antica Cavalleria** (www.vacanze-sicilia.com). A founding member of Produttori Etna Nord, Davide and his family focus their wine production on traditional Etna blends from Nerello Mascalese and some Nerello Cappuccio. A stylish Etna Rosato named *DAME* and an opulent Etna Rosso called *DAM* are sold internationally, in local establishments, and on the menu of their restaurant housed in the family's charming nineteenth-century palmento.

Tenuta Bastonaca (www.tenutabastonaca.it) is known for a range of wines grown around Vittoria, in the heart of southeast Sicily. A few years ago, they realized a dream of owning a single hectare of eighty-year-old vines in Contrada Piano dei Daini, on the north slope of the volcano. Here, with acclaimed enologist Carlo Ferrini, the company has adopted an organic scheme for the alberelli and low-impact vinification in the cellar. They make one classic Etna Bianco and an elegant award-winning Etna Rosso. Both carry the name of the cantina.

I was attending a tasting of white wines from small Etna wineries, when I stopped to taste **Tenuta Boccarossa's** (www.tenutaboccarossa.it) spry Etna Bianco. The husband and wife team of Michele and Claudia produce a single white wine from Contrada Pontale Palino and a single Etna Rosso from Contrada Arena, both on the north slope of the volcano. The artisanal wines are being made in Michele's family winery and distillery in the heart of Passopisciaro, where the Calabretta family established its business after helping to complete the Circumetnea train track at the end of the nineteenth century.

There are farms on Etna that you can't help notice. The estate owned by **Tenuta Ferrata** (www.tenutaferrata.it) captured my attention for its simplicity and historical structures. On the eastern side of Rovittello on Etna's north slope, the Oreste-Virlinzi family has reclaimed a part of their storied past to give it a new future. What began in 2014 as a restoration project has arrived at 20 hectares planted to vines, including a tasty Etna

Bianco, a vibrant Etna Rosato, and some Pinot Noir. Only Etna DOC wines are currently available: *Cielo Ceneris*, Etna Bianco; *Cimè*, Etna Rosato; and *Punta Drago*, Etna Rosso.

High on Mount Etna's historic southeast slope, in Nicolosi, **Tenute Foti Randazzese** (www.tenutefotirandazzese.it) produces three Etna classics from two spent volcanic craters—Monpilieri and Monti Rossi—which were created by massive lateral flank eruptions in 693 BCE and 1669 CE, respectively. From these two vineyard sites, located between 700 and 900 meters AMSL, Giacomo Foti Randazzese creates bright, easy-going wines that carry the names of and sentiments for his grandparents and the matriarch of the family, who have worked the vineyards around the Foti Randazzese villa since the nineteenth century.

When I think of **Tenuta Papale** (www.tenutapapale.it), I think of their cellar- and bottle-aged red wines from Nerello Mascalese. That's not to say that red wines are their focus. The winery produces traditional liqueurs as well as white, rosé, and red wines from two contrade on the southeast slope of the volcano, Valcorrente and Palmento Bianco, in Belpasso. While Etna's northern valley has drawn our attention for the last decade or so, it may be well worth our time to consider the potential for high-quality, age-worthy red wines from this historic corner of the mountain, which has been known for wine production for millennia.

Tenuta Rustìca (www.tenutarustica.com) is a large estate in Contrada Rustìca, on the north side of the Alcantara River. The villa, winery, and 140 hectares have been in the Fisauli family since the sixteenth century. In the 1960s, the Nerello vineyard was planted and trained in *tendone* on alluvial sandy soils. This wasn't the first time vines were planted here. The farm is home to a collection of outdoor *palmenti rupestri* (stone winemaking sites) and ancient ruins that are today adorned by olive groves and a breathtaking view of Mount Etna. It's well worth a visit if you're looking for a taste of Etna history.

I love a good Nerello Cappuccio. **Tenuta Stagliata** (www.facebook.com/Az.Agr.AgataSantangelo) surprised me during a recent tasting with their fresh and rich expression of this notoriously difficult-to-grow black grape. What's more, it's the only wine they are currently producing. When I asked what their secret is, owner Alfio Nicotra said, "We plant the right grapes in the right place and take very good care of them." The south-slope vineyard is trained in north-south oriented rows of spur-pruned cordon located in Belpasso, on the sunny southeast slope. The wine is currently produced in small quantities, but if my hunch is right, they may need to start making more.

Tenuta Vigna Patrizia (www.vignapatrizia.it) can be found in the sandy hills above Santa Venerina, in the hamlet of Monacella, on Mount Etna's east slope, where the company produces IGT Terre Siciliane and Etna DOC wines from Carricante, Catarratto, and Nerello Mascalese, as well as a grappa from Nerello Mascalese. In the late nineties, efforts were made to revive the farm, but the project stalled. Since 2020, the estate has reclaimed a history of winemaking that dates back to the end of the eighteenth century. In addition to wine tourism, Vigna Patrizia also provides bed and breakfast accommodations.

For cousins Claudio and Enrico Travaglianti, making wine is a vocation. **Travaglianti** (www.travaglianti.it) produces three Etna standards from old and young vines planted between 800 and 900 meters AMSL, near Santa Maria di Licodia. A divine Etna Bianco arrives from Carricante and 5% Catarratto trained in alberello and spur-pruned cordon with up to 70 years of age. A soft Etna Rosato and rich Etna Rosso are 100% Nerello Mascalese, from old and young vines. For now, you can buy Travaglianti wines directly through their website. The picturesque estate, with views of the southern valley and Mount Etna, will soon offer both rustic and luxury accommodations.

Unostru (www.produttorietnanord.it) is one of the latest additions to a growing catalogue of wines made by investors who admire Etna's volcanic wines on their own merits. After years of traveling to Etna from Holland with their families, Steven Tax and Job van Weeren—entrepreneurs and business partners—set their sights on a rolling vineyard of old alberello vines in Contrada Feudo di Mezzo-Porcaria, in Passopisciaro, on Etna's north slope. *U nostru* translates as our own. Their first wine, an Etna Rosso, shows an approachable style that should win over fans of unpretentious volcanic wines. An Etna Rosso Riserva is planned for future vintages.

The **Vino Arrigo** (www.instagram.com/vinoarrigo) estate was once used by the Lanza barons who, as legend has it, once possessed the tip of the spear that pierced the side of Jesus Christ as he was crucified. The original villa and cellar were built in 1858 in Contrada Pietramarina, one of Etna's oldest viticultural areas on the north slope. Today, Gaetano Arrigo's farm consists of a single vineyard of Nerello Mascalese surrounded by olive and fruit orchards. Thanks to this biodiversity and the additional hours of sunlight that the site receives, the Arrigo Nerello is worth finding. Look for the simple brown label.

Carmelo Vecchio and Rosa La Guzza launched **Vigneti Vecchio** (www.facebook.com/vignetivecchio) from a vineyard they inherited. It was hard work, but they knew what they were doing. Carmelo worked at the celebrated Passopisciaro winery for a decade-and-a-half before deciding to refocus his attention on their own project. The current portfolio arrives from young and old vines: two traditional Etna Rosso field blends, one DOC Sicilia skin-macerated Carricante with other white varieties, and a striking red Terre Siciliane that includes Nerello Mascalese and Cappuccio, Alicante, and 10% local white varieties.

The history of **Vini Calì** (www.vinicali.com) can be found in their vineyard located at 550 meters AMSL in Contrada Lavina, in Linguaglossa. Here, three generations ago, the family established a working farm sown with biodiversity—hazelnuts, chestnuts, fruit trees, and a small vineyard. In the beginning, it was a place for the relatives to gather. Since then, the vines have taken to their natural environs and the project has grown to produce a steady supply of traditional Etna blends that the family exports and sells locally. Each wine is affectionately named for a local legend—a playful child named Giufà, the nymph Galatea, and the tragedy of the Teste di Moro—which continues to live in the hearts and the minds of the Etna community.

Vini Pennisi (www.vinipennisi.com) produces three wines from vineyards at 580 meters AMSL, in the contrade of Verzella and Chiappemacine, in the Alcantara Valley on Etna's north slope. The company's three still wines all carry the name Etneide, but they are all the result of careful selection in the vineyard and a deft touch in the winery. A single Etna Bianco is produced in stainless steel from young vines of Carricante and a small quantity of Catarratto Bianco. Two Etna Rosso's are defined by the age of the vines used to make each wine, with the oldest vines producing a riserva-style Etna Rosso called *Maturo*, which spends three years in wood before being bottled.

Four years after the Etna DOC was legalized, Salvatore Zumbo planted and trained five hectares of vines at 750 meters AMSL, in Contrada Santo Spirito. Today, his granddaughters Erica and Ramona **Zumbo** (www.sorellezumbo.it) produce three wines from traditional Sicilian varieties and Etna DOC standards. The Terre Siciliane white *Pìnea* claims Inzolia on the label, but there is some Carricante and Catarratto in the blend. The Terre Siciliane Rosato, *Ciuriciuri*, and an Etna Rosso called *Àndico*, are made from 100% Nerello Mascalese. Recently, Erica and Ramona opened a tasting room between Rovittello and Solicchiata, bringing one of the family's long-held dreams to fruition.

Mount Etna's complex appellation system is a direct reflection of the intricacy of the volcanic terrain.

APPENDIX: LIST OF ETNA DOC CONTRADE

Etna Contrade—The production area includes part of the municipalities of Biancavilla, Santa Maria di Licodia, Paternò, Belpasso, Nicolosi, Pedara, Trecastagni, Viagrande, Aci Sant'Antonio, Acireale, Santa Venerina, Giarre, Mascali, Zafferana, Milo, Sant'Alfio, Piedimonte, Linguaglossa, Castiglione, Randazzo.

Vineyards that fall within the municipalities and boundaries of the Etna DOC that do not have legally defined districts can carry the Etna DOC denomination on the label.

Starting from the southern slope of Etna and moving from east to north, the name of the municipality is shown before each district listed within the administrative boundaries of the municipality.

Following are the municipalities, their location in reference to the central craters of the volcano, and the contrade registered within the delimited Etna DOC area as of 2021.

The Consortium of Etna producers is working to update the list of *contrade* to include additional districts within the Etna appellation. As of the publishing date, the total number of *contrade* remains at 133.

SOUTH SLOPE

BIANCAVILLA (South-west)
Maiorca, Torretta, Rapilli, Stella, Spadatrappo

SANTA MARIA DI LICODIA (South-west)
Cavaliere

TRECASTAGNI (Southeast craters, nine contrade)

Cavotta, Monte Ilice, Carpene, Grotta Comune, Eremo Di S.Emilia, Monte Gorna, Ronzini, Monte S. Nicolò, Tre Monti

VIAGRANDE (South-east)

Blandano, Cannarozzo, Monaci, Monte Rosso, Monte Serra, Muri Antichi, Paternostro, Sciarelle, Viscalori

EAST SLOPE

ZAFFERANA ETNEA (East-lower slope)

Fleri, San Giovannello, Cavotta, Pietralunga, Pisano, Pisanello, Fossa Gelata, Scacchieri, Sarro, Piricoco, Civita, Passo Pomo, Rocca d'api, Cancelliere–Spuligni, Airone, Valle San Giacomo, Piano dell'Acqua, Petrulli, Primoti, Algerazzi

MILO (East) Contrade included in Etna DOC Bianco Superiore

Villagrande, Pianogrande, Caselle, Rinazzo, Fornazzo, Praino, Volpare, Salice

NORTH SLOPE

LINGUAGLOSSA (North-east)

Pomiciaro, Lavina, Martinella, Arrigo, Friera, Vaccarile, Valle Galfina, Alboretto-Chiuse del Signore, Panella-Petto Dragone, Baldazza

CASTIGLIONE DI SICILIA (North-central)

Acquafredda, Cottanera, Diciasettesalme, Mille Cocchita, Carranco, Torreguarino, Feudo di Mezzo, Santo Spirito, Marchesa, Passo Chianche, Guardiola, Rampante, Montedolce, Zucconerò, Pettinociarelle, Schigliatore,

Imboscamento, Grotta della Paglia, Mantra Murata, Dafara Galluzzo, Dragala Gualtieri, Palmellata, Piano Filici, Picciolo, Caristia, Moscamento, Fossa San Marco, Pontale Palino, Crasà, Piano dei Daini, Zottorinoto, Malpasso, Pietra Marina, Verzella, Muganazzi, Arcurìa, Pietrarizzo, Bragaseggi, Sciambro, Vena, Iriti, Trimarchisa, Vignagrande, Canne, Barbabecchi, Collabbasso

RANDAZZO (North-west)
Imbischi, San Teodoro, Feudo, Ciarambella, Allegracore, Città Vecchia, Giunta, Campo Rè, San Lorenzo, Crocittà, Scimonetta, Bocca d'Orzo, Arena, Pignatuni, Chiusa Politi, Pianodario, Statella, Pignatone, Montelaguardia, Pino, Sciara Nuova, Croce Monaci, Taccione, Calderara Sottana

There's nothing like a wine tasting on Etna, especially when you get invited into the cellar or a winemaker's home and the service includes professional glassware that captures the essence of local varieties. Photo by Benjamin Spencer.

ABV: Alcohol by volume.

acqua tina: A coupage of wine and water; low-alcohol wine-water.

affinamento: The maturation of wine.

alberello: Small tree or sapling; an ancient training system that encourages grape vines to stand on their own.

allophane: An aluminum silicate mineral found in volcanic sands that contributes to root hydration and plant nutrition.

altri minori: Minor grapes included in Mount Etna's vineyards.

amphora: Terra cotta containers for wine storage; often buried.

angel's share: The amount of wine lost during aging via evaporation through semi-permeable containers.

anion: A negatively charged ion; the opposite of *cation*.

anteprima: Wine futures; a presentation of wine from the most recent vintage that is not yet in the market.

appassimento: The practice of drying grapes, in the sun or in drying rooms.

appellation: A defined area where wine grapes are grown for wine.

baglio: (See *masseria*)

barile/barili: A small wood barrel of 34.4 liters; usually hewn from chestnut trees.

barrique: A medium-size wood barrel capable of holding 225 to 230 liters.

bâttonage: A French term for stirring settled lees into wine.

bianco: White; a white wine.

bottai: A cooper or barrel maker.

bottaia: (See *dispensa*)

botte/botti: Large wood casks of 530 liters or more; currently in favor on Mount Etna.

botticelli: Medium-size wood casks of 320 liters or more.

cane: The growth of a grape vine shoot that has lignified (turned wooden) after the previous vintage growth.

cantina: Winery.

capu: Boss; leader of a team.

carusi: Boys.

cation: Ions with a positive charge; the opposite of *anion*.

Circumetnea: A train that circumnavigates most of the volcano, from Catania to Riposto.

colonna: Column; pillar; a meeting place for laborers in Passopisciaro

comune/comuni: A municipality or town.

conca: A depression created around the trunk of a vine during winter pruning.

contadino: Farmer.

contrada/contrade: An Italian neighborhood defined by administrative and natural boundaries.

conzu: Wine press; particularly those with a lever arm, screw, and counterweight.

cordone: A training method using wires to support the fruit-bearing arms of a grape vine; cordon.

coupage: The blending of wines, at times with water (French).

culleo: A water-tight leather bag capable of containing 525 liters, the equivalent of twenty clay amphorae; a legal Roman measurement.

cultivar: A specific variety of a plant that has evolved (through nature or nurture) to have particular qualities.

cuvée: A blend, mixture, or batch of wine.

dispensa: Storage room for fermenting and aging wine; the lowest room in a palmento.

dolium: Large, terra cotta vats for wine storage; similar to kvevri; often buried.

dosaggio: The amount of sugar in the liqueur d'expedition (a mix of sugar and wine) added immediately after disgorgement of a *metodo classico* wine.

ducea: duchy; the territory or dominions of a duke or duchess.

èlevage: (See *affinamento*).

emphyteusis: Long-term farming leases offered to peasants by landowners or the Christian Church.

Etna DOC (Denominazione di Origine Controllata [Controlled Designation of Origin]): A controlled and historic area of wine production based on local Sicilian wine grapes; includes twenty *comuni* and 133 *contrade* on the mid slope of Mount Etna.

fascia: A rope, or woven material, used to wrap wine grapes for pressing; any woven material dedicated to carrying or supporting a container or object.

fattorie: A working farm where large quantities of goods could be found; typically found outside of a city.

feudo: Fief; a land holding composed of a manor and connected small properties.

filare: A row or line of grape vines.

fioritura: The onset of pollination for a wine grape vine; flowering.

forbici: Shears; scissors.

gallon: A unit of liquid measure amounting to 3.785 liters.

ginestra: Scotch broom; a flowering bush and tree found throughout the Etna DOC.

graft: The union of a rootstock and a fruiting scion; features the characteristics of the scion and the capabilities of the root structure.

granita: A frozen dessert made from juice (or flavored liquid), sugar, and water.

grotta/grotte: A cave; on Mount Etna they are formed by the movement and hardening of lava.

invaiatura: Veraison; the moment during grape maturation when the berries change from green to yellow or black, depending on the variety.

indigenous: (*See* native)

jugera: A quarter hectare (0.623 acres); a Roman unit of measure for an area.

kylix: Wine-drinking cup.

lapilli: Pumice stones.

lees: Sediment in wine that falls out of solution by gravity.

liter: A liquid unit of measure amounting to 1,000 milliliters (0.26 gallons).

locanda: An inn; a structure designated for lodging.

mass selection: Method used for propagating a vineyard from a selection of vine material that's been removed from living vines during winter pruning. Cuttings are planted or grafted to other vines immediately.

masseria: A farm that consists of a centralized communal living area; usually walled for defensive reasons.

metodo classico: The French "classic method" technique for making sparkling wines in which a base wine is fermented for a second time in a bottle and allowed to rest for several months before being disgorged and sealed.

mosto: Unfermented and fermenting grape pulp, grape juice, and grape skins; must.

mousse: The frothy head that forms at the surface of a sparkling wine; the sensation of the carbon dioxide in a sparkling wine on the tongue.

munzeddu/munzeddi: Small mounds of earth collected between vines during winter pruning, in particular when the surface roots of the vines are removed.

muselet: The cage that connects the cork to the bottle on sparkling wines.

native: Of a place; applied to large and small areas.

nucidde/nocciole: hazelnuts

orbis: A wood disk attached to the lever of the press in a palmento; the contact point between the press and the grapes.

palmenti rupestri: Rock winemaking sites.

palmento: A gravity-operated vinification area composed of a maceration vat (*pista*) and a fermentation vat (*tino*); modern facilities include a press (*conzu*) and a roof.

parlamento: Parliament.

passaparola: Word of mouth.

passito: A shortening of *appassimento*; the drying of grapes in the sun or ventilated rooms.

permaculture: A permanent system of perpetual and sustainable agriculture.

phenotype: The genetic composition of an organism; variables among similar plants that produce distinctive organoleptic profiles.

pied de cuve: An early selection of grapes that are macerated and allowed to ferment, creating a natural yeast starter for the primary harvest.

pista: The treading area of a palmento.

pistamutta: A pale amber to rosy must or wine created from fresh, crushed grapes with little contact with the grape skins.

potatura: Pruning.

primo fiore: The juice that runs from macerated but not pressed grapes.

propaggine: Burying the cane of a grape vine under some earth to propagate another plant.

pruinose: The powdery appearance on the surface of a grape and its cluster.

quinconce: An ancient method for arranging a vineyard in a repeated pattern of rows; vines are arranged in a rectangle or square with four corners and a vine in the center, similar to the stars in an American flag.

quota mille: The 1,000-meter mark; the highest elevation of any border in the Etna DOC.

racking: Drafting clarified wine from sediment or lees, which has compacted at the bottom of a container.

rasola: A terrace or parcel within a vineyard, often separated by stone walkways called *rasole*.

riddling rack: A wood frame with holes that hold bottles of classic method sparkling wine at varying angles; wine bottles move from horizontal to vertical, in order to draw the *lees* toward the closure.

rimontaggio: The process of pumping red wine up from the bottom of the tank and splashing it over the top of the fermenting must.

ripiddu: Dense basalt rocks.

Riserva: A selection; an aged wine.

rosato: A pale, reddish wine.

rosso: Red; a red wine.

rupestre: Rock.

salasso: Drafting the pale must from a vat of mature red grapes for the purpose of concentrating the red wine and making a light red wine.

salma: A system of weights and measures used on Mount Etna and around Catania for eight centuries.

sboccatura: The act of removing lees from a bottle-fermented wine.

scanno: A seat or bench for patrons to rest.

sciara: A hardened effusive lava flow; desert.

scion: A notable variety selected for the fruiting part of a graft.

sfuso: Anything in bulk.

sparge: The removal of any particulate and displacement of oxygen inside a bottle using water and/or an inert gas, prior to filling the bottle; also refers to a procedure that forces gas through wine as a way of adjusting it.

spumante: Sparkling wine.

spur: The growth on the arm of a vine from where new shoots emerge.

subduction: The folding of one tectonic plate under another.

tannin: Astringent polyphenolic compound found in grape seeds, grape skins and stems.

terracotta: Baked earth; earthenware.

terroir: A complicated term that focuses on all the qualities that influence a wine.

tino: Collection or fermentation vat.

tonneau: A 500-liter barrel; currently in favor on Mount Etna.

torchio: (See *conzu*).

vendemmia verde: An intentional reduction of crop per vine; typically done after veraison.

veraison: the moment during grape maturation when the berries change from green to yellow or black, depending on the variety.

vigna vecchia: Old vines.

Vino da Pasto: Table wine.

Vino da Taglio: Cutting or blending wine.

Vino Semplice: Simple wine.

Vitaceae: A family of flowering plants that include the grape vine.

Vitis vinifera: The common grape vine; a climbing, fruiting, deciduous vine from Europe and Eurasia.

zappa: Hoe; a motorized rotovator is called a *motozappa*.

A traditional alberello vine trained with a chestnut stake in soft volcanic sands.

NOTES

1. Davide Tanasi et al., "1H-1H NMR 2D-TOCSY, ATR FT-IR and SEM-EDX for the identification of organic residues on Sicilian prehistoric pottery," *Microchemical Journal* 135, (November 2017). A recent excavation at Monte Kronio, near Sciacca on Sicily's southwest coast, reveals sophisticated ancient wine production and storage practices going back 6,000 years. DOI: https://doi.org/10.1016/j.microc.2017.08.010.

2. Hugh Johnson, *The Story of Wine* (London: Mitchell Beazley, 1999), 10–11.

3. Vitis species berlandieri, riparia, and rupestris are three American Vitis species that are used when grafting. The American species produce a sap that asphyxiates the phylloxera aphid. Following a wound, the vines develop a callous that protects further damage to the root ball. Grafting involves cutting an American Vitis rootstock and attaching a noble vinifera scion (Chardonnay, Pinot Noir, Cabernet Franc, etc.). The two Vitis species usually form a bond and begin producing quality wine within a year or two.

4. Hans Jörg Böhm, "*The Origin of Vines,*" *Vine to Wine Circle.* https://www.vinetowinecircle.com/en/history/the-origin-of-vines/.

5. Jancis Robinson, Julia Harding, and Jose Vouillamoz, *Wine Grapes: A Complete Guide to 1,368 Vine Varieties, Including Their Origins and Flavours* (London: Allen Lane, 2012), xiii.

6. Patrick E. McGovern, *Ancient Wine: The Search for the Origins of Viniculture* (Princeton: Princeton University Press, 2003), 1–3.

7. Nerello Mascalese is grown in other areas of Sicily, in Southern Italy, Turkey, and California.

8. Two days corresponds to the number of hours it takes for a fermentation in palmento to stratify. It also puts Etna Rosato firmly between a pistamutta and red wines meant for some aging.

9. A winemaking term that points to a lack of oxygen in the production and aging of a wine.

10. Luke Lavan, Enrico Zanini, and Alexander Constantine Sarantis, eds., *Technology in Transition A.D. 300-650.* Late Antique Archaeology, vol. 4, (Leiden: Brill, 2007), 83.

11. Fabio Guaitoli, Maria Gabriella Matranga, Vito Ferraro, "Valorizzazione dei vitigni autoctoni siciliani," Associazione Italiana Pedologi, Regione Sicilia Assessorato Agricoltura e Foreste, Palermo, 2006. http://www.aip-suoli.it/editoria/bollettino/n1-3a06/n1-3a06_06.htm.

12. Concentrations of clay can change within meters. Soils must be evaluated before planting.

13. Christy Campbell, *Phylloxera: How Wine was Saved for the World* (London: Harper Perennial, 2004), 130.

14. In Roman myth, Odysseus's name was changed to Ulysses.

15. Homer, *The Odyssey: A New Translation by Peter Green* (Oakland: University of California Press, 2018), 140.

16. While there is still some debate about the actual location of the island of the lotus eaters, it is recorded by scholars to be Djerba, off the coast of Tunisia, approximately 300 nautical miles south of Mount Etna. http://homes.chass.utoronto.ca/~jburgess/rop/pages/episodes/lotus-eaters.html.

17. This conversion of acids involves changes in citric, malic, tartaric and lactic acids.

18. Based on the "Maria Thun Biodynamic Calendar." This annual guide identifies optimum and avoidable wine-drinking days.

19. Monica Gagliano et al., "Tuned in: plant roots use sound to locate water," *Oecologia* 184, no. 1 (May 2017), 151-160. DOI:10.1007/s00442-017-3862-z

20. Guy D. Middleton, *Understanding Collapse: Ancient History and Modern Myths* (Cambridge: Cambridge University Press, 2017), 185.

21. Sandra Benjamin, *Sicily: Three Thousand Years of Human History* (Hanover, NH: Steerforth Press, 2006), iBook.

22. Bill Nesto and Frances Di Savino, *The World of Sicilian Wine* (Oakland: University of California Press, 2013), 5.

23. Johnson, *The Story of Wine* (London: Mitchell Beazley, 1999), 39.

24. R. Ross Holloway, *The Archaeology of Ancient Sicily* (New York: Routledge, 2000), 86.

25. Giovanni Casadio and Patricia A. Johnston, *Mystic Cults in Magna Graecia* (Austin: University of Texas Press, 2009), chap. 2, Google Play Books.

26. Edith Hamilton, *Mythology: Timeless Tales of Gods and Heroes* (New York: Mentor, 1962), 55.

27. Franco De Angelis, *Archaic and Classical Greek Sicily: A Social and Economic History* (Oxford: Oxford University Press, 2016), 91, 104, 125. At the time, a free and skilled laborer would have been paid about one drachma as a daily wage.

28. Nicolas Belfrage suggests in *Brunello to Zibibbo: The wines of Tuscany, Central and Southern Italy* (London: Mitchell Beazley, 2006), 345. *Centuripe is also known as Centorbi in ancient texts.*

29. Holloway, *Archaeology*, 127.

30. Pindar, "Selected Odes of Pindar: Nemean Ode; Pythian Ode," ed. Gilbert West (London: P. Wilson et al., 1753), 127.

31. Victors of the Nemea games would have been offered a wreath of celery leaf as well as the local wine—Phliasian— in celebration of their winnings. Phliasian wine was made in the hills west of Megara, between the Corinthian and Argolic gulfs. The offspring of Phliasian wine, Agiorgitiko, (S. Kourakou-Dragona, *Nemea: An Historical Wineland* [Athens: Foinikas, 2012]) was grown and produced on Mount Etna since the tenth century (Arnaldo Spitaleri di Muglia, *A Thousand Years of the History of the Best Wines of Etna* [Catania: Archi Grafiche Strano, 2017], 54). Agiorgitiko bears a similarity to Nerello Mascalese wines, but no DNA analysis has been completed on Agiorgitiko. Nerello Mascalese has its own confirmed parentage [See section on Etna grape varieties].

32. Johnson, *Story of Wine*, 68.

33. Robert Edward Zupko, Italian Weights and Measures from the Middle Ages to the Nineteenth Century (Philadelphia: American Philosophical Society,1981), 129. The Libbra or Libra became

synonymous with Lira, or Lire, the monetary system used throughout Italy until the twenty-first century. Libbra is abbreviated using lb. (like the imperial pound).

34. Johnson, *Story of Wine*, 73.

35. Andrew Dalby, *Cato: On Farming. De Agricultura: A Modern Translation with Commentary* (Blackawton, Devon: Prospect Books, 2010), 78.

36. Spitaleri di Muglia, *A Thousand Years*, 102.

37. Jancis Robinson, ed., *The Oxford Companion to Wine*, 3rd ed. (Oxford: Oxford University Press, 2006), 367. An intriguing element of note: In recent DNA analysis done by José Vouillamoz and his colleagues shows the Sangiovese (red) grape to be a natural crossing of Calabrese di Montenuovo (possibly plants brought from Murgentina) and Ciliegiolo. The Calabrese di Montenuovo is a black grape that grows well on volcanic soils, on a small hill west of Naples and the ancient city of Pompeii. Nerello Mascalese, the primary red wine grape of Mount Etna is a genetic offspring of Sangiovese and Mantonico Bianco, a red and a white grape. Is it possible that a relative Nerello Mascalese was born in the countryside west of Mount Etna?

38. Andrew Dalby, *Food in the Ancient World from A to Z* (London: Routledge, 2003), 3, 165, 166, 230.

39. Tamara Lewit, "Absent-Minded Landlords and Innovating Peasants? The Press in Africa and The Eastern Mediterranean," *Late Antique Archaeology* 4, (January 2008), 119–139. DOI: https://doi.org/10.1163/22134522-90000085.

40. Benjamin, *Sicily: Three Thousand Years,* iBook.

41. Ibid.

42. Today, known as Mazara del Vallo.

43. Benjamin, *Sicily: Three Thousand Years*, iBook.

44. Benjamin, *Sicily: Three Thousand Years*, iBook.

45. Manitta and Maugeri, *La Valle dell'Alcàntara*

46. Benjamin, *Sicily: Three Thousand Years*, iBook.

47. Johnson, *Story of Wine*, 103.

48. Jeremy Johns, *Arabic Administration in Norman Sicily: The Royal Diwan (Cambridge Studies in Islamic Civilization)* (Cambridge: Cambridge University Press, 2002), 147.

49. Johnson, *Story of Wine*, 104.

50. A.S. Fulton, "Fīrūzābādī's "Wine-List"," Bulletin of the School of Oriental and African Studies, University of London 12, no. 3/4 (1948), 579–85. http://www.jstor.org/stable/608714.

51. Benjamin, *Sicily: Three Thousand Years*, iBook.

52. Benjamin, *Sicily: Three Thousand Years*, iBook.

53. Donald Matthew, *The Norman Kingdom of Sicily* (Cambridge: Cambridge University Press, 2001), 9–10.

54. Joshua C. Birk, *Norman Kings of Sicily and the Rise of the Anti-Islamic Critique* (New York City: Palgrave MacMillan, 2016), 82–84.

55. Spitaleri di Muglia, *A Thousand Years*, 36.

56. Johns, *Arabic Administration*, xviii.

57. In Arabic, *salma* translates as "peaceful." *Salam* or *salaam* translates as "peace."

58. "Antiche misure," Le Produzione della provincia di Catania. http://www.ianomessina.it/curiosita/Antiche_misure.htm. Measures of liquid and weight changed from one district of the island to another, even if the words used to describe them were the same. In this case, I have focused on measurements used in the Catania area and on Mount Etna, within the Val Demone district.

59. Nesto and Di Savino, *Sicilian Wine*, 11.

60. Spitaleri di Muglia, *A Thousand Years*, 100.

61. Andrea Borruso, *Da oriente a occidente*, (Palermo: Officina di studi medievali, 2006), 72.

62. Stephano Tinti, ed., *"Tsunamis in the World: Fifteenth International Tsunami Symposium, 1991."* (Dordrecht: Kluwer Academic Publishers, 1991), 57.

63. The Svevi controlled Sicily from 1194–1268.

64. William C. Jordan, *Europe in the High Middle Ages* (London: Viking, 2003), Google Play Books.

65. "The War of the Sicilian Vespers, 1282–1302," the website for De Re Militari, The Society for Medieval Military History, Dec. 31, 2014. http://deremilitari.org/2014/12/the-war-of-the-sicilian-vespers-1282-1302/. Though this twenty-year war was fought between the Aragonese and Angevin—for control of Sicily, the Byzantine Empire, Genoa, Venice, Castile, England, and the Holy Roman Empire—even the kingdoms of North Africa would have a walk-on scene in the theatrics. The funny thing is, these were not land battles; almost every major fight was at sea.

66. Johnson, *Story of Wine*, 117.

67. Luke Lavan et al, *Technology in Transition A.D. 300-650*. (Leiden: Brill, 2007), 94–105.

68. Johnson, *Story of Wine*, 126.

69. Mario Ambrosoli, *The Wild and the Sown: Botany and Agriculture in Western Europe, 1350-1850* (Past and Present Publications) (New York: Cambridge University Press, 1997), 42.

70. David Burr, *The Spiritual Franciscans: From Protest to Persecution in the Century After Saint Francis* (University Park: Pennsylvania State University Press, 2015), 124.

71. "Camera Reginale," *Antonio Randazzo da Siracusa con Amore*, http://www.antoniorandazzo.it/palazzidipregio/camera-reginale.html. Other areas in the Camera Reginale included Mineo, Vizzini, Syracuse, Lentini, Avola, the village of Santo Stefano di Briga near Messina, and the island of Pantelleria.

72. C. R. Backman, *The Decline and Fall of Medieval Sicily: Politics, Religion, and Economy in the Reign of Frederick III, 1296–1337* (Cambridge: Cambridge Univ. Press. 2002), 226.

73. Backman, *Decline and Fall*, 75–79.

74. "Franciscan provinces with their custodies and convents, c. 1350," Franciscan Authors, 13th - 18th Century: A Catalogue in Progress last modified June 13, 2004, http://users.bart.nl/~roestb/franciscan/province.htm.

75. Nesto and Di Savino, *Sicilian Wine*, 15.

76. Helen Lowe, *Unprotected Females in Sicily, Calabria, and on the Top of Mount Ætna* (London: Routledge, Warnes, and Routledge. 1859).

77. Benjamin, *Sicily: Three Thousand Years.* iBook.

78. Stephan R. Epstein, *An Island for Itself: Economic Development and Social Change in Late Medieval Sicily* (Cambridge: Cambridge University Press, 2003), 179.

79. Aci was once known as the ancient Greek city of Xiphonia, which was later renamed Akis, by the Romans, and then divided into nine separate villages: Aci Bonaccorsi, Aci Castello, Aci Catena, Aci Platani, Aci San Filippo, Aci Sant'Antonio, Aci Santa Lucia, Aci Trezza, and Acireale.

80. Quatriglio, *Arabs to the Bourbons*, 82–83. It is worth noting that the Inquisition had less of an effect in Palermo and on the Italian Peninsula, where the Renaissance had (perhaps) a more positive influence on the concepts of multi-cultural interdependence. Members of the Jewish, Muslim, Greek, and Latin communities were invested in the local economy as merchants and landowners. Before deportation, some people were given the opportunity to convert. Those who did would spend their lives in fear of being identified as fakes. Indulgences were a way for 'sinners' to ameliorate the punishment for their sins by offering donations to the church.

81. Other properties—including the Castle of Calatabiano, now a luxury hotel—and the right to one third of the duties paid at the port of Catania were also included in the paperwork.

82. Paolo Nicolò Rossi, "Storico [di Mascali]," Comune di Mascali. http://www.comune.mascali.ct.it/la_citt_/storia.aspx. The church was lenient with tax payments up to a maximum of two years delinquency.

83. Nesto and Di Savino, *Sicilian Wine*, 16.

84. The area today encompasses Mascali, Giarre, Riposto, Sant'Alfio (which administratively included the villages of Fornazzo and Milo).

85. Eric Asimov, "Sicilian Reds Harness a Volcano's Energy," *New York Times*, Feb. 27, 2012, https://www.nytimes.com/2012/02/29/dining/reviews/etna-reds-wine-review.html?searchResultPosition=1.

86. Salvatore Mirone, *Monografia Storica dei Comuni di Nicolosi, Trecastagni, Pedara e Viagrande* (Catania; Tipografia di Eugenio Coco, 1875), 24.

87. Noted as 1,050 x 106 m³, the equivalence of forty-four Olympic swimming pools of lava.

88. Benjamin, *Sicily: Three Thousand Years*, iBook.

89. Flavia Girardi et al., "Discrimination of Tsunami Sources (Earthquake versus Landslide) on the Basis of Historical Data in Eastern Sicily and Southern Calabria," from *The Bulletin of the Seismological Society of America* 98, no. 6 (December 2008). https://doi.org/10.1785/0120070192.

90. Emanuela Guidoboni et al., "CFTI4Med, Catalogue of Strong Earthquakes in Italy (461 B.C.-1997) and Mediterranean Area (760 B.C.-1500)," *INGV-SGA* (January 2007). DOI: https://www.researchgate.net/publication/271078106_CFTI4Med_Catalogue_of_strong_earthquakes_in_Italy_461_BC-1997_and_Mediterranean_area_760_BC-1500

91. "Riposto" is past tense of the verb *riporre*: to leave; to stash; or to store

92. Fondachello was named so because it offered housing for international merchants and storage for local vendors. *Fondaco*, from the Greek, meaning "casa-magazzino" or house-storage.

93. Cupani included Viaspalora Minnavacchina, Poppa di Vacca, Greca di Palermo, Greca Bianca, Greca femmina, Greca di Napoli, Greco di Riposto, Greco Nero, Grecari ad acino grosso, Carnoso, Grenache Nero ossia l'Alicante, la Buttuna di Gaddu (Bottone di Gallo), la Zuccarina Mantonicu niuru e vrancu, l'Ammentellato, Giustalisa, Catarrattu vrancu, Catarratto semplice, Malvagia, Muscateddu vrancu, Muscateddu niuru (most likely *Vitis apiane*, the ancient variety named by Pliny The Elder as one of Rome's favorites), as well as Niuridduni and Niuriddu ordinariu, the local dialect for Nerello. Other varieties included Barbarossa, Calavrisi, Guarnaccia Nera, Gerosolimitana Nera, Inzolia Nera, Mandilaria, Mantonico Nero, Moscatella Nera, Moscato Nero, Nocera, Pitrusa Nera, Visparola dell'Etna, plus the remaining grapes of Saint George, planted by the Knights Hospitallers between Paternò and Bronte—namely Agiorgitiko, from the Greek Peloponnese.

94. Roughly 2.1 million 75cl / 750ml bottles.

95. Domenico Sestini, *Memorie sui vini siciliani*, ed. Alfio Signorelli (Palermo: Sellerio Editore, 1991), 46.

96. Sestini, 46

97. Robinson, Harding, and Vouillamoz, *Wine Grapes*, 195.

98. Sestini, *Memorie*, 48.

99. Daniele Palermo, *Dal Feudo alla Proprietà: Il Caso della Ducea di Bronte* (Palermo: Associazione Mediterranea, 2012. The reorganization of fiefs into the ducea, the annexation of Sant'Andrea, Samperi, Petrosino, Fioritta, and half of Ilichito, went to the Maniaci Abbey; to the monastery of San Filippo went San Nicola De Petra, Simantili, San Giorgio Agrappidà, and Gollia; plus Porticelli, Roccaro, Nave, Casitta, Corvo, Mangiuni, Tartaraci and San Pietro d'Ilichito, which belonged to the city of Bronte.

100. In 1805, Admiral Nelson was killed in action. A brother assumed control of the Ducea di Bronte. At first, he was unable to invest in any meaningful restoration. All he could do was pay for a small management team to remain on the property, to tend the citrus and vines.

101. A pipe is equivalent to 63 US gallons or 52.5 imperial gallons. This one order amounted to 63,000 gallons of Marsala.

102. Mario Carastro, "Il Vino della Ducea di Nelson," from Bronte Insieme Storia: La ducea inglese ai piedi dell'Etna (1799–1981), 2015. http://www.bronteinsieme.it/2st/Ducea/vino_2.htm.

103. Johnson, *Story of Wine*, 308.

104. Desmond Gregory, *Sicily: The Insecure Base: A History of the British Occupation of Sicily, 1806-1815* (Madison, NJ: Fairleigh Dickinson University Press, 1988), 23.

105. Nesto and Di Savino, *Sicilian Wine*, 22–23.

106. Clement King Shorter, *Charlotte Brontë and Her Circle* (London: Hodder and Stoughton, 1896), 144–233.

107. William Henry Smyth, *Memoir Descriptive of the Resources, Inhabitants, and Hydrography, of Sicily and Its Islands, Interspersed with Antiquarian and Other Notices* (London: John Murray, 1824), 130–157.

108. Approximately 1,000 vines could produce up to four pipes of wine depending on the weather and vintage and age of the vine. A pipe (also butt, pipa, ½ tun) of wine is a traditional measure used in bulk wine markets, with an approximate value of 475 liters, though the value changes depending on the country and region. Pipes represent portions of larger quantities divisible by smaller measures. This notation by Smyth secures the importance of Riposto in the international exchange of wine and the use of a unified system of measures for the production and shipment of wine.

109. Smyth, *Memoir Descriptive*, 131. On the north slope of Mount Etna, Smyth notes only that the area produces "an abundance of brush-wood—arbutus, myrtle, coronilla, several species of heath, broom, and evergreen oak"—which is cut down every three years. He almost completely avoids writing about the southern flank of the mountain, other than to name the towns he loathed.

110. Standard measurements for botticelli were between 100 and 344 liquid liters. They were measured in barile, or 34.4-liter quantities.

111. Sulfur was cheap. There was a sulfur mine southwest of Mount Etna.

112. Smyth, *Memoir Descriptive*, 131.

113. Salvo Foti, *Etna I Vini Del Vulcano* (Catania: Giuseppe Maimone Editore, 2005). The year was 1835.

114. Nesto and Di Savino, *Sicilian Wine*, 231.

115. Smyth, *Memoir Descriptive*, 131.

116. Leonardo Vigo, *Notizie storiche della città d'Aci-reale* (Palermo: Lao and Roberti, 1836).

117. Foti, *Vini Del Vulcano*.

118. Antonio Patanè, *I viaggi della neve: Raccolta, commercio e consumo della neve dell'Etna nei secoli XVII-XX* (Palermo: Associazione Mediterranea, 2014).

119. Stephen Skelton, *Viticulture—An Introduction to Commercial Grape Growing for Wine Production* (London: Stephen Skelton, 2007) 35–36.

120. Giuseppe Giarrizzo, *Un Comune Rurale della Sicilia Etnea (Biancavilla 1810-1860) Biblioteca, Serie IV, vol. 1* (Catania: Società di Storia Patria per la Sicilia orientale, 1963).

121. Spitaleri di Muglia, *A Thousand Years*, 88–177.

122. Ibid. By the time Spitaleri's vineyards were in full production, the disorder created by Italian unification had trashed the reputation of "Italian" wine.

123. Benjamin, *Three Thousand Years*, iBook.

124. Johnson, *Story of Wine*, 418–419.

125. The Bourbon Army and Navy were largely composed of drafted soldiers who were simply filling a uniform instead of going in front of a firing squad for deserting. Those who did not serve often joined a mercenary or brigand army financed by wealthy nobles. The Bourbon and new Italian Armies would have trouble with these trained runaway armies during and after the unification.

126. Lucy Riall, *Sicily and the Unification of Italy: Liberal Policy and Local Power, 1859-1866* (Oxford: Clarendon Press, 1998). 71.

127. Riall, *Sicily and the Unification*, 71.

128. "A short history of Bronte: The Facts from 2 to 5 August 1860," Bronte Insieme. Accessed July 2016. http://www.bronteinsieme.it/BrIns_en/2st_en/mo_60d_en.html.

129. Nesto and Di Savino, *Sicilian Wine*, 24–25.

130. Mirone, *Monografia storica*, 134.

131. Christopher Duggan, *Fascist Voices: An Intimate History of Mussolini's Italy* (Oxford: Oxford University Press 2013), 2.

132. Robinson, *Oxford Companion,* (Oxford: Oxford University Press, 2006), 543–544.

133. American Vitis species have evolved over eons to be resistant to the phylloxera aphid.

134. Campbell, *Phylloxera*, xxxv.

135. Robinson, *Oxford Companion,* (Oxford: Oxford University Press, 2006), 521–523

136. Mirone, *Monografia storica*, 110.

137. Spitaleri di Muglia, *A Thousand Years*, 272.

138. Spitaleri di Muglia, *A Thousand Years*, 260. His barrel maker, August Perch, worked for several years at Castello Solicchiata. Spitaleri didn't trust the Sicilian barrel makers in Riposto, Catania, or Marsala.

139. Between 1888 and 1894.

140. Nesto and Di Savino, *Sicilian Wine*, 29.

141. Carastro, *Il Vino della Ducea*, 52. The first trials were offered to laborers in lieu of payments.

142. It included the Catania Chamber of Commerce, the cities of Riposto, Giarre, Mascali, Piedimonte Etneo, Linguaglossa, Castiglione di Sicilia, Randazzo, Maletto, Bronte, Adrano, Biancavilla, Santa Maria di Licodia, Paternò, Belpasso, Misterbianco, and Catania.

143. Giuseppe Sergi, *La Ferrovia Circumetnea: Cento Anni Intorno al Vulcano* (Siracusa: ZangaraStampa, 1993), 37–40. The equivalent value of the Circumetnea investment—ITL (Italian Lire) 136,133 per mile of track—averages approximately $1.5 million USD per community based on 2015 currencies.

144. Sergi, *La Ferrovia Circumetnea*, 51.

145. Sergi, *La Ferrovia Circumetnea*, 76–77. The prices for a passenger/tourism ticket on the Circumetnea were advertised at a mere ITL 9.45 for first class, ITL 7.20 for second class, and ITL 5.50 for third class.

146. From the region of Sicily via the European Union.

147. Many of these editions were written by Sante Cettolini, a professor of agriculture from Sardegna who had risen to stardom at the end of the nineteenth century.

148. *Annuario Vinicolo d'Italia: Edizione 1927–1928*, (1927), 650–660.

149. No further than Motta Sant'Anastasia and Misterbianco.

150. *Annuario Vinicolo*, 652.

151. These were also compared to and named Trapanese (from Trapani) for their oxidized style.

152. Approximately 1,902 acres (770 ha).

153. Then called Abyssinia.

154. Nesto and Di Savino, *Sicilian Wine*, 32.

155. Carol King, "Operation Husky 70 Years Later: When the Allied Forces Landed in Sicily," Italy Magazine, July 8, 2013. http://www.italymagazine.com/featured-story/operation-husky-70-years-later-when-allied-forces-landed-sicily.

156. "Sicily Invaded by Allied Forces," Townsville Daily Bulletin, July 12, 1943, pg. 1.

157. The Axis armies included German, Italian, and Japanese fighters. Only the German and Italian were present in Sicily.

158. The Allied armies included fighters from the United States, Britain, Canada, France, and Australia. Other nations included in the Allied forces were not present during the operation.

159. Patrick K. O'Donnell, *Operatives, Spies, and Saboteurs: The Unknown Story of the Men and Women of World War II's OSS* (New York: Simon & Schuster, 2004), 49–50.

160. Monty S. Finkelstein, *Separatism, the Allies and the Mafia: The Struggle for Sicilian Independence, 1943–1948* (Bethlehem, PA: Lehigh University Press, 1998), 18–21. Benito Mussolini was named prime minister in 1922. A few years later, he launched an assault on the Mafia in Sicily.

161. Domenico Stimolo, "Estate 1943: Una Lunga Scia Di Sangue Nell'area Etnea. Le Stragi Naziste," *ANPI Palermo "Comandante Barbato"* (July 26, 2014) http://palermo.anpi.it/2014/07/26/estate-1943-una-lunga-scia-di-sangue-nellarea-etnea-le-stragi-naziste/. Castiglione di Sicilia, Randazzo, Bronte, Adrano, Paternò, Valverde, Nicolosi, Misterbianco, Fleri, Acireale, Trecastagni, and Aci Sant'Antonio were hit particularly hard by the advancing Allies and retreating Germans.

162. O'Donnell, *Operatives, Spies, and Saboteurs*, 25–26. After the war, these groups took over the politics and management of nearly all social and economic programs on the island.

163. Nesto and Di Savino, *Sicilian Wine*, 45.

164. F. S. Naiden, *Smoke Signals for the Gods: Ancient Greek Sacrifice from the Archaic Through Roman Periods* (Oxford: Oxford University Press, 2013), 117–118. The company made various shades of wine (white, rosé, red) plus a sweet Zibibbo, which they packaged in smaller bottles.

165. The family company continues producing and bottling Etna DOC still and sparkling wines in their modern facility in Contrada Crasà.

166. For my purposes here, "taste" includes color, aroma, flavor, and quality assessment.

167. The area written into the Etna DOC in 1968 included a delimited semi-circle of 56,810 acres (23,000 ha), of which 1,975 acres (800 ha) were planted with vines, between 1,324–3,281 ft. (400–1000 m) AMSL.

168. Joseph A. McMahon and Michael N. Cardwell, *Research Handbook on EU Agricultural Law* (Cheltenham: Edward Elgar Publishing, 2015), 140. The decree—75/268—specifically focused on mountain and hill-farming and "less favoured" areas.

169. Bernard O'Connor, *The Law of Geographical Indications* (London: Cameron May, 2007).

170. Terry Robards, "Wine Talk," *New York Times*, Feb 10, 1982. This article dedicated three paragraphs to a description of Torrepalino's 1975 Etna Rosso in a tasting of forty other Italian wines.

171. Giovanni Cordini, ed., *Domestic Protection of Food Safety and Quality Rights* (Torino: G. Giappichelli, 2013), 183.

172. Nesto and Di Savino, *Sicilian Wine*, 40--41.

173. Originally, Pietramarina, all one word. Now, Pietra Marina.

174. Nesto and Di Savino, *Sicilian Wine*, 50.

175. The original recipes of Champagne Etna included Pinot Noir, Chardonnay, and Pinot Blanc.

176. The *"Norme Generali - Classificazione Delle Denominazioni Di Origine, Delle Indicazioni Geografiche Tipiche e Ambito Di Applicazione,"* (Legge n. 164, 10 Feb. 1992) was billed as a way for wine producers to be creative. Instead, the new wine category established a change in course based on a proposal (C 276 vol. 21, 20 Nov. 1978) from *The Council of The European Communities.*

177. According to my notes, we ate pasta with a simple red sauce followed by grilled *suino di Nebrodi* sausages with sautéed *cauliceddi* (wild greens) that day.

178. Lucia Militi, "La viticoltura a Castiglione di Sicilia, volàno dell'economia e del rilancio del territorio," *Humanities* 5, no. 1 (January 2016). DOI: http://dx.doi.org/10.6092/2240-7715/2016.1.53-88

179. Roughly one meter between vine rows, spaced at 0.8 meters between plants.

180. Spitaleri di Muglia, *A Thousand Years*, 372–378.

181. Later it was owned by a wealthy family from around Acireale.

182. Benedetto is also winemaker at Alessandro di Camporeale, in West Sicily, and Monteleone, on Mount Etna.

183. On the list of miscellaneous changes: the delimited area of the Etna DOC was now mandatory for all stages of production and bottling; the chemical and organoleptic characteristics of DOC wines were more refined and clarified; and the size of glass bottles was limited to five liters or less.

184. Dr. Giuseppe Basile, *Rapporto Sugli Eventi Meteo Che Hanno Colpito La Sicilia I Giorni 21-25 Settembre 2009*, Regione Siciliana (Sicily: Dipartimento Della Protezione Civile: Servizio Rischi Idrogeologici e Ambientali, 2009). Accessed August 2016. http://www.regione.sicilia.it/presidenza/protezionecivile/documenti/documenti/rapportometeo_21-250909.pdf.

185. Tifeo was a dragon created by the earth goddess Gaea to slay Zeus.

INDEX OF SUBJECTS

Abbate, Roberto, 338; *See* Roberto Abbate Winery
absinthe. *See* Zambu
Aci Trezza, xx, 92, 148
Acireale, 132, 147, 163-163, 170, 188
Acknowledgements, ix
Adrano, 22, 26, 72, 114, 116, 125, 132, 150, 152, 155, 158, 196
Aeolian Islands: Archipelago, 128; Lipari, 141, 336; Salina, 24, 238
Aeris Winery, 234
Æschylus, 114
Ætna. *See* Catania
affinamento, 39
Africa, 12, 106, 128
Agatha, Saint, 122-124, 126, 132
Aitala Winery, 260
Akis (Acis), 128-129
Al-Cantàra Winery, 261
al-Idrisi al-Qurtubi al-Hasani as-Sabti, Abu Abdullah Muhammad (al-Idrisi), 125-128
alberello. *See* vine: vine training
Alcantara Valley, vii, 3, 71, 106, 112, 172
Alessandro, Benedetto, 203, 334, 337
Alfonso I (king), 135
Alleanza Viticultori Etnei (A.V.E.) Cantina Sociale, 167
Allies, the, 8, 165-166
Alta Montagna, 163
Alta Mora Winery, 43, 57, 262
Amaro, 163
amphora, 114, 207, 330, 335; amphorae, 5, 35
Angevins. *See* French
Annuario Vinicolo d'Italia, 162-163
Antichi Vinai 1877 Winery, 9, 57, 160, 263
Antichi Vini di Sicilia Winery, 235
Antonio Di Mauro Winery, 236
appassimento, 21, 25, 64, 67, 69, 322
Appendix (of Etna DOC Contrade names), 347-348
Aragonese, 129
Archaeological Museum Paolo Vagliasindi, 161
Arrigo, Gaetano. *See* Vino Arrigo Winery

Axis powers, the, 8, 165-166

Barone Beneventano della Corte Winery, 133, 328
Barone di Villagrande Winery, 8, 24-25, 32-33, 39-40, 47, 50, 54, 57, 166-169, 178, 238
barrels (wood containers) 5, 8, 38, 40, 145-146; *barrique*, x, 38, 56; *barili*, 40, 125, 138, 155; *botticelli*, 40, 146; *botti*, 8, 38, 40, 56-57, 138, 146, 153, 155, 195
Battiato, Francesco, 161
Belpasso, 72, 162, 342-343, 347
Benanti Winery, viii, xii, 9, 19, 38, 43, 47, 50, 53, 55, 57, 63, 65, 133, 155, 161, 173-176, 203, 239
Benanti, Antonio, 175, 223; Giuseppe, 9, 173, 239; Salvino, 175, 239
Benedictine, 5, 27, 131-132, 143, 195
Beneventano della Corte, Pierluca, 328; Roberto, 328
Bentivegna, Davide. *See* Etnella Winery
Bevilacqua, Nino, xii, 208, 314
Biancavilla, 71, 149, 152, 195, 203; contrade, 347
Biondi Winery, viii-xii, 43, 57, 133, 180, 198, 206, 210, 240
Biondi, Ciro, xi, 180, 188, 198, 206-207, 210, 240; Manfredi, xi, 206, 210; Stephanie, xi, 180, 188, 210, 240; Turi, 240
Birra Vulcano, 118
Birrificio dell'Etna, 118
Birrificio di Catania, 118
Birrificio Namasté, 118
Birrificio Timilia, 118
Bishops of Catania: Ansgarius, 124; Caracciolo, Nicola (Count of Mascali, c. 1540), 137
Bixio, Nino, Colonel, 152
Bizzantino Winery, 328-329
Bonaparte, Napoléon, 143
Bora. *See* wind
Bordeaux wine, 25-26, 156; Cru Bourgeois Bordeaux, 22
Bosco, Concetto; Sofia. *See* Tenute Bosco Winery
British Navy, 143-145
Bronte Madeira; Bronti Madiera; Bronti; Bronte Bronte, 143

Brontë, Anne; Charlotte; Emily; Patrick, 144-145
Bronte, 143-144, 152-153, 156, 158
bulk wine; *sfuso*, x, 6, 80, 167, 195, 215
Burgundy: wine, 22, 26, 176, 194; region, 194
Buscemi, Mirella, 22-23, 42, 53, 55, 329; Mirella
  Buscemi Winery, 329
bush vine. *See* vine: vine training
Byzantines, 118, 120

Cacciatori dell'Etna, 152
Caciorgna, Paolo, 59, 161, 199-200, 312
Calabretta, Claudia; *See* Tenuta Boccarossa
  Winery
Calabretta, Massimiliano; Massimo, 185, 267
Calabretta, Michele; *See* Tenuta Boccarossa
  Winery
Calabretta Winery, viii, 19, 25, 42, 53-55, 185-186,
  181, 267
Calabria, 14, 19, 111, 130, 133, 138, 208
Calatabiano, 110-11; Calatabiano Plain, 163
Calcagno Winery, 23, 47, 50, 57, 160, 210, 268
Calcagno, Francesco, 210; Gianni, 268; Giusy, 268
California, vii, ix-x, 5, 59, 74, 78, 99, 117, 139,
  203, 206-210
Camarda Winery, xiv, 42, 55, 160, 181, 269
Camarda, Gaetano; Graziella. *See* Camarda
  Winery
Cambria, Enzo, 183-184; Francesco, 183-184, 273;
  Guglielmo 183-184
Camera Reginale, 131
Campione Winery, 329
Campione, Giuseppe. *See* Campione Winery
Cannavò Winery, 327-328
Cantina del Malandrino Winery, 329-330
Cantina Malopasso Winery, 44, 50, 57, 133, 330
Cantina Maugeri Winery, 330-331
Cantine di Nessuno Winery, 330
Cantine Edomé Winery, 47, 57, 241
Cantine Iuppa Winery, 331
Cantine Nicosia Winery, 44, 58, 65, 134, 196, 242
Cantine Patria Winery, 58, 65, 160, 178, 184, 298
Cantine Russo Winery, 9, 44, 65, 167, 178, 270
Cantine Scudero Winery, 331
Cantine Tornatore Winery, 45, 51, 57, 59, 317
Cantine Valenti Winery, 24, 160, 183, 271,
Capo Schisò, 71, 108, 163
carbon dioxide, 61, 95, 210
Carella, Maria, 242
Carthaginians, 115
Caruso, Fabio, 338; *See* Rinanera Winery
Casa Cottone, 147
castagno. *See* chestnut
Castello di Calatabiano, 111
Castello Solicchiata Winery, 22, 26, 54, 62, 155,
  177, 196, 209
Castiglione di Sicilia, 131, 135, 158; contrade, 348

Catania, ix, 89, 98, 112, 114, 116, 122, 124, 129,
  132-137, 140, 148, 152, 155, 157-163, 166, 170,
  203; Province of Catania, 26
Cato, 4
Cave Ox, 207
Cédric Perraud Winery, 331-332
Centonze, Nicola, 296
Charles V (king), 137
chestnut, 5, 39-40, 81-82, 138, 156, 195, 208
Christ, 118, 344
Christian; Christianity, 118-120, 123-124, 130-
  131, 135-136
Church, the (Roman Catholic), 118, 123-124,
  131-132, 137, 153,
Cianci, Antonio; Paola. *See* Cantine Edomé
Cipresso, Roberto, 183, 273
Circumetnea Railway (Ferrovia Circumetnea),
  158-160
classic method. See *metodo classico*
closures: cork, 40, 62, 205-206; crown cap, 40,
  61-62; technical stoppers, 40
Coffa, Guido, 22, 42, 53-55, 200-201, 246
Consorzio per la Tutela dei Vini Etna, 3, 204, 347
Conta, Daniela. *See* Theresa Eccher Winery
Conte Uvaggio Winery, 243
Conti, Carlo; Giovanni, 337; *See* Mongibello33
  Winery
contrada (contrade [*pl.*]; *abbr.* Cda.), 72-73, 205-
  206; within Etna DOC, 347
Contrada Santo Spirito di Passopisciaro Winery,
  44, 272
Contrade dell'Etna, 74, 203-204
cooperative (co-op), 167, 171, 183
copper sulfate, 151, 154
cordone (cordon). *See* vine: vine training
cork. *See* closures
Cornelissen, Frank, 22, 35, 42, 49, 55, 160, 180,
  191, 197-198, 206, 287
Costa, Domenico, 338; *See* Oro d'Etna Winery
Costa d'Oro, 101
Costantino, Dino; Fabio, 36, 198-199, 255
Costanzo, Mimmo; Valeria. *See* Palmento
  Costanzo
Cotarella, Riccardo, 208, 314
Cottanera Winery, 9, 25, 28-29, 44, 54, 57, 273
crown cap. *See* closures
Cuore di Marchesa Winery, 332
Cupani, Francesco, 142
Curtaz, Federico, 44, 47, 202, 333
Cuseri, Antonio Moretti, 272
Cutuli, Mauro, 248
cycling, 160
Cyclops; Cyclopes, xx, 91

D'Urso, Alfio, 281
D'Agata, Ian, 13

De Crescentiis, Petrus, 131
De Grazia, Marco (Marc), viii, 180, 193-194, 198-199, 202, 308
Department of Agriculture, Food and Environment, University of Catania, 13
Destro Winery, 42, 44, 50, 57, 65, 68, 274
Destro, Antonio, 201-202, 274
Di Bella, Davide, 340-341; *See* Tenuta Antica Cavalleria Winery
Di Gaetano, Salvatore; Vinzia. *See* Firriato-Cavanera Winery
Di Giovanni, Pietro, 302, 328, 332
Di Grazia, Angelo, 317
Di Miceli, Bernardo, 184, 298
Di Stefano, Rocco, 173
dispensa (also *bottaia*), 32, 229
DNA, xxii, 13, 18, 20, 22-27, 126, 191
DOC. *See* Italian wine denominations
DOC/DOP Sicilia. *See* Italian wine denominations
DOCG. *See* Italian wine denominations
dolia, 5
Don Alfio, 190, 250
Don Michele Winery, 275
Donnafugata Winery, 44, 50, 173, 276
DOP. *See* Italian wine denominations
drinking; drunkenness, 222
Duca di Salaparuta Winery, 27, 54, 277
Ducea di Nelson (Duchy of Nelson), 28, 152, 156, 158, 189, 291; Porta Bigliardo (vineyard), 152

Eduardo Torres Acosta Winery, 23, 57, 278
Eleanor of Anjou, Queen, 129, 131, 132
élevage, 202, 205. See also *affinamento*
elevation, vii, 14, 19, 24, 37, 55-56, 71-72, 80, 100-101, 106, 146-147, 150, 155, 157, 192-194
Ellittico (volcano), 90
emphyteusis, 133, 138, 153
Enò-Trio Winery, 23, 25, 27, 42, 49, 58, 190, 279
Enologia magazine, 161-163
enology (winemaking), ix, 3-9, 37, 42, 48, 143, 161
Enoteca Etna Wine, 305
Enoteca Il Buongustaio dell'Etna, 161
Eredi Di Maio Winery, 47, 332
Etna Barrus Winery, 332-333
Etna Cognac, 155-156
Etna DOC wines, 13, 37-40; Etna Bianco, 43-45; Etna Bianco Superiore, 45-47; Etna Rosato, 49-51; Etna Rosso, 55-59; Etna Rosso Riserva, 55-59; Etna Spumante, 59-65
Etna Wine School, xi
Etna. *See* Mount Etna
Etna Urban Winery, 333
Etnella Winery, 244
Eudes Winery, 44, 58, 134, 245

Europe: general reference, 5, 7, 83, 134, 146, 148, 154, 157; European Council, 170; European Economic and Social Committee, 170; European Parliament, 170

Fabre, Louis, 156, 291
Falcone Winery, 228
Famiglia Statella, 333
Faro, Michele, 199, 299
Fascists. *See* Mussolini, Benito
Father-in-Law, Frank, 92
Fattorie Romeo del Castello Winery, 11, 50, 58, 280
Federico Curtaz Winery, 44, 47, 333
Federico Graziani Winery, 42, 283
Ferdinand II (king), 135
Ferdinand IV (king), 143
Ferlito, Giovanni, 237
fermentation, xi, 1-3, 6-8, 30, 36-39, 41-42, 47-48, 51-53, 56, 61, 99, 104, 205, 212
Ferrini, Bianca, 335; Carlo, 335
Ferrovia Circumetnea. *See* Circumetnea Railway
Feudo Arcurìa Winery, 281
Feudo Cavaliere Winery, 44, 58, 196, 229
Feudo Failla, 334
Feudo Plain, 163
Feudo Vagliasindi Winery, 19, 50, 53, 282
Fifth Estate, 334
Filippo Grasso Winery, 23, 42, 44, 50, 58, 160, 189, 284
filtration, 39
fining; fining agents, 39
Firriato-Cavanera Winery, 44, 50, 58, 65, 285
Fisauli. *See* Tenuta Rustìca
Fischetti Winery, 209, 286
Fischetti, Michela, 209, 286
Fiumefreddo, 163
Fondachello, 141-142
Forest of Catania, 162
Foreword, vii
Foti, Salvatore (Salvo), viii, 173, 234, 283
Francavilla di Sicilia, vii, 3, 131
France, 21-25, 57, 151, 154; Bordeaux, 22, 25-26, 156; Hermitage, 28, 150, 156
Francesco Modica Winery, 42, 58, 264
Franchetti, Andrea, viii, 54, 74, 192-193, 197-198, 203, 278, 297
Francis of Assisi, Saint, 130
Franciscans, 27, 130-131, 142
Franco, Nino, 101-102
Frank Cornelissen Winery, 42, 49, 55, 160, 287
Frederick III (king), 129, 131
French peoples, 143, 154, 156
friars, 130-132
Fulvio, Cesare. *See* Masseria Del Pino Winery

Gambino, Maria, 172, 320
Gangemi, Marco. *See* Antichi Vinai Winery
Garibaldi, Giuseppe, 150-154
Gela, 165
Generation Alessandro, 334-335
German. *See* Svevi
Giammanco, Salvo, 89-90
Giardini Naxos, 71, 112
Giarre, 107, 129, 158, 162-163, 167
Giodo Winery, 335
Giovanni Rosso Winery, 44, 58, 288
Girolamo Russo Winery, 44, 58, 160, 289
Glossary, 351
Gods: Adranus, 113; Dionysus, 113-114; Gaea,
    113; Uranus, 113; Zeus, 113
Gold Coast. *See* Costa d'Oro
Goria, Giovanni, 182
Goths, 117-118
Graci Winery, 44, 50, 55, 57-58, 160, 290
Graci, Alberto Aiello, vii, 66, 197-198, 290
grapevine, 11-12, 81, 86, 95, 105-106, 154
Grasso Fratelli (Etna Wine) Winery, 9; *See*
    Stanzaterrena Winery
Grasso, Filippo, 23, 42, 44, 50, 58, 160, 189, 284;
    Mariarita, 284
Graziani, Federico, 42, 283
grecale. *See* wind
Greece, 67, 114, 208
Greeks, 4, 20, 108, 112-116, 125, 167
Grottafumata Winery, 248
Guarrera, Serena, 336; *See* Mecori Winery
Guido Coffa Winery, 22, 42, 53-55, 200, 246
Gurrida Winery, 139, 225, 291

Harding, Julia, 13
Hargrave, Trente. *See* Terre di Trente
Harvey, Kevin, 234
Hieron, 114
Homer, xx, 91-92
Hospitallers. *See* Knights Hospitaller
hotels, 179, 219
House of Savoy, 153

I Custodi delle vigne dell'Etna Winery, 22, 24, 44,
    50, 53, 58, 201, 292
ice, 90, 147-148
IGP. *See* Italian wine denominations
IGT. *See* Italian wine denominations
IGT/IGP Terre Siciliane. *See* Italian wine
    denominations
INGV. *See* National Institute of Geophysics and
    Volcanology
Innocent III (pope), 130
Inquisition, the, 135-136
Ionian; Ionian Sea, viii, x, 7, 89, 106, 159, 172, 190
Irene Badalà Winery, 44, 160, 293

Isabella of Castile, Queen, 135
Islamic Sicily, 119-121
Israel, 90
Istituto Regionale del Vino e dell'Olio (IRVOS),
    13, 175
Italian wine denominations: DOP
    (Denominazione di Origine Protetta); DOC
    (Denominazione di Origine Controllata),
    8, 71-73, 166-167, 169-171; DOCG
    (Denominazione di Origine Controllata e
    Garantita), 72, 178; Sicilia DOC/DOP, 87; IGP
    (Indicazione Geografica Protetta), 54, 67-68,
    72, 87, 182, 196; IGT (Indicazione Geografica
    Tipica), 54, 67-68, 72, 87, 178, 182, 196
Italy, x, 8, 85, 112-114, 149, 153, 165, 172

Judaism, 120

Kesteloot, Filip. *See* Terre di Trente
King of Sardegna, 239
Kingdom of Sardegna, 153
Kingdom of Sicily, 125
Knights Hospitaller, 124, 126
Koran (Quran; Qur'an), 119-121

La Caverna del Mastro Birraio, 118
La Gelsomina Winery, 25, 64, 65, 68, 247
La Guzza, Rosa, 344
La Monaca, Giuseppe, 281
Lake Gurrida, 139
Laliman, Léo, 154
Lanati, Donato, 198
Lanza barons, 344
lapilli. See lava
lava, 11–12, 72, 90-94, 102, 139-141; lava stones,
    lapilli, 150, *ripiddu*, 66, 261
layering, 83, 190
Lazzaro, Giuseppe, 335; Giuseppe Lazzaro
    Winery 335
Le Due Tenute Winery, 335-336
Lentsch, Massimo, 336; Massimo Lentsch Winery,
    336
Licciardello, Arianna, 245, 251; Rosario, 181, 251;
    Santina, 251; Sebastiano, 210, 251
Licciardello, Salvo, 339; *See* Vini Licciardello
    Winery
light, vii, 81, 100-103, 146
Linguaglossa, 102, 159, 162, 167, 171, 183, 202,
    348
Lipari (Island), 141
Lizzio, Antonio; Dino. *See* Azienda Agricola La
    Vite dei F.lli Lizzio
Lo Guzzo, Luigi, 177
Lo Mauro, Vincenzo, 192-193
Lombardo di Monte Iato, Federico, 285
Lombardo di Villalonga, 311

Louis XVI (king), 143
Lowe, Helen, 133

Maestrelli, Silvia, 202-203, 310
Mafia, 165-166
malolactic fermentation, 41, 47, 99
Malta, 141, 144, 147
Maniace: Abbey, 131, 143; George, General, 122
Mannino, Giuseppe, 3, 65, 134, 186, 254
map, vi, 127, 168, 226, 232, 258
Marconi, Aurelio. *See* Monterosso Winery
Marie Antoinette, Queen, 143
Marie Caroline, Queen, 143
Marletta, Andrea, 209, 286, 301
Marletta, Giovanni, 195, 228
Marsala: city, 151; wine, 144, 164
Mascali, 19, 126, 136-142, 145-147, 149, 155-156, 162-164; Mascali Plain, 163
Mascalucia, 140, 162
mass selection, 21, 83, 190
Masseria Del Pino Winery, 49, 58, 294
Mecori Winery, 336-337
Messina (Zancle), 115, 134, 138, 152, 157, 166, 208
Messina, Giovanni; Laura Torrisi; Salvatore. *See* Eudes Winery
metodo classico 24, 27, 60-63, 156, 177, 190
Middle Ages, 5, 27, 134-135
Mikkelsen, Anne-Louise. *See* Tenuta di Aglaea
Milo, 8, 14, 43, 45, 84; contrade, 347-348
MLF. *See* malolactic fermentation
Modica, Francesco; Peppina; Salvatore. *See* Francesco Modica Winery
Monaci delle Terre Nere (resort), 53, 201, 246
Monastery of Saint Agatha. *See* Agatha, Saint
Mongibello33 Winery, 333
Monte Tauro, 108, 111
Monteleone Winery, 44, 58
Monteleone, Enrico; Giulia. *See* Monteleone Winery
Monterosso Winery, 58, 134, 237
Moors, 119, 235
Mount Etna, x-xi, 88-102; Sicilian dialect: Â Muntagna, viii; Mongibello, 90, 93-94; Mungibeddu, viii, 90
Muhammad, 120
Mulone, Riccardo; Sonia (Spadaro). *See* Santa Maria La Nave Winery
Murgo Winery, 9, 22, 27, 44, 54, 63, 65, 89, 177-178, 205, 249
Muslim, 119-121, 124-125, 127, 148
Mussolini, Benito, 164-165; Fascists, 165-166

Naples (Napoli), 135, 143, 152
National Institute of Geophysics and Volcanology (INGV) 89, 94

Naxos. *See* Giardini Naxos
Nebrodi Mountains, 106, 112, 172
Negro, Giandomenico, 174
Nelson, Admiral Horatio (Duke of Bronte), 143-144, 152
Neolithic, 4, 90
New World, 135-136
New York Times, the, 139, 171
Nibali Winery, 43, 68-69, 322
Nibali, Riccardo. *See* Nibali Winery
Nicola Gumina Winery, 295
Nicolosi-Asmundo, Carlo, 167-169, 238; Marco, 180, 238
Nicolosi, 28, 72, 139-140, 155, 162
Nicosia, Carmelo; Francesco (elder); Francesco (younger); Graziano. *See* Cantine Nicosia Winery
Nicotra, Alfio, 343; *See* Tenuta Stagliata Winery, 343
Noli, Benedetta; Daniele; Laura Davide. *See* Tenuta Benedetta Winery
Normans, 124-125, 129
Novella, Maria "Nuna". *See* Terre di Nuna Winery
Nuzzella Winery, 337-338

oak: Austrian, 40, 57; French, 57, 156; Slavonian, 40, 57, 171, 185; forests: Allier, Tronçais, Vosges, 57
Odysseus, 91-92, 148
Oenotria, 112-113
Ognina, 148
Oidium, 28, 149, 151, 154, 199; *Oidium tuckeri*, powdery mildew, *Uncinula necator*, 149
Operation Husky, 165-166
Oro d'Etna Winery, 338

Palermo, 138, 149, 151, 156-157
palmenti rupestri, 2, 342; *palmento*, 3-4, 6-7, 30-31, 36, 38, 137, 179, 195-196
Palmento Costanzo Winery, 38, 44, 50, 58, 65, 160, 296
Panozzo, Andrea. *See* Theresa Eccher Winery
Paoli, Giuseppe, 340; *See* Sive Natura Winery
Paoluzi, Manuela; Mario, 201
Parasiliti, Rori. *See* SRC Winery
Parco dell'Etna, 147
passito. See *appassimento*
Passopisciaro Winery, 22-23, 26, 42, 44, 54-55, 58, 74, 193, 203, 297
Passopisciaro: village, 72, 74, 101, 140, 159, 160, 192
Pasticceria Santo Musumeci, 161
Paternò, 126, 131-132
Patria Winery, 58, 65, 160, 178, 184, 298
Pedara, 28, 148, 152, 155, 162, 347
Peloritani Mountains, x, 106, 337

Pennisi, Don Michele; Giuseppina. *See* Don
  Michele Winery
Percolla, Fabio. *See* Terre di Nuna Winery
Perraud, Cédric. *See* Cédric Perraud Winery
Peynaud, Émile, 175-176
pH (potential of hydrogen), 41
Phoenicians, 4
Phylloxera, 7, 83-86, 154-157, 199; *Phylloxera
  vitifoliae*, 154-157; prephylloxera, 190, 199
Piano Provenzana, 107, 164
pied de cuve, 37–38, 192, 198
Piedimonte Etneo, 24, 73, 162-163
Pietradolce Winery, 42, 44, 50, 57, 58, 160, 199,
  299
pilgrims, 130, 171, 246; pilgrimage, 130
pirates, 136-137, 147
Planeta Winery, 27, 42, 44, 54, 65, 160, 300
Platania d'Antoni, Margherita. *See* Feudo
  Cavaliere Winery
Pliny the Elder, 5; Plinian, 5, 7
Poets; Hamdis, Ibn, 121; Khayyam, Omar, 121;
  Pindar, 114
Polyphemus. *See* Cyclops
Pometti, Orazio. *See* Nibali Winery
Porta Bigliardo. *See* Duchy of Nelson
Portale, Piero, 195, 231
Ports: Riposto, x, 7, 111, 145, 162, 167; Porto
  dell'Etna, 98
powdery mildew. *See* oidium
press, 2–7; *conzu*, 30–31
propaggine. See layering
Puglia, Rosario. *See* Don Saro Winery
Puglisi, Désirée; Nunzio; Stefany. *See* Enò-Trio
  Winery
Puglisi, Salvatore, 3
Punic Wars, 115

Quantico Winery, 24, 44, 58, 81, 302
Q'Assaggia Winery, 338
quinconce; quincunx, 82

Raciti Gambino, Delfo; Francesco; Maria Grazia.
  See Vini Gambino Winery
Raciti Family, 339; *See* Rupestre Winery
Raciti, Vittorio, 171-172, 320
Raiti, Giovanni. *See* Quantico Winery
Randazzo, 71, 73, 102, 132, 139-140, 161-162,
  185, 200; contrade, 347
Reale Vini Etna Winery, 230
red wine, 19, 37, 40, 51-59, 142, 162-163, 167,
  171, 205-206
reservations, 160, 220
restaurants, 98, 338, 341
Rinanera Winery, 338
ripe; ripeness; ripening, 17, 40-41, 48-49, 53, 71,
  74, 79-80, 174, 211-212

ripiddu. See lava
Riposto. *See* Ports
Ristorante San Giorgio e Il Drago, 161
Ristorante Veneziano, 161
Rizzo, Giovanni, 274
Rizzo, Lidia, 256
Robinson, Jancis, 13
Roger I (count), 124-125
Roger II (king), 125
Rome, 23, 115-116, 153; Eastern Roman Empire,
  118-119; Western Roman Empire, 115-117
Romeo, Giacinto; Pina Leone; Salvo. *See* Tenuta
  Monte Ilice Winery
rootstock, 83-86; American, 79, 83-86, 162; 775P
  (Paulsen 775), 86; 779P (Paulsen 779), 86;
  1103P (Paulsen 1103), 86; 140R (Ruggeri 140),
  86; graft, 7, 11, 20, 83-86, 79-82, 149, 154, 157,
  162, 177, 190. *See also* Vitis
rosé wine, 48-51
Rovittello, 159, 161, 175, 202-203, 337, 341, 345
Rupestre Winery, 339
Russo, Francesco; Gina; Vincenzo; Corsello,
  Robert. *See* Cantine Russo Winery
Russo, Girolamo; Giuseppe. *See* Girolamo Russo
  Winery

salasso, 48
Salina, 24, 238
San Bull, 118
San Martino, 164
Sant'Agata. *See* Agatha, Saint
Sant'Alfio, 201, 243, 337, 347
Santa Maria di Licodia, 132, 228, 229, 343;
  contrade, 347
Santa Maria La Nave Winery, 21, 24, 42, 44, 59,
  63, 65, 134, 189, 250
Santoro, Nino. *See* Donnafugata Winery
Sardegna, 21, 153
Sardo, Bruno Ferrara. *See* Vini Ferrara Sardo
  Winery
Scammacca, Michele, 9, 63, 177, 205, 249
Sciacca, Emilio, 332
Sciara Winery, 45, 68, 160, 266
Scilio Winery, 68, 303
Scilio, Salvatore. *See* Scilio Winery
Scirto Winery, 24, 35, 43, 51, 59, 160, 181, 321
Scirto, Giuseppe; Valeria. *See* Scirto Winery
Second World War. *See* World War II
Serafica Winery, 339-340
Sestini, Domenico, 142-143
sfuso. See bulk wine
Sicilia DOC/DOP. *See* Italian wine
  denominations
Siciliano Winery, 26, 49, 54, 160, 176, 178, 180,
  197, 265
Siciliano, Rocco, 26, 176, 180, 197, 265

Sicily: general reference, vii, ix, xii, 1, 8, 12, 92, 101, 112, 117-119, 127-131, 135, 142-143, 151-157, 165, 206; Sicilian, 4, 114, 153, 165-166; Sicani, Sicels, 4
Siegrist, Jean, 173-174
silk, 118-119, 147, 150
Siracusa, 114, 119
Sive Natura Winery, 340
ski; snowboard; ski resort, 107
Smyth, William H., 145-147
Sofia Winery, 328
Sofia, Angela; Carmelo; Gioacchino; Valentina. *See* Sofia Winery
soil, 72–73, 83-87, 94-98, 107
sommelier, ix, 76, 189, 204, 223
Spain, 130, 135, 137, 156, 278
sparkling wine. See *metodo classico*
Spitaleri di Muglia, Antonino (barone), 150, 155; Arnaldo, 196. *See also* Castello Solicchiata Winery
Spuches Winery, 328
SRC Winery, 22, 49, 53, 55, 57, 160, 304
Stagnitta, Dario. *See* Stagnita Winery
Stagnitta Winery, 340
Strabo, 95
Strano, Gianluca. *See* Monterosso Winery
sulfur, 93-95, 146, 149-150, 191-192
Svevi, 129

Tachis, Giacomo, 26, 175-176, 194
Taormina, 111, 116, 119, 132, 135, 138, 159
Tarderia, 89
tartaric (tartrate), 39, 147
Tasca, Alberto; Tasca d'Almerita. *See* Tenuta Tascante Winery
TDN (Trimethyl Dihydronapthalene), 17
tectonic plates: African, Eurasian, European, 12, 91-92
Tenuta Antica Cavalleria, 340-341
Tenuta Bastonaca Winery, 341
Tenuta Benedetta Winery, 27, 54, 59, 306
Tenuta Boccarossa, 341
Tenuta delle Terre Nere Winery, 38, 47, 59, 160, 193, 202, 308
Tenuta di Aglaea Winery, 59, 309
Tenuta di Castiglione Winery, 175-176
Tenuta di Fessina Winery, 19, 45, 47, 50, 53, 59, 161, 202-203, 310
Tenuta Ferrata Winery, 341-342
Tenuta Masseria Setteporte Winery, 45, 55, 58, 195, 231
Tenuta Monte Gorna Winery, 59, 134, 210, 225, 251
Tenuta Monte Ilice Winery, 43, 134, 252
Tenuta Papale Winery, 342
Tenuta Pietro Caciorgna Winery, 59, 161, 312; *See* Tenute delle Macchie Winery, 312

Tenuta Rustica Winery, 55
Tenuta Stagliata Winery, 343
Tenuta Tascante Winery, 43, 45, 160, 313
Tenuta Vigna Patrizia Winery, 343
Tenute Bosco Winery, 51, 59, 224, 307
Tenute Donna Elia Winery, 253
Tenute Foti Randazzese Winery, 342
Tenute Mannino di Plachi Winery, 3, 65, 134, 254
Tenute Paratore Winery, 311
Terra Costantino Winery, 36, 45, 49, 51, 57, 59, 134, 199, 255
terracotta, 5
Terrazze dell'Etna Winery, 22, 26-27, 30-31, 51, 54, 55, 59, 65, 208, 224, 314
Terre di Nuna Winery, 45, 256
Terre di Trente Winery, 315
Terre Forti, 163
Theresa Eccher Winery, 51, 59, 316
Thun, Matthias, 104-105
Tokash, Brandon, 256
Tóth, Patricia, 300
tourism, 159-160
traditional method. See *metodo classico*
train. *See* Circumetnea Railway
Travaglianti, Claudio; Enrico. *See* Travaglianti Winery, 343
Travaglianti Winery, 343
travel; travelers; traveling, 220-221
Trecastagni, xi, 28, 148, 155, 162, 206, 242; contrade, 347
Treffiletti, Valerio, 328
Trefiletti, Carmine; Rocco. *See* Aitala Winery
Trewhella, Robert. *See* Circumetnea railway
Trinoro, Tenuta de Trinoro Winery, 192
Tuscany, 132, 192, 202, 272, 310, 312, 335

United States; US, 164, 201, 260, 305
University of Catania, 13, 191, 238
Unostru Winery, 343-344

Valenti, Giovanni. *See* Cantine Valenti Winery
Valenti, Leonardo, 183, 273
Valle del Bove, 73, 89, 102, 249, 256, 257, 331, 332, 339
Vandals, 117
Vassallo, Corrado; Paolo. *See* Feudo Vagliasindi Winery
Vatican, 131
Vecchio, Carmelo. *See* Vigneti Vecchio Winery
Viagrande, 147, 149, 153, 155, 162, 186, 239; contrade, 347
Victor Emmanuel II (king), 153
Vigneti Vecchio Winery, 43, 59, 344
Vigo, Chiara, 11, 200, 280
Vine: general reference, 4, 12-14, 74-87, 138; vine training, 81-83

Vinci, Sebastiano, 336; *See* Mecori Winery
Vini Calì Winery, 344-345
Vini Ferrara Sardo Winery, 59, 319
Vini Gambino Winery, 45, 51, 59, 216, 320
Vini Licciardello Winery, 339
Vini Pennisi Winery, 345
Vinitaly, 175, 200, 210
Vino Arrigo Winery, 344
Vino Bianco. *See* Vino da Tavola
vino da taglio, 7, 146, 162-164, 331
Vino da Tavola (*vino da pasto*), 87, 171-172, 178,
Vino Rosato. *See* Vino da Tavola
Vino Rosso. *See* Vino da Tavola
vino sfuso. *See* bulk wine
Vitaceae, 12
Vitis, 12; *Vitis berlandieri*, *Vitis rupestris*, 78, 83,
    86, 154; *Vitis vinifera*, 12, 78, 83-85, 146, 154
Vivera Winery, 45, 59, 323
Vivera, Antonino; Armida; Loredana. *See* Vivera
    Winery
volcano, vii, ix-xi, 71-75, 87-98; volcanology, 89,
    94, 268

Vouillamoz, José, 13

walking, 159-160, 220
water, 77-78, 80, 86-87, 107
weather, 99-107
white wine, 40–47
Wiegner Winery, 23, 43, 54, 59, 160, 197, 324
Wiegner, Laura; Marco; Peter. *See* Wiegner
    Winery
wind, 79, 93-95, 98, 105-107
Woodhouse & Co., 144
World War II, 8, 11, 148, 165-166, 251, 280, 282,
    291

yield, 6, 14-29, 56, 80-86, 205-206
Yim, Stef. *See* Sciara Winery

Zafferana Etnea, 148, 162; contrade, 347
Zambu, 155
Zumbo Winery, 51, 59, 345
Zumbo, Erica; Ramona; Salvatore. *See* Zumbo
    Winery

INDEX OF GRAPE VARIETIES

Adrumenitanum, 116
Aglianico, 120, 197, 324
Albanello, 20–21, 42, 190
Alicante (*a.k.a.* Garnacha; Grenache; Cannonau),
    21–22, 53-54, 201, 225, 283, 292, 329, 337, 344
Alicante Bouschet, 22
Aminea/Aminnia, 115-116
Ansonica. *See* Inzolia

Barbarossa (*a.k.a.* Barbarussa), 126
Bracaù (*a.k.a.* Pampanuto/Verdeca), 330

Cabernet Franc, 22, 25, 54, 150, 156, 196,-197,
    324
Cabernet Sauvignon, 22, 54, 150, 156, 176-177,
    188, 249
Calabrese (*a.k.a.* Calavrisi), 26, 150
Carricante (*a.k.a.* Catanese Bianco), xi, 8, 13–15,
    17, 41, 43-47
Catarratto, 8, 13, 14, 17–18, 24, 42–43; Catarratto
    Comune; Catarratto Lucido; Catarratto Extra
    Lucido, 17-18
Catiniensis, 116
Cesanese d'Affile, 23, 26, 54
Chardonnay, 22, 42, 43, 59, 62, 65, 150, 193, 197,
    297, 314

Chimmunite, 126
Coda di Volpe Bianca, 23, 42, 289, 339

Durache, 126
Dureza, 28

Eugenia, 116

Fiano, 23, 42, 43, 197, 324
Furmint, 300

Garganega, 18, 23
Gerosolimitana Bianca, 126, 150
Gewürztraminer. *See* Traminer
Giustalisi, 126
Graecula, 116
Grecanico Dorato, 23–24, 42, 62, 63, 65, 190, 250
Greco di Tufo, 115;
Greco, 115; Greco Nero, 150
Grignolino, 150
Grillo, 24, 42, 43
Guarnaccia, 126; Guarnaccia Nera, 150

Inzolia (*a.k.a.* Ansonica), 22, 29, 42, 43, 126, 184,
    269, 273, 289, 345

Macabeo, 156
Madama Bianca, 24; Madama Nera, 24
Malvagie, 126
Malvasia delle Lipari, 24, 238
Mandilaria, 126
Mantonico Bianco, 19, 126; Mantonico Nero, 126, 150
Merlot, 25, 54, 150, 156, 184, 196, 273
Minella Bianca, 14, 25, 42, 43, 267, 269; Minella Nera, 25
Mondeuse, 25, 28, 29, 54, 184, 273; Mondeuse Blanche, 28–29
Montonico Pinto, 14
Moscato Bianco, 25, 64, 68, 247
Moscato d'Alessandria (*a.k.a.* Zibibbo), 24
Murgentina, 116
Muscadine, 126

Nebbiolo, 150, 171, 288
Nerello, general reference, xi, 8, 9, 13, 16, 18-20, 27, 40, 48-68, 176, 188, 205-206
Nerello Cappuccio (*a.k.a.* Nerello Mantellato), 18–19, 40, 52, 54-55, 239, 251, 267, 282, 310, 343
Nerello Mascalese, viii, 8–9, 13, 16, 19–20, 40, 48–69
Nero d'Avola (*a.k.a.* Calabrese), 26, 150, 176, 188, 303, 334
Nigrello, 142, 150; Nigrello Etneo, 150

Palomino, 156
Parellada, 156

Pedro Ximénez, 156
Petit Verdot, 23, 26, 54, 55, 176, 193, 208-209, 297, 314
Pinot Blanc, 150, 156
Pinot Grigio, 150
Pinot Nero (Pinot Noir), 26-27, 49, 54, 62-63, 180, 188, 196-197, 209, 265, 267, 277, 279, 300, 314
Pitrusa Bianca, 126; Pitrusa Nera, 126, 150

Riesling, 17, 27, 42, 47, 150, 300

Sangiovese, 19, 27–28, 54, 306, 335; Sangiovese Grosso, 27-28
Savagnin, 23
Scacco, 14
Syrah, 28, 156, 176, 184, 273

Tannat, 176
Terribile, 28
Tinto Nero, 156
Traminer, 23, 42, 176, 190, 279; Traminer Aromatico, 23, 42, 279
Trebbiano, 28, 43, 116

Viognier, 28–29, 42, 150, 184, 273
Vispalora, 126

Xarel-lo, 156

Zibibbo. *See* Moscato d'Alessandria
Zu' Matteo, 29, 330

One of Mount Etna's most striking features is the Valle del Bove. This massive valley was at one point a caldera that collapsed during a landslide around the sixth millennium BCE. This single event is credited with an historic tsunami that wiped out coastal villages throughout the Mediterranean Basin. Today, this breathtaking geologic wonder captures lava and excites those who see it.

Work is a perpetual reality for Etna wine producers. In the Biondi vineyard, like so many others, scores of chestnut posts are manually replaced each year.

ABOUT THE AUTHOR

Benjamin Spencer is an award-winning American author, journalist, and the founder of the Etna Wine School, a wine consulting company on Mount Etna, in Sicily. *The New Wines of Mount Etna* won *The Best European Wine Book* from Gourmand International in 2021.

ALSO FROM GEMELLI PRESS

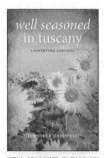

WELL SEASONED IN TUSCANY
Jennifer Criswell

COINS IN THE FOUNTAIN
Judith Works

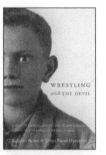

WRESTLING WITH THE DEVIL
Antonio Russo &
Tonya Russo Hamilton

TINO AND THE POMODORI
Tonya Russo Hamilton

TRUE VINES
Diana Strinati Baur

AT LEAST YOU'RE IN TUSCANY
Jennifer Criswell

BEYOND THE PASTA
Mark Leslie

PIECES OF SOMEDAY
Jan Vallone

**IMPARIAMO L'ITALIANO
CON L'AIUTO DELLA MANO**
Giuliana Sica

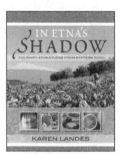

IN ETNA'S SHADOW
Karen Landes

www.gemellipress.com

Made in United States
North Haven, CT
09 September 2023

41327623R00222